AMERICAN SCIENCE SERIES, BRIEFER COURSE

PSYCHOLOGY

BY

WILLIAM JAMES

Professor of Psychology in Harvard University

ISBN: 979-8-89096-002-3

All Rights reserved. No part of this book maybe reproduced without written permission from the publishers, except by a reviewer who may quote brief passages in a review to be printed in a newspaper or magazine.

Printed: March 2023

Published and Distributed By:
Lushena Books
607 Country Club Drive, Unit E
Bensenville, IL 60106
www.lushenabks.com

ISBN: 979-8-89096-002-3

PREFACE.

IN preparing the following abridgment of my larger work, the Principles of Psychology, my chief aim has been to make it more directly available for class-room use. For this purpose I have omitted several whole chapters and rewritten others. I have left out all the polemical and historical matter, all the metaphysical discussions and purely speculative passages, most of the quotations, all the book-references, and (I trust) all the impertinences, of the larger work, leaving to the teacher the choice of orally restoring as much of this material as may seem to him good, along with his own remarks on the topics successively studied. Knowing how ignorant the average student is of physiology, I have added brief chapters on the various senses. In this shorter work the general point of view, which I have adopted as that of 'natural science,' has, I imagine, gained in clearness by its extrication from so much critical matter and its more simple and dogmatic statement. About two fifths of the volume is either new or rewritten, the rest is 'scissors and paste.' I regret to have been unable to supply chapters on pleasure and pain, æsthetics, and the moral sense. Possibly the defect may be made up in a later edition, if such a thing should ever be demanded.

I cannot forbear taking advantage of this preface to make a statement about the composition of the 'Principles of Psychology.' My critics in the main have been so indulgent that I must cordially thank them; but they have been unanimous in one reproach, namely, that my order of chapters is planless and unnatural; and in one charitable excuse for this, namely, that the work, being largely a collection of review-articles, could not be expected to show as much system as a treatise cast in a single mould. Both the reproach and the excuse misapprehend the facts of the case. The order of composition is doubtless unshapely, or it would not be found so by so many. But planless it is not, for I deliberately followed what seemed to me a good pedagogic order, in proceeding from the more concrete mental aspects with which we are best acquainted to the so-called elements which we naturally come to know later by way of abstraction. The opposite order, of 'building-up' the mind out of its 'units of composition,' has the merit of expository elegance, and gives a neatly subdivided table of contents; but it often purchases these advantages at the cost of reality and truth. I admit that my 'synthetic' order was stumblingly carried out; but this again was in consequence of what I thought were pedagogic necessities. On the whole, in spite of my critics, I venture still to think that the 'unsystematic' form charged upon the book is more apparent than profound, and that we really gain a more living understanding of the mind by keeping our attention as long as possible upon our entire conscious states as they are concretely given to us, than by the *post-mortem* study of their comminuted 'elements.' This last is the study of artificial abstractions, not of natural things.*

---

* In the present volume I have given so much extension to the details of 'Sensation' that I have obeyed custom and put that subject first, although by no means persuaded that such order intrinsically is the best. I feel now (when it is too late for the change to be made) that the chapters on the Production of Motion, on Instinct, and on Emotion ought, for purposes of teaching, to follow immediately upon that on Habit, and that the chapter on Reasoning ought to come in very early, perhaps immediately after that upon the Self. I advise teachers to adopt this modified order, in spite of the fact that with the change of place of 'Reasoning' there ought properly to go a slight amount of re-writing.

But whether the critics are right, or I am, on this first point, the critics are wrong about the relation of the magazine-articles to the book. With a single exception all the chapters were written for the book; and then by an afterthought some of them were sent to magazines, because the completion of the whole work seemed so distant. My lack of capacity has doubtless been great, but the charge of not having taken the utmost pains, according to my lights, in the composition of the volumes, cannot justly be laid at my door.

CONTENTS.

CHAPTER I.

INTRODUCTORY 1
Psychology defined; psychology as a natural science, its data, 1. The human mind and its environment, 3. The postulate that all consciousness has cerebral activity for its condition, 5.

CHAPTER II.

SENSATION IN GENERAL 9
Incoming nerve-currents, 9. Terminal organs, 10. 'Specific energies,' 11. Sensations cognize qualities, 13. Knowledge of acquaintance and knowledge-about, 14. Objects of sensation appear in space, 15. The intensity of sensations, 16. Weber's law, 17. Fechner's law, 21. Sensations are not psychic compounds, 23. The 'law of relativity,' 24. Effects of contrast, 26.

CHAPTER III.

SIGHT 28
The eye, 28. Accommodation, 32. Convergence, binocular vision, 33. Double images, 36. Distance, 39. Size, color, 40. After-images, 43. Intensity of luminous objects, 45.

CHAPTER IV.

HEARING 47
The ear, 47. The qualities of sound, 43. Pitch, 44. 'Timbre,' 45. Analysis of compound air-waves, 56. No fusion of elementary sensations of sound, 57. Harmony and discord, 58. Discrimination by the ear, 59.

vii

CHAPTER V.

TOUCH, THE TEMPERATURE SENSE, THE MUSCULAR SENSE, AND PAIN 60

End-organs in the skin, 60. Touch, sense of pressure, 60. Localization, 61. Sensibility to temperature, 63. The muscular sense, 65. Pain, 67.

CHAPTER VI.

SENSATIONS OF MOTION 70

The feeling of motion over surfaces, 70. Feelings in joints, 74. The sense of translation, the sensibility of the semicircular canals, 75.

CHAPTER VII.

THE STRUCTURE OF THE BRAIN 78

Embryological sketch, 78. Practical dissection of the sheep's brain, 81.

CHAPTER VIII.

THE FUNCTIONS OF THE BRAIN 91

General idea of nervous function, 91. The frog's nerve-centres, 92. The pigeon's nerve-centres, 96. What the hemispheres do, 97. The automaton-theory, 101. The localization of functions, 104. Brain and mind have analogous 'elements,' sensory and motor, 105. The motor zone, 106. Aphasia, 108. The visual region, 110. Mental blindness, 112. The auditory region, mental deafness, 113. Other centres, 116.

CHAPTER IX.

SOME GENERAL CONDITIONS OF NEURAL ACTIVITY . 120

The nervous discharge, 120. Reaction-time, 121. Simple reactions, 122. Complicated reactions, 124. The summation of stimuli, 128. Cerebral blood-supply, 130. Brain-thermometry, 131. Phosphorus and thought, 132.

CHAPTER X.

HABIT 134

Its importance, and its physical basis, 134. Due to pathways formed in the centres, 136. Its practical uses, 138. Concate-

CONTENTS. ix

PAGE

nated acts, 140. Necessity for guiding sensations in secondarily automatic performances, 141. Pedagogical maxims concerning the formation of habits, 142.

CHAPTER XI.

THE STREAM OF CONSCIOUSNESS 151
Analytic order of our study, 151. Every state of mind forms part of a personal consciousness, 152. The same state of mind is never had twice, 154. Permanently recurring ideas are a fiction, 156. Every personal consciousness is continuous, 157. Substantive and transitive states, 160. Every object appears with a 'fringe' of relations, 163. The 'topic' of the thought, 167. Thought may be rational in any sort of imagery, 168. Consciousness is always especially interested in some one part of its object, 170.

CHAPTER XII.

THE SELF 176
The Me and the I, 176. The material Me, 177. The social Me, 179. The spiritual Me, 181. Self-appreciation, 182. Self-seeking, bodily, social, and spiritual, 184. Rivalry of the Mes, 186. Their hierarchy, 190. Teleology of self-interest, 193. The I, or 'pure ego,' 195. Thoughts are not compounded of 'fused' sensations, 196. The 'soul' as a combining medium, 200. The sense of personal identity, 201. Explained by identity of function in successive passing thoughts, 203. Mutations of the self, 205. Insane delusions, 207. Alternating personalities, 210. Mediumships or possessions, 212. Who is the Thinker, 215.

CHAPTER XIII.

ATTENTION 217
The narrowness of the field of consciousness, 217. Dispersed attention, 218. To how much can we attend at once? 219. The varieties of attention, 220. Voluntary attention, its momentary character, 224. To keep our attention, an object must change, 226. Genius and attention, 227. Attention's physiological conditions, 228. The sense-organ must be adapted, 229. The idea of the object must be aroused, 232. Pedagogic remarks, 236. Attention and free-will, 237.

CHAPTER XIV.

CONCEPTION 239
Different states of mind can mean the same, 239. Conceptions of abstract, of universal, and of problematic objects, 240. The thought of 'the same' is not the same thought over again, 243.

CHAPTER XV.

DISCRIMINATION 244
Discrimination and association; definition of discrimination, 244. Conditions which favor it, 245. The sensation of difference, 246. Differences inferred, 248. The analysis of compound objects, 248. To be easily singled out, a quality should already be separately known, 250. Dissociation by varying concomitants, 251. Practice improves discrimination, 252.

CHAPTER XVI.

ASSOCIATION 253
The order of our ideas, 253. It is determined by cerebral laws, 255. The ultimate cause of association is habit, 256. The elementary law in association, 257. Indeterminateness of its results, 258. Total recall, 259. Partial recall, and the law of interest, 261. Frequency, recency, vividness, and emotional congruity tend to determine the object recalled, 264. Focalized recall, or 'association by similarity,' 267. Voluntary trains of thought, 271. The solution of problems, 273. Similarity no elementary law; summary and conclusion, 277.

CHAPTER XVII.

THE SENSE OF TIME 280
The sensible present has duration, 280. We have no sense for absolutely empty time, 281. We measure duration by the events which succeed in it, 283. The feeling of past time is a present feeling, 285. Due to a constant cerebral condition, 286.

CHAPTER XVIII.

MEMORY 287
What it is, 287. It involves both retention and recall, 289. Both elements explained by paths formed by habit in the brain, 290. Two conditions of a good memory, persistence and nu

CONTENTS.

merousness of paths, 292. Cramming, 295. One's native retentiveness is unchangeable, 296. Improvement of the memory, 298. Recognition, 299. Forgetting, 300. Pathological conditions, 301.

CHAPTER XIX.

IMAGINATION 302
What it is, 302. Imaginations differ from man to man; Galton's statistics of visual imagery, 303. Images of sounds, 306. Images of movement, 307. Images of touch, 308. Loss of images in aphasia, 309. The neural process in imagination, 310.

CHAPTER XX.

PERCEPTION 312
Perception and sensation compared, 312. The perceptive state of mind is not a compound, 313. Perception is of definite things, 316. Illusions, 317. First type: inference of the more usual object, 318. Second type: inference of the object of which our mind is full, 321. 'Apperception,' 326. Genius and old-fogyism, 327. The physiological process in perception, 329. Hallucinations, 330.

CHAPTER XXI.

THE PERCEPTION OF SPACE 335
The attribute of extensity belongs to all objects of sensation, 335. The construction of real space, 337. The processes which it involves: 1) Subdivision, 338; 2) Coalescence of different sensible data into one 'thing,' 339; 3) Location in an environment, 340; 4) Place in a series of positions, 341; 5) Measurement, 342. Objects which are signs, and objects which are realities, 345. The 'third dimension,' Berkeley's theory of distance, 346. The part played by the intellect in space-perception, 349.

CHAPTER XXII.

REASONING 351
What it is, 351. It involves the use of abstract characters, 353. What is meant by an 'essential' character, 354. The 'essence' varies with the subjective interest, 358. The two

great points in reasoning, 'sagacity' and 'wisdom,' 360. Sagacity, 362. The help given by association by similarity, 364. The reasoning powers of brutes, 367.

CHAPTER XXIII.

CONSCIOUSNESS AND MOVEMENT 370
All consciousness is motor, 370. Three classes of movement to which it leads, 372.

CHAPTER XXIV.

EMOTION 373
Emotions compared with instincts, 373. The varieties of emotion are innumerable, 374. The cause of their varieties, 375. The feeling, in the coarser emotions, results from the bodily expression, 375. This view must not be called materialistic, 380. This view explains the great variability of emotion, 381. A corollary verified, 382. An objection replied to, 383. The subtler emotions, 384. Description of fear, 385. Genesis of the emotional reactions, 386.

CHAPTER XXV.

INSTINCT 391
Its definition, 391. Every instinct is an impulse, 392. Instincts are not always blind or invariable, 395. Two principles of non-uniformity, 398. Enumeration of instincts in man, 406. Description of fear, 407.

CHAPTER XXVI.

WILL 415
Voluntary acts, 415. They are secondary performances, 415. No third kind of idea is called for, 418. The motor-cue, 420. Ideo-motor action, 422. Action after deliberation, 428. Five chief types of decision, 429. The feeling of effort, 434. Healthiness of will, 435. Unhealthiness of will, 436. The explosive will: (1) from defective inhibition, 437; (2) from exaggerated impulsion, 439. The obstructed will, 441. Effort feels like an original force, 442. Pleasure and pain as springs of action, 444. What holds attention determines action, 448. Will is a relation between the mind and its

'ideas,' 449. Volitional effort is effort of attention, 450. The question of free-will, 455. Ethical importance of the phenomenon of effort, 458.

EPILOGUE.

PSYCHOLOGY AND PHILOSOPHY 461

What the word metaphysics means, 461. Relation of consciousness to the brain, 462. The relation of states of mind to their 'objects,' 464. The changing character of consciousness, 466. States of consciousness themselves are not verifiable facts, 467.

PSYCHOLOGY.

CHAPTER I.

INTRODUCTORY.

The definition of Psychology may be best given in the words of Professor Ladd, as the *description and explanation of states of consciousness as such.* By states of consciousness are meant such things as sensations, desires, emotions, cognitions, reasonings, decisions, volitions, and the like. Their 'explanation' must of course include the study of their causes, conditions, and immediate consequences, so far as these can be ascertained.

Psychology is to be treated as a natural science in this book. This requires a word of commentary. Most thinkers have a faith that at bottom there is but one Science of all things, and that until all is known, no one thing can be completely known. Such a science, if realized, would be Philosophy. Meanwhile it is far from being realized; and instead of it, we have a lot of beginnings of knowledge made in different places, and kept separate from each other merely for practical convenience' sake, until with later growth they may run into one body of Truth. These provisioual beginnings of learning we call 'the Sciences' in the plural. In order not to be unwieldy, every such science has to stick to its own arbitrarily-selected problems, and to ignore all others. Every science thus accepts certain data unquestioningly, leaving it to the other parts of Philosophy to scrutinize their significance and truth. All the natural sciences, for example, in spite of the fact that farther reflection leads to Idealism, assume that a world of matter exists altogether independently of the perceiving mind. Mechanical Science assumes this matter to have 'mass' and to exert 'force,' defining these terms merely phenomenally, and not troubling itself about certain unintelligibilities which they present on nearer reflection. Motion similarly is assumed by mechanical science to exist independently of the mind, in spite of the difficulties involved in the assumption. So Physics assumes atoms, action at a distance, etc., uncritically; Chemistry uncritically adopts all the data of Physics; and Physiology adopts those of Chemistry. Psychology as a natural science deals with things in the same partial and provisional way. In addition to the 'material world' with all its determinations, which the other sciences of nature assume, she assumes additional data peculiarly her own, and leaves it to more developed parts of Philosophy to test their ulterior significance and truth. These data are—

1. *Thoughts and feelings,* or whatever other names transitory *states of consciousness* may be known by.

2. *Knowledge,* by these states of consciousness, of other things. These things may be material objects and events, or other states of mind. The material objects may be either near or distant in time and space, and the states of mind may be those of other people, or of the thinker himself at some other time.

How one thing *can* know another is the problem of what is called the Theory of Knowledge. How such a thing as a 'state of mind' can be at all is the problem of what has been called Rational, as distinguished from Empirical, Psychology. The *full* truth about states of mind cannot be known until both Theory of Knowledge and Rational Psychology have said their say. Meanwhile an immense amount of provisional truth about them can be got together, which will work in with the larger truth and be interpreted by it when the proper time arrives. Such a provisional body of propositions about states of mind, and about the cognitions which they enjoy, is what I mean by Psychology considered as a natural science. On any ulterior theory of matter, mind, and knowledge, the facts and laws of Psychology thus understood will have their value. If critics find that this natural-science point of view cuts things too arbitrarily short, they must not blame the book which confines itself to that point of view; rather must they go on themselves to complete it by their deeper thought. Incomplete statements are often practically necessary. To go beyond the usual 'scientific' assumptions in the present case, would require, not a volume, but a shelfful of volumes, and by the present author such a shelfful could not be written at all.

Let it also be added that the human mind is **all** that **can** be touched upon in this book. Although the mental life of lower creatures has been examined into of late years with some success, we have no space for its consideration here, and can only allude to its manifestations incidentally when they throw light upon our own.

Mental facts cannot be properly studied apart from the physical environment of which they take cognizance. The great fault of the older rational psychology was to set up the soul as an absolute spiritual being with certain faculties of its own by which the several activities of remembering, imagining, reasoning, willing, etc., were explained, almost without reference to the peculiarities of the world with which these activities deal. But the richer insight of modern days perceives that our inner faculties are *adapted* in advance to the features of the world in which we dwell, adapted, I mean, so as to secure our safety and prosperity in its midst. Not only are our capacities for forming new habits, for remembering sequences, and for abstracting general properties from things and associating their usual consequences with them, exactly the faculties needed for steering us in this world of mixed variety and uniformity, but our emofor our welfare, it interests and excites us the first time we come into its presence. Dangerous things fill us with involuntary fear; poisonous things with distaste; indispensable things with appetite. Mind and world in short have been evolved together, and in consequence are something of a mutual fit. The special interactions between the outer order and the order of consciousness, by which this harmony, such as it is, may in the course of time have come about, have been made the subject of many evolutionary speculations, which, though they cannot so far be said to be conclusive, have at least refreshed and enriched the whole subject, and brought all sorts of new questions to the light.

The chief result of all this more modern view is the gradually growing conviction that **mental life is primarily teleological**; that is to say, that our various ways of feeling and thinking have grown to be what they are because of their utility in shaping our *reactions* on the outer world. On the whole, few recent formulas have done more service in psychology than the Spencerian one that the essence of mental life and bodily life are one, namely, 'the adjustment of inner to outer relations.' The adjustment is to immediately present objects in lower animals and in infants. It is to objects more and more remote in time and space, and inferred by means of more and more complex and exact processes of reasoning, when the grade of mental development grows more advanced.

Primarily then, and fundamentally, the mental life is for the sake of action of a preservative sort. Secondarily and incidentally it does many other things, and may even, when ill 'adapted,' lead to its possessor's destruction. Psychology, taken in the widest way, ought to study every sort of mental activity, the useless and harmful sorts as well as that which is 'adapted.' But the study of the harmful in mental life has been made the subject of a special branch called 'Psychiatry'—the science of insanity—and the study of the useless is made over to 'Æsthetics.' Æsthetics and Psychiatry will receive no special notice in this book.

All mental states (no matter what their character as regards utility may be) are followed by bodily activity of some sort. They lead to inconspicuous changes in breathing, circulation, general muscular tension, and glandular or other visceral activity, even if they do not lead to conspicuous movements of the muscles of voluntary life. Not only certain particular states of mind, then (such as those called volitions, for example), but states of mind as such, *all* states of mind, even mere thoughts and feelings, are *motor* in their consequences. This will be made manifest in detail as our study advances. Meanwhile let it be set down as one of the fundamental facts of the science with which we are engaged.

It was said above that the 'conditions' of states of consciousness must be studied. **The immediate condition of a state of consciousness is an activity of some sort in the cerebral hemispheres.** This proposition is supported by so many pathological facts, and laid by physiologists at the base of so many of their reasonings, that to the medically educated mind it seems almost axiomatic. It would be hard, however, to give any short and peremptory proof of the unconditional dependence of mental action upon neural change. That a general and usual amount of dependence exists cannot possibly be ignored. One has only to consider how quickly consciousness may be (so far as we know) abolished by a blow on the head, by rapid loss of blood, by an epileptic discharge, by a full dose of alcohol, opium, ether, or nitrous oxide—or how easily it may be altered in quality by a smaller dose of any of these agents or of others, or by a fever,—to see how at the mercy of bodily happenings our spirit is. A little stoppage of the gall-duct, a swallow of cathartic medicine, a cup of strong coffee at the proper moment, will entirely overturn for the time a man's views of life. Our moods and resolutions are more determined by the condition of our circulation than by our logical grounds. Whether a man shall be a hero or a coward is a matter of his temporary 'nerves.' In many kinds of insanity, though by no means in all, distinct alterations of the brain-tissue have been found. Destruction of certain definite portions of the cerebral hemispheres involves losses of memory and of acquired motor faculty of quite determinate sorts, to which we shall revert again under the title of *aphasias*. Taking all such facts together, the simple and radical conception dawns upon the mind that mental action may be uniformly and absolutely a function of brain-action, varying as the latter varies, and being to the brain-action as effect to cause.

This conception is the 'working hypothesis' which underlies all the 'physiological psychology' of recent years, and it will be the working hypothesis of this book. Taken thus absolutely, it may possibly be too sweeping a statement of what in reality is only a partial truth. But the only way to make sure of its unsatisfactoriness is to apply it seriously to every possible case that can turn up. To work an hypothesis 'for all it is worth' is the real, and often the only, way to prove its insufficiency. I shall therefore assume without scruple at the outset that the uniform correlation of brain-states with mind-states is a law of nature. The interpretation of the law in detail will best show where its facilities and where its difficulties lie. To some readers such an assumption will seem like the most unjustifiable *a priori* materialism. In one sense it doubtless is materialism: it puts the Higher at the mercy of the Lower. But although we affirm that the *coming to pass* of thought is a consequence of mechanical laws,—for, according to another 'working hypothesis,' that namely of physiology, the laws of brain-action are at bottom mechanical laws,— we do not in the least explain the *nature* of thought by affirming this dependence, and in that latter sense our proposition is not materialism.] The authors who most unconditionally affirm the dependence of our thoughts on our brain to be a fact are often the loudest to insist that the fact is inexplicable, and that the intimate essence of consciousness can never be rationally accounted for by any material cause. It will doubtless take several generations of psychologists to test the hypothesis of dependence with anything like minuteness. The books which postulate it will be to some extent on conjectural ground But the student will remember that the Sciences constantly have to take these risks, and habitually advance by zigzagging from one absolute formula to another which corrects it by going too far the other way. At present Psychology is on the materialistic tack, and ought in the interests of ultimate success to be allowed full headway even by those who are certain she will never fetch the port without putting down the helm once more. The only thing that is perfectly certain is that when taken up into the total body of Philosophy, the formulas of Psychology will appear with a very different meaning from that which they suggest so long as they are studied from the point of view of an abstract and truncated 'natural science,' however practically necessary and indispensable their study from such a provisional point of view may be.

The Divisions of Psychology.—So far as possible, then, we are to study states of consciousness in correlation with their probable neural conditions. Now the nervous system is well understood to-day to be nothing but a machine for receiving impressions and discharging reactions preservative to the individual and his kind—so much of physiology the reader will surely know. Anatomically, therefore, the nervous system falls into three main divisions, comprising—

1) The fibres which carry currents in;
2) The organs of central redirection of them; and
3) The fibres which carry them out.

Functionally, we have sensation, central reflection, and motion, to correspond to these anatomical divisions. In Psychology we may divide our work according to a similar scheme, and treat successively of three fundamental conscious processes and their conditions. The first will be Sensation; the second will be Cerebration or Intellection; the third will be the Tendency to Action. Much vagueness results from this division, but it has practical conveniences for such a book as this, and they may be allowed to prevail over whatever objections may be urged.

CHAPTER II.

SENSATION IN GENERAL.

Incoming nerve-currents are the only agents which normally affect the brain. The human nerve-centres are surrounded by many dense wrappings of which the effect is to protect them from the direct action of the forces of the outer world. The hair, the thick skin of the scalp, the skull, and two membranes at least, one of them a tough one, surround the brain; and this organ moreover, like the spinal cord, is bathed by a serous fluid in which it floats suspended. Under these circumstances the only things that can *happen* to the brain are:

1) The dullest and feeblest mechanical jars;

2) Changes in the quantity and quality of the blood-supply; and

3) Currents running in through the so-called afferent or centripetal nerves.

The mechanical jars are usually ineffective; the effects of the blood-changes are usually transient; the nerve-currents, on the contrary, produce consequences of the most vital sort, both at the moment of their arrival, and later, through the invisible paths of escape which they plough in the substance of the organ and which, as we believe, remain as more or less permanent features of its structure, modifying its action throughout all future time.

Each afferent nerve comes from a determinate part of the periphery and is played upon and excited to its inward activity by a particular force of the outer world. Usually it is insensible to other forces: thus the optic nerves are not impressible by air-waves, nor those of the skin by light-waves. The lingual nerve is not excited by aromatic effluvia, the auditory nerve is unaffected by heat. Each selects from the vibrations of the outer world some one rate to which it responds exclusively. The result is that our sensations form a discontinuous series, broken by enormous gaps. There is no reason to suppose that the order of vibrations in the outer world is anything like as interrupted as the order of our sensations. Between the quickest audible air-waves (40,000 vibrations a second at the outside) and the slowest sensible heat-waves (which number probably billions), Nature must somewhere have realized innumerable intermediary rates which we have no nerves for perceiving. The process in the nerve-fibres themselves is very likely the same, or much the same, in all the different nerves. It is the so-called 'current'; but the current is *started* by one order of outer vibrations in the retina, and in the ear, for example, by another. This is due to the different *terminal organs* with which the several afferent nerves are armed. Just as we arm ourselves with a spoon to pick up soup, and with a fork to pick up meat, so our nerve-fibres arm themselves with one sort of end-apparatus to pick up air-waves, with another to pick up ether-waves. The terminal apparatus always consists of modified epithelial cells with which the fibre is continuous. The fibre itself is not directly excitable by the outer agent which impresses the terminal organ. The optic fibres are unmoved by the direct rays of the sun; a cutaneous nerve-trunk may be touched with ice without feeling cold.* The

---

* The subject may feel *pain*, however, in this experiment; and it must be admitted that nerve-fibres of every description, terminal organs as well, are to some degree excitable by mechanical violence and by the electric current.

fibres are mere transmitters; the terminal organs are so many imperfect telephones into which the material world speaks, and each of which takes up but a portion of what it says; the brain-cells at the fibres' central end are as many others at which the mind listens to the far-off call.

The 'Specific Energies' of the Various Parts of the Brain.—To a certain extent anatomists have traced definitely the paths which the sensory nerve-fibres follow after their entrance into the centres, as far as their termination in the gray matter of the cerebral convolutions.* It will be shown on a later page that the consciousness which accompanies the excitement of this gray matter varies from one portion of it to another. It is consciousness of things seen, when the occipital lobes, and of things heard, when the upper part of the temporal lobes, share in the excitement. Each region of the cerebral cortex responds to the stimulation which its afferent fibres bring to it, in a manner with which a peculiar quality of feeling seems invariably correlated. This is what has been called the law of 'specific energies' in the nervous system. Of course we are without even a conjectural explanation of the *ground* of such a law. Psychologists (as Lewes, Wundt, Rosenthal, Goldscheider, etc.) have debated a good deal as to whether the specific quality of the feeling depends solely on the *place* stimulated in the cortex, or on the *sort of current* which the nerve pours in. Doubtless the sort of outer force habitually impinging on the end-organ gradually modifies the end-organ, the sort of commotion received from the end-organ modifies the fibre, and the sort of current a so-modified fibre pours into the cortical centre modifies the centre. The modification of the centre in turn (though no man

---

* Thus the optic nerve-fibres are traced to the occipital lobes, the olfactory tracts go to the lower part of the temporal lobe (hippocampal convolution), the auditory nerve-fibres pass first to the cerebellum, and probably from thence to the upper part of the temporal lobe. These anatomical terms used in this chapter will be explained later. The *cortex* is the gray surface of the convolutions.

can guess how or why) seems to modify the resultant consciousness. But these adaptive modifications must be excessively slow; and as matters actually stand in any adult individual, it is safe to say that, more than anything else, the *place* excited in his cortex decides what kind of thing he shall feel. Whether we press the retina, or prick, cut, pinch, or galvanize the living optic nerve, the Subject always feels flashes of light, since the ultimate result of our operations is to stimulate the cortex of his occipital region. Our habitual ways of feeling outer things thus depend on which convolutions happen to be connected with the particular end-organs which those things impress. We *see* the sunshine and the fire, simply because the only peripheral end-organ susceptible of taking up the ether-waves which these objects radiate excites those particular fibres which run to the centres of sight. If we could interchange the inward connections, we should feel the world in altogether new ways. If, for instance, we could splice the outer extremity of our optic nerves to our ears, and that of our auditory nerves to our eyes, we should hear the lightning and see the thunder, see the symphony and hear the conductor's movements. Such hypotheses as these form a good training for neophytes in the idealistic philosophy!

Sensation distinguished from Perception.—It is impossible rigorously to *define* a sensation; and in the actual life of consciousness sensations, popularly so called, and perceptions merge into each other by insensible degrees. All we can say is that *what we mean by sensations are* FIRST *things in the way of consciousness.* They are the *immediate* results upon consciousness of nerve-currents as they enter the brain, and before they have awakened any suggestions or associations with past experience. But it is obvious that *such immediate sensations can only be realized in the earliest days of life.* They are all but impossible to adults with memories and stores of associations acquired. Prior to all impressions on sense-organs, the brain is plunged in deep sleep and consciousness is practically non-existent. Even the first weeks after birth are passed in almost unbroken sleep by human infants. It takes a strong message from the sense-organs to break this slumber. In a new-born brain this gives rise to an absolutely pure sensation. But the experience leaves its 'unimaginable touch' on the matter of the convolutions, and the next impression which a sense-organ transmits produces a cerebral reaction in which the awakened vestige of the last impression plays its part. Another sort of feeling and a higher grade of cognition are the consequence. 'Ideas' *about* the object mingle with the awareness of its mere sensible presence, we name it, class it, compare it, utter propositions concerning it, and the complication of the possible consciousness which an incoming current may arouse, goes on increasing to the end of life. In general, this higher consciousness about things is called Perception, the mere inarticulate feeling of their presence is Sensation, so far as we have it at all. To some degree we seem able to lapse into this inarticulate feeling at moments when our attention is entirely dispersed.

Sensations are cognitive. A sensation is thus an abstraction seldom realized by itself; and the object which a sensation knows is an abstract object which cannot exist alone. *'Sensible qualities' are the objects of sensation.* The sensations of the eye are aware of the *colors* of things, those of the ear are acquainted with their *sounds;* those of the skin feel their tangible *heaviness, sharpness, warmth* or *coldness,* etc., etc. From all the organs of the body currents may come which reveal to us the quality of *pain,* and to a certain extent that of *pleasure.*

Such qualities as *stickiness, roughness,* etc., are supposed to be felt through the coöperation of muscular sensations with those of the skin. The geometrical qualities of things, on the other hand, their *shapes, bignesses, distances,* etc. (so far as we discriminate and identify them), are by most psychologists supposed to be impossible without the evocation of memories from the past; and the cognition of these attributes is thus considered to exceed the power of sensation pure and simple.

'Knowledge of Acquaintance' and 'Knowledge about.'— Sensation, thus considered, differs from perception only in the extreme simplicity of its object or content. Its object, being a simple quality, is sensibly *homogeneous;* and its function is that of mere *acquaintance* with this homogeneous seeming fact. Perception's function, on the other hand, is that of knowing something *about* the fact. But we must know *what* fact we mean, all the while, and the various *whats* are what sensations give. [Our earliest thoughts are almost exclusively sensational.] They give us a set of *whats*, or *thats*, or *its*; of subjects of discourse in other words, with their relations not yet brought out. The first time we see *light*, in Condillac's phrase we *are* it rather than see it. But all our later optical knowledge is about what this experience gives. And though we were struck blind from that first moment, our scholarship in the subject would lack no essential feature so long as our memory remained. In training-institutions for the blind they teach the pupils as much *about* light as in ordinary schools. Reflection, refraction, the spectrum, the ether-theory, etc., are all studied. But the best taught born-blind pupil of such an establishment yet lacks a knowledge which the least instructed seeing baby has. They can never show him *what* light is in its 'first intention'; and the loss of that sensible knowledge no book-learning can replace. All this is so obvious that we usually find sensation 'postulated' as an element of experience, even by those philosophers who are least inclined to make much of its importance, or to pay respect to the knowledge which it brings.

Sensations distinguished from Images.—Both sensation and perception, for all their difference, are yet alike in that their objects appear *vivid, lively,* and *present*. Objects merely *thought of, recollected,* or *imagined,* on the contrary, are relatively faint and devoid of this pungency, or tang, this quality of *real presence* which the objects of sensation possess. Now the cortical brain-processes to which sensations are attached are due to incoming currents from the periphery of the body—an external object must excite the eye, ear, etc., before the sensation comes. Those cortical processes, on the other hand, to which mere ideas or images are attached are due in all probability to currents from other convolutions. It would seem, then, that the currents from the periphery normally awaken a kind of brain-activity which the currents from other convolutions are inadequate to arouse. To this sort of activity—a profounder degree of disintegration, perhaps—the quality of vividness, presence, or reality in the object of the resultant consciousness seems correlated.

The Exteriority of Objects of Sensation.—Every thing or quality felt is felt in outer space. It is impossible to conceive a brightness or a color otherwise than as extended and outside of the body. Sounds also appear in space. Contacts are against the body's surface; and pains always occupy some organ. An opinion which has had much currency in psychology is that sensible qualities are first apprehended as *in the mind itself*, and then ' projected ' from it, or ' extradited,' by a secondary intellectual or super-sensational mental act. There is no ground whatever for this opinion. The only facts which even seem to make for it can be much better explained in another way, as we shall see later on. The very first sensation which an infant gets *is* for him the outer universe. And the universe which he comes to know in later life is nothing but an amplification of that first simple germ which, by accretion on the one hand and intussusception on the other, has grown so big and complex and articulate that its first estate is unrememberable. In his dumb awakening to the consciousness of *something there*, a mere *this* as yet (or something for which even the term *this* would perhaps be too discriminative, and the intellectual acknowledgment of which would be better expressed by the bare interjection 'lo!'), the infant encounters an object in which (though it be given in a pure sensation) all the 'categories of the understanding' are contained. *It has externality, objectivity, unity, substantiality, causality, in the full sense in which any later object or system of objects has these things.* Here the young knower meets and greets his world; and the miracle of knowledge bursts forth, as Voltaire says, as much in the infant's lowest sensation as in the highest achievement of a Newton's brain.

The physiological condition of this first sensible experience is probably many nerve-currents coming in from various peripheral organs at once; but this multitude of organic conditions does not prevent the consciousness from being one consciousness. We shall see as we go on that it can be one consciousness, even though it be due to the coöperation of numerous organs and be a consciousness of many things together. The Object which the numerous inpouring currents of the baby bring to his consciousness is one big blooming buzzing Confusion. That Confusion is the baby's universe; and the universe of all of us is still to a great extent such a Confusion, potentially resolvable, and demanding to be resolved, but not yet actually resolved, into parts. It appears from first to last as a space-occupying thing. So far as it is unanalyzed and unresolved we may be said to know it sensationally; but as fast as parts are distinguished in it and we become aware of their relations, our knowledge becomes perceptual or even conceptual, and as such need not concern us in the present chapter.

The Intensity of Sensations.—A light may be so weak as not sensibly to dispel the darkness, a sound so low as not to be heard, a contact so faint that we fail to notice it. In other words, a certain finite amount of the outward stimulus is required to produce any sensation of its presence at all. This is called by Fechner the law of the *threshold*—something must be stepped over before the object can gain entrance to the mind. An impression just above the threshold is called the *minimum visibile, audibile,* etc

From this point onwards, as the impressing force increases, the sensation increases also, though at a slower rate, until at last an *acme* of the sensation is reached which no increase in the stimulus can make sensibly more great. Usually, before the acme, *pain* begins to mix with the specific character of the sensation. This is definitely observable in the cases of great pressure, intense heat, cold, light, and sound; and in those of smell and taste less definitely so only from the fact that we can less easily increase the force of the stimuli here. On the other hand, all sensations, however unpleasant when more intense, are rather agreeable than otherwise in their very lowest degrees. A faintly bitter taste, or putrid smell, may at least be *interesting*.

Weber's Law.—I said that the intensity of the sensation increases by slower steps than those by which its exciting

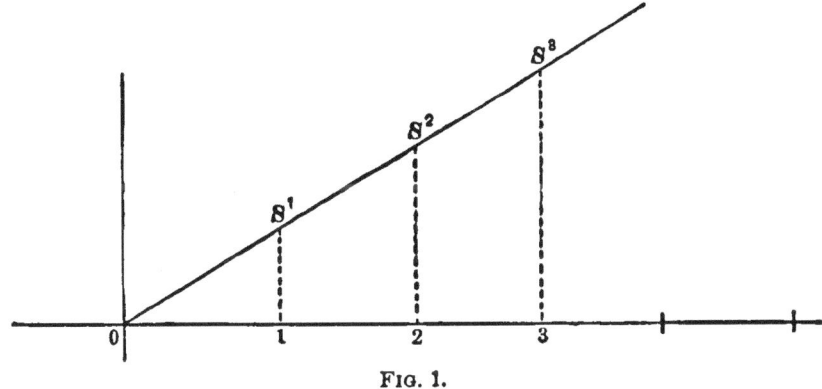

FIG. 1.

cause increases. If there were no threshold, and if every equal increment in the outer stimulus produced an equal increment in the sensation's intensity, a simple straight line would represent graphically the 'curve' of the relation between the two things. Let the horizontal line stand for the scale of intensities of the objective stimulus, so that at 0 it has no intensity, at 1 intensity 1, and so forth. Let the verticals dropped from the slanting line stand for the sensations aroused. At 0 there will be no sensation; at 1 there will be a sensation represented by the length of the vertical S'—1, at 2 the sensation will be represented by

S^2—2, and so on. The line of S's will rise evenly because by the hypothesis the verticals (or sensations) increase at the same rate as the horizontals (or stimuli) to which they severally correspond. But in Nature, as aforesaid, they increase at a slower rate. If each step forward in the horizontal direction be equal to the last, then each step upward in the vertical direction will have to be somewhat shorter than the last; the line of sensations will be convex on top instead of straight.

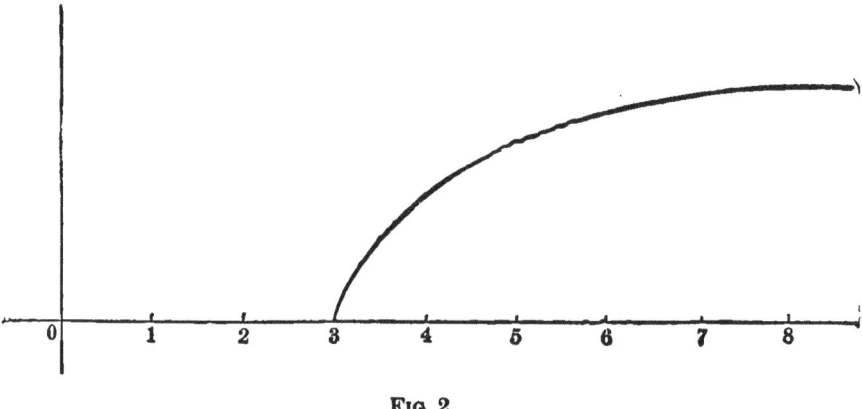

FIG. 2.

Fig. 2 represents this actual state of things, 0 being the zero-point of the stimulus, and conscious sensation, represented by the curved line, not beginning until the 'threshold' is reached, at which the stimulus has the value 3. From here onwards the sensation increases, but it increases less at each step, until at last, the 'acme' being reached, the sensation-line grows flat. The exact law of retardation is called *Weber's law*, from the fact that he first observed it in the case of weights. I will quote Wundt's account of the law and of the facts on which it is based.

"Every one knows that in the stilly night we hear things unnoticed in the noise of day. The gentle ticking of the clock, the air circulating through the chimney, the cracking of the chairs in the room, and a thousand other slight noises, impress themselves upon our ear It is equally well known that in the confused hubbub of the streets, or the clamor of a railway, we may lose not only what our neighbor says to us, but even not hear the sound of our own voice. The star*

SENSATION IN GENERAL. 19

which are brightest at night are invisible by day; and although we see the moon then, she is far paler than at night. Every one who has had to deal with weights knows that if to a pound in the hand a second pound be added, the difference is immediately felt; whilst if it be added to a hundredweight, we are not aware of the difference at all. . . .

' The sound of the clock, the light of the stars, the pressure of the pound, these are all *stimuli* to our senses, and stimuli whose outward amount remains the same. What then do these experiences teach? Evidently nothing but this, that one and the same stimulus, according to the circumstances under which it operates, will be felt either more or less intensely, or not felt at all. Of what sort now is the alteration in the circumstances upon which this alteration in the feeling may depend? On considering the matter closely we see that it is everywhere of one and the same kind. The tick of the clock is a feeble stimulus for our auditory nerve, which we hear plainly when it is alone, but not when it is added to the strong stimulus of the carriage-wheels and other noises of the day. The light of the stars is a stimulus to the eye. But if the stimulation which this light exerts be added to the strong stimulus of daylight, we feel nothing of it, although we feel it distinctly when it unites itself with the feebler stimulation of the twilight. The poundweight is a stimulus to our skin, which we feel when it joins itself to a preceding stimulus of equal strength, but which vanishes when it is combined with a stimulus a thousand times greater in amount.

" We may therefore lay it down as a general rule that a stimulus, in order to be felt, may be so much the smaller if the already preexisting stimulation of the organ is small, but must be so much the larger, the greater the preëxisting stimulation is. . . . The simplest relation would obviously be that the sensation should increase in identically the same ratio as the stimulus. . . . But if this simplest of all relations prevailed, . . . the light of the stars, e g., ought to make as great an addition to the daylight as it does to the darkness of the nocturnal sky, and this we know to be not the case. . . . So it is clear that the strength of the sensations does not increase in proportion to the amount of the stimuli, but more slowly. And now comes the question, in what proportion does the increase of the sensation grow less as the increase of the stimulus grows greater? To answer this question, every-day experiences do not suffice. We need exact measurements, both of the amounts of the various stimuli, and of the intensity of the sensations themselves.

" How to execute these measurements, however, is something which daily experience suggests. To measure the strength of sensations is, as we saw, impossible; we can only measure the difference of sensations. Experience showed us what very unequal differences of sensation might come from equal differences of outward stimulus But all these experiences expressed themselves in one kind of fact, that the same difference of stimulus could in one case be felt, and in another case not felt at all—a pound felt if added to another pound, but not if added to a hundredweight. . . . We can quickest reach a result with our observations if we start with an arbitrary strength of stimulus, notice what sensation it gives us, and then *see how much we can increase the stimulus without making the sensation seem to change.* If we carry out such observations with stimuli of varying absolute amounts, we shall be forced to choose in an equally varying way the amounts of addition to the stimulus which are capable of giving us a just barely perceptible feeling of *more*. A light to be just perceptible in the twilight need not be near as bright as the starlight; it must be far brighter to be just perceived during the day. If now we institute such observations for all possible strengths of the various stimuli, and note for each strength the amount of addition of the latter required to produce a barely perceptible alteration of sensation, we shall have a series of figures in which is immediately expressed the law according to which the sensation alters when the stimulation is increased. . . ."

Observations according to this method are particularly easy to make in the spheres of light, sound, and pressure. Beginning with the latter case,

"We find a surprisingly simple result. *The barely sensible addition to the original weight must stand exactly in the same proportion to it,* be the *same fraction* of it, no matter what the absolute value may be of the weights on which the experiment is made. . . . As the average of a number of experiments, this fraction is found to be about $\frac{1}{3}$; that is, no matter what pressure there may already be made upon the skin, an increase or a diminution of the pressure will be *felt*, as soon as the added or subtracted weight amounts to one third of the weight originally there."

Wundt then describes how differences may be observed in the muscular feelings, in the feelings of heat, in those of light, and in those of sound; and he concludes thus:

"So we have found that all the senses whose stimuli we are enabled to measure accurately, obey a uniform law. However various may be their several delicacies of discrimination, *this* holds true of all, that *the increase of the stimulus necessary to produce an increase* of the sensation bears a constant ratio to the total stimulus. The figures which express this ratio in the several senses may be shown thus in tabular form:

Sensation of light.......................... $\frac{1}{100}$
Muscular sensation........................ $\frac{1}{17}$
Feeling of pressure ⎱
"   " warmth,   ⎬ .... $\frac{1}{3}$
"   " sound,   ⎰

"These figures are far from giving as accurate a measure as might be desired. But at least they are fit to convey a general notion of the relative discriminative susceptibility of the different senses. . . . The important law which gives in so simple a form the relation of the sensation to the stimulus that calls it forth was first discovered by the physiologist Ernst Heinrich Weber to obtain in special cases."*

Fechner's Law.—Another way of expressing Weber's law is to say that to get equal positive additions to the sensation, one must make equal *relative* additions to the stimulus. Professor Fechner of Leipzig founded upon Weber's law a theory of the numerical measurement of sensations, over which much metaphysical discussion has raged. Each just perceptible addition to the sensation, as we gradually let the stimulus increase, was supposed by him to be a *unit* of sensation, and all these units were treated by him as equal, in spite of the fact that *equally perceptible* increments need by no means appear *equally big* when they once are perceived. The many pounds which form the just perceptible addition to a hundredweight feel bigger when added than the few ounces which form the just perceptible addition to a pound. Fechner ignored this fact. He considered that if n distinct perceptible steps of increase might be passed through in gradually increasing a stimulus from the threshold-value till the intensity s was felt, then the sensation of s was composed of n units, which were of the same value all along the line.† Sensations once

---

* Vorlesungen über Menschen u. Thierseele, Lecture VII.
† In other words, S standing for the sensation in general, and d for its noticeable increment, we have the equation $dS =$ const. The in

represented by numbers, psychology may become, according to Fechner, an 'exact' science, susceptible of mathematical treatment. His general formula for getting at the number of units in any sensation is $S = C \log R$, where S stands for the sensation, R for the stimulus numerically estimated, and C for a constant that must be separately determined by experiment in each particular order of sensibility. The sensation is proportional to the logarithm of the stimulus; and the absolute values, in units, of any series of sensations might be got from the ordinates of the curve in **Fig. 2**, if it were a correctly drawn logarithmic curve, with the thresholds rightly plotted out from experiments.

Fechner's psycho-physio formula, as he called it, has been attacked on every hand; and as absolutely nothing practical has come of it, it need receive no farther notice here. The main outcome of his book has been to stir up experimental investigation into the validity of Weber's law (which concerns itself merely with the just perceptible increase, and says nothing about the measurement of the sensation as a whole) and to promote discussion of statistical methods. Weber's law, as will appear when we take the senses, *seriatim*, is only approximately verified. The discussion of statistical methods is necessitated by the extraordinary fluctuations of our sensibility from one moment to the next. It is found, namely, when the difference of two sensations approaches the limit of discernibility, that at one moment we discern it and at the next we do not. Our incessant accidental inner alterations make it impossible to tell just what the least discernible increment of the sensation is without taking the average of a large number of appreciations. These *accidental errors* are as likely to increase as to diminish our sensibility, and are eliminated in such an average, for those above and those below

---

crement of stimulus which produces dS (call it dR) meanwhile varies Fechner calls it the 'differential threshold'; and as its *relative* value to R is always the same, we have the equation $\dfrac{dR}{R} = \text{const}$

the line then neutralize each other in the sum, and the normal sensibility, if there be one (that is, the sensibility due to constant causes as distinguished from these accidental ones), stands revealed. The methods of getting the average all have their difficulties and their snares, and controversy over them has become very subtle indeed. As an instance of how laborious some of the statistical methods are, and how patient German investigators can be, I may say that Fechner himself, in testing Weber's law for weights by the so-called 'method of true and false cases,' tabulated and computed no less than 24,576 separate judgments.

Sensations are not compounds. The fundamental objection to Fechner's whole attempt seems to be this, that although the outer *causes* of our sensations may have many parts, every distinguishable degree, as well as every distinguishable quality, of the *sensation itself* appears to be a unique fact of consciousness. Each sensation is a complete integer. "A strong one," as Dr. Münsterberg says, "is not the multiple of a weak one, or a compound of many weak ones, but rather something entirely new, and as it were incomparable, so that to seek a measurable difference between strong and weak sonorous, luminous, or thermic sensations would seem at first sight as senseless as to try to compute mathematically the difference between salt and sour, or between headache and toothache. It is clear that if in the stronger sensation of light the weaker sensation is not *contained*, it is unpsychological to say that the former differs from the latter by a certain *increment*."* Surely our feeling of scarlet is not a feeling of pink with a lot more pink added; it is something quite other than pink. Similarly with our sensation of an electric arc-light: it does not contain that of many smoky tallow candles in itself. Every sensation presents itself as an indivisible unit; and it is quite impossible to read any clear meaning into the notion that they are masses of units combined.

---

* Beiträge zur exp. Psychol., Heft 3, p. 4.

There is no inconsistency between this statement and the fact that, starting with a weak sensation and increasing it, we feel 'more,' 'more,' 'more,' as the increase goes on. It is not more of the same *stuff* added, so to speak; but it is more and more *difference*, more and more *distance*, from the starting-point, which we feel. In the chapter on Discrimination we shall see that Difference can be perceived between simple things. We shall see, too, that *differences themselves differ*—there are *various directions of difference;* and along any one of them a series of things may be arranged so as to increase steadily in that direction. In any such series the end differs more from the beginning than the middle does. Differences of 'intensity' form one such direction of possible increase—so our judgments of more intensity can be expressed without the hypothesis that more units have been added to a growing sum.

The so-called 'Law of Relativity.'—Weber's law seems only one case of the still wider law that the more we have to attend to the less capable we are of noticing any one detail. The law is obvious where the things differ in kind. How easily do we forget a bodily discomfort when conversation waxes hot; how little do we notice the noises in the room so long as our work absorbs us! *Ad plura intentus minus est ad singula sensus*, as the old proverb says. One might now add that the homogeneity of what we have to attend to does not alter the result; but that a mind with two strong sensations of the same sort already before it is incapacitated by their amount from noticing the detail of a difference between them which it would immediately be struck by, were the sensations themselves weaker and consequently endowed with less distracting power.

This particular idea may be taken for what it is worth.* Meanwhile it is an undoubted general fact that the psychi-

---

* I borrow it from Ziehen: Leitfaden d. Physiologischen Psychologie, 1891, p. 36, who quotes Hering's version of it.

cal effect of incoming currents does depend on what other currents may be simultaneously pouring in. Not only the *perceptibility* of the object which the current brings before the mind, but the *quality* of it, is changed by the other currents. "Simultaneous* sensations modify each other" is a brief expression for this law. "We feel all things in relation to each other" is Wundt's vaguer formula for this general 'law of relativity,' which in one shape or other has had vogue since Hobbes's time in psychology. Much mystery has been made of it, but although we are of course ignorant of the more intimate processes involved, there seems no ground to doubt that they are physiological, and come from the interference of one current with another. A current interfered with might naturally give rise to a modified sensation.

Examples of the modification in question are easy to find.† Notes make each other sweeter in a chord, and so do colors when harmoniously combined. A certain amount of skin dipped in hot water gives the perception of a certain heat. More skin immersed makes the heat much more intense, although of course the water's heat is the same. Similarly there is a *chromatic minimum* of size in objects. The image they cast on the retina must needs excite a sufficient number of fibres, or it will give no sensation of color at all. Weber observed that a thaler laid on the skin of the forehead feels heavier when cold than when warm. Urbantschitsch has found that all our sense-organs influence each other's sensations. The hue of patches of color so distant as not to be recognized was immediately, in his patients, perceived when a tuning-fork was sounded close to the ear. Letters too far off to be read could be read

---

* Successive ones also; but I consider simultaneous ones only, for simplicity's sake.

† The extreme case is where green light and red, *e g* light falling simultaneously on the retina, give a sensation of yellow. But I abstract from this because it is not certain that the incoming currents here affect different fibres of the optic nerve.

when the tuning-fork was heard, etc., etc. The most familiar examples of this sort of thing seem to be the increase of *pain* by noise or light, and the increase of *nausea* by all concomitant sensations.

Effects of Contrast.—The best-known examples of the way in which one nerve-current modifies another are the phenomena of what is known as 'simultaneous color-contrast.' Take a number of sheets of brightly and differently colored papers, lay on each of them a bit of one and the same kind of gray paper, then cover each sheet with some transparent white paper, which softens the look of both the gray paper and the colored ground. The gray patch will appear in each case tinged by the color *complementary* to the ground; and so different will the several pieces appear that no observer, before raising the transparent paper, will believe them all cut out of the same gray. Helmholtz has interpreted these results as being due to a false application of an inveterate habit—that, namely, of making allowance for the color of the medium through which things are seen. The same *thing*, in the blue light of a clear sky, in the reddish-yellow light of a candle, in the dark brown light of a polished mahogany table which may reflect its image, is always judged of its own proper color, which the mind *adds* out of its own knowledge to the appearance, thereby correcting the falsifying medium. In the cases of the papers, according to Helmholtz, the mind believes the color of the ground, subdued by the transparent paper, to be faintly spread *over* the gray patch. But a patch to *look* gray through such a colored film would have really to *be* of the complementary color to the film. Therefore it *is* of the complementary color, we think, and proceed to *see* it of that color.

This theory has been shown to be untenable by Hering. The discussion of the facts is too minute for recapitulation here, but suffice it to say that it proves the phenomenon to be physiological—a case of the way in which, when sensory nerve-currents run in together, the effect of each on consciousness is different from that which it would be if they ran in separately.

'*Successive contrast*' differs from the simultaneous variety, and is supposed to be due to fatigue. The facts will be noticed under the head of 'after-images,' in the section on Vision. It must be borne in mind, however, that after-images from previous sensations may coexist with present sensations, and the two may modify each other just as coexisting sensational processes do.

Other senses than sight show phenomena of contrast, but they are much less obvious, so I will not notice them here. We can now pass to a very brief survey of the various senses in detail.

CHAPTER III.

SIGHT.

The Eye's Structure is described in all the books on anatomy. I will only mention the few points which concern the psychologist.* It is a flattish sphere formed by a tough

---

* The student can easily verify the coarser features of the eye's anatomy upon a bullock's eye, which any butcher will furnish. Clean it first from fat and muscles and study its shape, etc., and then (following Golding Bird's method) make an incision with a pointed scalpel into the sclerotic half an inch from the edge of the cornea, so that the black choroid membrane comes into view. Next with one blade of a pair of scissors inserted into this aperature, cut through sclerotic, choroid, and retina (avoid wounding the membrane of the vitreous body!) all round the eyeball parallel to the cornea's edge.

The eyeball is thus divided into two parts, the anterior one containing the iris, lens, vitreous body, etc., whilst the posterior one contains most of the retina. The two parts can be separated by immersing the eyeball in water, cornea downwards, and simply pulling off the portion to which the optic nerve is attached. Floating this detached posterior cap in water, the delicate retina will be seen spread out over the choroid (which is partly iridescent in the ox tribe); and by turning the cup inside out, and working under water with a camel's-hair brush, the vessels and nerves of the eyeball may be detected.

The anterior part of the eyeball can then be attacked. Seize with forceps on each side the edge of the sclerotic and choroid (not including the retina), raise the eye with the forceps thus applied and shake it gently til' the vitreous body, lens, capsule, ligament, etc , drop out by their weight, and separate from the iris, ciliary processes, cornea, and sclerotic, which remains in the forceps. Examine these latter parts, and get a view of the ciliary muscle which appears as a white line, when with camel's-hair brush and scalpel the choroid membrane is detached from the sclerotic as far forward as it will go. Turning to the parts that cling to the vitreous body observe the clear ring around the lens, and radiating outside of it the marks made by the ciliary white membrane (the sclerotic), which encloses a nervous surface and certain refracting media (lens and 'humors') which cast a picture of the outer world thereon. It is in

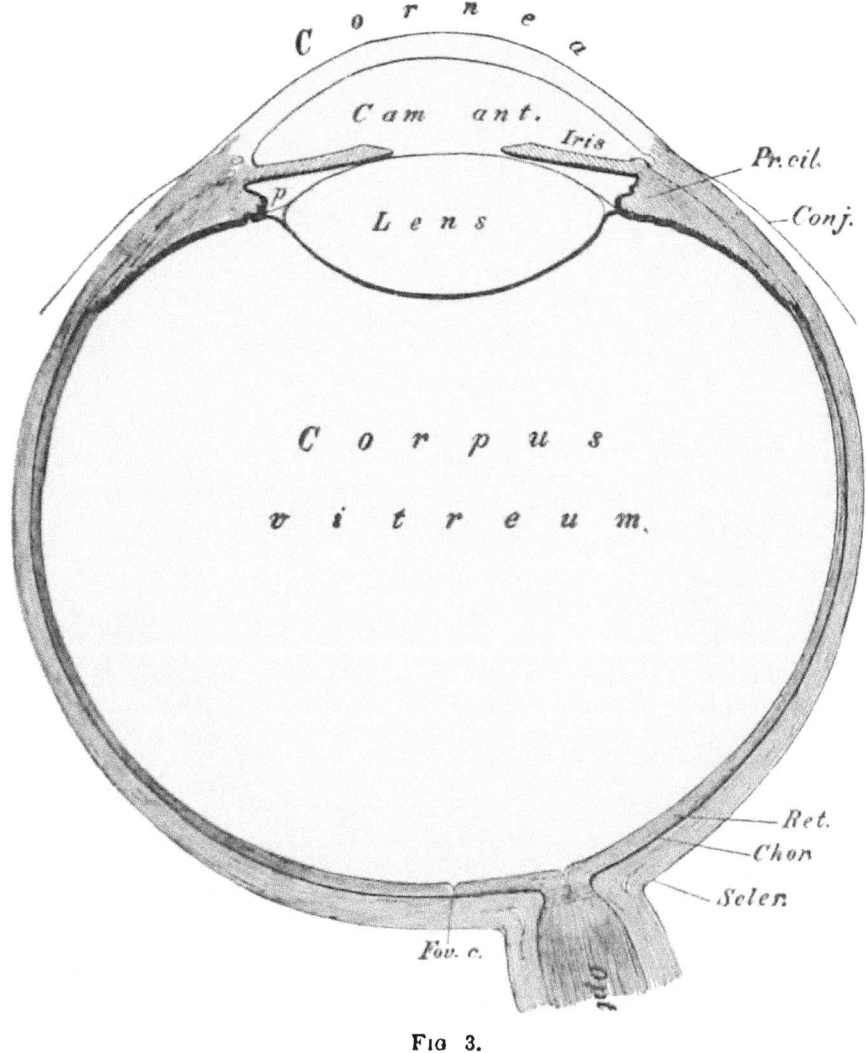

Fig 3.

processes before they were torn away from its suspensory ligament. A fine capillary tube may now be used to insufflate the clear ring, just below the letter p in Fig. 3, and thus to reveal the suspensory ligament itself.

All these parts can be seen in section in a frozen eye or one hardened in alcohol.

fact a little camera obscura, the essential part of which is the sensitive plate.

The retina is what corresponds to this plate. The optic nerve pierces the sclerotic shell and spreads its fibres radially in every direction over its inside, forming a thin translucent film (see Fig. 3, *Ret.*). The fibres pass into a complicated apparatus of cells, granules, and branches (Fig. 4), and finally end in the so-called rods and cones (Fig. 4,—9), which are the specific organs for taking up the influence of the waves of light. Strange to say, these end-organs are not pointed forward towards the light as it streams through the pupil, but backwards towards the sclerotic membrane itself, so

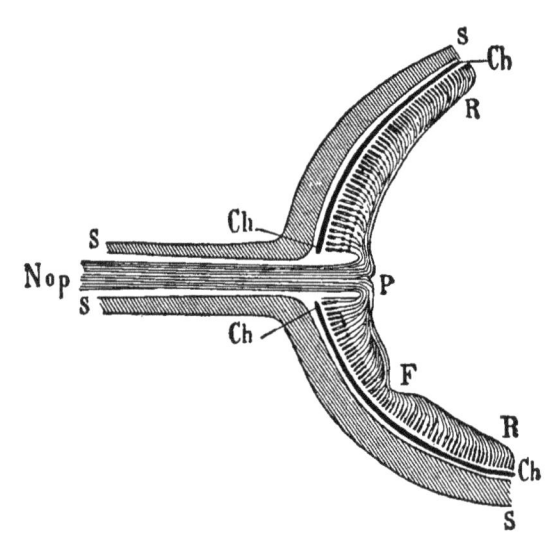

FIG. 4.

FIG. 5.—Scheme of retinal fibres, after Küss. *Nop.* optic nerve; *S*, sclerotic; *Ch*, choroid; *R*, retina; *P*, papilla (blind spot); *F*, fovea.

that the light-waves traverse the translucent nerve-fibres, and the cellular and granular layers of the retina, before they touch the rods and cones themselves. (See Fig. 5.)

SIGHT.

The Blind Spot.—The optic nerve-fibres must thus be unimpressible by light directly. The place where the nerve enters is in fact entirely blind, because nothing but fibres exist there, the other layers of the retina only beginning round about the entrance. Nothing is easier than to prove the existence of this blind spot. Close the right ye and look steadily with the left at the cross in Fig. 6,

FIG. 6.

holding the book vertically in front of the face, and moving it to and fro. It will be found that at about a foot off the black disk disappears; but when the page is nearer or farther, it is seen. During the experiment the gaze must be kept fixed on the cross. It is easy to show by measurement that this blind spot lies where the optic nerve enters.

The Fovea.—Outside of the blind spot the sensibility of the retina varies. It is greatest at the *fovea,* a little pit lying outwardly from the entrance of the optic nerve, and round which the radiating nerve-fibres bend without passing over it. The other layers also disappear at the fovea, leaving the cones alone to represent the retina there. The sensibility of the retina grows progressively less towards its periphery, by means of which neither colors, shapes, nor number of impressions can be well discriminated.

In the normal use of our two eyes, the eyeballs are rotated so as to cause the two images of any object which catches the attention to fall on the two foveæ, as the spots of acutest vision. This happens involuntarily, as any one may observe. In fact, it is almost impossible *not* to 'turn the eyes,' the moment any peripherally lying object does catch our attention, the turning of the eyes being only another name for such rotation of the eyeballs as will bring the foveæ under the object's image.

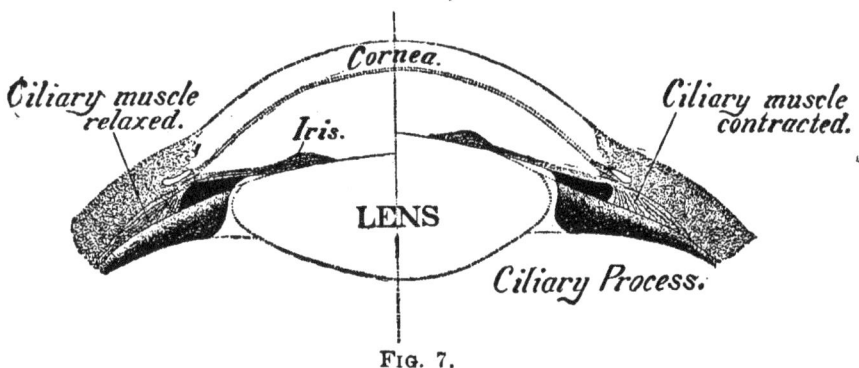

Fig. 7.

Accommodation.—The *focussing* or *sharpening* of the image is performed by a special apparatus. In every camera, the farther the object is from the eye the farther forward, and the nearer the object is to the eye the farther backward, is its image thrown. In photographers' cameras the back is made to slide, and can be drawn away from the lens when the object that casts the picture is near, and pushed forward when it is far. The picture is thus kept always sharp. But no such change of length is possible in the eyeball; and the same result is reached in another way. The lens, namely, grows more convex when a near object is looked at, and flatter when the object recedes. This change is due to the antagonism of the circular 'ligament' in which the lens is suspended, and the 'ciliary muscle.' The ligament, when the ciliary muscle is at rest, assumes such a spread-out shape as to keep the lens rather flat. But the lens is highly elastic; and it springs into the more convex form which is natural to it whenever the ciliary muscle, by contracting, causes the ligament to relax its pressure. The contraction of the muscle, by thus rendering the lens more refractive, adapts the eye for near objects ('accommodates' it for them, as we say); and its relaxation, by rendering the lens less refractive, adapts the eye for distant vision. Accommodation for the near is thus the more *active* change, since it involves contraction of the ciliary muscle. When we look far off, we simply let our eyes go passive. We feel this difference in the effort when we compare the two sensations of change.

Convergence accompanies accommodation. The two eyes act as one organ; that is, when an object catches the attention, both eyeballs turn so that its images may fall on the foveæ. When the object is near, this naturally requires them to turn inwards, or converge; and as accommodation then also occurs, the two movements of convergence and accommodation form a naturally associated couple, of which it is difficult to execute either singly. Contraction of the pupil also accompanies the accommodative act. When we come to stereoscopic vision, it will appear that by much practice one can learn to converge with relaxed accommodation, and to accommodate with parallel axes of vision. These are accomplishments which the student of psychological optics will find most useful.

Single Vision by the two Retinæ.—We hear single with two ears, and smell single with two nostrils, and we also see single with two eyes. The difference is that we also *can* see double under certain conditions, whereas under no conditions can we hear or smell double. The main conditions of single vision can be simply expressed.

In the first place, impressions on the two foveæ always appear in the same place. By no artifice can they be made to appear alongside of each other. The result is that one object, casting its images on the foveæ of the two converging eyeballs will necessarily always appear as what it is, namely, one object. Furthermore, if the eyeballs, instead of converging, are kept parallel, and two similar objects, one in front of each, cast their respective images on the foveæ, the two will also appear as one, or (in common parlance) 'their images will fuse.' To verify this, let the reader stare fixedly before him as if through the paper at infinite distance, with the black spots in Fig. 8 in front of his respective eyes. Ho will then see the two black spots swim together, as it were, and combine into one, which appears situated between their original two positions and as if opposite the root of his nose. This combined spot is the result of the spots opposite both eyes being seen in the same place. But in addition to the combined spot, each eye sees also the spot opposite the *other* eye. To the right eye this appears to the left of the combined spot, to the left eye it appears to the right of it; so that what is seen is *three* spots, of which the middle one is seen by both eyes, and is flanked by two

FIG 8.

others, each seen by one. That such are the facts can be tested by interposing some small opaque object so as to cut off the vision of either of the spots in the figure from the *other* eye. A vertical partition in the median plane, going from the paper to the nose, will effectually confine each eye's vision to the spot in front of it, and then the single combined spot will be all that appears.*

If, instead of two identical spots, we use two different figures, or two differently colored spots, as objects for the two foveæ to look at, they still are seen in the *same place;* but since they cannot appear as a single object, they appear there *alternately* displacing each other from the view. This is the phenomenon called *retinal rivalry.*

As regards the parts of the retinæ round about the foveæ, a similar correspondence obtains. Any impression on the

---

* This vertical partition is introduced into stereoscopes, which otherwise would give us three pictures instead of one.

upper half of either retina makes us see an object as below, on the lower half as above, the horizon; and on the right half of either retina, an impression makes us see an object to the left, on the left half one to the right, of the median line. Thus each quadrant of one retina corresponds as a whole to the geometrically *similar* quadrant of the other;

Fig 9.

and within two similar quadrants, *al* and *ar* for example, there should, if the correspondence were carried out in detail, be geometrically similar points which, if impressed at the same time by light emitted from the same object, should cause that object to appear in the same direction to either eye. Experiment verifies this surmise. If we look at the starry vault with parallel eyes, the stars all seem single; and the laws of perspective show that under the circumstances the parallel light-rays coming from each star must impinge on points within either retina which *are* geometrically similar to each other. Similarly, a pair of spectacles held an inch or so from the eyes seem like one large median glass. Or we may make an experiment like that with the spots. If we take two exactly similar pictures, no larger than those on an ordinary stereoscopic slide, and if we look at one with each eye (a median partition confining the view) we shall see but one flat picture, all of whose parts appear single. 'Identical retinal points' being impressed, both eyes see their object in the same direction, and the two objects consequently coalesce into one.

Here again retinal rivalry occurs if the pictures differ. And it must be noted that when the experiment is performed for the first time the combined picture is always far from sharp. This is due to the difficulty mentioned on p. 33, of accommodating for anything as near as the surface of the paper, whilst at the same time the convergence is relaxed so that each eye sees the picture in front of itself.

Double Images.—Now it is an immediate consequence of the law of identical location of images falling on geometrically similar points that *images which fall upon geometrically* DISPARATE *points of the two retinæ should be seen in* DISPARATE *directions, and that their objects should*

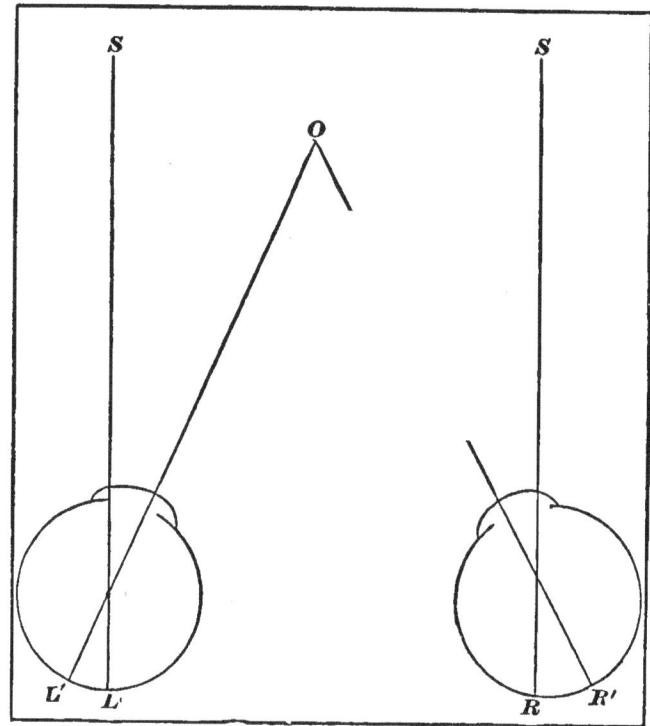

FIG. 10.

consequently appear in TWO *places, or* LOOK DOUBLE. Take the parallel rays from a star falling upon two eyes which converge upon a near object, O, instead of being parallel as in the previously instanced case. The two foveæ will receive the images of O, which therefore will look single. If then SL and SR in Fig. 10 be the parallel rays, each of them will fall upon the nasal half of the retina which it strikes. But the two nasal halves are disparate, geometrically *symmetrical*, not geometrically *similar*. The star's image on the left eye will therefore appear as if lying to the left of O; its image on the right eye will appear to the right of this point. The star will, in short, be seen double—'homonymously' double.

Conversely, if the star be looked at directly with parallel axes, any near object like O will be seen double, because its images will affect the onter or cheek halves of the two retinæ, instead of one outer and one nasal half. The position of the images will here be reversed from that of the previous case. The right eye's image will now appear to the left, the left eye's to the right; the double images will be 'heteronymous.'

The same reasoning and the same result ought to apply where the object's place with respect to the direction of the two optic axes is such as to make its images fall not on non-similar retinal halves, but on non-similar parts of similar halves. Here, of course, the positions seen will be less widely disparate than in the other case, and the double images will appear to lie less widely apart.

Careful experiments made by many observers according to the so-called haploscopic method confirm this law, and show that *corresponding points, of single visual direction*, exist upon the two retinæ. For the detail of these one must consult the special treatises.

Vision of Solidity.—This description of binocular vision follows what is called the theory of identical points. On the whole it formulates the facts correctly. The only odd thing is that we should be so little troubled by the innumerable double images which objects nearer and farther than the point looked at must be constantly producing. The answer to this is that *we have trained ourselves to habits of inattention* in regard to double images. So far as things interest us we turn our foveæ upon them, and they are necessarily seen single; so that if an object impresses disparate points, that may be taken as proof that it is so unimportant for us that we needn't notice whetner it appears in one place or in two. By long practice one may acquire great expertness in detecting double images, though, as some one says, it is an art which is not to be learned completely either in one year or in two.

Where the disparity of the images is but slight it is almost impossible to see them as if double. They give rather the perception of a solid object being there. To fix our ideas, take Fig. 11. Suppose we look at the dots in the

FIG. 11.

middle of the lines *a* and *b* just as we looked at the spots in Fig. 8. We shall get the same result—i.e., they will coalesce in the median line. But the entire lines will not coalesce, for, owing to their inclination, their tops fall on the temporal, and their bottoms on the nasal, retinal halves. What we see will be two lines crossed in the middle, thus (Fig. 12):

The moment we attend to the tops of these lines, however, our foveæ tend to abandon the dots and to move upwards, and in doing so, to converge somewhat, following the lines, which then appear coalescing at the top as in Fig. 13.

FIG. 12.

If we think of the bottom, the eyes descend and diverge, and what we see is Fig. 14.

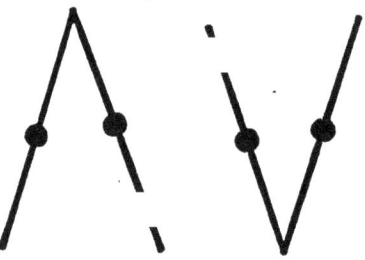

FIG. 13.   FIG. 14.

Running our eyes up and down the lines makes them converge and diverge just as they would were they running up and down some single line whose top was nearer to us than its bottom. Now, if the inclination of the lines be moderate, we may not see them double at all, but single throughout their length, when we look at the dots. Under these conditions their top does look nearer than their bottom—in other words, we see them stereoscopically; and we see them so even when our eyes are rigorously motionless. In other words, the slight disparity in the bottom-ends which *would* draw the foveæ divergently apart makes us see those ends farther, the slight disparity in the top ends which *would* draw them convergently together makes us see these ends nearer, than the point at which we look. The disparities, in short, affect our perception as the actual movements would.*

The Perception of Distance.—When we look about us at things, our eyes are incessantly moving, converging, diverging, accommodating, relaxing, and sweeping over the field. The field appears extended in three dimensions, with some of its parts more distant and some more near.

"With one eye our perception of distance is very imperfect, as illustrated by the common trick of holding a ring suspended by a string in front of a person's face, and telling him to shut one eye and pass a rod from one side through the ring. If a penholder be held erect before one eye, while the other is closed, and an attempt be made to touch it with a finger moved across towards it, an error will nearly always be made. In such cases we get the only clue from the amount of effort needed to 'accommodate' the eye to see the object distinctly. When we use both eyes our perception of distance is much better; when we look at an object with two eyes the visual axes are converged on it, and the nearer the object the greater the convergence. We have a pretty accurate knowledge of the degree of muscular effort required to converge the eyes on all tolerably near points. When objects are

---

* The simplest form of stereoscope is two tin tubes about one and one-half inches calibre, dead black inside and (for normal eyes) ten inches long. Close each end with paper not too opaque, on which an inch-long thick black line is drawn. The tubes can be looked through, one by each eye, and held either parallel or with their farther ends converging. When properly rotated, their images will show every variety of fusion and non-fusion, and stereoscopic effect.

farther off, their apparent size, and the modifications their retinal images experience by aërial perspective, come in to help. The relative distance of objects is easiest determined by moving the eyes; all stationary objects then appear displaced in the opposite direction (as for example when we look out of the window of a railway car) and those nearest most rapidly; from the different apparent rates of movement we can tell which are farther and which nearer." *

Subjectively considered, distance is an altogether peculiar content of consciousness. Convergence, accommodation, binocular disparity, size, degree of brightness, parallax, etc., all give us special feelings which are *signs* of the distance feeling, but not it. They simply suggest it to us. The best way to get it strongly is to go upon some hill-top and invert one's head. The horizon then looks very distant, and draws near as the head erects itself again.

The Perception of Size.—" The dimensions of the retinal image determine primarily the sensations on which conclusions as to size are based; and the larger the visual angle the larger the retinal image: since the visual angle depends on the distance of an object, the correct perception of size depends largely upon a correct perception of distance; having formed a judgment, conscious or unconscious, as to that, we conclude as to size from the extent of the retinal region affected. Most people have been surprised now and then to find that what appeared a large bird in the clouds was only a small insect close to the eye; the large apparent size being due to the previous incorrect judgment as to the distance of the object. The presence of an object of tolerably well-known height, as a man, also assists in forming conceptions (by comparison) as to size; artists for this purpose frequently introduce human figures to assist in giving an idea of the size of other objects represented." †

Sensations of Color.—The system of colors is a very complex thing. If one take any color, say green, one can pass

---

* Martin: The Human Body, p. 530.
† Ibid

away from it in more than one direction, through a series of greens more and more yellowish, let us say, towards yellow, or through another series more and more bluish towards blue. The result would be that if we seek to plot out on paper the various distinguishable tints, the arrangement cannot be that of a line, but has to cover a surface. With the tints arranged on a surface we can pass from any one of them to any other by various lines of gradually changing intermediaries. Such an arrangement is represented in Fig. 15. It is a merely classificatory diagram based on degrees of difference simply felt, and has no physical significance. Black is a color, but does not figure on the plane of the diagram. We cannot place it anywhere alongside of the other colors because we need both to represent the straight gradation from untinted white to black, and that from each pure color towards black as well as towards white.

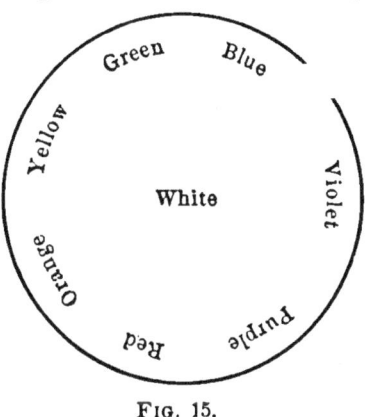

FIG. 15.

The best way is to put black into the third dimension, beneath the paper, *e.g.*, as is shown perspectively in Fig. 16, then all the transitions can be schematically shown. One can pass straight from black to white, or one can pass round by way of olive, green, and pale green; or one can change from dark blue to yellow through green, or by way of sky-blue, white and straw color; etc., etc. In any case the changes are continuous; and the color system thus forms what Wundt calls a tri-dimensional continuum.

Color-mixture. — Physiologically considered, the colors have this peculiarity, that many pairs of them, when they impress the retina together, produce the sensation of white. The colors which do this are called *complementaries*. Such are spectral red and green-blue, spectral yellow and indigo-blue. Green and purple, again, are complementaries. All the spectral colors added together also make white light, such as we daily experience in the sunshine. Furthermore, both homogeneous etherwaves and heterogeneous ones may make us feel the same color, when they fall on our retina. Thus yellow, which is a simple spectral color, is also felt when green light is added to red; blue is felt when violet and green lights are mixed. Purple, which is not a spectral color at all, results when the waves either of red and of violet or those of blue and of orange are superposed.*

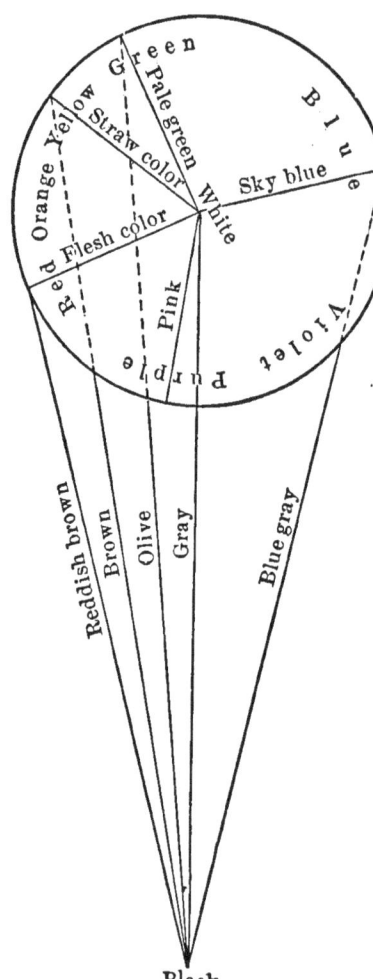

FIG. 16 (after Ziehen).

From all this it follows that there is no particular congruence between our system of color-sensations and the physical stimuli which excite them. Each color-feeling is a 'specific energy' (p. 11) which many different physical causes may arouse. Helmholtz, Hering, and others have sought to simplify the tangle of the facts, by physiological hypotheses which, differing much in detail, agree in principle, since they all postulate a limited number of elementary retinal processes to which, when excited singly,

---

* The ordinary mixing of *pigments* is not an addition, but rather, as Helmholtz has shown, a subtraction, of lights. To *add* one color to another we must either by appropriate glasses throw differently colored beams upon the same reflecting surface; or we must let the eye look at one color through an inclined plate of glass beneath which it lies, whilst the upper surface of the glass reflects into the same eye

certain 'fundamental' colors severally correspond. When excited in combination, as they may be by the most various physical stimuli, other colors, called 'secondary,' are felt. The secondary color-sensations are often spoken of as if they were compounded of the primary sensations. This is a great mistake. The *sensations as such* are not compounded—yellow, for example, a secondary on Helmholtz's theory, is as unique a quality of feeling as the primaries red and green, which are said to 'compose' it. What are compounded are merely the elementary retinal processes. These, according to their combination, produce diverse results on the brain, and thence the secondary colors result immediately in consciousness. The 'color-theories' are thus physiological, not psychological, hypotheses, and for more information concerning them the reader must consult the physiological books.

The Duration of Luminous Sensations.—" This is greater than that of the stimulus, a fact taken advantage of in making fireworks: an ascending rocket produces the sensation of a trail of light extending far behind the position of the bright part of the rocket itself at the moment, because the sensation aroused by it in a lower part of its course still persists. So, shooting stars appear to have luminous tails behind them. By rotating rapidly before the eye a disk with alternate white and black sectors we get for each point of the retina alternate stimulation (due to the passage of white sector) and rest (when a black sector is passing). If the rotation be rapid enough the sensation aroused is that of a uniform gray, such as would be produced if the white and black were mixed and spread evenly over the disk. In each revolution the eye gets as

---

another color placed alongside—the two lights then mix on the retina; or, finally, we must let the differently colored lights fall in succession upon the retina, so fast that the second is there before the impression made by the first has died away. This is best done by looking at a rapidly rotating disk whose sectors are of the several colors to be mixed.

much light as if that were the case, and is unable to distinguish that this light is made up of separate portions reaching it at intervals: the stimulation due to each lasts until the next begins, and so all are fused together. If one turns out suddenly the gas in a room containing no other light, the image of the flame persists a short time after the flame itself is extinguished."* If we open our eyes instantaneously upon a scene, and then shroud them in complete darkness, it will be as if we saw the scene in ghostly light through the dark screen. We can read off details in it which were unnoticed whilst the eyes were open. This is the primary positive after-image, so-called. According to Helmholtz, one third of a second is the most favorable length of exposure to the light for producing it.

Negative after-images are due to more complex conditions, in which fatigue of the retina is usually supposed to play the chief part.

" The nervous visual apparatus is easily fatigued. Usually we do not observe this because its restoration is also rapid, and in ordinary life our eyes, when open, are never at rest; we move them to and fro, so that parts of the retina receive light alternately from brighter and darker objects, and are alternately excited and rested. How constant and habitual the movement of the eyes is can be readily observed by trying to 'fix' for a short time a small spot without deviating the glance; to do so for even a few seconds is impossible without practice. If any small object is steadily 'fixed' for twenty or thirty seconds, it will be found that the whole field of vision becomes grayish and obscure, because the parts of the retina receiving most light get fatigued, and arouse no more sensation than those less fatigued and stimulated by light from less illuminated objects. Or look steadily at a black object, say a blot on a white page, for twenty seconds, and then turn the eye on a white wall; the latter will seem dark gray, with a white patch on it; an effect due to the greater excitability of the retinal parts previously rested by the black, when compared with the sensation aroused elsewhere by light from the white wall acting on the previously stimulated parts of the visual surface. All persons will recall many instances of such phenomena, which are especially noticeable soon after rising in the morning.

---

* Martin · *op. cit.*

Similar things may be noticed with colors; after looking at a red patch the eye turned on a white wall sees a blue-green patch; the elements causing red sensations having been fatigued, the white mixed light from the wall now excites on that region of the retina only the other primary color sensations. The blending of colors so as to secure their greatest effect depends on this fact; red and green go well together because each rests the parts of the visual apparatus most excited by the other, and so each appears bright and vivid as the eye wanders to and fro; while red and orange together, each exciting and exhausting mainly the same visual elements, render dull, or in popular phrase 'kill,' one another.

"If we fix steadily for thirty seconds a point between two white squares about 4 mm. (⅙ inch) apart on a large black sheet, and then close and cover our eyes, we get a negative after-image in which are seen two dark squares on a brighter surface; this surface is brighter close around the negative after-image of each square, and brightest of all between them. This luminous boundary is called the *corona*, and is explained usually as an effect of simultaneous contrast; the dark after-image of the square it is said makes us mentally err in judgment, and think the clear surface close to it brighter than elsewhere; and it is brightest between the two dark squares, just as a middle-sized man between two tall ones looks shorter than if alongside one only. If, however, the after-image be watched, it will often be noticed not only that the light band between the squares is intensely white, much more so than the normal idio-retinal light [see below], but, as the image fades away, often the two dark after-images of the squares disappear entirely with all of the corona, except that part between them which is still seen as a bright band on a uniform grayish field. Here there is no *contrast* to produce the error of judgment; and from this and other experiments Hering concludes that light acting on one part of the retina produces inverse changes in all the rest, and that this plays an important part in producing the phenomena of contrasts. Similar phenomena may be observed with colored objects, in their negative after-images each tint is represented by its complementary, as black is by white in colorless vision."*

This is one of the facts referred to on p. 27 which have made Hering reject the psychological explanation of simultaneous contrast.

The Intensity of Luminous Objects.—Black is an optical sensation. We have no black except in the field of view;

---

* Martin, pp. 525–8.

we do not, for instance, see black out of our stomach or out of the palm of our hand. *Pure* black is, however, only an 'abstract idea,' for the retina itself (even in complete objective darkness) seems to be always the seat of internal changes which give some luminous sensation. This is what is meant by the 'idio-retinal light,' spoken of a few lines back. It plays its part in the determination of all after-images with closed eyes. Any objective luminous stimulus, to be perceived, must be strong enough to give a sensible increment of sensation over and above the idio-retinal light. As the objective stimulus increases the perception is of an intenser luminosity; but the perception changes, as we saw on p. 18, more slowly than the stimulus. The latest numerical determinations, by König and Brodhun, were applied to six different colors and ran from an intensity arbitrarily called 1 to one which was 100,000 times as great. From intensity 2000 to 20,000 Weber's law held good; below and above this range discriminative sensibility declined. The relative increment discriminated here was the same for all colors of light, and lay (according to the tables) between 1 and 2 per cent of the stimulus. Previous observers have got different results.

A certain amount of luminous intensity must exist in an object for its color to be discriminated at all. "In the dark all cats are gray." But the colors rapidly become distincter as the light increases, first the blues and last the reds and yellows, up to a certain point of intensity, when they grow indistinct again through the fact that each takes a turn towards white. At the highest bearable intensity of the light all colors are lost in the blinding white dazzle. This again is usually spoken of as a 'mixing' of the sensation white with the original color-sensation. It is no mixing of two sensations, but the replacement of one sensation by another, in consequence of a changed neural process.

CHAPTER IV.

HEARING.*

The Ear.—" The auditory organ in man consists of three portions, known respectively as the *external ear,* the *middle ear* or *tympanum,* and the *internal ear* or *laby-*

FIG 17 —Semidiagrammatic section through the right ear (Czermak) *M,* concha, *G,* external auditory meatus; *T,* tympanic membrane; *P,* tympanic cavity. *o,* oval foramen; *r,* round foramen; *R,* pharyngeal opening of Eustachian tube. *V,* vestibule, *B,* a semicircular canal; *S,* the cochlea; *Vt,* scala vestibuli, *Pt,* scala tympani; *A,* auditory nerve.

rinth ; the latter contains the end-organs of the auditory nerve. The external ear consists of the expansion seen on the exterior of the head, called the *concha, M,* Fig. 17,

---

* In teaching the anatomy of the ear, great assistance will be yielded by the admirable model made by Dr. Auzoux, 56 Rue de Vaugirard, Paris, described in the catalogue of the firm as " No. 21 —*Oreille, temporal de* 60 cm , nouvelle édition," etc.

and a passage leading in from it, the *external auditory meatus*, G. This passage is closed at its inner end by the *tympanic* or *drum membrane*, T. It is lined by skin, through which numerous small glands, secreting the *wax* of the ear, open.

"*The Tympanum* (P, Fig. 17) is an irregular cavity in the temporal bone, closed externally by the drum membrane. From its inner side the *Eustachian tube* (R) proceeds and opens into the pharynx. The inner wall of the tympanum is bony except for two small apertures, the *oval* and *round foramens*, o and r, which lead into the labyrinth. During life the round aperture is closed by the lining mucous membrane, and the oval by the stirrup-bones. The *tympanic membrane* T, stretched across the outer side of the tympanum, forms a shallow funnel with its concavity outwards. It is pressed by the external air on its exterior, and by air entering the tympanic cavity through the Eustachian tube on its inner side. If the tympanum were closed these pressures would not be always equal when barometric pressure varied, and the membrane would be bulged in or out according as the external or internal pressure on it were the greater. On the other hand, were the Eustachian tube always open the sounds of our own voices would be loud and disconcerting, so it is usually closed; but every time we swallow it is opened, and thus the air-pressure in the cavity is kept equal to that in the external auditory meatus. On making a balloon ascent or going rapidly down a deep mine, the sudden and great change of aërial pressure outside frequently causes

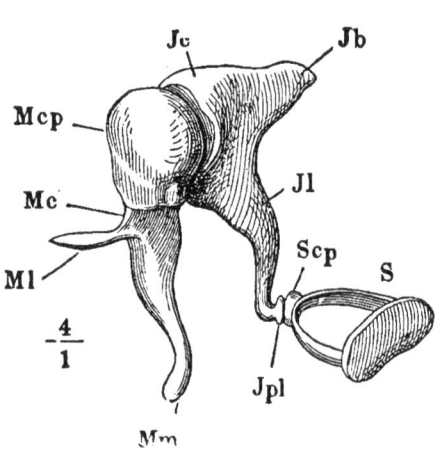

FIG 18 — *Mcp, Mc, Ml*, and *Mm* stand for different parts of the malleus; *Jc, Jb, Jl, Jpl*, for different parts of the incus *S* is the stapes.

painful tension of the drum-membrane, which may be greatly alleviated by frequent swallowing.

The Auditory Ossicles.—Three small bones lie in the tympanum forming a chain from the drum-membrane to the oval foramen. The external bone is the *malleus* or *hammer ;* the middle one, the *incus* or *anvil ;* and the internal one, the *stapes* or *stirrup.* They are represented in Fig. 18.*

Accommodation is provided for in the ear as well as in the eye. One muscle an inch long, the *tensor tympani,* arises in the petrous portion of the temporal bone (running in a canal parallel to the Eustachian tube) and is inserted into the malleus below its head. When it contracts, it makes the membrane of the tympanum more tense. Another smaller muscle, the *stapedius,* goes to the head of the stirrup-bone. These muscles are by many persons felt distinctly contracting when certain notes are heard, and some can make them contract at will. In spite of this, uncertainty still reigns as to their exact use in hearing, though it is highly probable that they give to the membranes which they influence the degree of tension best suited to take up whatever rates of vibration may fall upon them at the time. In listening, the head and ears in lower animals, and the head alone in man, are turned so as best to receive the sound. This also is a part of the reaction called 'adaptation' of the organ (see the chapter on Attention).

The Internal Ear.—" The labyrinth consists primarily of chambers and tubes hollowed out in the temporal bone and inclosed by it on all sides, except for the oval and round foramens on its exterior, and certain apertures for blood-vessels and the auditory nerve; during life all these are closed water-tight in one way or another. Lying in the *bony labyrinth* thus constituted are membranous parts, of the same general form but smaller, so that between the two

---

* This description is abridged from Martin's ' Human Body'

a space is left; this is filled with a watery fluid, called the *perilymph;* and the *membranous internal ear* is filled by a similar liquid, the *endolymph.*

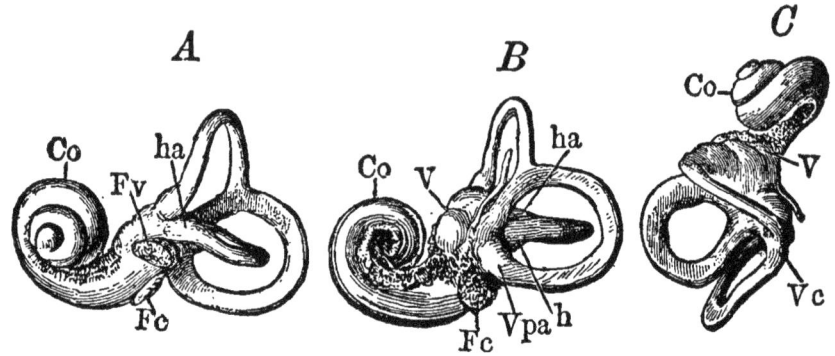

FIG. 19.—Casts of the bony labyrinth. *A*, left labyrinth seen from the outer side; *B*, right labyrinth from the inner side; *C*, left labyrinth from above; *Co*, cochlea; *V*, Vestibule; *Fc*, round foramen; *Fv*, oval foramen; *h*, horizontal semicircular canal; *ha*, its ampulla; *vaa*, ampulla of anterior vertical semicircular canal; *vpa*, ampulla of posterior vertical semicircular canal; *vc*, conjoined portion of the two vertical canals.

The Bony Labyrinth.—"The bony labyrinth is described in three portions, the *vestibule,* the *semicircular canals,* and the *cochlea;* casts of its interior are represented from different aspects in Fig. 19. The vestibule is the central part and has on its exterior the oval foramen (*Fv*) into which the base of the stirrup-bone fits. Behind the vestibule are three bony semicircular canals, communicating with the back of the vestibule at each end, and dilated near one end to form an *ampulla.* The bony cochlea is a tube coiled on itself somewhat like a snail's shell, and lying in front of the vestibule.

The Membranous Labyrinth.—"The membranous vestibule, lying in the bony, consists of two sacs communicating by a narrow aperture. The posterior is called the *utriculus,* and into it the membranous semicircular canals open. The anterior, called the *sacculus,* communicates by a tube with the membranous cochlea. The membranous semicircular canals much resemble the bony, and each has

HEARING.

an ampulla; in the ampulla one side of the **membranous** tube is closely adherent to its bony protector; at this point nerves enter the former. The relations of the membranous to the bony cochlea are more complicated. A section through this part of the auditory apparatus (Fig. 20) shows that its osseous portion consists of a tube wound two and a half times round a central bony axis, the *modiolus*.

FIG. 20.—A section through the cochlea in the line of its axis.

From the axis a shelf, the *lamina spiralis*, projects and partially subdivides the tube, extending farthest across in its lower coils. Attached to the outer edge of this bony plate is the membranous cochlea (*scala media*), a tube triangular in cross-section and attached by its base to the outer side of the bony cochlear spiral. The spiral lamina and the membranous cochlea thus subdivide the cavity of the bony tube (Fig. 21) into an upper portion, the *scala*

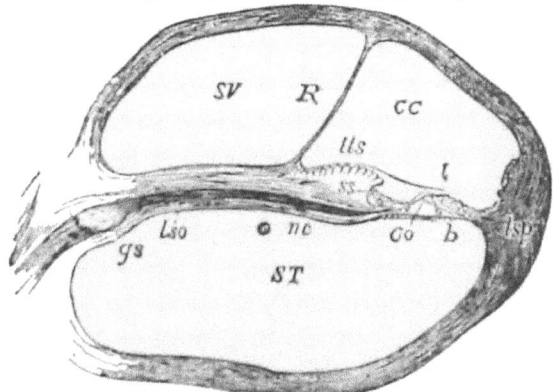

FIG. 21—Section of one coil of the cochlea, magnified. *SV, scala vestibuli; R*, membrane of Reissner, *CC*, membranous cochlea (*scala media*), *lls, limbus laminæ spiralis; t*, tectorial membrane, *ST, scala tympani; lso*, spiral lamina, *Co*, rods of Corti, *b*, basilar membrane

vestibuli, SV, and a lower, the *scala tympani, ST*. Between these lie the lamina spiralis (*lso*) and the membranous cochlea (CC), the latter being bounded above by the membrane of Reissner (R) and below by the basilar membrane (b)."*

The membranous cochlea does not extend to the tip of the bony cochlea; above its apex the scala vestibuli and scala tympani communicate. Both are filled with perilymph, so that when the stapes is pushed into the oval foramen, o, in Fig. 17, by the impact of an air-wave on the tympanic membrane, a wave of perilymph runs up the scala vestibuli to the top, where it turns into the scala tympani, down whose whorls it runs and pushes out the round foramen r, ruffling probably the membrane of Reissner and the basilar membrane on its way up and down.

The Terminal Organs.—"The membranous cochlea contains certain solid structures seated on the basilar membrane and forming the *organ of Corti*. This contains the end-organs of the cochlear nerves. Lining the sulcus

FIG 22.—The rods of Corti *A*, a pair of rods separated from the rest; *B*, a bit of the basilar membrane with several rods on it, showing how they cover in the *tunnel of Corti* ; i, inner, and e, outer rods; b, basilar membrane; r, reticular membrane.

spiralis, a groove in the edge of the bony lamina spiralis, are cuboidal cells; on the inner margin of the basilar membrane they become columnar, and then are succeeded by a row which bear on their upper ends a set of short stiff hairs, and constitute the *inner hair-cells*, which are fixed below by a narrow apex to the basilar membrane; nerve-fibres enter them. To the inner hair-cells succeed the

---

* Martin : *op. cit.*

HEARING.

rods of Corti (*Co*, Fig. 21), which are represented highly magnified in Fig. 22. These rods are stiff and arranged side by side in two rows, leaned against one another by their upper ends so as to cover in a tunnel; they are known respectively as the *inner* and *outer rods,* the former being nearer the *lamina spiralis*. The inner rods are more numerous than the outer, the numbers being about 6000 and 4500 respectively. Attached to the external sides of the heads of the outer rods is the *reticular membrane* (*r,* Fig. 22), which is stiff and perforated by holes. External to the outer rods come four rows of *outer hair-cells,* connected like the inner row with nerve-fibres; their bristles project into the holes of the reticular membrane. Beyond the outer hair-cells is ordinary columnar epithelium, which passes gradually into cuhoidal cells lining most of the membranous cochlea. From the upper lip of the sulcus spiralis projects the *tectorial membrane* (*t,* Fig. 21) which extends over the rods of Corti and the hair-cells."*

FIG. 23 —Sensory epithelium from ampulla or semicircular canal, and saccule At *n* a nerve-fibre pierces the wall, and after branching enters the two hair-cells, *c*. At *h* a 'columnar cell' with a long hair is shown, the nerve-fibre being broken away from its base The slender cells at *f* seem unconnected with nerves.

The hair-cells would thus seem to be the terminal organs for 'picking up' the vibrations which the air-waves communicate through all the intervening apparatus, solid and liquid, to the basilar membrane. Analogous hair-cells receive the terminal nerve-filaments in the walls of the saccule, utricle, and ampullæ (see Fig. 23).

The Various Qualities of Sound.—Physically, sounds consist of vibrations, and these are, generally speaking, *aërial waves.* When the waves are non-periodic the result is a

---

* Martin : *op. cit*

noise; when periodic it is what is nowadays called a *tone,* or *note.* The *loudness* of a sound depends on the *force* of the waves. When they recur periodically a peculiar quality called *pitch* is the effect of their *frequency.* In addition to loudness and pitch tones have each their *voice* or *timbre,* which may differ widely in different instruments giving equally loud tones of the same pitch. This voice depends on the *form* of the aërial wave.

Pitch.—A single puff of air, set in motion by no matter what cause, will give a sensation of sound; but it takes at least four or five puffs, or more, to convey a sensation of pitch. The pitch of the note *c,* for instance, is due to 132 vibrations a second, that of its octave *c'* is produced by twice as many, or 264 vibrations; but in neither case is it necessary for the vibrations to go on during a full second for the pitch to be discerned. "Sound vibrations may be too rapid or too slow in succession to produce sonorous sensations, just as the ultra-violet and ultra-red rays of the solar spectrum fail to excite the retina. The highest-pitched audible note answers to about 38,016 vibrations in a second, but it differs in individuals; many persons cannot hear the cry of a bat nor the chirp of a cricket, which lie near this upper audible limit. On the other hand, sounds of vibrational rate about 40 per second are not well heard, and a little below this they produce rather a 'hum' than a true tone-sensation, and are only used along with notes of higher octaves to which they give a character of greater depth." *

The entire system of pitches forms *a continuum of one dimension;* that is to say, you can pass from one pitch to another only by one set of intermediaries, instead of by more than one, as in the case of colors. (See p. 41.) The whole series of pitches is embraced in and between the terms of what is called the musical scale. The adoption of certain arbitrary points in this scale as 'notes' has an ex-

---

* Martin : *op. cit.*

planation partly historic and partly æsthetic, but too complex for exposition here.

The 'timbre' of a note is due to its *wave-form*. Waves are either simple ('pendular') or compound. Thus if a tuning-fork (which gives waves nearly simple) vibrate 132 times a second, we shall hear the note c. If simultaneously a fork of 264 vibrations be struck, giving the next higher octave, c', the aërial movement at any time will be the algebraic sum of the movements due to both forks; whenever both drive the air one way they reinforce one another; when on the contrary the recoil of one fork coincides with the forward stroke of another, they detract from each other's effect. The result is a movement which is still periodic, repeating itself at equal intervals of time, but no longer *pendular*, since it is not alike on the ascending and descending limbs of the curves. We thus get at the fact that non-pendular vibrations may be produced by the fusion of pendular, or, in technical phrase, by their *composition*.

Suppose several musical instruments, as those of an orchestra, to be sounded together. Each produces its own effect on the air-particles, whose movements, being an algebraical sum, must at any given instant be very complex; yet the ear can pick out at will and follow the tones of any one instrument. Now in most musical instruments it is susceptible of physical proof that with every single note that is sounded many upper octaves and other 'harmonics' sound simultaneously in fainter form. On the relative strength of this or that one or more of these Helmholtz has shown that the instrument's peculiar voice depends. The several vowel-sounds in the human voice also depend on the predominance of diverse upper harmonics accompanying the note on which the vowel is sung. When the two tuning-forks of the last paragraph are sounded together the new form of vibration has the same *period* as the lower-pitched fork; yet the ear can clearly distinguish the resultant sound from that of the lower fork alone, as a note of the same pitch but of different timbre; and within the compound sound the two components can by a trained ear be severally heard. Now how can one resultant wave-form make us hear so many sounds at once?

The analysis of compound wave-forms is supposed (after Helmholtz) to be effected through the different rates of sympathetic resonance of the different parts of the membranous cochlea. The basilar membrane is some twelve times broader at the apex of the cochlea than at the base where it begins, and is largely composed of radiating fibres which may be likened to stretched strings. Now the physical principle of sympathetic resonance says that when stretched strings are near a source of vibration those whose own rate agrees with that of the source also vibrate, the others remaining at rest. On this principle, waves of perilymph running down the scala tympani at a certain rate of frequency ought to set certain particular fibres of the basilar membrane vibrating, and ought to leave others unaffected. If then each vibrating fibre stimulated the hair-cell above it, and no others, and each such hair-cell, sending a current to the auditory brain-centre, awakened therein a specific process to which the sensation of one particular pitch was correlated, the physiological condition of our several pitch-sensations would be explained. Suppose now a chord to be struck in which perhaps twenty different physical rates of vibration are found: at least twenty different hair-cells or end-organs will receive the jar; and if the power of mental discrimination be at its maximum, twenty different 'objects' of hearing, in the shape of as many distinct pitches of sound, may appear before the mind.

The rods of Corti are supposed to be *dampers* of the fibres of the basilar membrane, just as the malleus, incus, and stapes are dampers of the tympanic membrane, as well as transmitters of its oscillations to the inner ear. There must be, in fact, an instantaneous *damping* of the physiological vibrations, for there are no such positive after-images, and no such blendings of rapidly successive tones, as the retina shows us in the case of light. Helmholtz's theory of the analysis of sounds is plausible and ingenious. One objection to it is that the keyboard of the cochlea does not seem extensive enough for the number of distinct resonances required. We can discriminate many more degrees of pitch than the 20,000 hair-cells, more or less, will allow for.

The so-called Fusion of Sensations in Hearing.—A very common way of explaining the fact that waves which singly give no feeling of pitch give one when recurrent, is to say that their several sensations *fuse into a compound sensation.* A preferable explanation is that which follows the analogy of muscular contraction. If electric shocks are sent into a frog's sciatic nerve at slow intervals, the muscle which the nerve supplies will give a series of distinct twitches, one for each shock. But if they follow each other at the rate of as many as thirty a second, no distinct twitches are observed, but a steady state of contraction instead. This steady contraction is known as *tetanus.* The experiment proves that there is a physiological cumulation or overlapping of processes in the muscular tissue. It takes a twentieth of a second or more for the latter to relax after the twitch due to the first shock. But the second shock comes in before the relaxation can occur, then the third again, and so on; so that continuous tetanus takes the place of discrete twitching. Similarly in the auditory nerve. One shock of air starts in it a current to the auditory brain-centre, and affects the latter, so that a dry stroke of sound is heard. If other shocks follow slowly, the brain-centre recovers its equilibrium after each, to be again upset in the same way by the next, and the result is that for each shock of air a distinct sensation of sound occurs. But if the shock comes in too quick succession, the later ones reach the brain before the effects of the earlier ones on that organ have died away. There is thus an overlapping of processes in the auditory centre, a physiological condition analogous to the muscle's tetanus, to which new condition a new quality of feeling, that of pitch, directly corresponds. This latter feeling is a new kind of sensation altogether, not a mere 'appearance' due to many sensations of dry stroke being compounded into one. No sensations of dry stroke can exist under these circumstances, for their physiological conditions have been replaced by others. What 'compounding' there is has already taken place in the brain-cells before the threshold of sensation was reached. Just so red light and green light beating on the retina in rapid enough alternation, arouse the central process to which the sensation *yellow* directly corresponds. The sensations of red and of green get no chance, under such conditions, to be born. Just so if the muscle could feel, it would have a certain sort of feeling when it gave a single twitch, but it would undoubtedly have a distinct sort of feeling altogether, when it contracted tetanically; and this feeling of the tetanic contraction would by no means be identical with a multitude of the feelings of twitching.

Harmony and Discord.—When several tones sound together we may get peculiar feelings of pleasure or displeasure designated as consonance and dissonance respectively. A note sounds most consonant with its octave. When with the octave the 'third' and the 'fifth' of the note are sounded, for instance c—e—g—c', we get the 'full chord' or maximum of consonance. The ratios of vibration here are as $4:5:6:8$, so that one might think simple ratios were the ground of harmony. But the interval c—d is discordant, with the comparatively simple ratio $8:9$. Helmholtz explains discord by the overtones making 'beats' together. This gives a subtle grating which is unpleasant. Where the overtones make no 'beats', or beats too rapid for their effect to be perceptible, there is consonance, according to Helmholtz, which is thus a negative rather than a positive thing. Wundt explains consonance by the presence of strong identical overtones in the notes which harmonize. No one of these explanations of musical harmony can be called quite satisfactory; and the subject is too intricate to be treated farther in this place.

Discriminative Sensibility of the Ear.—Weber's law holds fairly well for the intensity of sounds. If ivory or metal balls are dropped on an ebony or iron plate, they make a sound which is the louder as they are heavier or dropped from a greater height. Experimenting in this way (after others) Merkel found that the just perceptible increment of loudness required an increase of $\frac{3}{10}$ of the original stimulus everywhere between the intensities marked 20 and 5000 of his arbitrary scale. Below this the fractional increment of stimulus must be larger; above it, no measurements were made.

Discrimination of differences of *pitch* varies in different parts of the scale. In the neighborhood of 1000 vibrations per second, one fifth of a vibration more or less can make the sound sharp or flat for a good ear. It takes a much greater *relative* alteration to sound sharp or flat elsewhere on the scale. The chromatic scale itself has been used as an illustration of Weber's law. The notes seem to differ equally from each other, yet their vibration-numbers form a series of which each is a certain multiple of the last. This, however, has nothing to do with intensities or just perceptible differences; so the peculiar parallelism between the sensation series and the outer-stimulus series forms here a case all by itself, rather than an instance under Weber's more general law.

CHAPTER V.

TOUCH, THE TEMPERATURE SENSE, THE MUSCULAR SENSE, AND PAIN.

Nerve-endings in the Skin.—"Many of the afferent skin-nerves end in connection with hair-bulbs; the fine hairs over most of the cutaneous surface, projecting from the skin, transmit any movement impressed on them, with increased force, to the nerve-fibres at their fixed ends. Fine branches of axis-cylinders have also been described as penetrating between epidermic cells and ending there without terminal organs. In or immediately beneath the skin several peculiar forms of nerve end-organs have also been described; they are known as (1) *Touch-cells;* (2) *Pacinian corpuscles;* (3) *Tactile corpuscles;* (4) *End-bulbs.*" *

FIG. 24 —End-bulbs from the conjunctiva of the human eye, magnified.

These bodies all consist essentially of granules formed of connective tissue, in which or round about which one or more sensory nerve-fibres terminate. They probably magnify impressions just as a grain of sand does in a shoe, or a crumb does in a finger of a glove.

Touch, or the Pressure Sense.—"Through the skin we get several kinds of sensation; touch proper, heat and cold, and pain; and we can with more or less accuracy localize them on the surface of the body. The interior of the mouth possesses also three sensibilities. Through touch proper we recognize pressure or traction exerted on the skin, and the force of the pressure; the softness or hardness, roughness or smoothness, of the body producing it;

---

* Martin: *op. cit.*

and the form of this when not too large to be felt all over. When to learn the form of an object we move the hand over it, muscular sensations are combined with proper tactile, and such a combination of the two sensations is frequent; moreover, we rarely touch anything without at the same time getting temperature sensations; therefore pure tactile feelings are rare. From an evolution point of view, touch is probably the first distinctly differentiated sensation, and this primary position it still largely holds in our mental life." *

Objects are most important to us when in direct contact. The chief function of our eyes and ears is to enable us to prepare ourselves for contact with approaching bodies, or to ward such contact off. They have accordingly been characterized as organs of anticipatory touch.

"The delicacy of the tactile sense varies on different parts of the skin; it is greatest on the forehead, temples, and back of the forearm, where a weight of 2 milligr. pressing on an area of 9 sq. millim. can be felt.

"In order that the sense of touch may be excited neighboring skin-areas must be differently pressed. When the hand is immersed in a liquid, as mercury, which fits into all its inequalities and presses with practically the same weight on all neighboring immersed areas, the sense of pressure is only felt at a line along the surface, where the immersed and non-immersed parts of the skin meet.

The Localizing Power of the Skin.—" When the eyes are closed and a point of the skin is touched we can with some accuracy indicate the region stimulated; although tactile feelings are in general characters alike, they differ in something besides intensity by which we can distinguish them; some sub-sensation quality not rising definitely into prominence in consciousness must be present, comparable to the upper partials determining the timbre of a tone. The accuracy of the localizing power varies widely in different

---

* Martin : *op. cit.*

skin regions and is measured by observing the least distance which must separate two objects (as the blunted points of a pair of compasses) in order that they may be felt as two. The following table illustrates some of the differences observed:

Tongue-tip	1.1 mm.	(.04 inch)
Palm side of last phalanx of finger	2.2 mm.	(.08 inch)
Red part of lips	4.4 mm.	(.16 inch)
Tip of nose	6.6 mm.	(.24 inch)
Back of second phalanx of finger	11.0 mm.	(.44 inch)
Heel	22.0 mm.	(.88 inch)
Back of hand	30.8 mm.	(1.23 inches)
Forearm	39.6 mm.	(1.58 inches)
Sternum	44.0 mm.	(1.76 inches)
Back of neck	52.8 mm.	(2.11 inches)
Middle of back	66.0 mm.	(2.64 inches)

The localizing power is a little more acute across the long axis of a limb than in it; and is better when the pressure is only strong enough to just cause a distinct tactile sensation than when it is more powerful; it is also very readily and rapidly improvable by practice." It seems to be naturally delicate in proportion as the skin which possesses it covers a more movable part of the body.

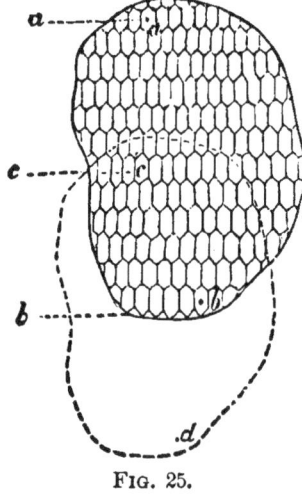

FIG. 25.

"It might be thought that this localizing power depended directly on nerve-distribution; that each touch-nerve had connection with a special brain-centre at one end (the excitation of which caused a sensation with a characteristic local sign), and at the other end was distributed over a certain skin-area, and that the larger this area the farther apart might two points be and still give rise to only one sensation. If this were so, however, the peripheral tactile areas (each being determined by the anatomical distribution of a nerve-fibre) must have definite unchangeable limits, which experiment shows that they do not possess. Suppose the small areas in Fig. 25 to each represent a peripheral area of nerve-distribution. If any two points in c were touched we should according to the theory get but a single sensation; but if, while the compass-points remained the same distance apart, or were even approximated, one were placed in c and the other on a contiguous area, two fibres would be stimulated and we ought to get two sensations; but such is not the case; on the same skin-region the points must be always the same distance apart, no matter how they be shifted, in order to give rise to two just distinguishable sensations.

"It is probable that the nerve-areas are much smaller than the tactile; and that several unstimulated must intervene between the excited, in order to produce sensations which shall be distinct. If we suppose twelve unexcited nerve-areas must intervene, then, in Fig. 25, a and b will be just on the limits of a single tactile area; and no matter how the points are moved, so long as eleven, or fewer, unexcited areas come between, we would get a single tactile sensation; in this way we can explain the fact that tactile areas have no fixed boundaries in the skin, although the nerve-distribution in any part must be constant. We also see why the back of a knife laid on the surface causes a continuous linear sensation, although it touches many distinct nerve-areas. If we could discriminate the excitations of each of these from that of its immediate neighbors we should get the sensation of a series of points touching us, one for each nerve-region excited; but in the absence of intervening unexcited nerve-areas the sensations are fused together.

The Temperature-sense. Its Terminal Organs.—" By this we mean our faculty of perceiving cold and warmth; and, with the help of these sensations, of perceiving temperature differences in external objects. Its organ is the whole skin, the mucuos membrane of mouth and fauces, pharynx and gullet, and the entry of the nares. Direct heating or cooling of a sensory nerve may stimulate it and cause pain, but not a true temperature-sensation; hence we assume the presence of temperature end-organs. [These have not yet been ascertained anatomically. Physiologically, however, the demonstration of special spots in the skin for feeling heat and cold is one of the most interesting discoveries of recent years. If one draw a pencil-point over the palm or cheek one will notice certain spots of sudden coolness. These are the cold-spots; the heat-spots are less easy to single out. Goldscheider, Blix, and Donaldson have made minute exploration of determinate tracts of skin and found the heat- and cold-spots thickset and permanently distinct. Between them no temperature-sensation is excited by contact with a pointed cold or hot object. Mechanical and faradic irritation also excites in these points their specific feelings respectively.]

FIG 26 — The figure marked C P shows the cold-spots, that marked H P the heat-spots, and the middle one the hairs on a certain patch of skin on one of Goldscheider's fingers.

The feeling of temperature is relative to the state of the skin. "In a comfortable room we feel at no part of the body either heat or cold, although different parts of its surface are at different temperatures; the fingers and nose being cooler than the trunk which is covered by clothes, and this, in turn, cooler than the interior of the mouth. The temperature which a given region of the temperature-organ has (as measured by a thermometer) when it feels neither heat nor cold, is its *temperature-sensation zero,* and is not associated with any one objective temperature; for not only, as we have just seen, does it vary in different parts of the organ, but also on the same part from time to time. Whenever a skin-region has a temperature above its sensation-zero we feel warmth; and *vice versa:* the sensation is more marked the greater the difference, and the more suddenly it is produced; touching a metallic body, which conducts heat rapidly to or from the skin, causes a more marked hot or cold sensation than touching a worse conductor, as a piece of wood, of the same temperature.

"The change of temperature in the organ may be brought about by changes in the circulatory apparatus (more blood flowing through the skin warms it and less leads to its cooling), or by temperature-changes in gases, liquids, or solids in contact with it. Sometimes we fail to distinguish clearly whether the cause is external or internal; a person coming in from a windy walk often feels a room uncomfortably warm which is not really so; the exercise has accelerated his circulation and tended to warm his skin, but the moving outer air has rapidly conducted off the extra heat; on entering the house the stationary air there does this less quickly, the skin gets hot, and the cause is supposed to be oppressive heat of the room. Hence, frequently, opening windows and sitting in a draught, with its concomitant risks; whereas keeping quiet for five or ten minutes, until the circulation has returned to its normal rate, would attain the same end without danger.

"The acuteness of the temperature-sense is greatest at temperatures within a few degrees of 30° C. (86° F.); at these differences of less than 0.1° C. can be discriminated. As a means of measuring absolute temperatures, however, the skin is very unreliable, on account of the changeability of its sensation-zero. We can localize temperature-sensations much as tactile, but not so accurately." *

Muscular Sensation.—The sensation in the muscle itself cannot well be distinguished from that in the tendon or in its insertion. In muscular fatigue the insertions are the places most painfully felt. In muscular rheumatism, however, the whole muscle grows painful; and violent contraction such as that caused by the faradic current, or known as cramp, produces a severe and peculiar pain felt in

---

* Martin · *op. cit* , with omissions

the whole mass of muscle affected. Sachs also thought that he had demonstrated, both experimentally and anatomically, the existence of special sensory nerve-fibres, distinct from the motor fibres, in the frog's muscle. The latter end in the 'terminal plates,' the former in a network.

Great importance has been attached to the muscular sense as a factor in our perceptions, not only of weight and pressure, but of the space-relations between things generally. Our eyes and our hands, in their explorations of space, move over it and through it. It is usually supposed that without this sense of an intervening motion performed we should not perceive two seen points or two touched points to be separated by an extended interval. I am far from denying the immense participation of experiences of motion in the construction of our space-perceptions. But it is still an open question *how* our muscles help us in these experiences, whether by their own sensations, or by awakening sensations of motion on our skin, retina, and articular surfaces. The latter seems to me the more probable view, and the reader may be of the same opinion after reading Chapter VI.

Sensibility to Weight.—When we wish to estimate accurately the weight of an object we always, when possible, lift it, and so combine muscular and articular with tactile sensations. By this means we can form much better judgments.

Weber found that whereas $\frac{1}{3}$ must be added to a weight resting on the hand for the increase to be felt, the same hand actively 'hefting' the weight could feel an addition of as little as $\frac{1}{17}$. Merkel's recent and very careful experiments, in which the finger pressed down the beam of a balance counterweighted by from 25 to 8020 grams, showed that between 200 and 2000 grams a constant fractional increase of about $\frac{1}{13}$ was felt when there was no movement of the finger, and of about $\frac{1}{13}$ when there was movement. Above and below these limits the discriminative power grew less.

PAIN.

Pain.—The physiology of pain is still an enigma. One might suppose separate afferent fibres with their own end-organs to carry painful impressions to a specific pain-centre. Or one might suppose such a specific centre to be reached by currents of overflow from the other sensory centres when the violence of their inner excitement should have reached a certain pitch. Or again one might suppose a certain extreme degree of inner excitement to produce the feeling of pain in all the centres. It is certain that sensations of every order, which in moderate degrees are rather pleasant than otherwise, become painful when their intensity grows strong. The rate at which the agreeableness and disagreeableness vary with the intensity of a sensation is roughly represented by the dotted curve in Fig. 27. The

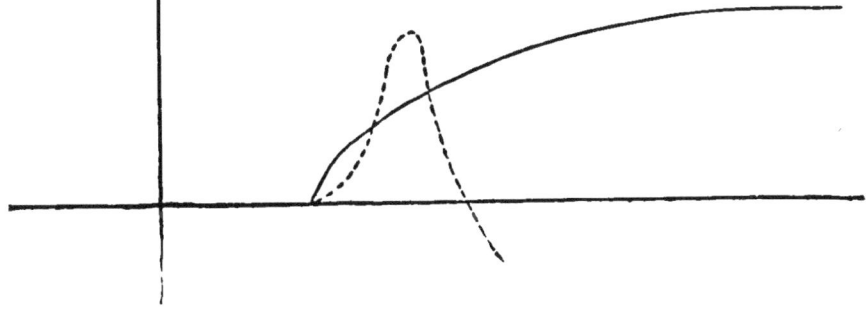

FIG. 27 (after Wundt).

horizontal line represents the threshold both of sensational and of agreeable sensibility. Below the line is the disagreeble. The continuous curve is that of Weber's law which we learned to know in Fig. 2, p. 18. With the minimal sensation the agreeableness is *nil*, as the dotted curve shows. It rises at first more slowly than the sensational intensity, then faster; and reaches its maximum before the sensation is near its acme. After its maximum of agreeableness the dotted line rapidly sinks, and soon tumbles below the horizontal into the realm of the disagreeable or painful in which it declines. That all sensations are painful when too strong is a piece of familiar knowledge. Light, sound, odors, the taste of sweet even, cold, heat, and all the skin-sensations, must be moderate to be enjoyed.

The quality of the sensation complicates the question, however, for in some sensations, as bitter, sour, salt, and certain smells, the turning point of the dotted curve must be drawn very near indeed to the beginning of the scale. In the skin the painful quality soon becomes so intense as entirely to overpower the specific quality of the sort of stimulus. Heat, cold, and pressure are indistinguishable when extreme —we only feel the pain. The hypothesis of separate end-organs in the skin receives some corroboration from recent experiments, for both Blix and Goldscheider have found, along with their special heat- and cold spots, also special 'pain-spots' on the skin. Mixed in with these are spots which are quite feelingless. However it may stand with the terminal pain-spots, separate paths of *conduction* to the brain, for painful and for merely tactile stimulations of the skin, are made probable by certain facts. In the condition termed *analgesia*, a touch is felt, but the most violent pinch, burn, or electric spark destructive of the tissue will awaken no sensation. This may occur in disease of the cord, by suggestion in hypnotism, or in certain stages of ether and chloroform intoxication. " In rabbits a similar state of things was produced by Schiff, by dividing the gray matter of the cord, leaving the posterior white columns intact. If, on the contrary, the latter were divided and the gray substance left, there was increased sensitive ness to pain, and possibly touch proper was lost. Such experiments make it pretty certain that when afferent impulses reach the spinal cord at any level and there enter its gray matter with the posterior root-fibres, they travel on in different tracts to conscious centres; the tactile ones coming soon out of the gray network and coursing on in a readily conducting white fibre, while the painful ones travel on farther in the gray substance. It is still uncertain if both impulses reach the cord in the same fibres. The gray network conducts nerve-impulses, but not easily; they tend soon to be blocked in it. A feeble (tactile) impulse reaching it by an afferent fibre might only spread a short way and then pass out into a single good conducting fibre in a white column, and proceed to the brain; while a stronger (painful) impulse would radiate farther in the gray matter, and perhaps break out of it by many fibres leading to the brain through the white columns, and so give rise to an incoördinate and ill-localized sensation. That pains are badly localized, and worse the more intense they are, is a well-known fact, which would thus receive an explanation." *

Pain also gives rise to ill-coördinated movements of defence. The stronger the pain the more violent the start. Doubtless in low animals pain is almost the only stimulus; and we have preserved the peculiarity in so far that to-day it is the stimulus of our most energetic, though not of our most discriminating, reactions.

Taste, smell, as well as hunger, thirst, nausea, and other so-called 'common' sensations need not be touched on in this book, as almost nothing of psychological interest is known concerning them.

---

* Martin: *op*

CHAPTER VI.

SENSATIONS OF MOTION.

I TREAT of these in a separate chapter in order to give them the emphasis which their importance deserves. They are of two orders:
1) Sensations of objects moving over our sensory surfaces; and
2) Sensations of our whole person's translation through space.

1) The Sensation of Motion over Surfaces.—This has generally been assumed by physiologists to be impossible until the positions of *terminus a quo* and *terminus ad quem* are severally cognized, and the successive occupancies of these positions by the moving body are perceived to be separated by a distinct interval of time. As a matter of fact, however, we cognize only the very slowest motions in this way. Seeing the hand of a clock at XII and afterwards at VI, I judge that it has moved through the interval. Seeing the sun now in the east and again in the west, I infer it to have passed over my head. But we can only *infer* that which we already generically know in some more direct fashion, and it is experimentally certain that we have the feeling of motion given us as a direct and simple *sensation*. Czermak long ago pointed out the difference between *seeing the motion* of the second-hand of a watch, when we look directly at it, and noticing the fact that it has *altered its position*, whilst our gaze is fixed upon some other point of the dial-plate. In the first case we have a specific quality of sensation which is absent in the second. If the reader will find a portion of his skin—the arm, for example—where a pair of compass-points an inch apart are felt as one impression, and if he will then trace lines a tenth of an inch long on that spot with a pencil-point, he will be distinctly aware of the point's motion and vaguely aware of the direction of the motion. The perception of the motion here is certainly not derived from a preëxisting knowledge that its starting and ending points are separate positions in space, because positions in space ten times wider apart fail to be discriminated as such when excited by the compass-points. It is the same with the retina. One's fingers when cast upon its peripheral portions cannot be counted—that is to say, the five retinal tracts which they occupy are not distinctly apprehended by the mind as five separate positions in space—and yet the slightest *movement* of the fingers is most vividly perceived as movement and nothing else. It is thus certain that our sense of movement, being so much more delicate than our sense of position, cannot possibly be derived from it.

Vierordt, at almost the same time, called attention to certain persistent illusions, amongst which are these: If another person gently trace a line across our wrist or finger, the latter being stationary, it will feel to us as if the member were moving in the opposite direction to the tracing point. If, on the contrary, we move our limb across a fixed point, it will seem as if the point were moving as well. If the reader will touch his forehead with his forefinger kept motionless, and then rotate the head so that the skin of the forehead passes beneath the finger's tip, he will have an irresistible sensation of the latter being itself in motion in the opposite direction to the head. So in abducting the fingers from each other; some may move and the rest be still, but the still ones will feel as if they were actively separating from the rest. These illusions, according to Vierordt, are survivals of a primitive form of perception, when motion was felt as such, but ascribed to the whole 'content' of consciousness, and not yet distinguished as belonging exclusively to one of its parts. When our perception is fully developed we go beyond the mere relative motion of thing and ground, and can ascribe absolute motion to one of these components of our total object, and absolute rest to another. When, in vision for example, the whole field of view seems to move together, we think it is ourselves or our eyes which are moving; and any object in the foreground which may seem to move relatively to the background is judged by us to be really still. But primitively this discrimination is not perfectly made. The sensation of the motion spreads over all that we see and infects it. Any relative motion of object and retina both makes the object seem to move, and makes us feel ourselves in motion. Even now when our whole field of view really does move we get giddy, and feel as if we too were moving; and we still see an apparent motion of the entire field of view whenever we suddenly jerk our head and eyes or shake them quickly to and fro. Pushing our eyeballs gives the same illusion. We *know* in all these cases what really happens, but the conditions are unusual, so our primitive sensation persists unchecked. So it does when clouds float by the moon. We *know* the moon is still; but we *see* it move faster than the clouds. Even when we slowly move our eyes the primitive sensation persists under the victorious conception. If we notice closely the experience, we find that any object towards which we look appears moving to meet our eye.

But the most valuable contribution to the subject is the paper of G. H. Schneider,* who takes up the matter zoölogically, and shows by examples from every branch of the animal kingdom that movement is the quality by which animals most easily attract each other's attention. The instinct of 'shamming death' is no shamming of death at all, but rather a paralysis through fear, which saves the insect, crustacean, or other creature from being *noticed at all* by his enemy. It is paralleled in the human race by

---

* Vierteljahrsch. für wiss. Philos., II. 377.

the breath-holding stillness of the boy playing 'I spy,' to whom the seeker is near; and its obverse side is shown in our involuntary waving of arms, jumping up and down, and so forth, when we wish to attract someone's attention at a distance. Creatures 'stalking' their prey and creatures hiding from their pursuers alike show how immobility diminishes conspicuity. In the woods, if we are quiet, the squirrels and birds will actually touch us. Flies will light on stuffed birds and stationary frogs. On the other hand, the tremendous shock of feeling the thing we are sitting on begin to move, the exaggerated start it gives us to have an insect unexpectedly pass over our skin, or a cat noiselessly come and snuffle about our hand, the excessive reflex effects of tickling, etc., show how exciting the sensation of motion is *per se*. A kitten cannot help pursuing a moving ball. Impressions too faint to be cognized at all are immediately felt if they move. A fly sitting is unnoticed,—we feel it the moment it crawls. A shadow may be too faint to be perceived. If we hold a finger between our closed eyelid and the sunshine we do not notice its presence. The moment we move it to and fro, however, we discern it. Such visual perception as this reproduces the conditions of sight among the radiates.

In ourselves, the main function of the peripheral parts of the retina is that of sentinels, which, when beams of light move over them, cry 'Who goes there?' and call the fovea to the spot. Most parts of the skin do but perform the same office for the finger-tips. Of course *movement of surface under object is (for purposes of stimulation) equivalent to movement of object over surface.* In exploring the shapes and sizes of things by either eye or skin the movements of these organs are incessant and unrestrainable. Every such movement draws the points and lines of the object across the surface, imprints them a hundred times more sharply, and drives them home to the attention. The immense part thus played by movements in our perceptive activity is held by many psychologists to prove that tho muscles are themselves the space-perceiving organ. Not surface-sensibility, but 'the muscular sense,' is for these writers the original and only revealer of objective extension. But they have all failed to notice with what peculiar intensity muscular movements call surface-sensibilities into play, and how largely the mere discernment of impressions depends on the mobility of the surfaces upon which they fall.

Our *articular surfaces are tactile organs* which become intensely painful when inflamed. Besides pressure, *the only stimulus they receive is their motion upon each other*. To the sensation of this motion more than anything else seems due the perception of the position which our limbs may have assumed. Patients cutaneously and muscularly anæsthetic in one leg can often prove that their articular sensibility remains, by showing (by movements of their well leg) the positions in which the surgeon may place their insensible one. Goldscheider in Berlin caused fingers, arms, and legs to be passively rotated upon their various joints in a mechanical apparatus which registered both the velocity of movement impressed and the amount of angular rotation. The minimal felt amounts of rotation were much less than a single angular degree in all the joints except those of the fingers. Such displacements as these, Goldscheider says, can hardly be detected by the eye. Anæsthesia of the skin produced by induction-currents had no disturbing effect on the perception, nor did the various degrees of pressure of the moving force upon the skin affect it. It became, in fact, all the more distinct in proportion as the concomitant pressure-feelings were eliminated by artificial anæsthesia. When the joints themselves, however, were made artificially anæsthetic, the perception of the movement grew obtuse and the angular rotations had to be much increased before they were perceptible. All these facts prove, according to Herr Goldscheider, that *the joint-surfaces and these alone are the seat of the impres-*

sions by which the movements of our members are immediately perceived.

2) **Sensations of Movement through Space.**—These may be divided into feelings of rotation and feelings of translation. As was stated at the end of the chapter on the ear, the labyrinth (semicircular canals, utricle and saccule) seems to have nothing to do with hearing. It is conclusively established to-day that the semicircular canals are the organs of a sixth special sense, that namely of rotation. When subjectively excited, this sensation is known as *dizziness* or *vertigo*, and rapidly engenders the farther feeling of nausea. Irritative disease of the inner ear causes intense vertigo (Menière's disease). Traumatic irritation of the canals in birds and mammals makes the animals tumble and throw themselves about in a way best explained by supposing them to suffer from false sensations of falling, etc., which they compensate by reflex muscular acts that throw them the other way. Galvanic irritation of the membranous canals in pigeons cause just the same compensatory movements of head and eye which actual rotations impressed on the creatures produce. Deaf and dumb persons (amongst whom many must have had their auditory nerves or labyrinths destroyed by the same disease which took away their hearing) are in a very large percentage of cases found quite insusceptible of being made dizzy by rotation. Purkinje and Mach have shown that, whatever the organ of the sense of rotation may be, it must have its seat in the head. The body is excluded by Mach's elaborate experiments.

The semicircular canals, being, as it were, six little spirit-levels in three rectangular planes, seem admirably adapted to be organs of a sense of rotation. We need only suppose that when the head turns in the plane of any one of them, the relative inertia of the endolymph momentarily increases its pressure on the nerve-termini in the appropriate ampulla, which pressure starts a current towards the central organ for feeling vertigo. This organ seems to be the cerebellum, and the teleology of the whole business would appear to be the maintenance of the upright position. If a man stand with shut eyes and attend to his body, he will find that he is hardly for a moment in equilibrium. Incipient fallings towards every side in succession are incessantly repaired by muscular contractions which restore the balance; and although impressions on the tendons, ligaments, foot-soles, joints, etc., doubtless are among the causes of the compensatory contractions, yet the strongest and most special reflex arc would seem to be that which has the sensation of incipient vertigo for its afferent member. This is experimentally proved to be much more easily excited than the other sensations referred to. When the cerebellum is disorganized the reflex response fails to occur properly and loss of equilibrium is the result. Irritation of the cerebellum produces vertigo, loss of balance, and nausea; and galvanic currents through the head produce various forms of vertigo correlated with their direction. It seems probable that direct excitement of the cerebellar centre is responsible for these feelings. In addition to these corporeal reflexes the sense of rotation causes compensatory rollings of the eyeballs in the opposite direction, to which some of the subjective phenomena of *optical vertigo* are due. Steady rotation gives no sensation ; it is only starting or stopping, or, more generally speaking, acceleration (positive or negative), which impresses the end-organs in the ampullæ. The sensation always has a little duration, however; and the feeling of reversed movement after whirling violently may last for nearly a minute, slowly fading out.

The cause of the *sense of translation* (movement forwards or backwards) is more open to dispute. The seat of this sensation has been assigned to the semicircular canals when compounding their currents to the brain; and also to the utricle. The latest experimenter, M. Delage, considers that it cannot possibly be in the head, and assigns it rather to the entire body, so far as its parts (blood-vessels, viscera, etc.) are movable against each other and suffer friction or pressure from their relative inertia when a movement of translation begins. M. Delage's exclusion of the labyrinth from this form of sensibility cannot, however, yet be considered definitively established, so the matter may rest with this mention.

CHAPTER VII.

THE STRUCTURE OF THE BRAIN.*

Embryological Sketch.—The brain is a sort of *pons asinorum* in anatomy until one gets a certain general conception of it as a clue. Then it becomes a comparatively simple affair. The clue is given by comparative anatomy and especially by embryology. At a certain moment in the development of all the higher vertebrates the cerebro-

Fig 28. Fig 29. Fig. 30.
(All after Huguenin.)

spinal axis is formed by a hollow tube containing fluid and terminated in front by an enlargement separated by transverse constrictions into three 'cerebral vesicles,' so called (see Fig. 28). The walls of these vesicles thicken in most

---

.* This chapter will be understood as a mere sketch for beginners. Models will be found of assistance. The best-is the 'Cerveau de Texture de Grande Dimension,' made by Auzoux, 56 Rue de Vaugirard, Paris. It is a wonderful work of art, and costs 300 francs. M. Jules **Talrich** of No. 97 Boulevard Saint-Germain, Paris, makes a series of five large plaster models, which I have found very useful for class-room purposes. They cost 350 francs, and are far better than any German models which I have seen

THE STRUCTURE OF THE BRAIN

places, change in others into a thin vascular tissue, and in others again send out processes which produce an appearance of farther subdivision. The middle vesicle or mid-brain (*Mb* in the figures) is the least affected by change. Its upper walls thicken into the optic lobes, or *corpora quadrigemina* as they are named in man; its lower walls become the so-called peduncles or *crura* of the brain; and its cavity dwindles into the aqueduct of Silvius. A section through the adult human mid-brain is shown in Fig. 31.

The anterior and posterior vesicles undergo much more considerable change. The walls of the posterior vesicle thicken enormously in their foremost portion and form the *cerebellum* on top

FIG. 32 (after Huxley).

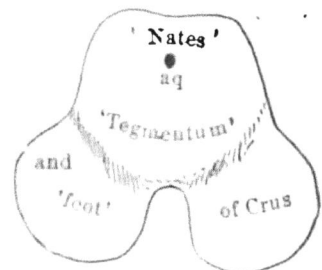

FIG. 31.—The 'nates' are the anterior corpora quadrigemina, the spot above *aq* is a section of the sylvian aqueduct, and the tegmentum and two 'feet' together make the Crura. These are marked *C C*, and a cross (+) marks the aqueduct, in Fig. 32.

(*Cb* in all the figures) and the *pons Varolii* below (*P.V.* in Fig. 33). In its hindmost portions the posterior vesicle thickens below into the medulla oblongata (*Mo* in all the figures), whilst on top its walls thin out and melt, so that one can pass a probe into the cavity without breaking through any truly nervous tissue. The cavity which one thus enters from without is named the *fourth ventricle* (4 in Figs. 32 and 33). One can run the probe forward through it, passing first under the cerebellum and then under a thin sheet of nervous tissue (the *valve of Vieussens*) just anterior thereto, as far as the *aqueduct of Silvius*. Passing through this, the probe emerges forward into what was once the cavity of the anterior vesicle. But the covering has melted away at this place, and the cavity now forms a deep compressed pit or groove between the two walls of the vesicle, and is called the *third ventricle* (3 in Figs. 32 and 33). The 'aqueduct of Sylvius' is in consequence of this connection often called the *iter a tertio ad quartum ventriculum*. The walls of the vesicle form the *optic thalami* (*Th* in all the figures).

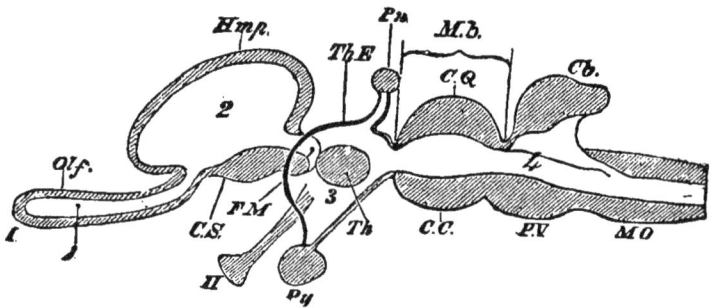

FIG. 33 (after Huxley).

From the anterior vesicle just in front of the thalami there buds out on either side an enlargement, into which the cavity of the vesicle continues, and which becomes the *hemisphere* of that side. In man its walls thicken enormously and form folds, the so-called *convolutions*, on their surface. At the same time they grow backwards rather than forwards of their starting-point just in front of the thalamus, arching over the latter; and growing fastest along their top circumference, they end by bending downwards and forwards again when they have passed the rear end of the thalamus. When fully developed in man, they overlay and cover in all the other parts of the brain. Their cavities form the *lateral ventricles*, easier to understand by a dissection than by a description. A probe can be passed into either of them from the third ventricle at its anterior end; and like the third ventricle, their wall is melted down along a certain line, forming a long cleft through which they can be entered without rupturing the nervous tissue. This cleft, on account of the growth of the hemisphere outwards, backwards, and then downwards from its starting point, has got rolled in and tucked away beneath the apparent surface.*

At first the two hemispheres are connected only with their respective thalami. But during the fourth and fifth months of embryonic life they become connected with each other above the thalami through the growth between them of a massive system of transverse fibres which crosses the median line like a great bridge and is called the *corpus callosum*. These fibres radiate in the walls of both hemispheres and form a direct connection between the convolutions of the right and of the left side. Beneath the corpus callosum another system of fibres called the *fornix* is formed, between which and the corpus callosum there is a peculiar connection. Just in front of the thalami, where the hemispheres begin their growth, a ganglionic mass called the *corpus striatum* (*C.S.*, Figs. 32 and 33) is formed in their wall. It is complex in structure, consisting of two main parts, called *nucleus lenticularis* and *nucleus caudatus* respectively. The figures, with their respective explanations, will give a better idea of the farther details of structure than any verbal description; so, after some practical directions for dissecting the organ, I will pass to a brief account of the physiological relations of its different parts to each other.

Dissection of Sheep's Brain.—The way really to understand the brain is to dissect it. The brains of mammals differ only in their proportions, and from the sheep's one can learn all that is essential in man's. The student is therefore strongly urged to dissect a sheep's brain. Full directions of the order of procedure are given in the human dis-

---

* All the places in the brain at which the cavities come through are filled in during life by prolongations of the membrane called *pia mater*, carrying rich plexuses of blood-vessels in their folds

secting books, e.g. Holden's Practical Anatomy (Churchill), Morrell's Student's Manual of Comparative Anatomy and Guide to Dissection (Longmans), and Foster and Langley's Practical Physiology (Macmillan). For the use of classes who cannot procure these books I subjoin a few practical notes. The instruments needed are a small saw, a chisel with a shoulder, and a hammer with a hook on its handle, all three of which form part of the regular medical autopsy-kit and can be had of surgical-instrument-makers. In addition a scalpel, a pair of scissors, a pair of dissecting-forceps, and a silver probe are required. The solitary student can find home-made substitutes for all these things but the forceps, which he ought to buy.

The first thing is to get off the skull-cap. Make two saw-cuts, through the prominent portion of each condyle (or articular surface bounding the hole at the back of the skull, where the spinal cord enters) and passing forwards to the temples of the animal. Then make two cuts, one on each side, which cross these and meet in an angle on the frontal bone. By actual trial, one will find the best direction for the saw-cuts. It is hard to saw entirely through the skull-bone without in some places also sawing into the brain. Here is where the chisel comes in—one can break by a smart blow on it with the hammer any parts of the skull not quite sawn through. When the skull-cap is ready to come off one will feel it 'wobble.' Insert then the hook under its forward end and pull firmly. The bony skull-cap alone will come away, leaving the periosteum of the inner surface adhering to that of the base of the skull, enveloping the brain, and forming the so-called *dura mater* or outer one of its 'meninges.' This dura mater should be slit open round the margins, when the brain will be exposed wrapped in its nearest membrane, the *pia mater*, full of blood-vessels whose branches penetrate the tissues.

The brain in its pia mater should now be carefully 'shelled out' Usually it is best to begin at the forward end, turning it up there and gradually working backwards. The *olfactory lobes* are liable to be torn; they must be carefully scooped from the pits in the base of the skull to which they adhere by the branches which they send through the bone into the nose-cavity. It is well to have a little blunt curved instrument expressly for this purpose. Next the *optic nerves* tie the brain down, and must be cut through—close to the chiasma is easiest. After that comes the *pituitary body*, which has to be left behind. It is attached by a neck, the so-called *infundibulum*, into the upper part of which the cavity of the third ventricle is prolonged downwards for a short distance. It has no known function and is probably a 'rudimentary organ.' Other nerves, into the detail of which I shall not go, must be cut successively. Their places in the human brain are shown in Fig. 34. When they

THE STRUCTURE OF THE BRAIN. 83

are divided, and the portion of dura mater (tentorium) which projects between the hemispheres and the cerebellum is cut through at its edges, the brain comes readily out.

It is best examined fresh. If numbers of brains have to be prepared and kept, I have found it a good plan to put them first in a solution of chloride of zinc, just dense enough at first to float them,

FIG 31.—The human brain from below, with its nerves numbered, after Henle I, olfactory, II, optic, III, oculo-motorius; IV, trochlearis; V, trifacial; VI, abducens oculi; VII, facial, VIII, auditory, IX, glosso-pharyngeal, X, pneumogastric; XI, spinal accessory; XII, hypoglossal; ncI, first cervical, etc

and to leave them for a fortnight or less. This softens the pia mater, which can then be removed in large shreds, after which it is enough to place them in quite weak alcohol to preserve them indefinitely, tough, elastic, and in their natural shape, though bleached to a uniform white color. Before immersion in the chloride all the more superficial adhesions of the parts must be broken through, to bring the fluid into contact with a maximum of surface. If the brain is used fresh, the pia mater had better be removed carefully in most places with the forceps, scalpel, and scissors. Over the grooves between the cerebellum and hemispheres, and between the cerebellum and medulla oblongata, thin cobwebby moist transparent vestiges of the *arachnoid* membrane will be found.

The subdivisions may now be examined in due order. For the convolutions, blood-vessels, and nerves the more special books must be consulted.

First, looked at from above, with the deep *longitudinal fissure* between them, the hemispheres are seen partly overlapping the intricately wrinkled *cerebellum*, which juts out behind, and covers in turn almost all the medulla oblongata. Drawing the hemispheres apart, the brilliant white *corpus callosum* is revealed, some half an inch below their surface. There is no median partition in the cerebellum, but a median elevation instead.

Looking at the brain from below, one still sees the longitudinal fissure in the median line in front, and on either side of it the *olfactory lobes*, much larger than in man; the *optic tracts* and *commissure* or 'chiasma'; the *infundibulum* cut through just behind them; and behind that the single *corpus albicans* or *mamillare*, whose function is unknown and which is double in man. Next the *crura* appear, converging upon the pons as if carrying fibres back from either side. The *pons* itself succeeds, much less prominent than in man; and finally behind it comes the medulla oblongata, broad and flat and relatively large. The pons looks like a sort of collar uniting the two halves of the cerebellum, and surrounding the medulla, whose fibres by the time they have emerged anteriorly from beneath the collar have divided into the two crura. The inner relations are, however, somewhat less simple than what this description may suggest.

Now turn forward the cerebellum ; pull out the vascular *choroid plexuses* of the pia, which fill the fourth ventricle ; and bring the upper surface of the *medulla oblongata* into view. The *fourth ventricle* is a triangular depression terminating in a posterior point called the *calamus scriptorius*. (Here a very fine probe may pass into the central canal of the spinal cord.) The lateral boundary of the ventricle on either side is formed by the *restiform body* or *column*, which runs into the cerebellum, forming its *inferior* or *posterior peduncle* on that side. Including the calamus scriptorius by their divergence, the posterior columns of the spinal cord continue into the medulla as the *fasciculi graciles*. These are at first separated from the broad restiform bodies by a slight groove. But this disappears anteriorly, and the 'slender' and 'ropelike' strands soon become outwardly indistinguishable.

THE STRUCTURE OF THE BRAIN. 85

Turn next to the ventral surface of the medulla, and note the *anterior pyramids*, two roundish cords, one on either side of the slight *median groove*. The pyramids are crossed and closed over anteriorly by the *pons Varolii*, a broad transverse band which surrounds them like a collar, and runs up into the cerebellum on either side, forming its *middle peduncles*. The pons has a slight median depression and its

Fig. 35 —Fourth ventricle, etc. (Henle) *III*, third Ventricle; *IV*, fourth ventricle, *P*, anterior, middle, and posterior peduncles of cerebellum cut through *Cr*, restiform body; *Fg*, funiculus gracilis; *Cq*, corpora quadrigemina.

posterior edge is formed by the *trapezium* on either side. The trapezium consists of fibres which, instead of surrounding the pyramid, seem to start from alongside of it. It is not visible in man. The *olivary bodies* are small eminences on the medulla lying just laterally of the pyramids and below the trapezium.

Now cut through the peduncles of the cerebellum, close to their entrance into that organ They give one surface of section on each side, though they receive contributions from three directions. The posterior and middle portions we have seen: the *anterior peduncles* pass forward to the *corpora quadrigemina*. The thin white layer of nerve-tissue between them and continuous with them is called the *valve of Vieussens*. It covers part of the canal from the fourth ventricle to the third. The cerebellum being removed, examine it, and cut sections to show the peculiar distribution of white and gray matter, forming an appearance called the *arbor vitæ* in the books.

Now bend up the posterior edge of the hemispheres, exposing the corpora quadrigemina (of which the anterior pair are dubbed the *nates* and the posterior the *testes*), and noticing the *pineal gland*, a small median organ situated just in front of them and probably, like the pituitary body, a vestige of something useful in premammalian times The rounded posterior edge of the corpus callosum is visible now passing from one hemisphere to the other. Turn it still farther up, letting the medulla, etc., hang down as much as possible and trace the under surface from this edge forward. It is broad behind but narrows forward, becoming continuous with the *fornix*. The anterior stem, so to speak, of this organ plunges down just in front of the *optic thalami*, which now appear with the fornix arching over them, and the median *third ventricle* between them. The margins of the fornix, as they pass backwards, diverge laterally farther than the margins of the corpus callosum, and under the name of *corpora fimbriata* are carried into the lateral ventricles, as will be seen again.

It takes a good topographical mind to understand these ventricles clearly, even when they are followed with eye and hand. A verbal description is absolutely useless. The essential thing to remember is that they are offshoots from the original cavity (now the third ventricle) of the anterior vesicle, and that a great split has occurred in the walls of the hemispheres so that they (the lateral ventricles) now communicate with the exterior along a cleft which appears sickle-shaped, as it were, and folded in.

The student will probably examine the relations of the parts in various ways. But he will do well to begin in any case by cutting horizontal slices off the hemispheres almost down to the level of the corpus callosum, and examining the distribution of gray and white matter on the surfaces of section, any one of which is the so-called *centrum ovale*. Then let him cut down in a fore-and-aft direction along the edge of the corpus callosum, till he comes 'through' and draw the hemispherical margin of the cut outwards—he will see a space which is the ventricle, and which farther cutting along the side and removing of its hemisphere-roof will lay more bare. The most conspicuous object on its floor is the *nucleus caudatus* of the *corpus striatum*.

THE STRUCTURE OF THE BRAIN.

Cut the corpus callosum transversely through near its posterior edge and bend the anterior portion of it forwards and sideways. The rear edge (*splenium*) left *in situ* bends round and downwards and becomes

FIG 35.—Horizontal section of human brain just above the thalami.—*Ccl*, corpus callosum in section; *Cs*, corpus striatum; *Sl*, septum lucidum; *Cf*, columns of the fornix; *Tho*, optic thalami, *Cn*, pineal gland. (After Henle.)

continuous with the *fornix*. The anterior part is also continuous with the fornix, but more along the median line, where a thinnish membrane, the *septum lucidum*, triangular in shape, reaching from the one body to the other, practically forms a sort of partition between the contiguous portion of the lateral ventricles on the two sides. Break through the *septum* if need be and expose the upper surface of the fornix, broad behind and narrow in front where its *anterior pillars* plunge down in front of the third ventricle (from a thickening in whose anterior walls they were originally formed), and finally penetrate the corpus albicans. Cut these pillars through and fold them back, exposing the thalamic portion of the brain, and noting the under surface of the fornix. Its diverging *posterior pillars* run backwards, downwards, and then forwards again, forming with their sharp edges the *corpora fimbriata*, which bound the cleft by which the ventricle lies open. The semi-cylindrical welts behind the *corpora fimbriata* and parallel thereto in the wall of the ventricle are the *hippocampi*. Imagine the fornix and corpus callosum shortened in the fore-and-aft direction to a transverse cord; imagine the hemispheres not having grown backwards and downwards round the thalamus; and the corpus fimbriatum on either side would then be the upper or anterior margin of a split in the wall of the hemispheric ventricle of which the lower and posterior margin would be the posterior border of the corpus striatum where it grows out of the thalamus.

The little notches just behind the anterior pillar of the fornix and between them and the thalami are the so-called *foramina of Monro* through which the plexus of vessels, etc., passes from the median to the lateral ventricles.

See the thick *middle commissure* joining the two thalami, just as the corpus callosum and fornix join the hemispheres. These are all embryological aftergrowths. Seek also the *anterior commissure* crossing just in front of the anterior pillars of the fornix, as well as the *posterior commissure* with its lateral prolongations along the thalami, just below the pineal gland.

On a median section, note the thinnish *anterior wall* of the third ventricle and its prolongation downwards into the *infundibulum*.

Turn up or cut off the rear end of one hemisphere so as to see clearly the optic tracts turning upwards towards the rear corner of the thalamus. The *corpora geniculata* to which they also go, distinct in man, are less so in the sheep. The lower ones are visible between the optic-tract band and the 'testes,' however.

The brain's principal parts are thus passed in review. A longitudinal section of the whole organ through the median line will be found most instructive (Fig. 37). The student should also (on a *fresh* brain, or one hardened in bichromate of potash or ammonia to save the contrast of color between white and gray matter) make transverse sections through the *nates* and *crura*, and through the

Fig. 87.—Median section of human brain below the hemispheres. *Th*, thalamus; *Cq*, corpora quadrigemina; *V'''*, third Ventricle; *Com*, middle commissure; *F*, columns of fornix; *Inf*, infundibulum, *Op n*, optic nerve; *Pit*, pituitary body; *Av*, arbor Vitæ (After Obersteiner)

hemispheres just in front of the corpus albicans. The latter section shows on each side the *nucleus lenticularis* of the corpus striatum, and also the *inner capsule* (see Fig. 38, *Nl*, and *Ic*).

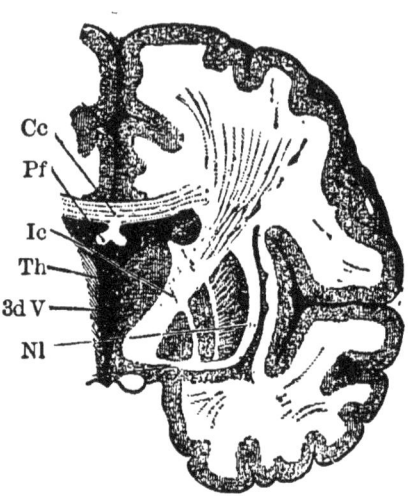

FIG. 38.—Transverse section through right hemisphere (after Gegenbaur). *Cc*, corpus callosum; *Pf*, pillars of fornix; *Ic*, internal capsule; *V*, third ventricle; *Nl*, nucleus lenticularis

When all is said and done, the fact remains that, for the beginner, the understanding of the brain's structure is not an easy thing. It must be gone over and forgotten and learned again many times before it is definitively assimilated by the mind. But patience and repetition, here as elsewhere, will bear their perfect fruit.

CHAPTER VIII.

THE FUNCTIONS OF THE BRAIN.

General Idea of Nervous Function.—If I begin chopping the foot of a tree, its branches are unmoved by my act, and its leaves murmur as peacefully as ever in the wind. If, on the contrary, I do violence to the foot of a fellow-man, the rest of his body instantly responds to the aggression by movements of alarm or defence. The reason of this difference is that the man has a nervous system, whilst the tree has none; and the function of the nervous system is to bring each part into harmonious coöperation with every other. The afferent nerves, when excited by some physical irritant, be this as gross in its mode of operation as a chopping axe or as subtle as the waves of light, conveys the excitement to the nervous centres. The commotion set up in the centres does not stop there, but discharges through the efferent nerves, exciting movements which vary with the animal and with the irritant applied. These acts of response have usually the common character of being of service. They ward off the noxious stimulus and support the beneficial one; whilst if, in itself indifferent, the stimulus be a sign of some distant circumstance of practical importance, the animal's acts are addressed to this circumstance so as to avoid its perils or secure its benefits, as the case may be. To take a common example, if I hear the conductor calling 'All aboard!' as I enter the station, my heart first stops, then palpitates, and my legs respond to the air-waves falling on my tympanum by quickening their movements. If I stumble as I run, the sensation of falling provokes a movement of the hands towards the direction of the fall, the effect of which is to shield the body from too sudden a shock. If a cinder enter my eye, its lids close forcibly and a copious flow of tears tends to wash it out.

These three responses to a sensational stimulus differ, however, in many respects. The closure of the eye and the lachrymation are quite involuntary, and so is the disturbance of the heart. Such involuntary responses we know as 'reflex' acts. The motion of the arms to break the shock of falling may also be called reflex, since it occurs too quickly to be deliberately intended. It is, at any rate, less automatic than the previous acts, for a man might by conscious effort learn to perform it more skilfully, or even to suppress it altogether. Actions of this kind, into which instinct and volition enter upon equal terms, have been called 'semi-reflex.' The act of running towards the train, on the other hand, has no instinctive element about it. It is purely the result of education, and is preceded by a consciousness of the purpose to be attained and a distinct mandate of the will. It is a 'voluntary act.' Thus the animal's reflex and voluntary performances shade into each other gradually, being connected by acts which may often occur automatically, but may also be modified by conscious intelligence.

The Frog's Nerve-centres.—Let us now look a little more closely at what goes on.

The best way to enter the subject will be to take a lower creature, like a frog, and study by the vivisectional method the functions of his different nerve-centres. The frog's nerve-centres are figured in the diagram over the page, which needs no further explanation. I shall first proceed to state what happens when various amounts of the anterior parts are removed, in different frogs, in the way in which an ordinary student removes them—that is, with no extreme precautions as to the purity of the operation.

If, then, we reduce the frog's nervous system to the spinal cord alone, by making a section behind the base of the skull, between the spinal cord and the medulla ob-

THE FUNCTIONS OF THE BRAIN. 93

longata, thereby cutting off the brain from all connection with the rest of the body, the frog will still continue to live, but with a very peculiarly modified activity. It ceases to breathe or swallow; it lies flat on its oelly, and does not, like a normal frog, sit up on its forepaws, though its hind-legs are kept, as usual, folded against its body and immediately resume this position if drawn out. If thrown on its back it lies there quietly, without turning over like a normal frog. Locomotion and voice seem entirely abolished. If we suspend it by the nose, and irritate different portions of its skin by acid, it performs a set of remarkable 'defensive' movements calculated to wipe away the irritant. Thus, if the breast be touched, both fore-paws will rub it vigorously; if we touch the outer

FIG 39 —C, H, cerebial hemispheres; O Th, optic thalami; O L, optic lobes; Cb, cerebellum; M O, medulla oblongata, S C, spinal cord.

side of the elbow, the hind-foot of the same side will rise directly to the spot and wipe it. The back of the foot will rub the knee if that be attacked, whilst if the foot be cut away, the stump will make ineffectual movements, and then, in many frogs, a pause will come, as if for deliberation, succeeded by a rapid passage of the opposite unmutilated foot to the acidulated spot.

The most striking character of all these movements, after their teleological appropriateness, is their precision. They vary, in sensitive frogs and with a proper amount of irritation, so little as almost to resemble in their machine-like regularity the performances of a jumping-jack, whose legs must twitch whenever you pull the string. The spinal cord of the frog thus contains arrangements of cells and fibres fitted to convert skin-irritations into movements of defence. We may call it the *centre for defensive movements* in this animal. We may indeed go farther than this, and by cutting the spinal cord in various places find that its separate segments are independent mechanisms, for appropriate activities of the head and of the arms and legs respectively. The segment governing the arms is especially active, in male frogs, in the breeding season; and these members alone, with the breast and back appertaining to them, and everything else cut away, will actively grasp a finger placed between them and remain hanging to it for a considerable time.

Similarly of the medulla oblongata, optic lobes, and other centres between the spinal cord and the hemispheres of the frog. Each of them is proved by experiment to contain a mechanism for the accurate execution, in response to definite stimuli, of certain special acts. Thus with the medulla the animal swallows; with the medulla and cerebellum together he jumps, swims, and turns over from his back; with his optic lobes he croaks when pinched; etc. *A frog which has lost his cerebral hemispheres alone is by an unpractised observer indistinguishable from a normal animal.*

Not only is he capable, on proper instigation, of all the acts already mentioned, but he guides himself by sight, so that if an obstacle be set up between him and the light, and he be forced to move forward, he either jumps over it or swerves to one side. He manifests the sexual instinct at the proper seasons, and discriminates between male and female individuals of his own species. He is, in short, so similar in every respect to a normal frog that it would take a person very familiar with these animals to suspect anything wrong or wanting about him; but even then such a person would soon remark the almost entire absence of spontaneous motion—that is, motion unprovoked by any present incitation of sense. The continued movements of swimming, performed by the creature in the water, seem to be the fatal result of the contact of that fluid with its skin. They cease when a stick, for example, touches his hands. This is a sensible irritant towards which the feet are automatically drawn by reflex action, and on which the animal remains sitting. He manifests no hunger, and will

THE FUNCTIONS OF THE BRAIN. 95

suffer a fly to crawl over his nose unsnapped at. Fear, too, seems to have deserted him. In a word, he is an extremely complex machine whose actions, so far as they go, tend to self-preservation; but still a *machine,* in this sense—that it seems to contain no incalculable element. By applying the right sensory stimulus to him we are almost as certain of getting a fixed response as an organist is of hearing a certain tone when he pulls out a certain stop.

But now if to the lower centres we add the cerebral hemispheres, or if, in other words, we make an intact animal the subject of our observations, all this is changed. In addition to the previous responses to present incitements of sense, our frog now goes through long and complex acts of locomotion *spontaneously,* or as if moved by what in ourselves we should call an idea. His reactions to outward stimuli vary their form, too. Instead of making simple defensive movements with his hind-legs, like a headless frog, if touched; or of giving one or two leaps and then sitting still like a hemisphereless one, he makes persistent and varied efforts of escape, as if, not the mere contact of the physiologist's hand, but the notion of danger suggested by it were now his spur. Led by the feeling of hunger, too, he goes in search of insects, fish, or smaller frogs, and varies his procedure with each species of victim. The physiologist cannot by manipulating him elicit croaking, crawling up a board, swimming or stopping, at will. His conduct has become incalculable—we can no longer foretell it exactly. Effort to escape is his dominant reaction, but he *may* do anything else, even swell up and become perfectly passive in our hands.

Such are the phenomena commonly observed, and such the impressions which one naturally receives. Certain general conclusions follow irresistibly First of all the following:

The acts of all the centres involve the use of the same muscles. When a brainless frog's hind-leg wipes the acid, he calls into play all the leg-muscles which a frog with his full medulla oblongata and cerebellum uses when he turns from his back to his belly. Their contractions are, however, *combined* differently in the two cases, so that the results vary widely. We must consequently conclude that specific arrangements of cells and fibres exist in the cord for wiping, in the medulla for turning over, etc. Similarly they exist in the thalami for jumping over seen obstacles and for balancing the moved body; in the optic lobes for creeping backwards, or what not. But in the hemispheres, since the presence of these organs *brings no new elementary form of movement* with it, but only *determines differently the occasions* on which the movements shall occur, making the usual stimuli less fatal and machine-like, we need suppose no such machinery *directly* coördinative of muscular contractions to exist. We may rather assume, when the mandate for a wiping-movement is sent forth by the hemispheres, that a current goes straight to the wiping-arrangement in the spinal cord, exciting this arrangement as a whole. Similarly, if an intact frog wishes to jump, all he need do is to excite from the hemispheres the jumping-centre in the thalami or wherever it may be, and the latter will provide for the details of the execution. It is like a general ordering a colonel to make a certain movement, but not telling him how it shall be done.

The same muscle, then, is repeatedly represented at different heights; and at each it enters into a different combination with other muscles to coöperate in some special form of concerted movement. At each height the movement is discharged by some particular form of sensorial stimulus, whilst the stimuli which discharge the hemispheres would seem not so much to be elementary sorts of sensation, as groups of sensations forming determinate *objects* or *things*.

The Pigeon's Lower Centres.—The results are just the same if, instead of a frog, we take a pigeon, cut out his hemispheres carefully and wait till he recovers from the operation. There is not a movement natural to him which this brainless bird cannot execute; he seems, too, after some days to execute movements from some inner irritation, for he moves spontaneously. But his emotions and instincts exist no longer. In Schrader's striking words:

"The hemisphereless animal moves in a world of bodies which ... are all of equal value for him. ... He is, to use Goltz's apt expression, *impersonal*. ... Every object is for him only a space-occupying mass, he turns out of his path for an ordinary pigeon no otherwise than for a stone. He may try to climb over both. All authors agree that they never found any difference, whether it was an inanimate body, a cat, a dog, or a bird of prey which came in their pigeon's way. The creature knows neither friends nor enemies, in the thickest company it lives like a hermit. The languishing cooing of the male awakens no more impression than the rattling of the peas, or the call-whistle which in the days before the injury used to make the birds hasten to be fed. Quite as little as the earlier observers have I seen hemisphereless she-birds answer the courting of the male. A hemisphereless male will coo all day long and show distinct signs of sexual excitement, but his activity is without any object, it is entirely indifferent to him whether the she-bird be there or not. If one is placed near him, he leaves her unnoticed. ... As the male pays no attention to the female, so she pays none to her young The brood may follow the mother ceaselessly calling for food, but they might as well ask it from a stone. ... The hemisphereless pigeon is in the highest degree tame, and fears man as little as cat or bird of prey."

General Notion of Hemispheres.—All these facts lead us, when we try to formulate them broadly, to some such conception as this: *The lower centres act from present sensational stimuli alone ; the hemispheres act from considerations*, the sensations which they may receive serving only as suggesters of these. But what are considerations but expectations, in the fancy, of sensations which will be felt one way or another according as action takes this course or that? If I step aside on seeing a rattlesnake, from considering how dangerous an animal he is, the mental materials which constitute my prudential reflection are images more or less vivid of the movement of his head, of a sudden pain in my leg, of a state of terror, a swelling of the limb, a chill, delirium, death, etc., etc., and the ruin of my hopes. But all these images are constructed out of my past experiences. They are *reproductions* of what I have felt or witnessed. They are, in short, *remote* sensations; and the main difference between the hemisphereless animal and the whole one may be concisely expressed by saying that *the one obeys absent, the other only present, objects.*

The hemispheres would then seem to be the chief seat of memory. Vestiges of past experience must in some way be stored up in them, and must, when aroused by present stimuli, first appear as representations of distant goods and evils; and then must discharge into the appropriate motor channels for warding off the evil and securing the benefits of the good. If we liken the nervous currents to electric currents, we can compare the nervous system, C, below the hemispheres to a direct circuit from sense-organ to muscle along the line $S\ldots C\ldots M$ of Fig. 40). The hemisphere, H, adds the long circuit or loop-line through which the current may pass when for any reason the direct line is not used.

Thus, a tired wayfarer on a hot day throws himself on the damp earth beneath a maple-tree. The sensations of delicions rest and coolness pouring themselves through the direct line would naturally discharge into the muscles of complete extension: he would abandon himself to the dangerous repose. But the loop-line being open, part of the current is drafted along it, and awakens rheumatic or catarrhal reminiscences, which prevail over the instigations of sense, and make the man arise and pursue his way

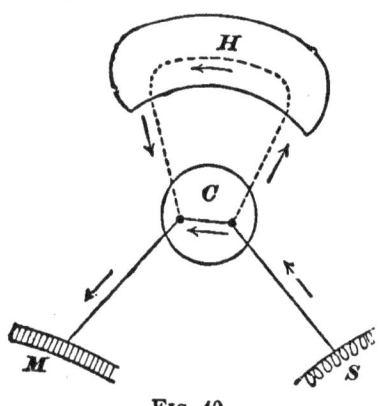

FIG. 40.

THE FUNCTIONS OF THE BRAIN. 99

to where he may enjoy his rest more safely. Presently we shall examine the manner in which the hemispheric loop-line may be supposed to serve as a reservoir for such reminiscences as these. Meanwhile I will ask the reader to notice some corollaries of its being such a reservoir.

First, no animal without it can deliberate, pause, postpone, nicely weigh one motive against another, or compare. Prudence, in a word, is for such a creature an impossible virtue. Accordingly we see that nature removes those functions in the exercise of which prudence is a virtue from the lower centres and hands them over to the cerebrum. Wherever a creature has to deal with complex features of the environment, prudence is a virtue. The higher animals have so to deal; and the more complex the features, the higher we call the animals. The fewer of his acts, then, can *such* an animal perform without the help of the organs in question. In the frog many acts devolve wholly on the lower centres; in the bird fewer; in the rodent fewer still; in the dog very few indeed; and in apes and men hardly any at all.

The advantages of this are obvious. Take the prehension of food as an example and suppose it to be a reflex performance of the lower centres. The animal will be condemned fatally and irresistibly to snap at it whenever presented, no matter what the circumstances may be; he can no more disobey this prompting than water can refuse to boil when a fire is kindled under the pot. His life will again and again pay the forfeit of his gluttony. Exposure to retaliation, to other enemies, to traps, to poisons, to the dangers of repletion, must be regular parts of his existence. His lack of all thought by which to weigh the danger against the attractiveness of the bait, and of all volition to remain hungry a little while longer, is the direct measure of his lowness in the mental scale. And those fishes which, like our cunners and sculpins, are no sooner thrown back from the hook into the water than they automatically seize the hook again, would soon expiate the degradation of their intelligence by the extinction of their type, did not their extraordinary fecundity atone for their imprudence. Appetite and the acts it prompts have consequently become in all higher vertebrates functions of the cerebrum. They disappear when the physiologist's knife has left the subordinate centres alone in place. The brainless pigeon will starve though left on a corn-heap.

Take again the sexual function. In birds this devolves exclusively upon the hemispheres. When these are shorn away the pigeon pays no attention to the billings and cooings of its mate. It is the same, according to Goltz, with male dogs who have suffered large losses of cerebral tissue. Those who have read Darwin's Descent of Man will recollect what an importance this author ascribes to the agency of sexual selection in the amelioration of the breeds of birds. The females are naturally coy, and their coyness must be overcome by the exhibition of the gorgeous plumage, and various accomplishments in the way of strutting and fighting, of the males. In frogs and toads, on the other hand, where (as we saw on page 94) the sexual instinct devolves upon the lower centres, we find a machine-like obedience to the present incitements of sense, and an almost total exclusion of the power of choice. The consequence is that every spring an immense waste of batrachian life, involving numbers of adult animals and innumerable eggs, takes place from no other cause than the blind character of the sexual impulse in these creatures.

No one need be told how dependent all human social elevation is upon the prevalence of chastity. Hardly any factor measures more than this the difference between civilization and barbarism. Physiologically interpreted, chastity means nothing more than the fact that present solicitations of sense are overpowered by suggestions of æsthetic and moral fitness which the circumstances awaken in the cerebrum; and that upon the inhibitory or permissive influence of these alone action directly depends.

Within the psychic life due to the cerebrum itself the

same general distinction obtains, between considerations of the more immediate and considerations of the more remote. In all ages the man whose determinations are swayed by reference to the most distant ends has been held to possess the highest intelligence. The tramp who lives from hour to hour; the bohemian whose engagements are from day to day; the bachelor who builds but for a single life; the father who acts for another generation; the patriot who thinks of a whole community and many generations; and, finally, the philosopher and saint whose cares are for humanity and for eternity,—these range themselves in an unbroken hierarchy, wherein each successive grade results from an increased manifestation of the special form of action by which the cerebral centres are distinguished from all below them.

The Automaton-Theory.—In the 'loop-line' along which the memories and ideas of the distant are supposed to lie, the action, so far as it is a physical process, must be interpreted after the type of the action in the lower centres. If regarded here as a reflex process, it must be reflex there as well. The current in both places runs out into the muscles only after it has first run in; but whilst the path by which it runs out is determined in the lower centres by reflections few and fixed amongst the cell-arrangements, in the hemispheres the reflections are many and instable. This, it will be seen, is only a difference of degree and not of kind, and does not change the reflex type. The conception of *all* action as conforming to this type is the fundamental conception of modern nerve-physiology. This conception, now, has led to two quite opposite theories about the relation to consciousness of the nervous functions. Some authors, finding that the higher voluntary functions seem to require the guidance of feeling, conclude that over the lowest reflexes some such feeling also presides, though it may be a feeling connected with the spinal cord, of which the higher conscious self connected with the hemispheres remains unconscious. Others, finding that reflex and semi-automatic acts may, notwithstanding their appropriateness, take place with an unconsciousness apparently complete, fly to the opposite extreme and maintain that the appropriateness even of the higher voluntary actions connected with the hemispheres owes nothing to the fact that consciousness attends them. They are, according to these writers, results of physiological mechanism pure and simple.

To comprehend completely this latter doctrine one should apply it to examples. The movements of our tongues and pens, the flashings of our eyes in conversation, are of course events of a physiological order, and as such their causal antecedents may be exclusively mechanical. If we knew thoroughly the nervous system of Shakespeare, and as thoroughly all his environing conditions, we should be able, according to the theory of automatism, to show why at a given period of his life his hand came to trace on certain sheets of paper those crabbed little black marks which we for shortness' sake call the manuscript of Hamlet. We should understand the rationale of every erasure and alteration therein, and we should understand all this without in the slightest degree acknowledging the existence of the thoughts in Shakespeare's mind. The words and sentences would be taken, not as signs of anything beyond themselves, but as little outward facts, pure and simple. In like manner, the automaton-theory affirms, we might exhaustively write the biography of those two hundred pounds, more or less, of warmish albuminoid matter called Martin Luther, without ever implying that it felt.

But, on the other hand, nothing in all this could prevent us from giving an equally complete account of either Luther's or Shakespeare's spiritual history, an account in which every gleam of thought and emotion should find its place. The mind-history would run alongside of the body-history of each man, and each point in the one would correspond to, but not react upon, a point in the other. So the melody floats from the harp-string, but neither checks nor quickens its vibrations; so the shadow runs alongside the pedestrian, but in no way influences his steps.

As a mere *conception*, and so long as we confine our view to the nervous centres themselves, few things are more seductive than this radically mechanical theory of their action. And yet our consciousness *is there*, and has in all probability been evolved, like all other functions, for a use—it is to the highest degree improbable *a priori* that it should have no use. Its use *seems* to be that of *selection ;* but to select, it must be efficacious. States of consciousness which feel right are held fast to; those which feel wrong are checked. If the 'holding' and the 'checking' of the conscious states severally mean also the efficacions reinforcing or inhibiting of the correlated neural processes, then it would seem as if the presence of the states of mind might help to steer the nervous system and keep it in the path which to the consciousness seemed best. Now on the average what seems best to consciousness is really best for the creature. It is a well-known fact that pleasures are generally associated with beneficial, pains with detrimental, experiences. All the fundamental vital processes illustrate this law. Starvation; suffocation; privation of food, drink, and sleep; work when exhausted; burns, wounds, inflammation; the effects of poison, are as disagreeable as filling the hungry stomach, enjoying rest and sleep after fatigue, exercise after rest, and a sound skin and unbroken bones at all times, are pleasant. Mr. Spencer and others have suggested that these coincidences are due, not to any preëstablished harmony, but to the mere action of natural selection, which would certainly kill off in the long-run any breed of creatures to whom the fundamentally noxious experience seemed enjoyable. An animal that should take pleasure in a feeling of suffocation would, if that pleasure were efficacious enough to make him keep his head under water, enjoy a longevity of four or five minutes. But if conscious pleasure does not reinforce, and conscious pain does not inhibit, anything, one does not see (without some such *a priori* rational harmony as would be scouted by the 'scientific' champions of the automaton-theory) why the most noxious acts, such as burning, might not with perfect impunity give thrills of delight, and the most necessary ones, such as breathing, cause agony. The only considerable attempt that has been made to explain the *distribution* of our feelings is that of Mr. Grant Allen in his suggestive little work, *Physiological Æsthetics;* and his reasoning is based exclusively on that causal efficacy of pleasures and pains which the partisan of pure automatism so strenuously deny.

Probability and circumstantial evidence thus run dead against the theory that our actions are *purely* mechanical in their causation. From the point of view of descriptive Psychology (even though we be bound to assume, as on p. 6, that all our feelings have brain-processes for their condition of existence, and can be remotely traced in every instance to currents coming from the outer world) we have no clear reason to doubt that the feelings may react so as to further or to dampen the processes to which they are due. I shall therefore not hesitate in the course of this book to use the language of common-sense. I shall talk as if consciousness kept actively pressing the nerve-centres in the direction of its own ends, and was no mere impotent and paralytic spectator of life's game.

The Localization of Functions in the Hemispheres —The hemispheres, we lately said, must be the organ of memory, and in some way retain vestiges of former currents, by means of which mental considerations drawn from the past may be aroused before action takes place. The vivisections of physiologists and the observations of physicians have of late years given a concrete confirmation to this notion which the first rough appearances suggest. The various convolutions have had special functions assigned to them in relation to this and that sense-organ, as well as to this or that portion of the muscular system. This book is no place for going over the evidence in detail, so I will simply indicate the conclusions which are most probable at the date of writing.

Mental and Cerebral Elements.—In the first place, there is a very neat parallelism between the analysis of brain-functions by the physiologists and that of mental functions by the 'analytic' psychologists.

The phrenological brain-doctrine divided the brain into 'organs,' each of which stood for the man in a certain partial attitude. The organ of 'Philoprogenitiveness,' with its concomitant consciousness, is an entire man so far as he loves children, that of 'Reverence' is an entire man worshipping, etc. The spiritualistic psychology, in turn, divided the Mind into 'faculties,' which were also entire mental men in certain limited attitudes. But 'faculties' are not mental *elements* any more than 'organs' are brain-elements. Analysis breaks both into more elementary constituents.

Brain and mind alike consist of simple elements, sensory and motor. "All nervous centres," says Dr. Hughlings Jackson, "from the lowest to the very highest (the substrata of consciousness), are made up of nothing else than nervous arrangements, representing impressions and movements. . . . I do not see of what other materials the brain *can* be made." Meynert represents the matter similarly when he calls the cortex of the hemispheres the surface of projection for every muscle and every sensitive point of the body. The muscles and the sensitive points are *represented* each by a cortical point, and the Brain is little more than the sum of all these cortical points, to which, on the mental side, as many sensations and *ideas* correspond. The sensations and ideas of sensation and of motion are, in turn, the elements out of which the Mind is built according to the analytic school of psychology. The relations between objects are explained by 'associations' between the ideas; and the emotional and instinctive tendencies, by associations between ideas and movements

The same diagram can symbolize both the inner and the outer world; dots or circles standing indifferently for cells or ideas, and lines joining them, for fibres or associations. The associationist doctrine of 'ideas' may be doubted to be a literal expression of the truth, but it probably will always retain a didactic usefulness. At all events, it is interesting to see how well physiological analysis plays into its hands. To proceed to details.

The Motor Region.—The one thing which is *perfectly* well established is this, that the 'central' con-

FIG. 41.—Left hemisphere of monkey's brain. Outer surface.

volutions, on either side of the fissure of Rolando, and (at least in the monkey) the calloso-marginal convolution (which is continuous with them on the mesial surface where one hemisphere is applied against the other), form the region by which all the motor incitations which leave the cortex pass out, on their way to those executive centres in the region of the pons, medulla, and spinal cord from

THE FUNCTIONS OF THE BRAIN. 107

which the muscular contractions are discharged in the last resort. The existence of this so-called 'motor zone' is established by anatomical as well as vivisectional and pathological evidence.

The accompanying figures (Figs. 41 and 42), from Schaefer and Horsley, show the topographical arrangement of the monkey's motor zone more clearly than any description.

Fig. 42.—Left hemisphere of monkey's brain. Mesial surface.

Fig. 43, after Starr, shows how the fibres run downwards. All sensory currents entering the hemispheres run out from the Rolandic region, which may thus be regarded as a sort of funnel of escape, which narrows still more as it plunges beneath the surface, traversing the inner capsule, pons, and parts below. The dark ellipses on the left half of the diagram stand for hemorrhages or tumors, and the reader can easily trace, by following the course of the fibres, what the effect of them in interrupting motor currents may be.

108   PSYCHOLOGY.

One of the most instructive proofs of motor localization in the cortex is that furnished by the disease now called aphemia, or *motor aphasia*. Motor aphasia is neither loss of voice nor paralysis of the tongue or lips. The patient's voice is as strong as ever, and all the innervations of his

Fig.] 43.—Schematic transverse section of the human brain, through the rolandic region. *S*, fissure of Sylvius; *N.C.*, *nucleus candatus*, and *N.L.*, *nucleus lenticularis*, of the corpus striatum; *O.T.*, thalamus; *C*, crus; *M*, medulla oblongata; *VII*, the facial nerves passing out from their nucleus in the region of the *pons*. The fibres passing between *O.T.* and *N.L.* constitute the socalled internal capsule.

hypoglossal and facial nerves, except those necessary for speaking, may go on perfectly well. He can laugh and cry, and even sing; but he either is unable to utter any words at all; or a few meaningless stock phrases form his only speech; or else he speaks incoherently and confusedly.

mispronouncing, misplacing, and misusing his words in various degrees. Sometimes his speech is a mere broth of unintelligible syllables. In cases of pure motor aphasia the patient recognizes his mistakes and suffers acutely from them. Now whenever a patient dies in such a condition as this, and an examination of his brain is per-

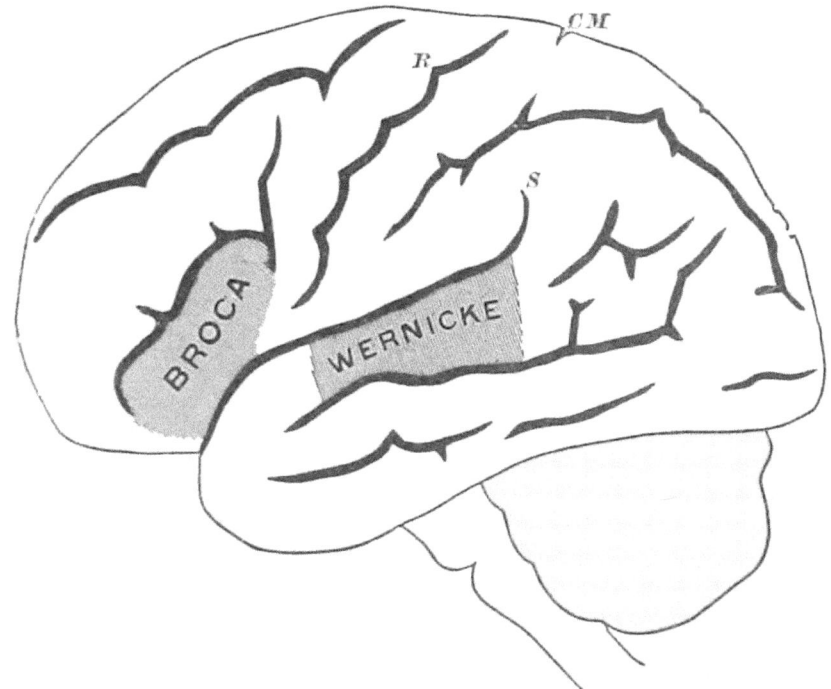

FIG. 41 —Schematic profile of left hemisphere, with the parts shaded whose destruction causes motor ('Broca') and sensory ('Wernicke') aphasia.

mitted, it is found that the lowest frontal gyrus (see Fig. 44) is the seat of injury. Broca first noticed this fact in 1861, and since then the gyrus has gone by the name of Broca's convolution. The injury in right-handed people is found on the left hemisphere, and in left-handed people on the right hemisphere. Most people, in fact, are left-brained, that is, all their delicate and specialized movements are handed over to the charge of the left hemisphere. The ordinary right-handedness for such movements is only a consequence of that fact, a consequence which shows outwardly on account of that extensive crossing of the fibres from the left hemisphere to the right half of the body only, which is shown in Fig. 43, below the letter *M*. But the left-brainedness might exist and *not* show outwardly. This would happen wherever organs on *both* sides of the body could be governed by the left hemisphere; and just such a case seems offered by the vocal organs, in that highly delicate and special motor service which we call speech. Either hemisphere *can* innervate them bilaterally, just as either seems able to innervate bilaterally the muscles of the trunk, ribs, and diaphragm. Of the special movements of speech, however, it would appear (from these very facts of aphasia) that the left hemisphere in most persons habitually takes exclusive charge. With that hemisphere thrown out of gear, speech is undone; even though the opposite hemisphere still be there for the performance of less specialized acts, such as the various movements required in eating.

The visual centre is in the *occipital lobes*. This also is proved by all the three kinds of possible evidence. It seems that the fibres from the *left* halves of *both* retinæ go to the *left* hemisphere, those from the right half to the right hemisphere. The consequence is that when the right occipital lobe, for example, is injured, 'hemianopsia' results in both eyes, that is, both retinæ grow blind as to their right halves, and the patient loses the leftward half of his field of view. The diagram on p. 111 will make this matter clear (see Fig. 45).

Quite recently, both Schaefer and Munk, in studying the movements of the eyeball produced by galvanizing the visual cortex in monkeys and dogs, have found reason to plot out an analogous correspondence between the upper and lower portions of the retinæ and certain parts of the visual cortex. If both occipital lobes were destroyed, we should have double hemiopia, or, in other words, total blindness. In human hemiopic blindness there is insensibility to light on one half of the field of view, but mental images of visible things remain. In *double* hemiopia there is every reason to believe that not only the sensation of light must go, but that all memories and images

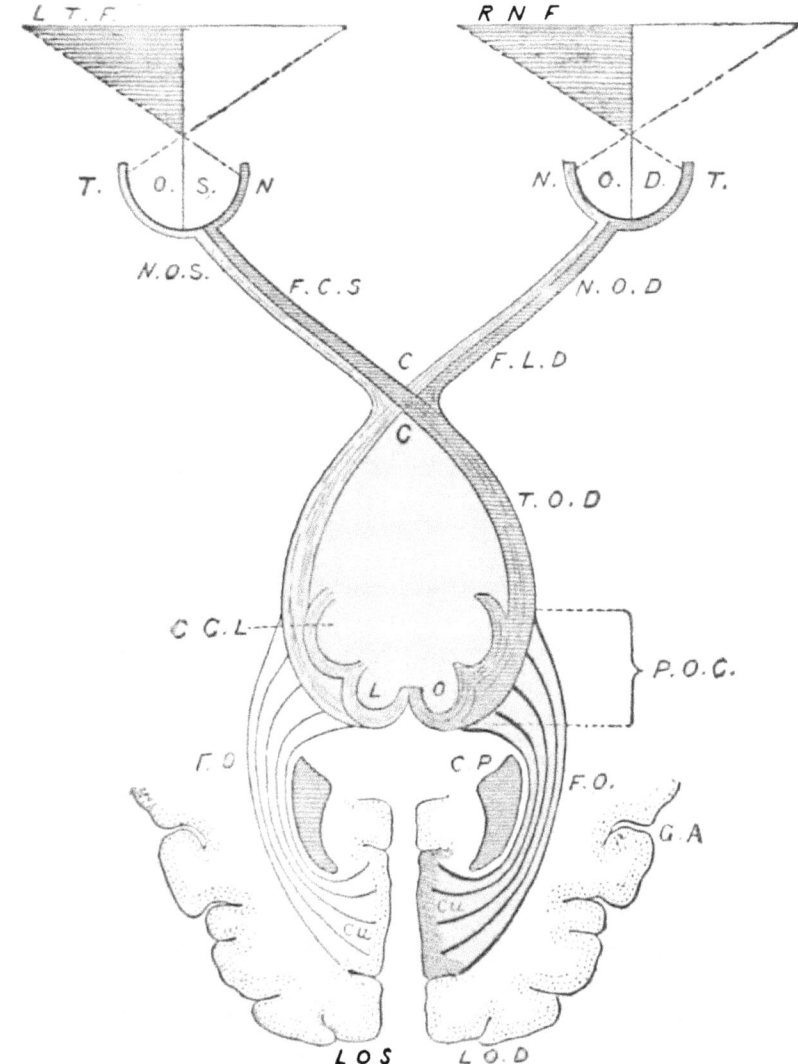

FIG. 45.—Scheme of the mechanism of vision, after Seguin. The *cuneus* convolution (*Cu*) of the right occipital lobe is supposed to be injured, and all the parts which lead to it are darkly shaded to show that they fail to exert their function. *F.O.* are the intra hemispheric optical fibres. *P.O.C.* is the region of the lower optic centres (corpora geniculata and quadrigemina). *T.O.D.* is the right optic tract; *C*, the chiasma; *F.L.D.* are the fibres going to the lateral or temporal half *T* of the right retina, and *F.C.S.* are those going to the central or nasal half of the left retina. *O.D.* is the right, and *O.S.* the left, eyeball. The rightward half of each is therefore blind; in other words, the right nasal field, *R N F*., and the left temporal field, *L T F*., have become invisible to the subject with the lesion at *Cu*.

of a visual order must be annihilated also. The man loses his visual 'ideas.' Only 'cortical' blindness can produce this effect on the ideas. Destruction of the retinæ or of the visual tracts anywhere between the cortex and the eyes impairs the retinal sensibility to light, but not the power of visual imagination.

Mental Blindness.—A most interesting effect of cortical disorder is *mental blindness*. This consists not so much

FIG. 46.—Fibres associating the cortical centres together. (Schematic, after Starr.)

in insensibility to optical impressions, as in *inability to understand them*. Psychologically it is interpretable as *loss of associations* between optical sensations and what they signify; and any interruption of the paths between the optic centres and the centres for other ideas ought to bring it about. Thus, printed letters of the alphabet, or words, signify both certain sounds and certain articulatory movements. But the connection between the articulating or auditory centres and those for sight being ruptured, we ought *a priori* to expect that the sight of words would fail to awaken the idea of their sound, or of the movement for pronouncing them. We ought, in short, to have *alexia*, or inability to read; and this is just what we do have as a complication of *aphasic* disease in many cases of extensive injury about the fronto-temporal regions.

Where an object fails to be recognized by sight, it often happens that the patient will recognize and name it as soon as he touches it with his hand. This shows in an interesting way how numerous are the incoming paths which all end by running out of the brain through the channel of speech. The hand-path is open, though the eye-path be closed. When mental blindness is most complete, neither sight, touch, nor sound avails to steer the patient, and a sort of dementia which has been called *asymbolia* or *apraxia* is the result. The commonest articles are not understood. The patient will put his breeches on one shoulder and his hat upon the other, will bite into the soap and lay his shoes on the table, or take his food into his hand and throw it down again, not knowing what to do with it, etc. Such disorder can only come from extensive brain-injury.

The centre for hearing is situated in man in the upper convolution of the temporal lobe (see the part marked 'Wernicke' in Fig. 44). The phenomena of aphasia show this. We studied motor aphasia a few pages back; we must now consider *sensory aphasia*. Our knowledge of aphasia has had three stages: we may talk of the period of Broca, the period of Wernicke, and the period of Charcot. What Broca's discovery was we have seen. Wernicke was the first to discriminate those cases in which the patient can *not even understand* speech from those in which he can understand, only not talk; and to ascribe the former condition to lesion of the temporal lobe. The condition in question is *word-deafness*, and the disease is *auditory aphasia*. The latest statistical survey of the subject is that by Dr. Allen Starr. In the seven cases of *pure* word-deafness which he has collected (cases in which the patient could read, talk, and write, but not understand what was said to him), the lesion was limited to the first and second temporal convolutions in their posterior two thirds. The lesion (in right-handed, i.e. left-brained, persons) is always on the left side, like the lesion in motor aphasia. Crude hearing would not be abolished even were the left centre for it utterly destroyed; the right centre would still provide for that. But the *linguistic use* of hearing appears bound up with the integrity of the left centre more or less exclusively. Here it must be that words heard enter into association with the things which they represent, on the one hand, and with the movements necessary for pronouncing them, on the other. In most of us (as Wernicke said) speech must go on from auditory cues; that is, our visual, tactile, and other ideas probably do not innervate our motor centres directly, but only after first arousing the mental sound of the words. This is the immediate stimulus to articulation; and where the possibility of this is abolished by the destruction of its usual channel in the left temporal lobe, the articulation must suffer. In the few cases in which the channel is abolished with no bad effect on speech we must suppose an idiosyncrasy. The patient must innervate his speech-organs either from the corresponding portion of the other hemisphere or directly from the centres of vision, touch, etc., without leaning on the auditory region. It is the minuter analysis of such individual differences as these which constitutes Charcot's contribution towards clearing up the subject.

Every namable thing has numerous properties, qualities, or aspects. In our minds the properties together with the name form an associated group. If different parts of the brain are severally concerned with the several properties, and a farther part with the hearing, and still another with the uttering, of the name, there must inevitably be brought about (through the law of association which we shall later study) such a connection amongst all these brain-parts that the activity of any one of them will be likely to awaken the activity of all the rest. When we are talking whilst we think, the *ultimate* process is utterance. If the brain-part for *that* be injured, speech is impossible or disorderly, even though all the other brain-parts be intact: and this is just the condition of things which, on p. 109, we found to be brought about by lesion of the convolution of Broca. But back of that last act various orders of succession are possible in the associations of a talking man's ideas. The more usual order is, as aforesaid, from the tactile, visual, or other properties of the things thought-about to the sound of their names, and then to the latter's utterance. But if in a certain individual's mind the *look* of an object or the *look* of its name be what habitually precedes articulation, then the loss of the *hearing* centre will *pro tanto* not affect that individual's speech or reading. He will be mentally deaf, i.e. his *understanding* of the human voice will suffer, but he will not be aphasic. In this way it is possible to explain the seven cases of word-deafness without motor aphasia which figure in Dr. Starr's table.

If this order of association be ingrained and habitual in that individual, injury to his *visual* centres will make him not only word-blind, but aphasic as well. His speech will become confused in consequence of an occipital lesion. Naunyn, consequently, plotting out on a diagram of the hemisphere the 71 irreproachably reported cases of aphasia which he was able to collect, finds that the lesions concentrate themselves in three places: first, on Broca's centre; second, on Wernicke's; third, on the supra-marginal and angular convolutions under which those fibres pass which connect the visual centres with the rest of the brain (see Fig. 47, p. 116). With this result Dr. Starr's analysis of purely sensory cases agrees.

In the chapter on Imagination we shall return to these differences in the sensory spheres of different individuals. Meanwhile few things show more beautifully than the history of our knowledge of aphasia how the sagacity and patience of many banded workers are in time certain to

116   PSYCHOLOGY.

analyze the darkest confusion into an orderly display
There is no 'organ' of Speech in the brain any more than
there is a 'faculty' of Speech in the mind. The entire
mind and the entire brain are more or less at work in a

Fig. 47.

man who uses language. The subjoined diagram, from
Ross, shows the four parts most vitally concerned, and,
in the light of our text, needs no farther explanation (see
Fig. 48, p. 117).

Centres for Smell, Taste, and Touch.—The other sensory
centres are less definitely made out. Of smell and taste I
will say nothing; and of muscular and cutaneous feeling
only this, that it seems most probably seated in the motor
zone, and possibly in the convolutions immediately backwards and midwards thereof. The incoming tactile currents must enter the cells of this region by one set of fibres,
and the discharges leave them by another, but of these
refinements of anatomy we at present know nothing.

THE FUNCTIONS OF THE BRAIN. 117

Conclusion.—We thus see the postulate of Meynert and Jackson, with which we started on p. 105, to be on the whole most satisfactorily corroborated by objective research. *The highest centres do probably contain nothing but arrange-*

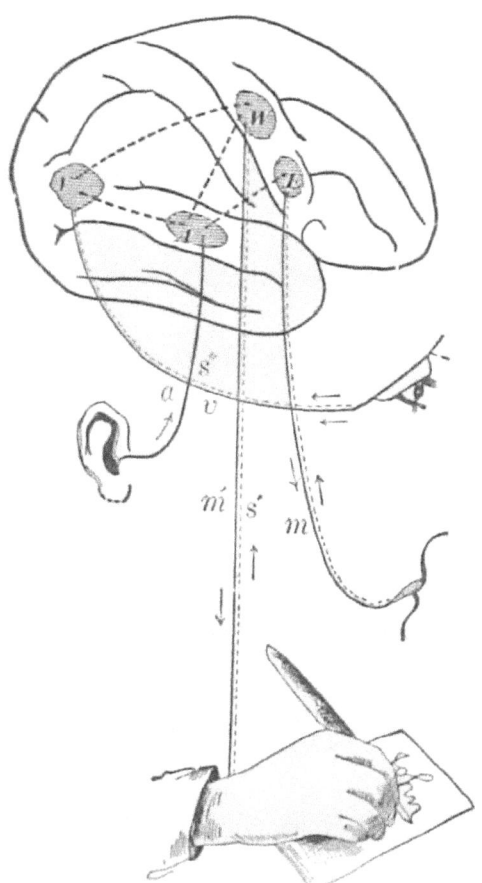

FIG. 48.—*A* is the auditory centre, *V* the visual, *W* the writing, and *E* that for speech.

ments for representing impressions and movements, and other arrangements for coupling the activity of these arrangements together. Currents pouring in from the sense-organs first excite some arrangements, which in turn excite others, until at last a discharge downwards of some sort occurs. When this is once clearly grasped there remains little ground for asking whether the motor zone is exclusively motor, or sensitive as well. The whole cortex, inasmuch as currents run through it, is both. All the currents probably have feelings going with them, and sooner or later bring movements about. In one aspect, then, every centre is afferent, in another efferent, even the motor cells of the spinal cord having these two aspects inseparably conjoined. Marique, and Exner and Paneth have shown that by cutting *round* a 'motor' centre and so separating it from the influence of the rest of the cortex, the same disorders are produced as by cutting it out, so that it is really just what I called it, only the funnel through which the stream of innervation, starting from elsewhere, escapes; *consciousness accompanying the stream, and being mainly of things seen if the stream is strongest occipitally, of things heard if it is strongest temporally, of things felt, etc., if the stream occupies most intensely the 'motor zone.'* It seems to me that some broad and vague formulation like this is as much as we can safely venture on in the present state of science— so much at least is not likely to be overturned. But it is obvious how little this tells us of the detail of what goes on in the brain when a certain thought is before the mind. The general forms of relation perceived between things, as their identities, likenesses, or contrasts; the forms of the consciousness itself, as effortless or perplexed, attentive or inattentive, pleasant or disagreeable; the phenomena of interest and selection, etc., etc., are all lumped together as effects correlated with the currents that connect one centre with another. Nothing can be more vague than such a formula. Moreover certain portions of the brain, as the lower frontal lobes, escape formulation altogether. Their destruction gives rise to no local trouble of either motion or sensibility in dogs, and in monkeys neither stimulation nor excision of these lobes produces any symptoms whatever. One monkey of Horsley and Schaefer's was as tame, and did certain tricks as well, after as before the operation.

It is in short obvious that our knowledge of our mental states infinitely exceeds our knowledge of their concomitant cerebral conditions. Without introspective analysis of the mental elements of speech, the doctrine of Aphasia, for instance, which is the most brilliant jewel in Physiology, would have been utterly impossible. Our assumption, therefore (p. 5), that mind-states are absolutely dependent on brain-conditions, must still be understood as a mere postulate. We may have a general faith that it must be true, but any exact insight as to *how* it is true lags wofully behind.

Before taking up the study of conscious states properly so called, I will in a separate chapter speak of two or three aspects of brain-function which have a general importance and which coöperate in the production of all our mental states.

CHAPTER IX.

SOME GENERAL CONDITIONS OF NEURAL ACTIVITY.

The Nervous Discharge.—The word discharge is constantly used, and must be used in this book, to designate the escape of a current downwards into muscles or other internal organs. The reader must not understand the word figuratively. From the point of view of dynamics the passage of a current out of a motor cell is probably altogether analogous to the explosion of a gun. The matter of the cell is in a state of internal tension, which the incoming current resolves, tumbling the molecules into a more stable equilibrium and liberating an amount of energy which starts the current of the outgoing fibre. This current is stronger than that of the incoming fibre. When it reaches the muscle it produces an analogous disintegration of pent-up molecules and the result is a stronger effect still. Matteuci found that the work done by a muscle's contraction was 27,000 times greater than that done by the galvanic current which stimulated its motor nerve. When a frog's leg-muscle is made to contract, first directly, by stimulation of its motor nerve, and second reflexly, by stimulation of a sensory nerve, it is found that the reflex way requires a stronger current and is more tardy, but that the contraction is stronger when it does occur. These facts prove that the cells in the spinal cord through which the reflex takes place offer a resistance which has first to be overcome, but that a relatively violent outward current outwards then escapes from them. What is this but an explosive discharge on a minute scale?

Reaction-time.—The measurement of the time required for the discharge is one of the lines of experimental investigation most diligently followed of late years. Helmholtz led the way by discovering the rapidity of the outgoing current in the sciatic nerve of the frog. The methods he used were soon applied to sensory reactions, and the results caused much popular admiration when described as measurements of the 'velocity of thought.' The phrase 'quick as thought' had from time immemorial signified all that was wonderful and elusive of determination in the line of speed; and the way in which Science laid her doomful hand upon this mystery reminded people of the day when Franklin first *'eripuit cœlo fulmen,'* foreshadowing the reign of a newer and colder race of gods. I may say, however, immediately, that the phrase 'velocity of *thought'* is misleading, for it is by no means clear in any of the cases what particular act of thought occurs during the time which is measured. What the times in question really represent is the total duration of certain *reactions upon stimuli.* Certain of the conditions of the reaction are prepared beforehand; they consist in the assumption of those motor and sensory tensions which we name the expectant state. Just what happens during the actual time occupied by the reaction (in other words, just what is added to the preëxistent tensions to produce the actual discharge) is not made out at present, either from the neural or from the mental point of view.

The method is essentially the same in all these investigations. A signal of some sort is communicated to the subject, and at the same instant records itself on a time-registering apparatus. The subject then makes a muscular movement of some sort, which is the 'reaction,' and which also records itself automatically. The time found to have elapsed between the two records is the total time of that reaction. The time-registering instruments are of various types. One type is that of the revolving drum covered with smoked paper, on which one electric pen traces a line which the signal breaks and the 'reaction' draws again; whilst another electric pen (connected with a rod of metal vibrating at a known rate) traces alongside of the former line a 'time-line' of which each undulation or link stands for a certain fraction of a second, and against which the break in the reaction-line can be measured. Compare Fig. 49, where the line is broken by the signal at the first

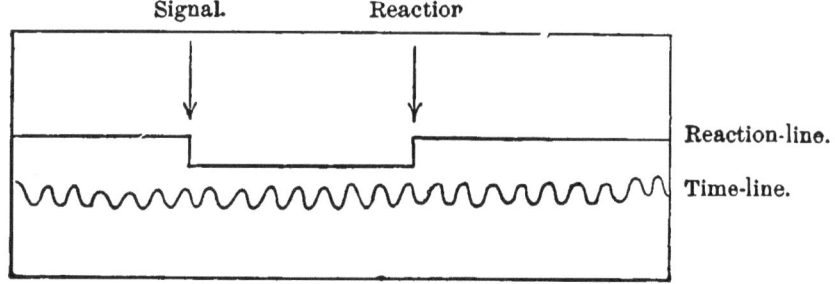

FIG. 49.

arrow, and continued again by the reaction at the second. The machine most often used is Hipp's chronoscopic clock. The hands are placed at zero, the signal starts them (by an electric connection), and the reaction stops them. The duration of their movement, down to 1000ths of a second, is then read off from the dial-plates.

Simple Reactions.—It is found that the reaction-time differs in the same person according to the direction of his expectant attention. If he thinks as little as possible of the movement which he is to make, and concentrates his mind upon the signal to be received, it is longer; if, on the contrary, he bends his mind exclusively upon the muscular response, it is shorter. Lange, who first noticed this fact when working in Wundt's laboratory, found his own 'muscular' reaction-time to average 0″.123, whilst his 'sensorial' reaction-time averaged as much as 0″.230. It is obvious that experiments, to have any *comparative* value, must always be made according to the 'muscular' method, which reduces the figure to its minimum and makes it more constant. In general it lies between one and two tenths of a second. It seems to me that under these circumstances the reaction is essentially a reflex act. The preliminary *making-ready* of the muscles for the movement means the excitement of the paths of discharge to a point just short of actual discharge before the signal comes in. In other words, it means the temporary formation of a real 'reflex-arc' in the centres, through which the incoming current instantly can pour out again. But when, on the other hand, the expectant attention is exclusively addressed to the signal, the excitement of the motor tracts can only begin after this latter has come in, and under this condition the reaction takes more time. In the hair-trigger condition in which we stand when making reactions by the 'muscular' method, we sometimes respond to a wrong signal, especially if it be of the same *kind* with the one we expect. The signal is but the spark which touches off a train already laid. There is no thought in the matter; the hand jerks by an involuntary start.

These experiments are thus in no sense measurements of the swiftness of *thought*. Only when we complicate them is there a chance for anything like an intellectual operation to occur. They may be complicated in various ways. The reaction may be withheld until the signal has consciously awakened a distinct idea (Wundt's discrimination-time, association-time), and may then be performed. Or there may be a variety of possible signals, each with a different reaction assigned to it, and the reacter may be uncertain which one he is about to receive. The reaction would then hardly seem to occur without a preliminary recognition and choice. Even here, however, the discrimination and choice are widely different from the intellectual operations of which we are ordinarily conscious under those names. Meanwhile the simple reaction-time remains as the starting point of all these superinduced complications, and its own variations must be briefly passed in review.

The reaction-time varies with the *individual* and his *age*. Old and uncultivated people have it long (nearly a second, in an old pauper observed by Exner). Children have it long (half a second, according to Herzen).

Practice shortens it to a quantity which is for each individual a minimum beyond which no farther reduction can be made. The aforesaid old pauper's time was, after much practice, reduced to 0.1866 sec.

Fatigue lengthens it, and *concentration of attention* shortens it. The *nature of the signal* makes it vary. I here bring together the averages which have been obtained by some observers:

	Hirsch.	Hankel.	Exner.	Wundt.
Sound	0.149	0.1505	0.1360	0.167
Light	0.200	0.2246	0.1506	0.222
Touch	0.182	0.1546	0.1337	0.213

It will be observed that *sound* is more promptly reacted on than either *sight* or *touch*. *Taste* and *smell* are slower than either. The *intensity of the signal* makes a difference. The intenser the stimulus the shorter the time. Herzen compared the reaction from a *corn* on the toe with that from the skin of the hand of the same subject. The two places were stimulated simultaneously, and the subject tried to react simultaneously with both hand and foot, but the foot always went quickest. When the sound skin of the foot was touched instead of the corn, it was the hand which always reacted first. *Intoxicants* on the whole lengthen the time, but much depends on the dose.

Complicated Reactions.—These occur when some kind of intellectual operation accompanies the reaction. The rational place in which to report of them would be under the head of the various intellectual operations concerned. But certain persons prefer to see all these measurements bunched together regardless of context; so, to meet their views, I give the complicated reactions here.

When we have to think before reacting it is obvious that there is no definite reaction-time of which we can talk—it all depends on how long we think. The only times we can measure are the *minimum* times of certain determinate and very simple intellectual operations. The *time required for discrimination* has thus been made a subject of experimental measurement. Wundt calls it *Unterscheidungszeit*.

His subjects (whose simple reaction-time had previously been determined) were required to make a movement, always the same, the instant they discerned *which* of two or more signals they received. The *excess* of time occupied by these reactions *over the simple reaction-time*, in which only one signal was used and known in advance, measured, according to Wundt, the time required for the act of discrimination. It was found longer when four different signals were irregularly used than when only two were used. When two were used (the signals being the sudden appearance of a black or of a white object), the average times of three observers were respectively (in seconds)

0.050   0.047   0.079

When four signals were used, a red and a green light being added to the others, it became, for the same observers,

0.157   0.073   0.132

Prof. Cattell found he could get no results by this method, and reverted to one used by observers previous to Wundt and which Wundt had rejected. This is the *einfache Wahlmethode*, as Wundt calls it. The reacter awaits the signal and reacts if it is of one sort, but omits to act if it is of another sort. The reaction thus occurs after discrimination; the motor impulse cannot be sent to the hand until the subject knows what the signal is. Reacting in this way, Prof. Cattell found the increment of time required for distinguishing a white signal from no signal to be, in two observers,

0.030   and   0.050;

that for distinguishing one color from another was similarly

0.100   and   0.110;

that for distinguishing a certain color from ten other colors,

0.105   and   0.117;

that for distinguishing the letter A in ordinary print from the letter Z,

0.142   and   0.137;

that for distinguishing a given letter from all the rest of the alphabet (not reacting until that letter appeared),

0.119 and 0.116;

that for distinguishing a word from any of twenty-five other words, from

0.118 to 0.158 sec.

—the difference depending on the length of the words and the familiarity of the language to which they belonged.

Prof. Cattell calls attention to the fact that the time for distinguishing a word is often but little more than that for distinguishing a letter: "We do not, therefore," he says, "distinguish separately the letters of which a word is composed, but the word as a whole. The application of this in teaching children to read is evident."

He also finds a great difference in the time with which various letters are distinguished, E being particularly bad.

The time required for association of one idea with another has been measured. Galton, using a very simple apparatus, found that the sight of an unforeseen word would awaken an associated 'idea' in about $\frac{5}{6}$ of a second. Wundt next made determinations in which the 'cue' was given by single-syllabled words called out by an assistant. The person experimented on had to press a key as soon as the sound of the word awakened an associated idea. Both word and reaction were chronographically registered, and the total time-interval between the two amounted, in four observers, to 1.009, 0.896, 1.037, and 1.154 seconds respectively. From this the simple reaction-time and the time of merely identifying the word's sound (the 'apperception-time,' as Wundt calls it) must be subtracted, to get the exact time required for the associated idea to arise. These times were separately determined and subtracted. The difference, called by Wundt *association-time*, amounted, in the same four persons, to 706, 723, 752, and 874 thousandths of a second respectively. The length of the last figure is due to the fact that the person reacting was an American, whose associations with German words would naturally be slower than those of natives. The shortest association-time noted was when the word 'Sturm' suggested to Wundt the word 'Wind' in 0.341 second. Prof. Cattell made some interesting observations upon the association-time between the look of letters and their names. "I pasted letters," he says, "on a revolving drum, and determined at what rate they could be read aloud as they passed by a slit in a screen." He found it to vary according as one, or more than one, letter was visible at a time through the slit, and gives half a second as about the time which it takes to see and name a single letter seen alone. The rapidity of a man's *reading* is of course a measure of that of his associations, since each seen word must call up its name, at least, ere it is read. "I find," says Prof. Cattell, "that it takes about twice as long to read (aloud, as fast as possible) words which have no connection, as words which make sentences, and letters which have no connection, as letters which make words. When the words make sentences and the letters words, not only do the processes of seeing and naming overlap, but by one mental effort the subject can recognize a whole group of words or letters, and by one will-act choose the motions to be made in naming, so that the rate at which the words and letters are read is really only limited by the maximum rapidity at which the speech-organs can be moved. . . . For example, when reading as fast as possible the writer's rate was, English 138, French 167, German 250, Italian 327, Latin 434, and Greek 484; the figures giving the thousandths of a second taken to read each word. Experiments made on others strikingly confirm these results. The subject does not know that he is reading the foreign language more slowly than his own; this explains why foreigners seem to talk so fast. . . .

"The time required to see and name colors and pictures of objects was determined in the same way. The time was found to be about the same (over ¼ sec.) for colors as for pictures, and about twice as long as for words and letters. Other experiments I have made show that we can recognize a single color or picture in a slightly shorter time than a word or letter, but take longer to name it. This is because, in the case of words and letters, the association between the idea and the name has taken place so often that the process has become automatic, whereas in the case of colors and pictures we must by a voluntary effort choose the name."

Dr. Romanes has found "astonishing differences in the *maximum* rate of reading which is possible to different individuals, all of whom have been accustomed to extensive reading. That is to say, the difference may amount to 4 to 1; or, otherwise stated, in a given time one individual may be able to read four times as much as another. Moreover, it appeared that there was no relationship between slowness of reading and power of assimilation; on the contrary, when all the efforts are directed to assimilating as much as possible in a given time, the rapid readers (as shown by their written notes) usually give a better account of the portions of the paragraph which have been compassed by the slow readers than the latter are able to give; and the most rapid reader I have found is also the best at assimilating. I should further say," Dr. R. continues, "that there is no relationship between rapidity of perception as thus tested and intellectual activity as tested by the general results of intellectual work; for I have tried the experiment with several highly distinguished men in science and literature, most of whom I found to be slow readers."

The degree of concentration of the attention has much to do with determining the reaction-time. Anything which baffles or distracts us beforehand, or startles us in the signal, makes the time proportionally long.

The Summation of Stimuli.—Throughout the nerve-centres it is a law that *a stimulus which would be inadequate by itself to excite a nerve-centre to effective discharge may, by acting with one or more other stimuli (equally ineffectual by themselves alone) bring the discharge about*

The natural way to consider this is as a summation of tensions which at last overcome a resistance. The first of them produce a 'latent excitement' or a 'heightened irritability'—the phrase is immaterial so far as practical consequences go;—the last is the straw which breaks the camel's back.

This is proved by many physiological experiments which cannot here be detailed; but outside of the laboratory we constantly apply the law of summation in our practical appeals. If a car-horse balks, the final way of starting him is by applying a number of customary incitements at once. If the driver uses reins and voice, if one bystander pulls at his head, another lashes his hind-quarters, the conductor rings the bell, and the dismounted passengers shove the car, all at the same moment, his obstinacy generally yields, and he goes on his way rejoicing. If we are striving to remember a lost name or fact, we think of as many 'cues' as possible, so that by their joint action they may recall what no one of them can recall alone. The sight of a dead prey will often not stimulate a beast to pursuit, but if the sight of movement be added to that of form, pursuit occurs. "Brücke noted that his brainless hen which made no attempt to peck at the grain under her very eyes, began pecking if the grain were thrown on the ground with force, so as to produce a rattling sound." "Dr. Allen Thomson hatched out some chickens on a carpet, where he kept them for several days. They showed no inclination to scrape, . . . but when Dr. Thomson sprinkled a little gravel on the carpet, . . . the chickens immediately began their scraping movements." A strange person, and darkness, are both of them stimuli to fear and mistrust in dogs (and for the matter of that, in men). Neither circumstance alone may awaken outward manifestations, but together, i.e. when the strange man is met in the dark, the dog will be excited to violent defiance. Street hawkers well know the efficacy of summation, for they arrange themselves in a line on the sidewalk, and the passer often buys from the last one of them, through the effect of the reiterated solicitation, what he refused to buy from the first in the row.

Cerebral Blood-supply.—All parts of the cortex, when electrically excited, produce alterations both of respiration and circulation. The blood-pressure somewhat rises, as a rule, all over the body, no matter where the cortical irritation is applied, though the motor zone is the most sensitive region for the purpose. Slowing and quickening of the heart are also observed. Mosso, using his 'plethysmograph' as an indicator, discovered that the blood-supply to the arms diminished during intellectual activity, and found furthermore that the arterial tension (as shown by the sphygmograph) was increased in these members (see Fig. 50). So

FIG. 50.—Sphygmographic pulse-tracing. *A*, during intellectual repose; *B*, during intellectual activity. (Mosso.)

slight an emotion as that produced by the entrance of Professor Ludwig into the laboratory was instantly followed by a shrinkage of the arms. The brain itself is an execssively vascular organ, a sponge full of blood, in fact; and another of Mosso's inventions showed that when less blood went to the legs, more went to the head. The subject to be observed lay on a delicately balanced table which could tip downward either at the head or at the foot if the weight of either end were increased. The moment emotional or intellectual activity began in the subject, down went the head-end, in consequence of the redistribution of blood in his system. But the best proof of the immediate afflux of blood to the brain during mental activity is due to Mosso's observations on three persons whose brain had been laid bare by lesion of the skull.

By means of apparatus described in his book, this physiologist was enabled to let the brain-pulse record itself directly by a tracing. The intra-cranial blood-pressure rose immediately whenever the subject was spoken to, or when he began to think actively, as in solving a problem in mental arithmetic. Mosso gives in his work a large number of reproductions of tracings which show the instantaneity of the change of blood-supply, whenever the mental activity was quickened by any cause whatever, intellectual or emotional. He relates of his female subject that one day whilst tracing her brain-pulse he observed a sudden rise with no apparent outer or inner cause. She however confessed to him afterwards that at that moment she had caught sight of a *skull* on top of a piece of furniture in the room, and that this had given her a slight emotion.

Cerebral Thermometry.—*Brain-activity seems accompanied by a local disengagement of heat.* The earliest careful work in this direction was by Dr. J. S. Lombard in 1867. He noted the changes in delicate thermometers and electric piles placed against the scalp in human beings, and found that any intellectual effort, such as computing, composing, reciting poetry silently or aloud, and especially that emotional excitement such as an angry fit, caused a general rise of temperature, which rarely exceeded a degree Fahrenheit. In 1870 the indefatigable Schiff took up the subject, experimenting on live dogs and chickens by plunging thermo-electric needles into the substance of their brain. After habituation was established, he tested the animals with various sensations, tactile, optic, olfactory, and auditory. He found very regularly an abrupt alteration of the intra-cerebral temperature. When, for instance, he presented an empty roll of paper to the nose of his dog as it lay motionless, there was a small deflection, but when a piece of meat was in the paper the deflection was much greater. Schiff concluded from these and other experiments that sensorial activity heats the brain-tissue, but he did not try to localize the increment of heat beyond finding that it was in both hemispheres, whatever might be the sensation applied. Dr. Amidon in 1880 made a farther step forward, in localizing the heat produced by voluntary muscular contractions. Applying a number of delicate surface-thermometers simultaneously against the scalp, he found that when different muscles of the body were made to contract vigorously for ten minutes or more, different regions of the scalp rose in temperature, that the regions were well focalized, and that the rise of temperature was often considerably over a Fahrenheit degree. To a large extent these regions correspond to the centres for the same movements assigned by Ferrier and others on other grounds; only they cover more of the skull.

Phosphorus and Thought.—Considering the large amount of popular nonsense which passes current on this subject I may be pardoned for a brief mention of it here. '*Ohne Phosphor, kein Gedanke,*' was a noted war-cry of the 'materialists' during the excitement on that subject which filled Germany in the '60s. The brain, like every other organ of the body, contains phosphorus, and a score of other chemicals besides. Why the phosphorus should be picked out as its essence, no one knows. It would be equally true to say, 'Ohne Wasser, kein Gedanke,' or 'Ohne Kochsalz, kein Gedanke'; for thought would stop as quickly if the brain should dry up or lose its NaCl as if it lost its phosphorus. In America the phosphorus-delusion has twined itself round a saying quoted (rightly or wrongly) from Professor L. Agassiz, to the effect that fishermen are more intelligent than farmers because they eat so much fish, which contains so much phosphorus. All the alleged facts may be doubted.

The only straight way to ascertain the importance of phosphorus to thought would be to find whether more is excreted by the brain during mental activity than during rest. Unfortunately we cannot do this directly, but can only gauge the amount of PO_5 in the urine, and this procedure has been adopted by a variety of observers, some of whom found the phosphates in the urine diminished, whilst others found them increased, by intellectual work. On the whole, it is impossible to trace any constant relation. In maniacal excitement less phosphorus than usual seems to be excreted. More is excreted during sleep. The fact that phosphorus-preparations may do good in nervous exhaustion proves nothing as to the part played by phosphorus in mental activity. Like iron, arsenic, and other remedies it is a stimulant or tonic, of whose intimate workings in the system we know absolutely nothing, and which moreover does good in an extremely small number of the cases in which it is prescribed.

The phosphorus-philosophers have often compared thought to a secretion. "The brain secretes thought, as the kidneys secrete urine, or as the liver secretes bile," are phrases which one sometimes hears. The lame analogy need hardly be pointed out. The materials which the brain *pours into the blood* (cholesterin, creatin, xanthin, or whatever they may be) are the analogues of the urine and the bile, being in fact real material excreta. As far as these matters go, the brain is a ductless gland. But we know of nothing connected with liver- and kidney-activity which can be in the remotest degree compared with the stream of thought that accompanies the brain's material secretions.

CHAPTER X.

HABIT.

Its Importance for Psychology.—There remains a condition of general neural activity so important as to deserve a chapter by itself—I refer to the aptitude of the nerve-centres, especially of the hemispheres, for acquiring habits. *An acquired habit, from the physiological point of view, is nothing but a new pathway of discharge formed in the brain, by which certain incoming currents ever after tend to escape.* That is the thesis of this chapter; and we shall see in the later and more psychological chapters that such functions as the association of ideas, perception, memory, reasoning, the education of the will, etc. etc., can best be understood as results of the formation *de novo* of just such pathways of discharge.

Habit has a physical basis. The moment one tries to define what habit is, one is led to the fundamental properties of matter. The laws of Nature are nothing but the immutable habits which the different elementary sorts of matter follow in their actions and reactions upon each other. In the organic world, however, the habits are more variable than this. Even instincts vary from one individual to another of a kind; and are modified in the same individual, as we shall later see, to suit the exigencies of the case. On the principles of the atomistic philosophy the habits of an elementary particle of matter cannot change, because the particle is itself an unchangeable thing; but those of a compound mass of matter can change, because they are in the last instance due to the structure of the compound, and either outward forces or inward tensions can, from one hour to another, turn that structure into something different from what it was. That is, they can do so if the body be plastic enough to maintain its integrity, and be not disrupted when its structure yields. The change of structure here spoken of need not involve the outward shape; it may be invisible and molecular, as when a bar of iron becomes magnetic or crystalline through the action of certain outward causes, or india-rubber becomes friable, or plaster 'sets.' All these changes are rather slow; the material in question opposes a certain resistance to the modifying cause, which it takes time to overcome, but the gradual yielding whereof often saves the material from being disintegrated altogether. When the structure has yielded, the same inertia becomes a condition of its comparative permanence in the new form, and of the new habits the body then manifests. *Plasticity*, then, in the wide sense of the word, means the possession of a structure weak enough to yield to an influence, but strong enough not to yield all at once. Each relatively stable phase of equilibrium in such a structure is marked by what we may call a new set of habits. Organic matter, especially nervous tissue, seems endowed with a very extraordinary degree of plasticity of this sort; so that we may without hesitation lay down as our first proposition the following: that *the phenomena of habit in living beings are due to the plasticity of the organic materials of which their bodies are composed.*

The philosophy of habit is thus, in the first instance, a chapter in physics rather than in physiology or psychology. That it is at bottom a physical principle, is admitted by all good recent writers on the subject. They call attention to analogues of acquired habits exhibited by dead matter. Thus, M. Léon Dumont writes:

"Every one knows how a garment, after having been worn a certain time, clings to the shape of the body better than when it was new; there has been a change in the tissue, and this change is a new habit of cohesion. A lock works better after being used some time; at the outset more force was required to overcome certain roughness in the mechanism. The overcoming of their resistance is a phenomenon of habituation. It costs less trouble to fold a paper when it has been folded already; . . . and just so in the nervous system the impressions of outer objects fashion for themselves more and more appropriate paths, and these vital phenomena recur under similar excitements from without, when they have been interrupted a certain time."

Not in the nervous system alone. A scar anywhere is a *locus minoris resistentiæ*, more liable to be abraded, inflamed, to suffer pain and cold, than are the neighboring parts. A sprained ankle, a dislocated arm, are in danger of being sprained or dislocated again; joints that have once been attacked by rheumatism or gout, mucous membranes that have been the seat of catarrh, are with each fresh recurrence more prone to a relapse, until often the morbid state chronically substitutes itself for the sound one. And in the nervous system itself it is well known how many so-called functional diseases seem to keep themselves going simply because they happen to have once begun; and how the forcible cutting short by medicine of a few attacks is often sufficient to enable the physiological forces to get possession of the field again, and to bring the organs back to functions of health. Epilepsies, neuralgias, convulsive affections of various sorts, insomnias, are so many cases in point. And, to take what are more obviously habits, the success with which a 'weaning' treatment can often be applied to the victims of unhealthy indulgence of passion, or of mere complaining or irascible disposition, shows us how much the morbid manifestations themselves were due to the mere inertia of the nervous organs, when once launched on a false career.

Habits are due to pathways through the nerve-centres. If habits are due to the plasticity of materials to outward agents, we can immediately see to what outward influences, if to any, the brain-matter is plastic. Not to mechanical pressures, not to thermal changes, not to any of the forces to which all the other organs of our body are exposed; for, as we saw on pp. 9–10, Nature has so blanketed and wrapped the brain about that the only impressions that can be made upon it are through the blood, on the one hand, and the sensory nerve-roots, on the other; and it is to the infinitely attenuated currents that pour in through these latter channels that the hemispherical cortex shows itself to be so peculiarly susceptible. The currents, once in, must find a way out. In getting out they leave their traces in the paths which they take. The only thing they *can* do, in short, is to deepen old paths or to make new ones; and the whole plasticity of the brain sums itself up in two words when we call it an organ in which currents pouring in from the sense-organs make with extreme facility paths which do not easily disappear. For, of course, a simple habit, like every other nervous event—the habit of snuffling, for example, or of putting one's hands into one's pockets, or of biting one's nails—is, mechanically, nothing but a reflex discharge; and its anatomical substratum must be a path in the system. The most complex habits, as we shall presently see more fully, are, from the same point of view, nothing but *concatenated* discharges in the nerve-centres, due to the presence there of systems of reflex paths, so organized as to wake each other up successively—the impression produced by one muscular contraction serving as a stimulus to provoke the next, until a final impression inhibits the process and closes the chain.

It must be noticed that the growth of structural modification in living matter may be more rapid than in any lifeless mass, because the incessant nutritive renovation of which the living matter is the seat tends often to corroborate and fix the impressed modification, rather than to counteract it by renewing the original constitution of the tissue that has been impressed. Thus, we notice after exercising our muscles or our brain in a new way, that we can do so no longer at that time; but after a day or two of rest, when we resume the discipline, our increase in skill not seldom surprises us. I have often noticed this in learning a tune; and it has led a German author to say that we learn to swim during the winter, and to skate during the summer.

Practical Effects of Habit.—First, habit simplifies our movements, makes them accurate, and diminishes fatigue.

Man is born with a tendency to do more things than he has ready-made arrangements for in his nerve-centres. Most of the performances of other animals are automatic. But in him the number of them is so enormous that most of them must be the fruit of painful study. If practice did not make perfect, nor habit economize the expense of nervous and muscular energy, he would be in a sorry plight. As Dr. Maudsley says:*

"If an act became no easier after being done several times, if the careful direction of consciousness were necessary to its accomplishment on each occasion, it is evident that the whole activity of a lifetime might be confined to one or two deeds—that no progress could take place in development. A man might be occupied all day in dressing and undressing himself; the attitude of his body would absorb all his attention and energy; the washing of his hands or the fastening of a button would be as difficult to him on each occasion as to the child on its first trial; and he would, furthermore, be completely exhausted by his exertions. Think of the pains necessary to teach a child to stand, of the many efforts which it must make, and of the ease with which it at last stands, unconscious of any effort. For while secondarily-automatic acts are accomplished with comparatively little weariness—in this regard approaching the organic movements, or the original reflex movements— the conscious effort of the will soon produces exhaustion. A spinal cord without . . . memory would simply be an idiotic spinal cord. . . . It is impossible for an individual

---

* The Physiology of Mind, p. 155.

HABIT. 139

to realize how much he owes to its automatic agency until disease has impaired its functions."

Secondly, *habit diminishes the conscious attention with which our acts are performed.*

One may state this abstractly thus: If an act require for its execution a chain, A, B, C, D, E, F, G, etc., of successive nervous events, then in the first performances of the action the conscious will must choose each of these events from a number of wrong alternatives that tend to present themselves; but habit soon brings it about that each event calls up its own appropriate successor without any alternative offering itself, and without any reference to the conscious will, until at last the whole chain, A, B, C, D, E, F, G, rattles itself off as soon as A occurs, just as if A and the rest of the chain were fused into a continuous stream. Whilst we are learning to walk, to ride, to swim, skate, fence, write, play, or sing, we interrupt ourselves at every step by unnecessary movements and false notes. When we are proficients, on the contrary, the results follow not only with the very minimum of muscular action requisite to bring them forth, but they follow from a single instantaneous 'cue.' The marksman sees the bird, and, before he knows it, he has aimed and shot. A gleam in his adversary's eye, a momentary pressure from his rapier, and the fencer finds that he has instantly made the right parry and return. A glance at the musical hieroglyphics, and the pianist's fingers have rippled through a shower of notes. And not only is it the right thing at the right time that we thus involuntarily do, but the wrong thing also, if it be an habitual thing. Who is there that has never wound up his watch on taking off his waistcoat in the daytime, or taken his latch-key out on arriving at the door-step of a friend? Persons in going to their bedroom to dress for dinner have been known to take off one garment after another and finally to get into bed, merely because that was the habitual issue of the first few movements when performed at a later hour. We all have a definite routine manner of performing certain daily offices connected with the toilet, with the opening and shutting of familiar cupboards, and the like. But our higher thought-centres know hardly anything about the matter. Few men can tell off-hand which sock, shoe, or trousers-leg they put on first. They must first mentally rehearse the act; and even that is often insufficient—the act must be *performed*. So of the questions, Which valve of the shutters opens first? Which way does my door swing? etc. I cannot *tell* the answer; yet my *hand* never makes a mistake. No one can *describe* the order in which he brushes his hair or teeth; yet it is likely that the order is a pretty fixed one in all of us.

These results may be expressed as follows:

In action grown habitual, what instigates each new muscular contraction to take place in its appointed order is not a thought or a perception, but the *sensation occasioned by the muscular contraction just finished*. A strictly voluntary act has to be guided by idea, perception, and volition, throughout its whole course. In habitual action, mere sensation is a sufficient guide, and the upper regions of brain and mind are set comparatively free. A diagram will make the matter clear:

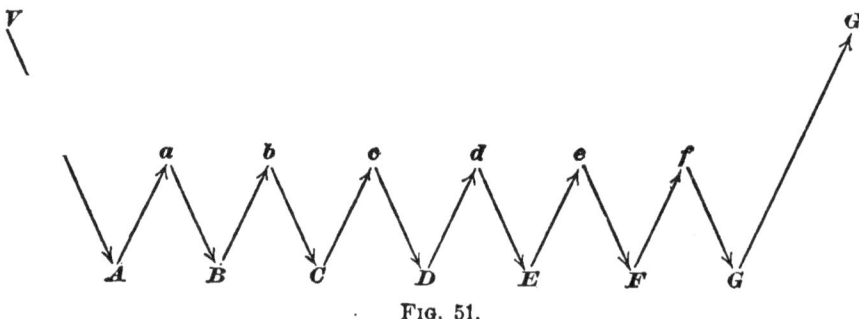

FIG. 51.

Let A, B, C, D, E, F, G represent an habitual chain of muscular contractions, and let a, b, c, d, e, f stand for the several sensations which these contractions excite in us when they are successively performed. Such sensations will usually be in the parts moved, but they may also be effects of the movement upon the eye or the ear. Through them, and through them alone, we are made aware whether or not the contraction has occurred. When the series, *A, B, C, D, E, F, G,* is being learned, each of these sensations becomes the object of a separate act of attention by the mind. We test each movement intellectually, to see if it have been rightly performed, before advancing to the next. We hesitate, compare, choose, revoke, reject, etc.; and the order by which the next movement is discharged is an express order from the ideational centres after this deliberation has been gone through.

In habitual action, on the contrary, the only impulse which the intellectual centres need send down is that which carries the command to *start*. This is represented in the diagram by V; it may be a thought of the first movement or of the last result, or a mere perception of some of the habitual conditions of the chain, the presence, e.g., of the keyboard near the hand. In the present example, no sooner has this conscious thought or volition instigated movement *A*, than *A*, through the sensation *a* of its own occurrence, awakens *B* reflexly; *B* then excites *C* through *b*, and so on till the chain is ended, when the intellect generally takes cognizance of the final result. The intellectual perception at the end is indicated in the diagram by the sensible effect of the movement *G* being represented at G'', in the ideational centres above the merely sensational line. The sensational impressions, *a, b, c, d, e, f*, are all supposed to have their seat below the ideational level.

Habits depend on sensations not attended to. We have called *a, b, c, d, e, f*, by the name of 'sensations.' If sensations, they are sensations to which we are usually inattentive; but that they are more than unconscious nerve-currents seems certain, for they catch our attention if they go wrong. Schneider's account of these sensations deserves to be quoted. In the act of walking, he says, even when our attention is entirely absorbed elsewhere, it is doubtful whether we could preserve equilibrium if no sensation of our body's attitude were there, and doubtful whether we should advance our leg if we had no sensation of its movement as executed, and not even a minimal feeling of impulse to set it down. Knitting appears altogether mechanical, and the knitter keeps up her knitting even while she reads or is engaged in lively talk. But if we ask her how this is possible, she will hardly reply that the knitting goes on of itself. She will rather say that she has a feeling of it, that she feels in her hands that she knits and how she must knit, and that therefore the movements of knitting are called forth and regulated by the sensations associated therewithal, even when the attention is called away. . . ." Again: " When a pupil begins to play on the violin, to keep him from raising his right elbow in playing a book is placed under his right armpit, which he is ordered to hold fast by keeping the upper arm tight against his body. The muscular feelings, and feelings of contact connected with the book, provoke an impulse to press it tight. But often it happens that the beginner, whose attention gets absorbed in the production of the notes, lets drop the book. Later, however, this never happens; the faintest sensations of contact suffice to awaken the impulse to keep it in its place, and the attention may be wholly absorbed by the notes and the fingering with the left hand. *The simultaneous combination of movements is thus in the first instance conditioned by the facility with which in us, alongside of intellectual processes, processes of inattentive feeling may still go on.*"

Ethical and Pedagogical Importance of the Principle of Habit.—" Habit a second nature! Habit is ten times nature," the Duke of Wellington is said to have exclaimed; and the degree to which this is true no one probably can appreciate as well as one who is a veteran soldier himself. The daily drill and the years of discipline end by fashioning a man completely over again, as to most of the possibilities of his conduct.

"There is a story," says Prof. Huxley, "which is credible enough, though it may not be true, of a practical joker who, seeing a discharged veteran carrying home his dinner, suddenly called out, 'Attention!' whereupon the man instantly brought his hands down, and lost his mutton and potatoes in the gutter. The drill had been thorough, and its effects had become embodied in the man's nervous structure."

Riderless cavalry-horses, at many a battle, have been seen to come together and go through their customary evolutions at the sound of the bugle-call. Most domestic beasts seem machines almost pure and simple, undoubtingly, unhesitatingly doing from minute to minute the duties they have been taught, and giving no sign that the possibility of an alternative ever suggests itself to their mind. Men grown old in prison have asked to be readmitted after being once set free. In a railroad accident a menagerie-tiger, whose cage had broken open, is said to have emerged, but presently crept back again, as if too much bewildered by his new responsibilities, so that he was without difficulty secured.

Habit is thus the enormous fly-wheel of society, its most precious conservative agent. It alone is what keeps us all within the bounds of ordinance, and saves the children of fortune from the envious uprisings of the poor. It alone prevents the hardest and most repulsive walks of life from being deserted by those brought up to tread therein. It keeps the fisherman and the deck-hand at sea through the winter; it holds the miner in his darkness, and nails the countryman to his log-cabin and his lonely farm through all the months of snow; it protects us from invasion by the natives of the desert and the frozen zone. It dooms us all to fight out the battle of life upon the lines of our nurture or our early choice, and to make the best of a pursuit that disagrees, because there is no other for which we are fitted, and it is too late to begin again. It keeps different social strata from mixing. Already at the age of twenty-five you see the professional mannerism settling down on the young commercial traveller, on the young doctor, on the young minister, on the young counsellor-at-law. You see the little lines of cleavage running through the character, the tricks of thought, the prejudices, the ways of the 'shop,' in a word, from which the man can by-and-by no more escape than his coat-sleeve can suddenly fall into a new set of folds. On the whole, it is best he should not escape. It is well for the world that in most of us, by the age of thirty, the character has set like plaster, and will never soften again.

If the period between twenty and thirty is the critical one in the formation of intellectual and professional habits, the period below twenty is more important still for the fixing of *personal* habits, properly so called, such as vocalization and pronunciation, gesture, motion, and address. Hardly ever is a language learned after twenty spoken without a foreign accent; hardly ever can a youth transferred to the society of his betters unlearn the nasality and other vices of speech bred in him by the associations of his growing years. Hardly ever, indeed, no matter how much money there be in his pocket, can he even learn to *dress* like a gentleman-born. The merchants offer their wares as eagerly to him as to the veriest 'swell,' but he simply *cannot* buy the right things. An invisible law, as strong as gravitation, keeps him within his orbit, arrayed this year as he was the last; and how his better-clad acquaintances contrive to get the things they wear will be for him a mystery till his dying day.

The great thing, then, in all education, is to *make our nervous system our ally instead of our enemy.* It is to fund and capitalize our acquisitions, and live at ease upon the interest of the fund. *For this we must make automatic and habitual, as early as possible, as many useful actions as we can*, and guard against the growing into ways that are likely to be disadvantageous to us, as we should guard against the plague. The more of the details of our daily life we can hand over to the effortless custody of automatism, the more our higher powers of mind will be set free for their own proper work. There is no more miserable human being than one in whom nothing is habitual but indecision, and for whom the lighting of every cigar, the drinking of every cup, the time of rising and going to bed every day, and the beginning of every bit of work, are subjects of express volitional deliberation. Full half the time of such a man goes to the deciding, or regretting, of matters which ought to be so ingrained in him as practically not to exist for his consciousness at all. If there be such daily duties not yet ingrained in any one of my readers, let him begin this very hour to set the matter right.

In Professor Bain's chapter on 'The Moral Habits' there are some admirable practical remarks laid down. Two great maxims emerge from his treatment. The first is that in the acquisition of a new habit, or the leaving off of an old one, we must take care to *launch ourselves with as strong and decided an initiative as possible.* Accumulate all the possible circumstances which shall re-enforce the right motives; put yourself assiduously in conditions that encourage the new way; make engagements incompatible with the old; take a public pledge, if the case allows; in short, envelop your resolution with every aid you know. This will give your new beginning such a momentum that the temptation to break down will not occur as soon as it otherwise might; and every day during which a breakdown is postponed adds to the chances of its not occurring at all.

The second maxim is: *Never suffer an exception to occur till the new habit is securely rooted in your life.* Each lapse is like the letting fall of a ball of string which one is carefully winding up; a single slip undoes more than a great many turns will wind again. *Continuity* of training is the great means of making the nervous system act infallibly right. As Professor Bain says:

"The peculiarity of the moral habits, contradistinguishing them from the intellectual acquisitions, is the presence of two hostile powers, one to be gradually raised into the ascendant over the other. It is necessary, above all things, in such a situation, never to lose a battle. Every gain on the wrong side undoes the effect of many conquests on the right. The essential precaution, therefore, is so to regulate the two opposing powers that the one may have a series of uninterrupted successes, until repetition has fortified it to such a degree as to enable it to cope with the opposition, under any circumstances. This is the theoretically best career of mental progress."

The need of securing success at the *outset* is imperative. Failure at first is apt to damp the energy of all future attempts, whereas past experiences of success nerve one to future vigor. Goethe says to a man who consulted him about an enterprise but mistrusted his own powers: "Ach! you need only blow on your hands!" And the remark illustrates the effect on Goethe's spirits of his own habitually successful career.

The question of "tapering-off," in abandoning such habits as drink and opium-indulgence comes in here, and is a question about which experts differ within certain limits, and in regard to what may be best for an individual case. In the main, however, all expert opinion would agree that abrupt acquisition of the new habit is the best way, *if there be a real possibility of carrying it out*. We must be careful not to give the will so stiff a task as to insure its defeat at the very outset; but, *provided one can stand it*, a sharp period of suffering, and then a free time, is the best thing to aim at, whether in giving up a habit like that of opium, or in simply changing one's hours of rising or of work. It is surprising how soon a desire will die of inanition if it be *never* fed.

"One must first learn, unmoved, looking neither to the right nor left, to walk firmly on the strait and narrow path, before one can begin 'to make one's self over again.' He who every day makes a fresh resolve is like one who, arriving at the edge of the ditch he is to leap, forever stops and returns for a fresh run. Without *unbroken* advance there is no such thing as *accumulation* of the ethical forces possible, and to make this possible, and to exercise us and habituate us in it, is the sovereign blessing of regular work."*

A third maxim may be added to the preceding pair: *Seize the very first possible opportunity to act on every resolution you make, and on every emotional prompting you may experience in the direction of the habits you aspire to gain.* It is not in the moment of their forming, but in the moment of their producing *motor effects*, that resolves and aspirations communicate the new 'set' to the brain. As the author last quoted remarks:

"The actual presence of the practical opportunity alone furnishes the fulcrum upon which the lever can rest, by means of which the moral will may multiply its strength, and raise itself aloft. He who has no solid ground to press against will never get beyond the stage of empty gesture-making."

No matter how full a reservoir of *maxims* one may possess, and no matter how good one's *sentiments* may be, if one have not taken advantage of every concrete opportunity to *act*, one's character may remain entirely unaffected for the better. With mere good intentions, hell is proverbially paved. And this is an obvious consequence of the principles we have laid down. A 'character,' as J. S. Mill says, 'is a completely fashioned will'; and a will, in the sense in which he means it, is an aggregate of tendencies to act in a firm and prompt and definite way upon all the principal emergencies of life. A tendency to act only becomes effectively ingrained in us in proportion to the uninterrupted frequency with which the actions actually occur, and the brain 'grows' to their use. When a resolve or a fine glow of feeling is allowed to evaporate without

---

* J. Bahnsen : 'Beiträge zu Charakterologie' (1867), vol. I. p. 209.

bearing practical fruit it is worse than a chance lost; it works so as positively to hinder future resolutions and emotions from taking the normal path of discharge. There is no more contemptible type of human character than that of the nerveless sentimentalist and dreamer, who spends his life in a weltering sea of sensibility and emotion, but who never does a manly concrete deed. Rousseau, inflaming all the mothers of France, by his eloquence, to follow Nature and nurse their babies themselves, while he sends his own children to the foundling hospital, is the classical example of what I mean. But every one of us in his measure, whenever, after glowing for an abstractly formulated Good, he practically ignores some actual ease, among the squalid 'other particulars' of which that same Good lurks disguised, treads straight on Rousseau's path. All Goods are disguised by the vulgarity of their concomitants, in this work-a-day world; but woe to him who can only recognize them when he thinks them in their pure and abstract form ! The habit of excessive novel-reading and theatre-going will produce true monsters in this line. The weeping of the Russian lady over the fictitious personages in the play, while her coachman is freezing to death on his seat outside, is the sort of thing that everywhere happens on a less glaring scale. Even the habit of excessive indulgence in music, for those who are neither performers themselves nor musically gifted enough to take it in a purely intellectual way, has probably a relaxing effect upon the character. One becomes filled with emotions which habitually pass without prompting to any deed, and so the inertly sentimental condition is kept up. The remedy would be, never to suffer one's self to have an emotion at a concert, without expressing it afterward in *some* active way. Let the expression be the least thing in the world—speaking genially to one's grandmother, or giving up one's seat in a horse-car, if nothing more heroic offers —but let it not fail to take place.

These latter cases make us aware that it is not simply

particular lines of discharge, but also *general forms* of discharge, that seem to be grooved out by habit in the brain. Just as, if we let our emotions evaporate, they get into a way of evaporating; so there is reason to suppose that if we often flinch from making an effort, before we know it the effort-making capacity will be gone; and that, if we suffer the wandering of our attention, presently it will wander all the time. Attention and effort are, as we shall see later, but two names for the same psychic fact. To what brain-processes they correspond we do not know. The strongest reason for believing that they do depend on brain-processes at all, and are not pure acts of the spirit, is just this fact, that they seem in some degree subject to the law of habit, which is a material law. As a final practical maxim, relative to these habits of the will, we may, then, offer something like this: *Keep the faculty of effort alive in you by a little gratuitous exercise every day.* That is, be systematically ascetic or heroic in little unnecessary points, do every day or two something for no other reason than that you would rather not do it, so that when the hour of dire need draws nigh, it may find you not unnerved and untrained to stand the test. Asceticism of this sort is like the insurance which a man pays on his house and goods. The tax does him no good at the time, and possibly may never bring him a return. But if the fire *does* come, his having paid it will be his salvation from ruin. So with the man who has daily inured himself to habits of concentrated attention, energetic volition, and self-denial in unnecessary things. He will stand like a tower when everything rocks around him, and when his softer fellow-mortals are winnowed like chaff in the blast.

The physiological study of mental conditions is thus the most powerful ally of hortatory ethics. The hell to be endured hereafter, of which theology tells, is no worse than the hell we make for ourselves in this world by habitually fashioning our characters in the wrong way. Could the young but realize how soon they will become mere walking bundles of habits, they would give more heed to their conduct while in the plastic state. We are spinning our own fates, good or evil, and never to be undone. Every smallest stroke of virtue or of vice leaves its never so little scar. The drunken Rip Van Winkle, in Jefferson's play, excuses himself for every fresh dereliction by saying, 'I won't count this time!' Well! he may not count it, and a kind Heaven may not count it; but it is being counted none the less. Down among his nerve-cells and fibres the molecules are counting it, registering and storing it up to be used against him when the next temptation comes. Nothing we ever do is, in strict scientific literalness, wiped out. Of course this has its good side as well as its bad one. As we become permanent drunkards by so many separate drinks, so we become saints in the moral, and authorities and experts in the practical and scientific spheres, by so many separate acts and hours of work. Let no youth have any anxiety about the upshot of his education, whatever the line of it may be. If he keep faithfully busy each hour of the working day, he may safely leave the final result to itself. He can with perfect certainty count on waking up some fine morning, to find himself one of the competent ones of his generation, in whatever pursuit he may have singled out. Silently, between all the details of his business, the *power of judging* in all that class of matter will have built itself up within him as a possession that will never pass away. Young people should know this truth in advance. The ignorance of it has probably engendered more discouragement and faint-heartedness in youths embarking on arduous careers than all other causes put together.

CHAPTER XI.

THE STREAM OF CONSCIOUSNESS.

The order of our study must be analytic. We are now prepared to begin the introspective study of the adult consciousness itself. Most books adopt the so-called synthetic method. Starting with 'simple ideas of sensation,' and regarding these as so many atoms, they proceed to build up the higher states of mind out of their 'association,' 'integration,' or 'fusion,' as houses are built by the agglutination of bricks. This has the didactic advantages which the synthetic method usually has. But it commits one beforehand to the very questionable theory that our higher states of consciousness are compounds of units; and instead of starting with what the reader directly knows, namely his total concrete states of mind, it starts with a set of supposed 'simple ideas' with which he has no immediate acquaintance at all, and concerning whose alleged interactions he is much at the mercy of any plausible phrase. On every ground, then, the method of advancing from the simple to the compound exposes us to illusion. All pedants and abstractionists will naturally hate to abandon it. But a student who loves the fulness of human nature will prefer to follow the 'analytic' method, and to begin with the most concrete facts, those with which he has a daily acquaintance in his own inner life. The analytic method will discover in due time the elementary parts, if such exist, without danger of precipitate assumption. The reader will bear in mind that our own chapters on sensation have dealt mainly with the physiological conditions thereof. They were put first as a mere matter of convenience, because incoming currents come first. *Psychologically* they might better have come last. Pure sensations were described on page 12 as processes which in adult life are well-nigh unknown, and nothing was said which could for a moment lead the reader to suppose that they were the *elements of composition* of the higher states of mind.

The Fundamental Fact.—The first and foremost concrete fact which every one will affirm to belong to his inner experience is the fact that *consciousness of some sort goes on*. '*States of mind*' *succeed each other in him*. If we could say in English 'it thinks,' as we say 'it rains' or 'it blows,' we should be stating the fact most simply and with the minimum of assumption. As we cannot, we must simply say that *thought goes on*.

Four Characters in Consciousness.—How does it go on? We notice immediately four important characters in the process, of which it shall be the duty of the present chapter to treat in a general way:

1) Every 'state' tends to be part of a personal consciousness.

2) Within each personal consciousness states are always changing.

3) Each personal consciousness is sensibly continuous.

4) It is interested in some parts of its object to the exclusion of others, and welcomes or rejects—*chooses* from among them, in a word—all the while.

In considering these four points successively, we shall have to plunge *in medias res* as regards our nomenclature and use psychological terms which can only be adequately defined in later chapters of the book. But every one knows what the terms mean in a rough way; and it is only in a rough way that we are now to take them. This chapter is like a painter's first charcoal sketch upon his canvas, in which no niceties appear.

When I say *every* '*state*' *or* '*thought*' *is part of a personal consciousness*, 'personal consciousness' is one of the terms in question. Its meaning we know so long as no one asks us to define it, but to give an accurate account of it is the most difficult of philosophic tasks. This task we must confront in the next chapter; here a preliminary word will suffice.

In this room—this lecture-room, say—there are a multitude of thoughts, yours and mine, some of which cohere mutually, and some not. They are as little each-for-itself and reciprocally independent as they are all-belonging-together. They are neither: no one of them is separate, but each belongs with certain others and with none beside. My thought belongs with *my* other thoughts, and your thought with *your* other thoughts. Whether anywhere in the room there be a *mere* thought, which is nobody's thought, we have no means of ascertaining, for we have no experience of its like. The only states of consciousness that we naturally deal with are found in personal consciousnesses, minds, selves, concrete particular I's and you's.

Each of these minds keeps its own thoughts to itself. There is no giving or bartering between them. No thought even comes into direct *sight* of a thought in another personal consciousness than its own. Absolute insulation, irreducible pluralism, is the law. It seems as if the elementary psychic fact were not *thought* or *this thought* or *that thought*, but *my thought*, every thought being *owned*. Neither contemporaneity, nor proximity in space, nor similarity of quality and content are able to fuse thoughts together which are sundered by this barrier of belonging to different personal minds. The breaches between such thoughts are the most absolute breaches in nature. Every one will recognize this to be true, so long as the existence of *something* corresponding to the term 'personal mind' is all that is insisted on, without any particular view of its nature being implied. On these terms the personal self rather than the thought might be treated as the immediate datum in psychology. The universal conscious fact is not 'feelings and thoughts exist,' but 'I think' and 'I feel.' No psychology, at any rate, can question the *existence* of personal selves. Thoughts connected as we feel them to be connected are *what we mean* by personal selves. The worst a psychology can do is so to interpret the nature of these selves as to rob them of their *worth.*

Consciousness is in constant change. I do not mean by this to say that no one state of mind has any duration— even if true, that would be hard to establish. What I wish to lay stress on is this, that *no state once gone can recur and be identical with what it was before.* Now we are seeing, now hearing; now reasoning, now willing; now recollecting, now expecting; now loving, now hating; and in a hundred other ways we know our minds to be alternately engaged. But all these are complex states, it may be said, produced by combination of simpler ones;—do not the simpler ones follow a different law? Are not the *sensations* which we get from the same object, for example, always the same? Does not the same piano-key, struck with the same force, make us hear in the same way? Does not the same grass give us the same feeling of green, the same sky the same feeling of blue, and do we not get the same olfactory sensation no matter how many times we put our nose to the same flask of cologne? It seems a piece of metaphysical sophistry to suggest that we do not; and yet a close attention to the matter shows that *there is no proof that an incoming current ever gives us just the same bodily sensation twice.*

What is got twice is the same OBJECT. We hear the same *note* over and over again; we see the same *quality* of green, or smell the same objective perfume, or experience the same *species* of pain. The realities, concrete and abstract, physical and ideal, whose permanent existence we believe in, seem to be constantly coming up again before our thought, and lead us, in our carelessness, to suppose that our 'ideas' of them are the same ideas. When we come, some time later, to the chapter on Perception, we shall see how inveterate is our habit of simply using our sensible impressions as stepping-stones to pass over to the recognition of the realities whose presence they reveal. The grass out of the window now looks to me of the same green in the sun as in the shade, and yet a painter would have to paint one part of it dark brown, another part bright yellow, to give its real sensational effect. We take no heed, as a rule, of the different way in which the same things look and sound and smell at different distances and under different circumstances. The sameness of the *things* is what we are concerned to ascertain; and any sensations that assure us of that will probably be considered in a rough way to be the same with each other. This is what makes off-hand testimony about the subjective identity of different sensations well-nigh worthless as a proof of the fact. The entire history of what is called Sensation is a commentary on our inability to tell whether two sensible qualities received apart are exactly alike. What appeals to our attention far more than the absolute quality of an impression is its *ratio* to whatever other impressions we may have at the same time. When everything is dark a somewhat less dark sensation makes us see an object white. Helmholtz calculates that the white marble painted in a picture representing an architectural view by moonlight is, when seen by daylight, from ten to twenty thousand times brighter than the real moonlit marble would be.

Such a difference as this could never have been *sensibly* learned; it had to be inferred from a series of indirect considerations. These make us believe that our sensibility is altering all the time, so that the same object cannot easily give us the same sensation over again. We feel things differently accordingly as we are sleepy or awake, hungry or full, fresh or tired; differently at night and in the morning, differently in summer and in winter; and above all, differently in childhood, manhood, and old age. And yet we never doubt that our feelings reveal the same world, with the same sensible qualities and the same sensible things occupying it. The difference of the sensibility is shown best by the difference of our emotion about the things from one age to another, or when we are in different organic moods. What was bright and exciting becomes weary, flat, and unprofitable. The bird's song is tedious, the breeze is mournful, the sky is sad.

To these indirect presumptions that our sensations, following the mutations of our capacity for feeling, are always undergoing an essential change, must be added another presumption, based on what must happen in the brain. Every sensation corresponds to some cerebral action. For an identical sensation to recur it would have to occur the second time *in an unmodified brain.* But as this, strictly speaking, is a physiological impossibility, so is an unmodified feeling an impossibility; for to every brain-modification, however small, we suppose that there must correspond a change of equal amount in the consciousness which the brain subserves.

But if the assumption of 'simple sensations' recurring in immutable shape is so easily shown to be baseless, how much more baseless is the assumption of immutability in the larger masses of our thought!

For there it is obvious and palpable that our state of mind is never precisely the same. Every thought we have of a given fact is, strictly speaking, unique, and only bears a resemblance of kind with our other thoughts of the same fact. When the identical fact recurs, we *must* think of it in a fresh manner, see it under a somewhat different angle, apprehend it in different relations from those in which it last appeared. And the thought by which we cognize it is the thought of it-in-those-relations, a thought suffused with the consciousness of all that dim context. Often we are ourselves struck at the strange differences in our successive views of the same thing. We wonder how we ever could have opined as we did last month about a certain matter. We have outgrown the possibility of that state of mind, we know not how. From one year to another we see things in new lights. What was unreal has grown real, and what was exciting is insipid. The friends we used to care the world for are shrunken to shadows;

the women once so divine, the stars, the woods, and the waters, how now so dull and common!—the young girls that brought an aura of infinity, at present hardly distinguishable existences; the pictures so empty; and as for the books, what *was* there to find so mysteriously significant in Goethe, or in John Mill so full of weight? Instead of all this, more zestful than ever is the work, the work; and fuller and deeper the import of common duties and of common goods.

I am sure that this concrete and total manner of regarding the mind's changes is the only true manner, difficult as it may be to carry it out in detail. If anything seems obscure about it, it will grow clearer as we advance. Meanwhile, if it be true, it is certainly also true that no two 'ideas' are ever exactly the same, which is the proposition we started to prove. The proposition is more important theoretically than it at first sight seems. For it makes it already impossible for us to follow obediently in the footprints of either the Lockian or the Herbartian school, schools which have had almost unlimited influence in Germany and among ourselves. No doubt it is often *convenient* to formulate the mental facts in an atomistic sort of way, and to treat the higher states of consciousness as if they were all built out of unchanging simple ideas which 'pass and turn again.' It is convenient often to treat curves as if they were composed of small straight lines, and electricity and nerve-force as if they were fluids. But in the one case as in the other we must never forget that we are talking symbolically, and that there is nothing in nature to answer to our words. *A permanently existing 'Idea' which makes its appearance before the footlights of consciousness at periodical intervals is as mythological an entity as the Jack of Spades.*

Within each personal consciousness, thought is sensibly continuous. I can only define 'continuous' as that which is without breach, crack, or division. The only breaches that can well be conceived to occur within the limits of a single mind would either be *interruptions, time*-gaps during which the consciousness went out; or they would be breaks in the content of the thought, so abrupt that what followed had no connection whatever with what went before. The proposition that consciousness feels continuous, means two things:

a. That even where there is a time-gap the consciousness after it feels as if it belonged together with the consciousness before it, as another part of the same self;

b. That the changes from one moment to another in the quality of the consciousness are never absolutely abrupt.

The case of the time-gaps, as the simplest, shall be taken first.

a. When Paul and Peter wake up in the same bed, and recognize that they have been asleep, each one of them mentally reaches back and makes connection with but *one* of the two streams of thought which were broken by the sleeping hours. As the current of an electrode buried in the ground unerringly finds its way to its own similarly buried mate, across no matter how much intervening earth; so Peter's present instantly finds out Peter's past, and never by mistake knits itself on to that of Paul. Paul's thought in turn is as little liable to go astray. The past thought of Peter is appropriated by the present Peter alone. He may have a *knowledge*, and a correct one too, of what Paul's last drowsy states of mind were as he sank into sleep, but it is an entirely different sort of knowledge from that which he has of his own last states. He *remembers* his own states, whilst he only *conceives* Paul's. Remembrance is like direct feeling; its object is suffused with a warmth and intimacy to which no object of mere conception ever attains. This quality of warmth and intimacy and immediacy is what Peter's *present* thought also possesses for itself. So sure as this present is me, is mine, it says, so sure is anything else that comes with the same warmth and intimacy and immediacy, me and mine. What the qualities called warmth and intimacy may in themselves be will have to be matter for future consideration. But whatever past states appear with those qualities must be admitted to receive the greeting of the present mental state, to be owned by it, and accepted as belonging together with it in a common self. This community of self is what the time-gap cannot break in twain, and is why a present thought, although not ignorant of the time-gap, can still regard itself as continuous with certain chosen portions of the past.

Consciousness, then, does not appear to itself chopped up in bits. Such words as 'chain' or 'train' do not describe it fitly as it presents itself in the first instance. It is nothing jointed; it flows. A 'river' or a 'stream' are the metaphors by which it is most naturally described. *In talking of it hereafter, let us call it the* **stream** *of thought, of consciousness, or of subjective life.*

b. But now there appears, even within the limits of the same self, and between thoughts all of which alike have this same sense of belonging together, a kind of jointing and separateness among the parts, of which this statement seems to take no account. I refer to the breaks that are produced by sudden *contrasts in the quality* of the successive segments of the stream of thought. If the words 'chain' and 'train' had no natural fitness in them, how came such words to be used at all? Does not a loud explosion rend the consciousness upon which it abruptly breaks, in twain? No; for even into our awareness of the thunder the awareness of the previous silence creeps and continues; for what we hear when the thunder crashes is not thunder *pure*, but thunder-breaking-upon-silence-and-contrasting-with-it. Our feeling of the same objective thunder, coming in this way, is quite different from what it would be were the thunder a continuation of previous thunder. The thunder itself we believe to abolish and exclude the silence; but the *feeling* of the thunder is also a feeling of the silence as just gone; and it would be difficult to find in the actual concrete consciousness of man a feeling so limited to the present as not to have an inkling of anything that went before.

'Substantive' and 'Transitive' States of Mind.—When we take a general view of the wonderful stream of our consciousness, what strikes us first is the different pace of its parts. Like a bird's life, it seems to be an alternation of flights and perchings. The rhythm of language expresses this, where every thought is expressed in a sentence, and every sentence closed by a period. The resting-places are usually occupied by sensorial imaginations of some sort, whose peculiarity is that they can be held before the mind for an indefinite time, and contemplated without changing; the places of flight are filled with thoughts of relations, static or dynamic, that for the most part obtain between the matters contemplated in the periods of comparative rest.

Let us call the resting-places the 'substantive parts,' and the places of flight the 'transitive parts,' of the stream of thought. It then appears that our thinking tends at all times towards some other substantive part than the one from which it has just been dislodged. And we may say that the main use of the transitive parts is to lead us from one substantive conclusion to another.

Now it is very difficult, introspectively, to see the transitive parts for what they really are. If they are but flights to a conclusion, stopping them to look at them before the conclusion is reached is really annihilating them. Whilst if we wait till the conclusion *be* reached, it so exceeds them in vigor and stability that it quite eclipses and swallows them up in its glare. Let anyone try to cut a thought across in the middle and get a look at its section, and he will see how difficult the introspective observation of the transitive tracts is. The rush of the thought is so headlong that it almost always brings us up at the conclusion before we can arrest it. Or if our purpose is nimble enough and we do arrest it, it ceases forthwith to be itself. As a snowflake crystal caught in the warm hand is no longer a crystal but a drop, so, instead of catching the feeling of relation moving to its term, we find we have caught some substantive thing, usually the last word we were pronouncing, statically taken, and with its function, tendency, and particular meaning in the sentence quite evaporated. The attempt at introspective analysis in these cases is in fact like seizing a spinning top to catch its motion, or trying to turn up the gas quickly enough to see how the darkness looks. And the challenge to *produce* these transitive states of consciousness, which is sure to be thrown by doubting psychologists at anyone who contends for their existence, is as unfair as Zeno's treatment of the advocates of motion, when, asking them to point out in what place an arrow *is* when it moves, he argues the falsity of their thesis from their inability to make to so preposterous a question an immediate reply.

The results of this introspective difficulty are baleful. If to hold fast and observe the transitive parts of thought's stream be so hard, then the great blunder to which all schools are liable must be the failure to register them, and the undue emphasizing of the more substantive parts of the stream. Now the blunder has historically worked in two ways. One set of thinkers have been led by it to *Sensationalism*. Unable to lay their hands on any substantive feelings corresponding to the innumerable relations and forms of connection between the sensible things of the world, finding no *named* mental states mirroring such relations, they have for the most part denied that any such states exist; and many of them, like Hume, have gone on to deny the reality of most relations *out* of the mind as well as in it. Simple substantive 'ideas,' sensations and their copies, juxtaposed like dominoes in a game, but really separate, everything else verbal illusion,—such is the upshot of this view. The *Intellectualists*, on the other hand, unable to give up the reality of relations *extra mentem*, but equally unable to point to any distinct substantive feelings in which they were known, have made the same admission that such feelings do not exist. But they nave drawn an opposite conclusion. The relations must be known, they say, in something that is no feeling, no mental 'state,' continuous and consubstantial with the subjective tissue out of which sensations and other substantive conditions of consciousness are made. They must be known by something that lies on an entirely different plane, by an *actus purus* of Thought, Intellect, or Reason, all written with capitals and considered to mean something unutterably superior to any passing perishing fact of sensibility whatever.

But from our point of view both Intellectualists and Sensationalists are wrong. If there be such things as feelings at all, *then so surely as relations between objects exist* in rerum naturâ, *so surely, and more surely, do feelings exist to which these relations are known.* There is not a conjunction or a preposition, and hardly an adverbial phrase, syntactic form, or inflection of voice, in human speech, that does not express some shading or other of relation which we at some moment actually feel to exist between the larger objects of our thought. If we speak objectively, it is the real relations that appear revealed; if we speak subjectively, it is the stream of consciousness that matches each of them by an inward coloring of its own. In either case the relations are numberless, and no existing language is capable of doing justice to all their shades.

We ought to say a feeling of *and*, a feeling of *if*, a feeling of *but*, and a feeling of *by*, quite as readily as we say a feeling of *blue* or a feeling of *cold*. Yet we do not: so inveterate has our habit become of recognizing the existence of the substantive parts alone, that language almost refuses to lend itself to any other use. Consider once again the analogy of the brain. We believe the brain to be an organ whose internal equilibrium is always in a state of change—the change affecting every part. The pulses of change are doubtless more violent in one place than in another, their rhythm more rapid at this time than at that. As in a kaleidoscope revolving at a uniform rate, although the figures are always rearranging themselves, there are instants during which the transformation seems minute and interstitial and almost absent, followed by others when it shoots with magical rapidity, relatively stable forms thus alternating with forms we should not distinguish if seen again; so in the brain the perpetual rearrangement must result in some forms of tension lingering relatively long, whilst others simply come and pass. But if consciousness corresponds to the fact of rearrangement itself, why, if the rearrangement stop not, should the consciousness ever cease? And if a lingering rearrangement brings with it one kind of consciousness, why should not a swift rearrangement bring another kind of consciousness as peculiar as the rearrangement itself?

The object before the mind always has a 'Fringe.' There are other unnamed modifications of consciousness just as important as the transitive states, and just as cognitive as they. Examples will show what I mean.

Suppose three successive persons say to us: 'Wait!' 'Hark!' 'Look!' Our consciousness is thrown into three quite different attitudes of expectancy, although no definite object is before it in any one of the three cases. Probably no one will deny here the existence of a real conscious affection, a sense of the direction from which an impression is about to come, although no positive impression is yet there. Meanwhile we have no names for the psychoses in question but the names hark, look, and wait.

Suppose we try to recall a forgotten name. The state of our consciousness is peculiar. There is a gap therein; but no mere gap. It is a gap that is intensely active. A sort of wraith of the name is in it, beckoning us in a given direction, making us at moments tingle with the sense of our closeness, and then letting us sink back without the longed-for term. If wrong names are proposed to us, this singularly definite gap acts immediately so as to negate them. They do not fit into its mould. And the gap of one word does not feel like the gap of another, all empty of content as both might seem necessarily to be when described as gaps. When I vainly try to recall the name of Spalding, my consciousness is far removed from what it is when I vainly try to recall the name of Bowles. There are innumerable consciousnesses of *want*, no one of which taken in itself has a name, but all different from each other. Such a feeling of want is *toto cœlo* other than a want of feeling: it is an intense feeling. The rhythm of a lost word may be there without a sound to clothe it; or the evanescent sense of something which is the initial vowel or consonant may mock us fitfully, without growing more distinct. Every one must know the tantalizing effect of the blank rhythm of some forgotten verse, restlessly dancing in one's mind, striving to be filled out with words.

What is that first instantaneous glimpse of some one's meaning which we have, when in vulgar phrase we say we 'twig' it? Surely an altogether specific affection of our mind. And has the reader never asked himself what kind of a mental fact is his *intention of saying a thing* before he has said it? It is an entirely definite intention, distinct from all other intentions, an absolutely distinct state of consciousness, therefore; and yet how much of it consists of definite sensorial images, either of words or of things? Hardly anything! Linger, and the words and things come into the mind; the anticipatory intention, the divination is there no more. But as the words that replace it arrive, it welcomes them successively and calls them right if they agree with it, it rejects them and calls them wrong if they do not. The intention *to-say-so-and-so* is the only name it can receive. One may admit that a good third of our psychic life consists in these rapid premonitory perspective views of schemes of thought not yet articulate. How comes it about that a man reading something aloud for the first time is able immediately to emphasize all his words aright, unless from the very first he have a sense of at least the form of the sentence yet to come, which sense is fused with his consciousness of the present word, and modifies its emphasis in his mind so as to make him give it the proper accent as he utters it? Emphasis of this kind almost altogether depends on grammatical construction. If we read 'no more,' we expect presently a 'than'; if we read 'however,' it is a 'yet,' a 'still,' or a 'nevertheless,' that we expect. And this foreboding of the coming verbal and grammatical scheme is so practically accurate that a reader incapable of understanding four ideas of the book he is reading aloud can nevertheless read it with the most delicately modulated expression of intelligence.

It is, the reader will see, the reinstatement of the vague and inarticulate to its proper place in our mental life which I am so anxious to press on the attention. Mr. Galton and Prof. Huxley have, as we shall see in the chapter on Imagination, made one step in advance in exploding the ridiculous theory of Hume and Berkeley that we can have no images but of perfectly definite things. Another is made if we overthrow the equally ridiculous notion that, whilst simple objective qualities are revealed to our knowledge in 'states of consciousness,' relations are not. But these reforms are not half sweeping and radical enough. What must be admitted is that the definite images of traditional psychology form but the very smallest part of our minds as they actually live. The traditional psychology talks like one who should say a river consists of nothing but pailsful, spoonsful, quartpotsful, barrelsful, and other moulded forms of water. Even were the pails and the pots all actually standing in the stream, still between them the free water would continue to flow. It is just this free water of consciousness that psychologists resolutely overlook. Every definite image in the mind is steeped and dyed in the free water that flows round it. With it goes the sense of its relations, near and remote, the dying echo of whence it came to us, the dawning sense of whither it is to lead. The significance, the value, of the image is all in this halo or penumbra that surrounds and escorts it,—or rather that is fused into one with it and has become bone of its bone and flesh of its flesh; leaving it, it is true, an image of the same *thing* it was before, but making it an image of that thing newly taken and freshly understood.

Let us call the consciousness of this halo of relations around the image by the name of 'psychic overtone' or 'fringe.'

Cerebral Conditions of the 'Fringe.'—Nothing is easier than to symbolize these facts in terms of brain-action. Just as the echo of the *whence,* the sense of the starting point of our thought, is probably due to the dying excitement of processes but a moment since vividly aroused; so the sense of the whither, the foretaste of the terminus, must be due to the waxing excitement of tracts or processes whose psychical correlative will a moment hence be the vividly present feature of our thought. Represented by a curve, the neurosis underlying consciousness must at any moment be like this:

Let the horizontal in Fig. 52 be the line of time, and

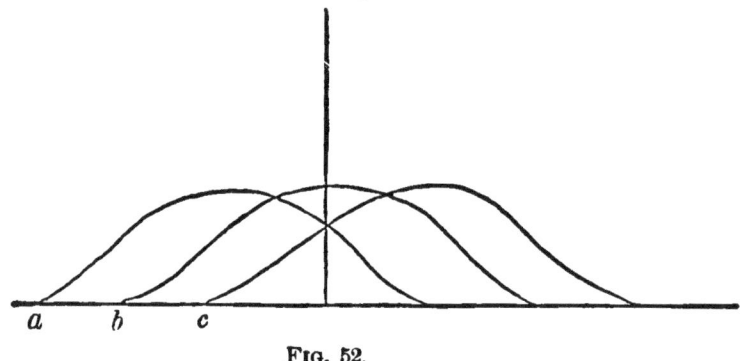

FIG. 52.

let the three curves beginning at *a, b,* and *c* respectively stand for the neural processes correlated with the thoughts of those three letters. Each process occupies a certain time during which its intensity waxes, culminates, and wanes. The process for *a* has not yet died out, the process for c has already begun, when that for b is culminating. At the time-instant represented by the vertical line all three processes are *present*, in the intensities shown by the curve. Those before c's apex *were* more intense a moment ago; those after it *will be* more intense a moment hence. If I recite a, b, c, then, at the moment of uttering b, neither a nor c is out of my consciousness altogether, but both, after their respective fashions, 'mix their dim lights' with the stronger b, because their processes are both awake in some degree.

It is just like 'overtones' in music: they are not separately heard by the ear; they blend with the fundamental note, and suffuse it, and alter it; and even so do the waxing and waning brain-processes at every moment blend with and suffuse and alter the psychic effect of the processes which are at their culminating point.

The 'Topic' of the Thought.—If we then consider the *cognitive function* of different states of mind, we may feel assured that the difference between those that are mere 'acquaintance' and those that are 'knowledges-*about*' is reducible almost entirely to the absence or presence of psychic fringes or overtones. Knowledge *about* a thing is knowledge of its relations. Acquaintance with it is limitation to the bare impression which it makes. Of most of its relations we are only aware in the penumbral nascent way of a 'fringe' of unarticulated affinities about it. And, before passing to the next topic in order, I must say a little of this sense of affinity, as itself one of the most interesting features of the subjective stream.

Thought may be equally rational in any sort of terms. *In all our voluntary thinking there is some* TOPIC *or* SUBJECT about which all the members of the thought revolve. Relation to this topic or interest is constantly felt in the fringe, and particularly the relation of harmony and discord, of furtherance or hindrance of the topic. Any thought the quality of whose fringe lets us feel ourselves 'all right.' may be considered a thought that furthers the topic. Provided we only feel its object to have a place in the scheme of relations in which the topic also lies, that is sufficient to make of it a relevant and appropriate portion of our train of ideas.

Now we may think about our topic mainly in words, or we may think about it mainly in visual or other images, but this need make no difference as regards the furtherance of our knowledge of the topic. If we only feel in the terms, whatever they be, a fringe of affinity with each other and with the topic, and if we are conscious of approaching a conclusion, we feel that our thought is rational and right. The words in every language have contracted by long association fringes of mutual repugnance or affinity with each other and with the conclusion, which run exactly parallel with like fringes in the visual, tactile, and other ideas. The most important element of these fringes is, I repeat, the mere feeling of harmony or discord, of a right or wrong direction in the thought.

If we know English and French and begin a sentence in French, all the later words that come are French; we hardly ever drop into English. And this affinity of the French words for each other is not something merely operating mechanically as a brain-law, it is something we feel at the time. Our understanding of a French sentence heard never falls to so low an ebb that we are not aware that the words linguistically belong together. Our attention can hardly so wander that if an English word be suddenly introduced we shall not start at the change. Such a vague sense as this of the words belonging together is the very minimum of fringe that can accompany them, if 'thought' at all. Usually the vague perception that all the words we hear belong to the same language and to the same special vocabulary in that language, and that the grammatical sequence is familiar, is practically equivalent to an admission that what we hear is sense. But if an unusual foreign word be introduced, if the grammar trip, or if a term from an incongruous vocabulary suddenly appear, such as 'rat-trap' or 'plumber's bill' in a philosophical discourse, the sentence detonates as it were, we receive a shock from the incongruity, and the drowsy assent is gone. The feeling of rationality in these cases seems rather a negative than a positive thing, being the mere absence of shock, or sense of discord, between the terms of thought.

Conversely, if words do belong to the same vocabulary, and if the grammatical structure is correct, sentences with absolutely no meaning may be uttered in good faith and pass unchallenged. Discourses at prayer-meetings, re-shuffling the same collection of cant phrases, and the whole genus of penny-a-line-isms and newspaper-reporter's flourishes give illustrations of this. "The birds filled the tree-tops with their morning song, making the air moist, cool, and pleasant," is a sentence I remember reading once in a report of some athletic exercises in Jerome Park. It was probably written unconsciously by the hurried reporter, and read uncritically by many readers.

We see, then, that it makes little or no difference in what sort of mind-stuff, in what quality of imagery, our thinking goes on. The only images *intrinsically* important are the halting-places, the substantive conclusions, provisional or final, of the thought. Throughout all the rest of the stream, the feelings of relation are everything, and the terms related almost naught. These feelings of relation, these psychic overtones, halos, suffusions, or fringes about the terms, may be the same in very different systems of imagery. A diagram may help to accentuate this indifference of the mental means where the end is the same. Let A be some experience from which a number of thinkers start. Let Z be the practical conclusion rationally inferrible from it. One gets to this conclusion by one line, another

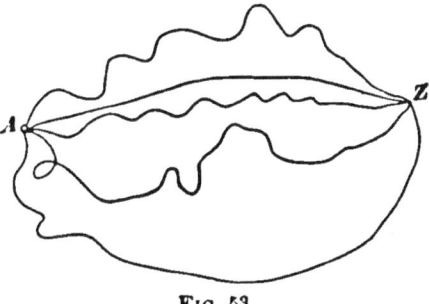

FIG 53.

by another; one follows a course of English, another of German, verbal imagery. With one, visual images predominate; with another, tactile. Some trains are tinged with emotions, others not; some are very abridged, synthetic and rapid; others, hesitating and broken into many steps. But when the penultimate terms of all the trains, however differing *inter se,* finally shoot into the same conclusion, we say, and rightly say, that all the thinkers have had substantially the same thought. It would probably astound each of them beyond measure to be let into his neighbor's mind and to find how different the scenery there was from that in his own.

The last peculiarity to which attention is to be drawn in this first rough description of thought's stream is that—

Consciousness is always interested more in one part of its object than in another, and welcomes and rejects, or chooses, all the while it thinks.

The phenomena of selective attention and of deliberative will are of course patent examples of this choosing activity. But few of us are aware how incessantly it is at work in operations not ordinarily called by these names. Accentuation and Emphasis are present in every perception we have. We find it quite impossible to disperse our attention impartially over a number of impressions. A monotonous succession of sonorous strokes is broken up into rhythms, now of one sort, now of another, by the different accent which we place on different strokes. The simplest of these rhythms is the double one, tick-tóck, tick-tóck, tick-tóck. Dots dispersed on a surface are perceived in rows and groups. Lines separate into diverse figures. The ubiquity of the distinctions, *this* and *that, here* and *there, now* and *then,* in our minds is the result of our laying the same selective emphasis on parts of place and time.

But we do far more than emphasize things, and unite some, and keep others apart. We actually *ignore* most of the things before us. Let me briefly show how this goes on.

To begin at the bottom, what are our very senses themselves, as we saw on pp. 10-12, but organs of selection? Out of the infinite chaos of movements, of which physics teaches us that the outer world consists, each sense-organ picks out those which fall within certain limits of velocity. To these it responds, but ignores the rest as completely as if they did not exist. Out of what is in itself an nudistinguishable, swarming *continuum*, devoid of distinction or emphasis, our senses make for us, by attending to this motion and ignoring that, a world full of contrasts, of sharp accents, of abrupt changes, of picturesque light and shade.

If the sensations we receive from a given organ have their causes thus picked out for us by the conformation of the organ's termination, Attention, on the other hand, out of all the sensations yielded, picks out certain ones as worthy of its notice and suppresses all the rest. We notice only those sensations which are signs to us of *things* which happen practically or æsthetically to interest us, to which we therefore give substantive names, and which we exalt to this exclusive status of independence and dignity. But in itself, apart from my interest, a particular dust-wreath on a windy day is just as much of an individual *thing*, and just as much or as little deserves an individual name, as my own body does.

And then, among the sensations we get from each separate thing, what happens? The mind selects again. It chooses certain of the sensations to represent the thing most *truly*, and considers the rest as its appearances, modified by the conditions of the moment. Thus my table-top is named *square*, after but one of an infinite number of retinal sensations which it yields, the rest of them being sensations of two acute and two obtuse angles; but I call the latter *perspective* views, and the four right angles the *true* form of the table, and erect the attribute squareness into the table's essence, for æsthetic reasons of my own. In like manner, the real form of the circle is deemed to be the sensation it gives when the line of vision is perpendicular to its centre—all its other sensations are *signs* of this sensation. The real sound of the cannon is the sensation it makes when the ear is close by. The real color of the brick is the sensation it gives when the eye looks squarely at it from a near point, out of the sunshine and yet not in the gloom; under other circumstances it gives us other color-sensations which are but signs of this—we then see it looks pinker or bluer than it really is. The reader knows no object which he does not represent to himself by preference as in some typical attitude, of some normal size, at some characteristic distance, of some standard tint, etc., etc. But all these essential characteristics, which together form for us the genuine objectivity of the thing and are contrasted with what we call the subjective sensations it may yield us at a given moment, are mere sensations like the latter. The mind chooses to suit itself, and decides what particular sensation shall be held more real and valid than all the rest.

Next, in a world of objects thus individualized by our mind's selective industry, what is called our 'experience' is almost entirely determined by our habits of attention. A thing may be present to a man a hundred times, but if he persistently fails to notice it, it cannot be said to enter into his experience. We are all seeing flies, moths, and beetles by the thousand, but to whom, save an entomologist, do they say anything distinct? On the other hand, a thing met only once in a lifetime may leave an indelible experience in the memory. Let four men make a tour in Europe. One will bring home only picturesque impressions—costumes and colors, parks and views and works of architecture, pictures and statues. To another all this will be non-existent; and distances and prices, populations and drainage-arrangements, door- and window-fastenings, and other useful statistics will take their place. A third will give a rich account of the theatres, restaurants, and public halls, and naught beside; whilst the fourth will perhaps have been so wrapped in his own subjective broodings as to be able to tell little more than a few names of places through which he passed. Each has selected, out of the same mass of presented objects, those which suited his private interest and has made his experience thereby.

If now, leaving the empirical combination of objects, we ask how the mind proceeds *rationally* to connect them, we find selection again to be omnipotent. In a future chapter we shall see that all Reasoning depends on the ability of the mind to break up the totality of the phenomenon reasoned about, into parts, and to pick out from among these the particular one which, in the given emergency, may lead to the proper conclusion. The man of genius is he who will always stick in his bill at the right point, and bring it out with the right element—'reason' if the emergency be theoretical, 'means' if it be practical—transfixed upon it.

If now we pass to the æsthetic department, our law is still more obvious. The artist notoriously selects his items, rejecting all tones, colors, shapes, which do not harmonize with each other and with the main purpose of his work. That unity, harmony, 'convergence of characters,' as M. Taine calls it, which gives to works of art their superiority over works of nature, is wholly due to *elimination*. Any natural subject will do, if the artist has wit enough to pounce upon some one feature of it as characteristic, and suppress all merely accidental items which do not harmonize with this.

Ascending still higher, we reach the plane of Ethics, where choice reigns notoriously supreme. An act has no ethical quality whatever unless it be chosen out of several all equally possible. To sustain the arguments for the good course and keep them ever before us, to stifle our longing for more flowery ways, to keep the foot unflinchingly on the arduous path, these are characteristic ethical energies. But more than these; for these but deal with the means of compassing interests already felt by the man to be supreme. The ethical energy *par excellence* has to go farther and choose which *interest* out of several, equally coercive, shall become supreme. The issue here is of the utmost pregnancy, for it decides a man's entire career. When he debates, Shall I commit this crime? choose that profession? accept that office, or marry this fortune?—his choice really lies between one of several equally possible future Characters. What he shall *become* is fixed by the conduct of this moment. Schopenhauer, who enforces his determinism by the argument that with a given fixed character only one reaction is possible under given circumstances, forgets that, in these critical ethical moments, what consciously *seems* to be in question is the complexion of the character itself. The problem with the man is less what act he shall now resolve to do than what being he shall now choose to become.

Taking human experience in a general way, the choosings of different men are to a great extent the same. The race as a whole largely agrees as to what it shall notice and name; and among the noticed parts we select in much the same way for accentuation and preference, or subordination and dislike. There is, however, one entirely extraordinary case in which no two men ever are known to choose alike. One great splitting of the whole universe into two halves is made by each of us; and for each of us almost all of the interest attaches to one of the halves; but we all draw the line of division between them in a different place. When I say that we all call the two halves by the same names, and that those names are '*me*' and '*not-me*' respectively, it will at once be seen what I mean. The altogether unique kind of interest which each human mind feels in those parts of creation which it can call *me* or *mine* may be a moral riddle, but it is a fundamental psychological fact. No mind can take the same interest in his neighbor's *me* as in his own. The neighbor's me falls together with all the rest of things in one foreign mass against which his own *me* stands out in startling relief.

Even the trodden worm, as Lotze somewhere says, contrasts his own suffering self with the whole remaining universe, though he have no clear conception either of himself or of what the universe may be. He is for me a mere part of the world; for him it is I who am the mere part. Each of us dichotomizes the Kosmos in a different place.

Descending now to finer work than this first general sketch, let us in the next chapter try to trace the psychology of this fact of self-consciousness to which we have thus once more been led

CHAPTER XII.

THE SELF

The Me and the I.—Whatever I may be thinking of, 1 am always at the same time more or less aware of *myself*, of my *personal existence*. At the same time it is *I* who am aware; so that the total self of me, being as it were duplex, partly known and partly knower, partly object and partly subject, must have two aspects discriminated in it, of which for shortness we may call one the *Me* and the other the *I*. I call these 'discriminated aspects,' and not separate things, because the identity of *I* with *me*, even in the very act of their discrimination, is perhaps the most ineradicable dictum of common-sense, and must not be undermined by our terminology here at the outset, whatever we may come to think of its validity at our inquiry's end.

I shall therefore treat successively of A) the self as known, or the *me*, the 'empirical ego' as it is sometimes called; and of B) the self as knower, or the I, the 'pure ego' of certain authors.

A) The Self as Known.

The Empirical Self or Me.—Between what a man calls *me* and what he simply calls *mine* the line is difficult to draw. We feel and act about certain things that are ours very much as we feel and act about ourselves. Our fame, our children, the work of our hands, may be as dear to us as our bodies are, and arouse the same feelings and the same acts of reprisal if attacked. And our bodies themselves, are they simply ours, or are they *us?* Certainly men have been ready to disown their very bodies and to regard them as mere vestures, or even as prisons of clay from which they should some day be glad to escape.

We see then that we are dealing with a fluctuating material; the same object being sometimes treated as a part of me, at other times as simply mine, and then again as if I had nothing to do with it at all. *In its widest possible sense,* however, *a man's Me is the sum total of all that he* CAN *call his*, not only his body and his psychic powers, but his clothes and his house, his wife and children, his ancestors and friends, his reputation and works, nis lands and horses, and yacht and bank-account. All these things give him the same emotions. If they wax and prosper, he feels triumphant; if they dwindle and die away, he feels cast down,—not necessarily in the same degree for each thing, but in much the same way for all. Understanding the Me in this widest sense, we may begin by dividing the history of it into three parts, relating respectively to—

a. Its constituents;

b. The feelings and emotions they arouse,—*self-appreciation;*

c. The acts to which they prompt,—*self-seeking and self-preservation.*

a. The constituents of the Me may be divided into two classes, those which make up respectively—

> The material me;
> The social me; and
> The spiritual me.

The Material Me.—The *body* is the innermost part of the material me in each of us; and certain parts of the body seem more intimately ours than the rest. The clothes come next. The old saying that the human person is composed of three parts—soul, body and clothes—is more than a joke. We so appropriate our clothes and identify ourselves with them that there are few of us who, if asked to choose between having a beautiful body clad in raiment perpetually shabby and unclean, and having an ugly and blemished form always spotlessly attired, would not hesitate a moment before making a decisive reply. Next, our immediate family is a part of ourselves. Our father and mother, our wife and babes, are bone of our bone and flesh of our flesh. When they die, a part of our very selves is gone. If they do anything wrong, it is our shame. If they are insulted, our anger flashes forth as readily as if we stood in their place. Our home comes next. Its scenes are part of our life; its aspects awaken the tenderest feelings of affection; and we do not easily forgive the stranger who, in visiting it, finds fault with its arrangements or treats it with contempt. All these different things are the objects of instinctive preferences coupled with the most important practical interests of life. We all have a blind impulse to watch over our body, to deck it with clothing of an ornamental sort, to cherish parents, wife, and babes, and to find for ourselves a house of our own which we may live in and 'improve.'

An equally instinctive impulse drives us to collect property; and the collections thus made become, with different degrees of intimacy, parts of our empirical selves. The parts of our wealth most intimately ours are those which are saturated with our labor. There are few men who would not feel personally annihilated if a life-long construction of their hands or brains—say an entomological collection or an extensive work in manuscript—were suddenly swept away. The miser feels similarly towards his gold; and although it is true that a part of our depression at the loss of possessions is due to our feeling that we must now go without certain goods that we expected the possessions to bring in their train, yet in every case there remains, over and above this, a sense of the shrinkage of our personality, a partial conversion of ourselves to nothingness, which is a psychological phenomenon by itself. Wr are all at once assimilated to the tramps and poor devils whom we so despise, and at the same time removed farther than ever away from the happy sons of earth who lord it over land and sea and men in the full-blown lustihood that wealth and power can give, and before whom, stiffen ourselves as we will by appealing to anti-snobbish first principles, we cannot escape an emotion, open or sneaking, of respect and dread.

The Social Me —A man's social me is the recognition which he gets from his mates. We are not only gregarious animals, liking to be in sight of our fellows, but we have an innate propensity to get ourselves noticed, and noticed favorably, by our kind. No more fiendish punishment could be devised, were such a thing physically possible, than that one should be turned loose in society and remain absolutely unnoticed by all the members thereof. If no one turned round when we entered, answered when we spoke, or minded what we did, but if every person we met 'cut us dead,' and acted as if we were non-existing things, a kind of rage and impotent despair would ere long well up in us, from which the cruellest bodily tortures would be a relief; for these would make us feel that, however bad might be our plight, we had not sunk to such a depth as to be unworthy of attention at all.

Properly speaking, *a man has as many social selves as there are individuals who recognize him* and carry an image of him in their mind. To wound any one of these his images is to wound him. But as the individuals who carry the images fall naturally into classes, we may practically say that he has as many different social selves as there are distinct *groups* of persons about whose opinion he cares. He generally shows a different side of himself to each of these different groups. Many a youth who is demure enough before his parents and teachers, swears and swaggers like a pirate among his 'tough' young friends. We do not show ourselves to our children as to our club-companions, to our customers as to the laborers we employ, to our own masters and employers as to our intimate friends. From this there results what practically is a division of the man into several selves; and this may be a discordant splitting, as where one is afraid to let one set of his acquaintances know him as he is elsewhere; or it may be a perfectly harmonious division of labor, as where one tender to his children is stern to the soldiers or prisoners under his command.

The most peculiar social self which one is apt to have is in the mind of the person one is in love with. The good or bad fortunes of this self cause the most intense elation and dejection—unreasonable enough as measured by every other standard than that of the organic feeling of the individual. To his own consciousness he *is* not, so long as this particular social self fails to get recognition, and when it is recognized his contentment passes all bounds.

A man's *fame*, good or bad, and his *honor* or dishonor, are names for one of his social selves. The particular social self of a man called his honor is usually the result of one of those splittings of which we have spoken. It is his image in the eyes of his own 'set,' which exalts or condemns him as he conforms or not to certain requirements that may not be made of one in another walk of life. Thus a layman may abandon a city infected with cholera; but a priest or a doctor would think such an act incompatible with his honor. A soldier's honor requires him to fight or to die under circumstances where another man can apologize or run away with no stain upon his social self. A judge, a statesman, are in like manner debarred by the honor of their cloth from entering into pecuniary relations perfectly honorable to persons in private life. Nothing is commoner than to hear people discriminate between their different selves of this sort: "As a man I pity you, but as an official I must show you no mercy"; "As a politician I regard him as an ally, but as a moralist I loathe him"; etc., etc. What may be called 'club-opinion' is one of the very strongest forces in life. The thief must not steal from other thieves; the gambler must pay his gambling-debts, though he pay no other debts in the world. The code of honor of fashionable society has throughout history been full of permissions as well as of vetoes, the only reason for following either of which is that so we best serve one of our social selves. You must not lie in general, but you may lie as much as you please if asked about your relations with a lady; you must accept a challenge from an equal, but if challenged by an inferior you may laugh him to scorn: these are examples of what is meant.

The Spiritual Me.—By the 'spiritual me,' so far as it belongs to the empirical self, I mean no one of my passing states of consciousness. I mean rather the entire collection of my states of consciousness, my psychic faculties and dispositions taken concretely. This collection can at any moment become an object to my thought at that moment and awaken emotions like those awakened by any of the other portions of the Me. When we *think of ourselves as thinkers*, all the other ingredients of our Me seem relatively external possessions. Even within the spiritual *Me* some ingredients seem more external than others. Our capacities for sensation, for example, are less intimate possessions, so to speak, than our emotions and desires; our intellectual processes are less intimate than our volitional decisions. The more *active-feeling* states of consciousness are thus the more central portions of the spiritual Me. The very core and nucleus of our self, as we know it, the very sanctuary of our life, is the sense of activity which certain inner states possess. This sense of activity is often held to be a direct revelation of the living substance of our Soul. Whether this be so or not is an ulterior question. I wish now only to lay down the peculiar *internality* of whatever states possess this quality of seeming to be active. It is as if they *went out to meet* all the other elements of our experience. In thus feeling about them probably all men agree.

b. The feelings and emotions of self come after the constituents.

Self-appreciation.—This is of two sorts, *self-complacency* and *self-dissatisfaction*. 'Self-love' more properly belongs under the division *C*, of *acts,* since what men mean by that name is rather a set of motor tendencies than a kind of feeling properly so called.

Language has synonyms enough for both kinds of self-appreciation. Thus pride, conceit, vanity, self-esteem, arrogance, vainglory, on the one hand; and on the other modesty, humility, confusion, diffidence, shame, mortification, contrition, the sense of obloquy, and personal despair. These two opposite classes of affection seem to be direct and elementary endowments of our nature. Associationists would have it that they are, on the other hand, secondary phenomena arising from a rapid computation of the sensible pleasures or pains to which our prosperous or debased personal predicament is likely to lead, the sum of the represented pleasures forming the self-satisfaction, and the sum of the represented pains forming the opposite feeling of shame. No doubt, when we are self-satisfied, we do fondly rehearse all possible rewards for our desert, and when in a fit of self-despair we forebode evil. But the mere expectation of reward *is* not the self-satisfaction, and the mere apprehension of the evil *is* not the self-despair; for there is a certain average tone of self-feeling which each one of us carries about with him, and which is independent of the objective reasons we may have for satisfaction or discontent. That is, a very meanly-conditioned man may abound in unfaltering conceit, and one whose success in life is secure, and who is esteemed by all, may remain diffident of his powers to the end.

One may say, however, that the normal *provocative* of self-feeling is one's actual success or failure, and the good or bad actual position one holds in the world. " He put in his thumb and pulled out a plum, and said, 'What a good boy am I!'" A man with a broadly extended empirical Ego, with powers that have uniformly brought him success, with place and wealth and friends and fame, is not likely to be visited by the morbid diffidences and doubts about himself which he had when he was a boy. "Is not this great Babylon, which I have planted?" Whereas he who has made one blunder after another, and still lies in middle life among the failures at the foot of the hill, is liable to grow all sicklied o'er with self-distrust, and to shrink from trials with which his powers can really cope.

The emotions themselves of self-satisfaction and abasement are of a unique sort, each as worthy to be classed as a primitive emotional species as are, for example, rage or pain. Each has its own peculiar physiognomical expression. In self-satisfaction the extensor muscles are innervated, the eye is strong and glorious, the gait rolling and elastic, the nostril dilated, and a peculiar smile plays upon the lips. This whole complex of symptoms is seen in an exquisite way in lunatic asylums, which always contain some patients who are literally mad with conceit, and whose fatuous expression and absurdly strutting or swaggering gait is in tragic contrast with their lack of any valuable personal quality. It is in these same castles of despair that we find the strongest examples of the opposite physiognomy, in good people who think they have committed 'the unpardonable sin' and are lost forever, who crouch and cringe and slink from notice, and are unable to speak aloud or look us in the eye. Like fear and like anger, in similar morbid conditions, these opposite feelings of Self may be aroused with no adequate exciting cause. And in fact we ourselves know how the barometer of our self-esteem and confidence rises and falls from one day to another through causes that seem to be visceral and organic rather than rational, and which certainly answer to no corresponding variations in the esteem in which we are held by our friends.

c. Self-seeking and self-preservation come next.

These words cover a large number of our fundamental instinctive impulses. We have those of *bodily self-seeking*, those of *social self-seeking*, and those of *spiritual self-seeking*.

Bodily Self-seeking.—All the ordinary useful reflex actions and movements of alimentation and defence are acts of bodily self-preservation. Fear and anger prompt to acts that are useful in the same way. Whilst if by self-seeking we mean the providing for the future as distinguished from maintaining the present, we must class both anger and fear, together with the hunting, the acquisitive, the home-constructing and the tool-constructing instincts, as impulses to self-seeking of the bodily kind. Really, however, these latter instincts, with amativeness, parental fondness, curiosity and emulation, seek not only the development of the bodily Me, but that of the material Me in the widest possible sense of the word.

Our social self-seeking, in turn, is carried on directly through our amativeness and friendliness, our desire to please and attract notice and admiration, our emulation and jealousy, our love of glory, influence, and power, and indirectly through whichever of the material self-seeking impulses prove serviceable as means to social ends. That the direct social self-seeking impulses are probably pure instincts is easily seen. The noteworthy thing about the desire to be 'recognized' by others is that its strength has so little to do with the worth of the recognition computed in sensational or rational terms. We are crazy to get a visiting-list which shall be large, to be able to say when any one is mentioned, "Oh! I know him well," and to be bowed to in the street by half the people we meet. Of course distinguished friends and admiring recognition are the most desirable—Thackeray somewhere asks his readers to confess whether it would not give each of *them* an exquisite pleasure to be met walking down Pall Mall with a duke on either arm. But in default of dukes and envious salutions almost anything will do for some of us; and there is a whole race of beings to-day whose passion is to keep their names in the newspapers, no matter under what heading, 'arrivals and departures,' 'personal paragraphs,' 'interviews,'—gossip, even scandal, will suit them if nothing better is to be had. Guiteau, Garfield's assassin, is an example of the extremity to which this sort of craving for the notoriety of print may go in a pathological case. The newspapers bounded his mental horizon; and in the poor wretch's prayer on the scaffold, one of the most heart-felt expressions was: "The newspaper press of this land has a big bill to settle with thee, O Lord!"

Not only the people but the places and things I know enlarge my Self in a sort of metaphoric social way. '*Ça me connait*,' as the French workman says of the implement he can use well. So that it comes about that persons for whose *opinion* we care nothing are nevertheless persons whose notice we woo; and that many a man truly great, many a woman truly fastidious in most respects, will take a deal of trouble to dazzle some insignificant cad whose whole personality they heartily despise.

Under the head of spiritual self-seeking ought to be included every impulse towards psychic progress, whether intellectual, moral, or spiritual in the narrow sense of the term. It must be admitted, however, that much that commonly passes for spiritual self-seeking in this narrow sense is only material and social self-seeking beyond the grave. In the Mohammedan desire for paradise and the Christian aspiration not to be damned in hell, the materiality of the goods sought is undisguised. In the more positive and refined view of heaven, many of its goods, the fellowship of the saints and of our dead ones, and the presence of God, are but social goods of the most exalted kind. It is only the search of the redeemed inward nature, the spotlessness from sin, whether here or hereafter, that can count as spiritual self-seeking pure and undefiled.

But this broad external review of the facts of the life of the Me will be incomplete without some account of the

Rivalry and Conflict of the Different Mes.—With most objects of desire, physical nature restricts our choice to but one of many represented goods, and even so it is here. I am often confronted by the necessity of standing by one of my empirical selves and relinquishing the rest. Not that I would not, if I could, be both handsome and fat and well dressed, and a great athlete, and make a million a year, be a wit, a *bon-vivant*, and a lady-killer, as well as a philosopher; a philanthropist, statesman, warrior, and African explorer, as well as a 'tone-poet' and saint. But the thing is simply impossible. The millionaire's work would run counter to the saint's; the *bon-vivant* and the philanthropist would trip each other up; the philosopher and the lady-killer could not well keep house in the same tenement of clay. Such different characters may conceivably at the outset of life be alike *possible* to a man. But to make any one of them actual, the rest must more or less be suppressed. So the seeker of his truest, strongest, deepest self must review the list carefully, and pick out the one on which to stake his salvation. All other selves thereupon become unreal, but the fortunes of this self are real. Its failures are real failures, its triumphs real triumphs, carrying shame and gladness with them. This is as strong an example as there is of that selective industry of the mind on which I insisted some pages back (p. 173 ff.). Our thought, incessantly deciding, among many things of a kind, which ones for it shall be realities, here chooses one of many possible selves or characters, and forthwith reckons it no shame to fail in any of those not adopted expressly as its own.

So we have the paradox of a man shamed to death because he is only the second pugilist or the second oarsman in the world That he is able to beat the whole population of the globe minus one is nothing; he has 'pitted' himself to beat that one; and as long as he doesn't do that nothing else counts. He is to his own regard as if he were not, indeed he *is* not. Yonder puny fellow, however, whom every one can beat, suffers no chagrin about it, for he has long ago abandoned the attempt to 'carry that line,' as the merchants say, of self at all. With no attempt there can be no failure; with no failure, no humiliation. So our self-feeling in this world depends entirely on what we *back* ourselves to be and do. It is determined by the ratio of our actualities to our supposed potentialities; a fraction of which our pretensions are the denominator and the numerator our success: thus,

$$\text{Self-esteem} = \frac{\text{Success}}{\text{Pretensions}}.$$

Such a fraction may be increased as well by diminishing the denominator as by increasing the numerator. To give up pretensions is as blessed a relief as to get them gratified; and where disappointment is incessant and the struggle unending, this is what men will always do. The history of evangelical theology, with its conviction of sin, its self-despair, and its abandonment of salvation by works, is the deepest of possible examples, but we meet others in every walk of life. There is the strangest lightness about the heart when one's nothingness in a particular line is once accepted in good faith. *All* is not bitterness in the lot of the lover sent away by the final inexorable 'No.' Many Bostonians, *crede experto* (and inhabitants of other cities, too, I fear), would be happier women and men to-day, if they could once for all abandon the notion of keeping up a Musical Self, and without shame let people hear them call a symphony a nuisance. How pleasant is the day when we give up striving to be young,—or slender! Thank God! we say, *those* illusions are gone. Everything added to the Self is a burden as well as a pride. A certain man who lost every penny during our civil war went and actually rolled in the dust, saying he had not felt so free and happy since he was born.

Once more, then, our self-feeling is in our power. As Carlyle says: " Make thy claim of wages a zero, then hast thou the world under thy feet. Well did the wisest of our time write, it is only with *renunciation* that life, properly speaking, can be said to begin."

Neither threats nor pleadings can move a man unless they touch some one of his potential or actual selves. Only thus can we, as a rule, get a 'purchase' on another's will. The first care of diplomatists and monarchs and all who wish to rule or influence is, accordingly, to find out their victim's strongest principle of self-regard, so as to make that the fulcrum of all appeals. But if a man has given up those things which are subject to foreign fate, and ceased to regard them as parts of himself at all, we are well-nigh powerless over him. The Stoic receipt for contentment was to dispossess yourself in advance of all that was out of your own power,—then fortune's shocks might rain down unfelt. Epictetus exhorts us, by thus narrowing and at the same time solidifying our Self to make it invulnerable: " I must die; well, but must I die groaning too? I will speak what appears to be right, and if the despot says, 'Then I will put you to death,' I will reply, 'When did I ever tell you that I was immortal? You will do your part, and I mine; it is yours to kill, and mine to die intrepid; yours to banish, mine to depart untroubled.' How do we act in a voyage? We choose the pilot, the sailors, the hour. Afterwards comes a storm. What have I to care for? My part is performed. This matter belongs to the pilot. But the ship is sinking; what then have I to do? That which alone I can do—submit to being drowned without fear, without clamor or accusing of God, but as one who knows that what is born must likewise die."

This Stoic fashion, though efficacious and heroic enough in its place and time, is, it must be confessed, only possible as an habitual mood of the soul to narrow and unsympathetic characters. It proceeds altogether by exclusion. If I am a Stoic, the goods I cannot appropriate cease to be *my* goods, and the temptation lies very near to deny that they are goods at all. We find this mode of protecting the Self by exclusion and denial very common among people who are in other respects not Stoics. All narrow people *intrench* their Me, they *retract* it,—from the region of what they cannot securely possess. People who don't resemble them, or who treat them with indifference, people over whom they gain no influence, are people on whose existence, however meritorious it may intrinsically be, they look with chill negation, if not with positive hate. Who will not be mine I will exclude from existence altogether; that is, as far as I can make it so, such people shall be as if they were not. Thus may a certain absoluteness and definiteness in the outline of my Me console me for the smallness of its content.

Sympathetic people, on the contrary, proceed by the entirely opposite way of expansion and inclusion. The outline of their self often gets uncertain enough, but for this the spread of its content more than atones. *Nil humani a me alienum.* Let them despise this little person of mine, and treat me like a dog, *I* shall not negate *them* so long as I have a soul in my body. They are realities as much as I am. What positive good is in them shall be mine too, etc., etc. The magnanimity of these expansive natures is often touching indeed. Such persons can feel a sort of delicate rapture in thinking that, however sick, ill-favored, mean-conditioned, and generally forsaken they may be, they yet are integral parts of the whole of this brave world, have a fellow's share in the strength of the dray-horses, the happiness of the young people, the wisdom of the wise ones, and are not altogether without part or lot in the good fortunes of the Vanderbilts and the Hohenzollerns themselves. Thus either by negating or by embracing, the Ego may seek to establish itself in reality. He who, with Marcus Aurelius, can truly say, "O Universe, I wish all that thou wishest," has a self from which every trace of negativeness and obstructiveness has been removed—no wind can blow except to fill its sails.

The Hierarchy of the Mes.—A tolerably unanimous opinion ranges the different selves of which a man may be 'seized and possessed,' and the consequent different orders of his self-regard, in an *hierarchical scale, with the bodily me at the bottom, the spiritual me at top, and the extra-corporeal material selves and the various social selves between* Our merely natural self-seeking would lead us to aggran dize all these selves; we give up deliberately only those among them which we find we cannot keep. Our unselfishness is thus apt to be a 'virtue of necessity'; and it is not without all show of reason that cynics quote the fable of the fox and the grapes in describing our progress therein. But this is the moral education of the race; and if we agree in the result that on the whole the selves we can keep are the intrinsically best, we need not complain of being led to the knowledge of their superior worth in such a tortuous way.

Of course this is not the only way in which we learn to subordinate our lower selves to our higher. A direct ethical judgment unquestionably also plays its part, and last, not least, we apply to our own persons judgments originally called forth by the acts of others. It is one of the strangest laws of our nature that many things which we are well satisfied with in ourselves disgust us when seen in others. With another man's bodily 'hoggishness' hardly anyone has any sympathy; almost as little with his cupidity, his social vanity and eagerness, his jealousy, his despotism, and his pride. Left absolutely to myself I should probably allow all these spontaneous tendencies to luxuriate in me unchecked, and it would be long before I formed a distinct notion of the order of their subordination. But having constantly to pass judgment on my associates, I come ere long to see, as Herr Horwicz says, my own lusts in the mirror of the lusts of others, and to *think* about them in a very different way from that in which I simply *feel*. Of course, the moral generalities which from childhood have been instilled into me accelerate enormously the advent of this reflective judgment on myself.

So it comes to pass that, as aforesaid, men have arranged the various selves which they may seek in an hierarchical scale according to their worth. A certain amount of bodily selfishness is required as a basis for all the other selves. But too much sensuality is despised, or at best condoned on account of the other qualities of the individual. The wider material selves are regarded as higher than the immediate body. He is esteemed a poor creature who is unable to forego a little meat and drink and warmth and sleep for the sake of getting on in the world. The social self as a whole, again, ranks higher than the material self as a whole. We must care more for our honor, our friends, our human ties, than for a sound skin or wealth. And the spiritual self is so supremely precious that, rather than lose it, a man ought to be willing to give up friends and good fame, and property, and life itself.

In each kind of Me, material, social, and spiritual, men distinguish between the immediate and actual, and the remote and potential, between the narrower and the wider view, to the detriment of the former and the advantage of the latter. One must forego a present bodily enjoyment for the sake of one's general health; one must abandon the dollar in the hand for the sake of the hundred dollars to come; one must make an enemy of his present interlocutor if thereby one makes friends of a more valued circle; one must go without learning and grace and wit, the better to compass one's soul's salvation.

Of all these wider, more potential selves, *the potential social Me* is the most interesting, by reason of certain apparent paradoxes to which it leads in conduct, and by reason of its connection with our moral and religious life. When for motives of honor and conscience I brave the condemnation of my own family, club, and 'set'; when, as a Protestant, I turn Catholic; as a Catholic, freethinker; as a 'regular practitioner,' homœopath, or what not, I am always inwardly strengthened in my course and steeled against the loss of my actual social self by the thought of other and better *possible* social judges than those whose verdict goes against me now. The ideal social self which I thus seek in appealing to their decision may be very remote: it may be represented as barely possible. I may not hope for its realization during my lifetime; I may even expect the future generations, which would approve me if they knew me, to know nothing about me when I am dead and gone. Yet still the emotion that beckons me on is indubitably the pursuit of an ideal social self, of a self that is at least *worthy* of approving recognition by the highest *possible* judging companion, if such companion there be. This self is the true, the intimate, the ultimate, the permanent me which I seek. This judge is God, the Absolute Mind, the 'Great Companion.' We hear, in these days of scientific enlightenment, a great deal of discussion about the efficacy of prayer; and many reasons are given us why we should not pray, whilst others are given us why we should. But in all this very little is said of the reason why we *do* pray, which is simply that we cannot help praying. It seems probable that, *in* spite of all that 'science' may do to the contrary, men will continue to pray to the end of time, unless their mental nature changes in a manner which nothing we know should lead us to expect. The impulse to pray is a necessary consequence of the fact that whilst the innermost of the empirical selves of a man is a Self of the *social* sort, it yet can find its only adequate *Socius* in an ideal world.

All progress in the social Self is the substitution of higher tribunals for lower; this ideal tribunal is the highest; and most men, either continually or occasionally, carry a reference to it in their breast. The humblest outcast on this earth can feel himself to be real and valid by means of this higher recognition. And, on the other hand, for most of us, a world with no such inner refuge when the outer social self failed and dropped from us would be the abyss of horror. I say 'for most of us,' because it is probable that individuals differ a good deal in the degree in which they are haunted by this sense of an ideal spectator. It is a much more essential part of the consciousness of some men than of others. Those who have the most of it are possibly the most *religious* men. But I am sure that even those who say they are altogether without it deceive themselves, and really have it in some degree. Only a non-gregarious animal could be completely without it. Probably no one can make sacrifices for 'right,' without to some degree personifying the principle of right for which the sacrifice is made, and expecting thanks from it. *Complete* social unselfishness, in other words, can hardly exist; *complete* social suicide hardly occur to a man's mind. Even such texts as Job's, "Though He slay me, yet will I trust Him," or Marcus Aurelius's, "If gods hate me and my children, there is a reason for it," can least of all be cited to prove the contrary. For beyond all doubt Job revelled in the thought of Jehovah's recognition of the worship after the slaying should have been done; and the Roman emperor felt sure the Absolute Reason would not be all indifferent to his acquiescence in the gods' dislike. The old test of piety, "Are you willing to be damned for the glory of God?" was probably never answered in the affirmative except by those who felt sure in their heart of hearts that God would 'credit' them with their willingness, and set more store by them thus than if in His unfathomable scheme He had not damned them at all.

Teleological Uses of Self-interest.—On zoölogical principles it is easy to see why we have been endowed with impulses of self-seeking and with emotions of self-satisfaction and the reverse. Unless our consciousness were something more than cognitive, unless it experienced a partiality for certain of the objects, which, in succession, occupy its ken, it could not long maintain itself in existence; for, by an inscrutable necessity, each human mind's appearance on this earth is conditioned upon the integrity of the body with which it belongs, upon the treatment which that body gets from others, and upon the spiritual dispositions which use it as their tool, and lead it either towards longevity or to destruction. *Its own body, then, first of all, its friends next, and finally its spiritual dis positions,* MUST *be the supremely interesting objects for each human mind.* Each mind, to begin with, must have a certain minimum of selfishness in the shape of instincts of bodily self-seeking in order to exist. This minimum must be there as a basis for all farther conscious acts, whether of self-negation or of a selfishness more subtle still. All minds must have come, by the way of the survival of the fittest, if by no directer path, to take an intense interest in the bodies to which they are yoked, altogether apart from any interest in the pure Ego which they also possess.

And similarly with the images of their person in the minds of others. I should not be extant now had I not become sensitive to looks of approval or disapproval on the faces among which my life is cast. Looks of contempt cast on other persons need affect me in no such peculiar way. My spiritual powers, again, must interest me more than those of other people, and for the same reason. I should not be here at all unless I had cultivated them and kept them from decay. And the same law which made me once care for them makes me care for them still.

All these three things form the *natural Me.* But all these things are *objects,* properly so called, to the thought which at any time may be doing the thinking; and if the zoological and evolutionary point of view is the true one, there is no reason why one object *might* not arouse passion and interest as primitively and instinctively as any other. The phenomenon of passion is in origin and essence the same, whatever be the target upon which it is discharged; and what the target actually happens to be is solely a question of fact. I might conceivably be as much fascinated, and as primitively so, by the care of my neighbor's body as by the care of my own. I *am* thus fascinated by the care of my child's body. The only check to such exuberant non-egoistic interests is natural selection, which would weed out such as were very harmful to the individual or to his tribe. Many such interests, however, remain unweeded out—the interest in the opposite sex, for example, which seems in mankind stronger than is called for by its utilitarian need; and alongside of them remain interests, like that in alcoholic intoxication, or in musical sounds, which, for aught we can see, are without any utility whatever. The sympathetic instincts and the egoistic ones are thus coördinate. They arise, so far as we can tell, on the same psychologic level. The only difference between them is that the instincts called egoistic form much the larger mass.

Summary.—The following table may serve for a summary of what has been said thus far. The empirical life of Self is divided, as below, into

	MATERIAL.	SOCIAL.	SPIRITUAL.
SELF-SEEKING.	Bodily Appetites and Instincts Love of Adornment, Foppery, Acquisitiveness, Constructiveness. Love of Home, etc.	Desire to Please, be Noticed, Admired, etc. Sociability, Emulation, Envy, Love, Pursuit of Honor, Ambition, etc.	Intellectual, Moral and Religious Aspirations, Conscientiousness.
SELF-ESTIMATION.	Personal Vanity, Modesty, etc. Pride of Wealth, Fear of Poverty.	Social and Family Pride, Vainglory, Snobbery, Humility, Shame, etc	Sense of Moral or Mental Superiority, Purity, etc. Sense of Inferiority or of Guilt.

B) THE SELF AS KNOWER.

The I, or 'pure ego,' is a very much more difficult subject of inquiry than the Me. It is that which at any given moment *is* conscious, whereas the Me is only one of the things which it is conscious *of*. In other words, it is the *Thinker;* and the question immediately comes up *what* is the thinker? Is it the passing state of consciousness itself, or is it something deeper and less mutable? The passing state we have seen to be the very embodiment of change (see p. 155 ff.). Yet each of us spontaneously considers that by 'I,' he means something always the same. This has led most philosophers to postulate behind the passing state of consciousness a permanent Substance or Agent whose modification or act it is. This Agent is the thinker; the 'state' is only its instrument or means. 'Soul' 'transcendental Ego,' 'Spirit,' are so many names for this more permanent sort of Thinker. Not discriminating them just yet, let us proceed to define our idea of the passing state of consciousness more clearly.

The Unity of the Passing Thought.—Already, in speaking of 'sensations,' from the point of view of Fechner's idea of measuring them, we saw that there was no ground for calling them compounds. But what is true of sensations cognizing simple qualities is also true of thoughts with complex objects composed of many parts. This proposition unfortunately runs counter to a wide-spread prejudice, and will have to be defended at some length. Common-sense, and psychologists of almost every school, have agreed that whenever an object of thought contains many elements, the thought itself must be made up of just as many ideas, one idea for each element, all fused together in appearance, but really separate.

"There can be no difficulty in admitting that association *does* form the ideas of an indefinite number of individuals into one complex idea," says James Mill, "because it is an acknowledged fact. Have we not the idea of an army? And is not that precisely the ideas of an indefinite number of men formed into one idea?"

Similar quotations might be multiplied, and the reader's own first impressions probably would rally to their support. Suppose, for example, he thinks that "the pack of cards is on the table." If he begins to reflect, he is as likely as not to say: "Well, isn't that a thought of the pack of cards? Isn't it of the cards as included in the pack? Isn't it of the table? And of the legs of the table as well? Hasn't my thought, then, all these parts—one part for the pack and another for the table? And within the pack-part a part for each card, as within the table-part a part for each leg? And isn't each of these parts an idea? And can thought, then, be anything but an assemblage or pack of ideas, each answering to some element of what it knows?"

Plausible as such considerations may seem, it is astonishing how little force they have. In assuming a pack of ideas, each cognizant of some one element of the fact one has assumed, nothing has been assumed which knows the whole fact *at once*. The idea which, on the hypothesis the pack of ideas. knows, *e.g.*, the ace of spades must be ignorant of the leg of the table, since to account for that knowledge another special idea is by the same hypothesis invoked ; and so on with the rest of the ideas, all equally ignorant of each other's objects. And yet in the actual living human mind what knows the cards also knows the table, its legs, etc., for all these things are known in relation to each other and at once. Our notion of the abstract numbers eight, four, two is as truly one feeling of the mind as our notion of simple unity. Our idea of a couple is not a couple of ideas. " But," the reader may say, " is not the taste of lemonade composed of that of lemon *plus* that of sugar?" No! I reply, this is taking the combining of objects for that of feelings. The physical lemonade contains both the lemon and the sugar, but its taste does not contain their tastes ; for if there are any two things which are certainly *not* present in the taste of lemonade, those are the pure lemon-sour on the one hand and the pure sugar-sweet on the other. These tastes are absent utterly. A taste somewhat *like* both of them is there, but that is a distinct state of mind altogether.

Distinct mental states cannot 'fuse.' But not only is

the notion that our ideas are combinations of smaller ideas improbable, it is logically unintelligible; it leaves out the essential features of all the 'combinations' which we actually know.

All the 'combinations' which we actually know are EFFECTS, *wrought by the units said to be 'combined,'* UPON SOME ENTITY OTHER THAN THEMSELVES. Without this feature of a medium or vehicle, the notion of combination has no sense.

In other words, no possible number of entities (call them as you like, whether forces, material particles, or mental elements) can sum *themselves* together. Each remains, in the sum, what it always was; and the sum itself exists only *for a bystander* who happens to overlook the units and to apprehend the sum as such; or else it exists in the shape of some other effect on an entity external to the sum itself. When H_2 and O are said to combine into 'water,' and thenceforward to exhibit new properties, the 'water' is just the old atoms in the new position, H-O-H; the 'new properties' are just their combined *effects*, when in this position, upon external media, such as our sense-organs and the various reagents on which water may exert its properties and be known. Just so, the strength of many men may combine when they pull upon one rope, of many muscular fibres when they pull upon one tendon.

In the parallelogram of forces, the 'forces' do not combine *themselves* into the diagonal resultant; a *body* is needed on which they may impinge, to exhibit their resultant effect. No more do musical sounds combine *per se* into concords or discords. Concord and discord are names for their combined effects on that external medium, the *ear.*

Where the elemental units are supposed to be feelings, the case is in no wise altered. Take a hundred of them, shuffle them and pack them as close together as you can (whatever that may mean); still each remains the same

THE SELF.

feeling it always was, shut in its own skin, windowless, ignorant of what the other feelings are and mean. There would be a hundred-and-first feeling there, if, when a group or series of such feelings were set up, a consciousness *belonging to the group as such* should emerge, and this one hundred and first feeling would be a totally new fact. The one hundred original feelings might, by a curious physical law, be a signal for its *creation*, when they came together—we often have to learn things separately before we know them as a sum—but they would have no substantial identity with the new feeling, nor it with them; and one could never deduce the one from the others, or (in any intelligible sense) say that they *evolved* it out of themselves.

Take a sentence of a dozen words, and take twelve men and tell to each one word. Then stand the men in a row or jam them in a bunch, and let each think of his word as intently as he will: nowhere will there be a consciousness of the whole sentence. We talk, it is true, of the 'spirit of the age,' and the 'sentiment of the people,' and in various ways we hypostatize 'public opinion.' But we know this to be symbolic speech, and never dream that the spirit, opinion, or sentiment constitutes a consciousness other than, and additional to, that of the several individuals whom the words 'age,' 'people,' or 'public' denote. The private minds do not agglomerate into a higher compound mind. This has always been the invincible contention of the spiritualists against the associationists in Psychology. The associationists say the mind is constituted by a multiplicity of distinct 'ideas' *associated* into a unity. There is, they say, an idea of a, and also an idea of b. *Therefore*, they say, there is an idea of $a + b$, or of a and b together. Which is like saying that the mathematical square of a plus that of b is equal to the square of $a + b$, a palpable untruth. Idea of a + idea of b is *not* identical with idea of $(a + b)$. It is one, they are two; in it, what knows a also knows b; in them, what knows a is expressly posited as not knowing b; etc. In short, the two separate ideas can never by any logic be made to figure as one idea. If one idea (of $a + b$, for example) come as a matter of fact after the two separate ideas (of a and of b), then we must hold it to be as direct a product of the later conditions as the two separate ideas were of the earlier conditions.

The simplest thing, therefore, if we are to assume the existence of a stream of consciousness at all, would be to suppose that things that are known together are known in single pulses of that stream. The things may be many, and may occasion many currents in the brain. But the psychic phenomenon correlative to these many currents is one integral 'state,' transitive or substantive (see p. 161), to which the many things appear.

The Soul as a Combining Medium.—The spiritualists in philosophy have been prompt to see that things which are known together are known by one *something*, but that something, they say, is no mere passing thought, but a simple and permanent spiritual being on which many ideas combine their effects. It makes no difference in this connection whether this being be called Soul, Ego, or Spirit, in either case its chief function is that of a combining medium. This is a different vehicle of knowledge from that in which we just said that the mystery of knowing things together might be most simply lodged. Which is the real knower, this permanent being, or our passing state? If we had other grounds, not yet considered, for admitting the Soul into our psychology, then getting there on those grounds, she might turn out to be the knower too. But if there be no *other* grounds for admitting the Soul, we had better cling to our passing 'states' as the exclusive agents of knowledge; for we have to assume their existence anyhow in psychology, and the knowing of many things together is just as well accounted for when we call it one of their functions as when we call it a reaction of the Soul. *Explained* it is not by either conception, and has to figure in psychology as a datum that is **ultimate.**

But there are other alleged grounds for admitting the Soul into psychology, and the chief of them is

The Sense of Personal Identity.—In the last chapter it was stated (see p. 154) that the thoughts which we actually know to exist do not fly about loose, but seem each to belong to some one thinker and not to another. Each thought, out of a multitude of other thoughts of which it may think, is able to distinguish those which belong to it from those which do not. The former have a warmth and intimacy about them of which the latter are completely devoid, and the result is a Me of yesterday, judged to be in some peculiarly subtle sense the *same* with the I who now make the judgment. As a mere subjective phenomenon the judgment presents no special mystery. It belongs to the great class of judgments of sameness; and there is nothing more remarkable in making a judgment of sameness in the first person than in the second or the third. The intellectual operations seem essentially alike, whether I say ' I am the same as I was,' or whether I say ' the pen is the same as it was, yesterday.' It is as easy to think this as to think the opposite and say ' neither of us is the same.' The only question which we have to consider is whether it be a right judgment. *Is the sameness predicated really there?*

Sameness in the Self as Known.—If in the sentence "I am the same that I was yesterday," we take the ' I ' broadly, it is evident that in many ways I am *not* the same. As a concrete Me, I am somewhat different from what I was: then hungry, now full; then walking, now at rest; then poorer, now richer; then younger, now older; etc. And yet in other ways I *am* the same, and we may call these the essential ways. My name and profession and relations to the world are identical, my face, my faculties and store of memories, are practically indistinguishable, now and then. Moreover the Me of now and the Me of then are *continuous:* the alterations were gradual and never affected the whole of me at once. So far, then, my personal identity is just like the sameness predicated of any other aggregate thing. It is a conclusion grounded either on the resemblance in essential respects, or on the continuity of the phenomena compared. And it must not be taken to mean more than these grounds warrant, or treated as a sort of metaphysical or absolute Unity in which all differences are overwhelmed. The past and present selves compared are the same just so far as they *are* the same, and no farther. They are the same in *kind*. But this generic sameness coexists with generic differences just as real; and if from the one point of view I am one self, from another I am quite as truly many. Similarly of the attribute of continuity: it gives to the self the unity of mere connectedness, or unbrokenness, a perfectly definite phenomenal thing—but it gives not a jot or tittle more.

Sameness in the Self as Knower.—But all this is said only of the Me, or Self as known. In the judgment I am the same,' etc., the 'I' was taken broadly as the concrete person. Suppose, however, that we take it narrowly, as the *Thinker*, as '*that to which*' all the concrete determinations of the Me belong and are known: does there not then appear an absolute identity at different times? That something which at every moment goes out and knowingly appropriates the *Me* of the past, and discards the non-me as foreign, is it not a permanent abiding principle of spiritual activity identical with itself wherever found?

That it is such a principle is the reigning doctrine both of philosophy and common-sense, and yet reflection finds it difficult to justify the idea. *If there were no passing states of consciousness*, then indeed we might suppose an abiding principle, absolutely one with itself, to be the ceaseless thinker in each one of us. But if the states of consciousness be accorded as realities, no such 'substantial' identity in the thinker need be supposed. Yesterday's and to-day's states of consciousnesses have no *substantial* identity, for when one is here the other is irrevocably dead and gone. But they have a *functional* identity, for both know the same objects, and so far as the by-gone me is one of those objects, they react upon it in an identical way, greeting it and calling it *mine*, and opposing it to all the other things they know. This functional identity seems really the only sort of identity in the thinker which the facts require us to suppose. Successive thinkers, numerically distinct, but all aware of the same past in the same way, form an adequate vehicle for all the experience of personal unity and sameness which we actually have. And just such a train of successive thinkers is the stream of mental states (each with its complex object cognized and emotional and selective reaction thereupon) which psychology treated as a natural science has to assume (see p. 2).

The logical conclusion seems then to be that *the states of consciousness are all that psychology needs to do her work with. Metaphysics or theology may prove the Soul to exist; but for psychology the hypothesis of such a substantial principle of unity is superfluous.*

How the I appropriates the Me.—But *why* should each successive mental state appropriate the same past Me? I spoke a while ago of my own past experiences appearing to me with a 'warmth and intimacy' which the experiences thought of by me as having occurred to other people lack. This leads us to the answer sought. My present Me is felt with warmth and intimacy. The heavy warm mass of my body is there, and the nucleus of the 'spiritual me,' the sense of intimate activity (p. 184), is there. We cannot realize our present self without simultaneously feeling one or other of these two things. Any other object of thought which brings these two things with it into consciousness will be thought with a warmth and an intimacy like those which cling to the present me.

Any *distant* object which fulfils this condition will be thought with such warmth and intimacy. But which distant objects *do* fulfil the condition, when represented?

Obviously those, and only those, which fulfilled it when they were alive. *Them* we shall still represent with the animal warmth upon them; to them may possibly still cling the flavor of the inner activity taken in the act. And by a natural consequence, we shall assimilate them to each other and to the warm and intimate self we now feel within us as we think, and separate them as a collection from whatever objects have not this mark, much as out of a herd of cattle let loose for the winter on some wide Western prairie the owner picks out and sorts together, when the round-up comes in the spring, all the beasts on which he finds his own particular brand. Well, just such objects are the past experiences which I now call mine. Other men's experiences, no matter how much I may know about them, never bear this vivid, this peculiar brand. This is why Peter, awakening in the same bed with Paul, and recalling what both had in mind before they went to sleep, reidentifies and appropriates the 'warm' ideas as his, and is never tempted to confuse them with those cold and pale-appearing ones which he ascribes to Paul. As well might he confound Paul's body, which he only sees, with his own body, which he sees but also feels. Each of us when he awakens says, Here's the same old Me again, just as he says, Here's the same old bed, the same old room, the same old world.

And similarly in our waking hours, though each pulse of consciousness dies away and is replaced by another, yet that other, among the things it knows, knows its own predecessor, and finding it 'warm,' in the way we have described, greets it, saying: "Thou art *mine*, and part of the same self with me." Each later thought, knowing and including thus the thoughts that went before, is the final receptacle—and appropriating them is the final owner—of all that they contain and own. As Kant says, it is as if elastic balls were to have not only motion but knowledge of it, and a first ball were to transmit both its motion and its consciousness to a second, which took both up into *its* consciousness and passed them to a third, until the last ball held all that the other balls had held, and realized it as its own. It is this trick which the nascent thought has of immediately taking up the expiring thought and 'adopting' it, which leads to the appropriation of most of the remoter constituents of the self. Who owns the last self owns the self before the last, for what possesses the possessor possesses the possessed. It is impossible to discover any *verifiable* features in personal identity which this sketch does not contain, impossible to imagine how any transcendent principle of Unity (were such a principle there) could shape matters to any other result, or be known by any other fruit, than just this production of a stream of consciousness each successive part of which should know, and knowing, hug to itself and adopt, all those that went before,—thus standing as the *representative* of an entire past stream with which it is in no wise to be identified.

Mutations and Multiplications of the Self.—The Me, like every other aggregate, changes as it grows. The passing states of consciousness, which should preserve in their succession an identical knowledge of its past, wander from their duty, letting large portions drop from out of their ken, and representing other portions wrong. The identity which we recognize as we survey the long procession can only be the relative identity of a slow shifting in which there is always some common ingredient retained. The commonest element of all, the most uniform, is the possession of some common memories. However different the man may be from the youth, both look back on the same childhood and call it their own.

Thus the identity found by the *I* in its *Me* is only a loosely construed thing : an identity 'on the whole,' just like that which any outside observer might find in the same assemblage of facts. We often say of a man 'he is so changed one would not know him'; and so does a man, less often, speak of himself. These changes in the *Me*, recognized by the I, or by outside observers, may be grave or slight. They deserve some notice here.

The mutations of the Self may be divided into two main classes:

a. Alterations of memory; and

b. Alterations in the present bodily and spiritual selves.

a. Of the alterations of memory little need be said—they are so familiar. Losses of memory are a normal incident in life, especially in advancing years, and the person's *me*, as 'realized,' shrinks *pari passu* with the facts that disappear. The memory of dreams and of experiences in the hypnotic trance rarely survives.

False memories, also, are by no means rare occurrences, and whenever they occur they distort our consciousness of our Me. Most people, probably, are in doubt about certain matters ascribed to their past. They may have seen them, may have said them, done them, or they may only have dreamed or imagined they did so. The content of a dream will oftentimes insert itself into the stream of real life in a most perplexing way. The most frequent source of false memory is the accounts we give to others of our experiences. Such accounts we almost always make both more simple and more interesting than the truth. We quote what we should have said or done, rather than what we really said or did; and in the first telling we may be fully aware of the distinction. But ere long the fiction expels the reality from memory and reigns in its stead alone. This is one great source of the fallibility of testimony meant to be quite honest. Especially where the marvellous is concerned, the story takes a tilt that way, and the memory follows the story.

b. When we pass beyond alterations of memory to abnormal *alterations in the present self* we have graver disturbances. These alterations are of three main types, but our knowledge of the elements and causes of these changes of personality is so slight that the division into types must not be regarded as having any profound significance. The types are:

α. Insane delusions;
β. Alternating selves;
γ. Mediumships or possessions.

α. In insanity we often have delusions projected into the past, which are melancholic or sanguine according to the character of the disease. But the worst alterations of the self come from present perversions of sensibility and impulse which leave the past undisturbed, but induce the patient to think that the present *Me* is an altogether new personage. Something of this sort happens normally in the rapid expansion of the whole character, intellectual as well as volitional, which takes place after the time of puberty. The pathological cases are curious enough to merit longer notice.

The basis of our personality, as M. Ribot says, is that feeling of our vitality which, because it is so perpetually present, remains in the background of our consciousness.

" It is the basis because, always present, always acting, without peace or rest, it knows neither sleep nor fainting, and lasts as long as life itself, of which it is one form. It serves as a support to that self-conscious *me* which memory constitutes, it is the medium of association among its other parts. . . . Suppose now that it were possible at once to change our body and put another into its place: skeleton, vessels, viscera, muscles, skin, everything made new, except the nervous system with its stored-up memory of the past. There can be no doubt that in such a case the afflux of unaccustomed vital sensations would produce the gravest disorders. Between the old sense of existence engraved on the nervous system, and the new one acting with all the intensity of its reality and novelty, there would be irreconcilable contradiction."

What the particular perversions of the bodily sensibility may be which give rise to these contradictions is, for the most part, impossible for a sound-minded person to conceive. One patient has another self that repeats all his thoughts for him. Others, amongst whom are some of the first characters in history, have internal dæmons who speak with them and are replied to. Another feels that someone 'makes' his thoughts for him. Another has two bodies, lying in different beds. Some patients feel as if they had lost parts of their bodies, teeth, brain, stomach, etc. In some it is made of wood, glass, butter, etc. In some it does not exist any longer, or is dead, or is a foreign object quite separate from the speaker's self. Occasionally, parts of the body lose their connection for consciousness with the rest, and are treated as belonging to another person and moved by a hostile will. Thus the right hand may fight with the left as with an enemy. Or the cries of the patient himself are assigned to another person with whom the patient expresses sympathy. The literature of insanity is filled with narratives of such illusions as these. M. Taine quotes from a patient of Dr. Krishaber an account of sufferings, from which it will be seen how completely aloof from what is normal a man's experience may suddenly become:

"After the first or second day it was for some weeks impossible to observe or analyze myself. The suffering—angina pectoris—was too overwhelming. It was not till the first days of January that I could give an account to myself of what I experienced. . . . Here is the first thing of which I retain a clear remembrance. I was alone, and already a prey to permanent visual trouble, when I was suddenly seized with a visual trouble infinitely more pronounced. Objects grew small and receded to infinite distances—men and things together. I was myself immeasurably far away. I looked about me with terror and astonishment; *the world was escaping from me.* . . . I remarked at the same time that my voice was extremely far away from me, that it sounded no longer as if mine. I struck the ground with my foot, and perceived its resistance; but this resistance seemed illusory—not that the soil was soft, but that the weight of my body was reduced to almost nothing. . . . I had the feeling of being without weight. . . ." In addition to being so distant, "objects appeared to me *flat*. When I spoke with anyone, I saw him like an image cut out of paper with no relief. . . . This sensation lasted intermittently for two years. . . . Constantly it seemed as if my legs did not belong to me. It was almost as bad with my arms. As for my head, it seemed no longer to exist. . . . I appeared to myself to act automatically, by an impulsion foreign to myself. . . . There was inside of me a new being, and another part of myself, the old being, which took no interest in the newcomer. I distinctly remember saying to myself that the sufferings of this new being were to me indifferent. I was never really dupe of these illusions, but my mind grew often tired of incessantly correcting the new impressions, and I let myself go and live the unhappy life of this new entity. I had an ardent desire to see my old world again, to get back to my old self. This desire kept me from killing myself. . . . I was another, and I hated, I despised this other; he was perfectly odious to me; it was certainly another who had taken my form and assumed my functions." *

In cases like this, it is as certain that the *I* is unaltered as that the *Me* is changed. That is to say, the present Thought of the patient is cognitive of both the old Me and the new, so long as its memory holds good. Only, within that objective sphere which formerly lent itself so simply to the judgment of recognition and of egoistic appropriation, strange perplexities have arisen. The present and the past, both seen therein, will not unite. Where is my old Me? What is this new one? Are they the same? Or have I two? Such questions, answered by whatever theory the patient is able to conjure up as plausible, form the beginning of his insane life.

---

* De l'Intelligence, 3me édition (1878), vol. II. p. 461, note.

β. The phenomenon of *alternating personality* in its simplest phases seems based on lapses of memory. Any man becomes, as we say, *inconsistent* with himself if he forgets his engagements, pledges, knowledges, and habits; and it is merely a question of degree at what point we shall say that his personality is changed. But in the pathological cases known as those of double or alternate personality the loss of memory is abrupt, and is usually preceded by a period of unconsciousness or syncope lasting a variable length of time. In the hypnotic trance we can easily produce an alteration of the personality, either by telling the subject to forget all that has happened to him since such or such a date, in which case he becomes (it may be) a child again, or by telling him he is another altogether imaginary personage, in which case all facts about himself seem for the time being to lapse from out his mind, and he throws himself into the new character with a vivacity proportionate to the amount of histrionic imagination which he possesses. But in the pathological cases the transformation is spontaneous. The most famous case, perhaps, on record is that of Félida X., reported by Dr. Azam of Bordeaux. At the age of fourteen this woman began to pass into a 'secondary' state characterized by a change in her general disposition and character, as if certain 'inhibitions,' previously existing, were suddenly removed. During the secondary state she remembered the first state, but on emerging from it into the first state she remembered nothing of the second. At the age of forty-four the duration of the secondary state (which was on the whole superior in quality to the original state) had gained upon the latter so much as to occupy most of her time. During it she remembers the events belonging to the original state, **but** her complete oblivion of the secondary state when the original state recurs is often very distressing to her, as, for example, when the transition takes place in a carriage on her way to a funeral, and she has no idea which **one of her friends** may be dead. She actually became pregnant during one of her early secondary states, and during her first state had no knowledge of how it had come to pass. Her distress at these blanks of memory is sometimes intense and once drove her to attempt suicide.

M. Pierre Janet describes a still more remarkable case as follows: " Léonie B., whose life sounds more like an improbable romance than a genuine history, has had attacks of natural somnambulism since the age of three years. She has been hypnotized constantly by all sorts of persons from the age of sixteen upwards, and she is now forty-five. Whilst her normal life developed in one way in the midst of her poor country surroundings, her second life was passed in drawing-rooms and doctors' offices, and naturally took an entirely different direction. To-day, when in her normal state, this poor peasant woman is a serious and rather sad person, calm and slow, very mild with every one, and extremely timid: to look at her one would never suspect the personage which she contains. But hardly is she put to sleep hypnotically when a metamorphosis occurs. Her face is no longer the same. She keeps her eyes closed, it is true, but the acuteness of her other senses supplies their place. She is gay, noisy, restless, sometimes insupportably so. She remains good-natured, but has acquired a singular tendency to irony and sharp jesting. Nothing is more curious than to hear her after a sitting when she has received a visit from strangers who wished to see her asleep. She gives a word-portrait of them, apes their manners, claims to know their little ridiculous aspects and passions, and for each invents a romance. To this character must be added the possession of an enormous number of recollections, whose existence she does not even suspect when awake, for her amnesia is then complete. . . . She refuses the name of Léonie and takes that of Léontine (Léonie 2) to which her first magnetizers had accustomed her. 'That good woman is not myself,' she says, 'she is too stupid!' To herself, Léontine, or Léonie 2, she attributes all the sensations and all the actions, in a word all the conscious experiences, which she has undergone *in somnambulism*, and knits them together to make the history of her already long life. To Léonie 1 [as M. Janet calls the waking woman], on the other hand, she exclusively ascribes the events lived through in waking hours. I was at first struck by an important exception to the rule, and was disposed to think that there might be something arbitrary in this partition of her recollections. In the normal state Léonie has a husband and children; but Léonie 2, the somnambulist, whilst acknowledging the children as her own, attributes the husband to 'the other.' This choice was perhaps explicable, but it followed no rule. It was not till later that I learned that her magnetizers in early days, as audacious as certain hypnotizers of recent date, had somnambulized her for her first *accouchements*, and that she had lapsed into that state spontaneously in the later ones. Léonie 2 was thus quite right in ascribing to herself the children—it was she who had had them, and the rule that her first trance-state forms a different personality was not broken. But it is the same with her second or deepest state of trance. When after the renewed passes, syncope, etc., she reaches the condition which I have called Léonie 3, she is another person still. Serious and grave, instead of being a restless child, she speaks slowly and moves but little. Again she separates herself from the waking Léonie 1. 'A good but rather stupid woman,' she says, 'and not me.' And she also separates herself from Léonie 2: 'How can you see anything of me in that crazy creature?' she says. 'Fortunately I am nothing for her.'"

γ. In '*mediumships*' or '*possessions*' the invasion and the passing away of the secondary state are both relatively abrupt, and the duration of the state is usually short—i.e., from a few minutes to a few hours. Whenever the secondary state is well developed, no memory for aught that happened during it remains after the primary consciousness comes back. The subject during the secondary consciousness speaks, writes, or acts as if animated by a foreign person, and often names this foreign person and gives his history. In old times the foreign 'control' was usually a demon, and is so now in communities which favor that belief. With us he gives himself out at the worst for an Indian or other grotesquely speaking but harmless personage. Usually he purports to be the spirit of a dead person known or unknown to those present, and the subject is then what we call a 'medium.' Mediumistic possession in all its grades seems to form a perfectly natural special type of alternate personality, and the susceptibility to it in some form is by no means an uncommon gift, in persons who have no other obvious nervous anomaly. The phenomena are very intricate, and are only just beginning to be studied in a proper scientific way. The lowest phase of mediumship is automatic writing, and the lowest grade of that is where the Subject knows what words are coming, but feels impelled to write them as if from without. Then comes writing unconsciously, even whilst engaged in reading or talk. Inspirational speaking, playing on musical instruments, etc., also belong to the relatively lower phases of possession, in which the normal self is not excluded from conscious participation in the performance, though their initiative seems to come from elsewhere. In the highest phase the trance is complete, the voice, language, and everything are changed, and there is no after-memory whatever until the next trance comes. One curious thing about trance-utterances is their generic similarity in different individuals. The 'control' here in America is either a grotesque, slangy, and flippant personage ('Indian' controls, calling the ladies 'squaws,' the men 'braves,' the house a 'wigwam,' etc., etc., are excessively common; or, if he ventures on higher intellectual flights, he abounds in a curiously vague optimistic philosophy-and-water, in which phrases about spirit, harmony, beauty, law, progression, development, etc., keep recurring. It seems exactly as if one author composed more than half of the trance-messages, no matter by whom they are uttered. Whether all sub-conscious selves are peculiarly susceptible to a certain stratum of the *Zeitgeist,* and get their inspiration from it, I know not; but this is obviously the case with the secondary selves which become 'developed' in spiritualist circles. There the beginnings of the medium trance are indistinguishable from effects of hypnotic suggestion. The subject assumes the rôle of a medium simply because opinion expects it of him under the conditions which are present; and carries it out with a feebleness or a vivacity proportionate to his histrionic gifts. But the odd thing is that persons unexposed to spiritualist traditions will so often act in the same way when they become entranced, speak in the name of the departed, go through the motions of their several death-agonies, send messages about their happy home in the summer-land, and describe the ailments of those present.

I have no theory to publish of these cases, the actual beginning of several of which I have personally seen. I am, however, persuaded by abundant acquaintance with the trances of one medium that the 'control' may be altogether different from any *possible* waking self of the person. In the case I have in mind, it professes to be a certain departed French doctor; and is, I am convinced, acquainted with facts about the circumstances, and the living and dead relatives and acquaintances, of numberless sitters whom the medium never met before, and of whom she has never heard the names. I record my bare opinion here unsupported by the evidence, not, of course, in order to convert anyone to my view, but because I am persuaded that a serious study of these trance-phenomena is one of the greatest needs of psychology, and think that my personal confession may possibly draw a reader or two into a field which **the** *soi-disant* 'scientist' usually refuses to explore.*

---

* Some of the evidence for this medium's supernormal powers is

Review, and Psychological Conclusion.—To sum up this long chapter:—The consciousness of Self involves a stream of thought, each part of which as 'I' can remember those which went before, know the things they knew, and care paramountly for certain ones among them as '*Me*,' and *appropriate to these* the rest. This Me is an empirical aggregate of things objectively known. The *I* which knows them cannot itself be an aggregate; neither for psychological purposes need it be an unchanging metaphysical entity like the Soul, or a principle like the transcendental Ego, viewed as 'out of time.' It is a *thought*, at each moment different from that of the last moment, but *appropriative* of the latter, together with all that the latter called its own. All the experiential facts find their place in this description, unencumbered with any hypothesis save that of the existence of passing thoughts or states of mind.

If passing thoughts be the directly verifiable existents which no school has hitherto doubted them to be, then they are the only 'Knower' of which Psychology, treated as a natural science, need take any account. The only pathway that I can discover for bringing in a more transcendental Thinker would be to deny that we have any such *direct* knowledge of the existence of our 'states of consciousness' as common-sense supposes us to possess. The existence of the 'states' in question would then be a mere hypothesis, or one way of asserting that there *must be* a knower correlative to all this known; but the problem *who that knower is* would have become a metaphysical problem. With the question once stated in these terms, the notion either of a Spirit of the world which thinks through us, or that of a set of individual substantial souls, must be considered as *primâ facie* on a par with our own 'psychological' solution, and discussed impartially. I myself believe that

---

given in The Proceedings of the Society for Psychical Research, vol. VI. p. 436, and in the last Part of vol. VII (1892).

room for much future inquiry lies in this direction. The
'states of mind' which every psychologist believes in are by
no means clearly apprehensible, if distinguished from their
objects. But to doubt them lies beyond the scope of our
natural-science (see p. 1) point of view. And in this book
the provisional solution which we have reached must be
the final word: the thoughts themselves are the thinkers.

CHAPTER XIII.

ATTENTION.

The Narrowness of Consciousness —One of the most extraordinary facts of our life is that, although we are besieged at every moment by impressions from our whole sensory surface, we notice so very small a part of them. The sum total of our impressions never enters into our *experience*, consciously so called, which runs through this sum total like a tiny rill through a broad flowery mead. Yet the physical impressions which do not count are *there* as much as those which do, and affect our sense-organs just as energetically. Why they fail to pierce the mind is a mystery, which is only named and not explained when we invoke *die Enge des Bewusstseins*, 'the narrowness of consciousness,' as its ground.

Its Physiological Ground.—Our consciousness certainly is narrow, when contrasted with the breadth of our sensory surface and the mass of incoming currents which are at all times pouring in. Evidently no current can be recorded in conscious experience unless it succeed in penetrating to the hemispheres and filling their pathways by the processes set up. When an incoming current thus occupies the hemispheres with its consequences, other currents are for the time kept out. They may show their faces at the door, but are turned back until the actual possessors of the place are tired. Physiologically, then, the narrowness of consciousness seems to depend on the fact that the activity of the hemispheres tends at all times to be a consolidated and unified affair, determinable now by this current and now by that, but determinable only as a whole. The ideas correlative to the reigning system of processes are those which are said to 'interest' us at the time; and thus that selective character of our attention on which so much stress was laid on pp. 173 ff. appears to find a physiological ground. At all times, however, there is a liability to disintegration of the reigning system. The consolidation is seldom quite complete, the excluded currents are not wholly abortive, their presence affects the 'fringe' and margin of our thought.

Dispersed Attention.—Sometimes, indeed, the normal consolidation seems hardly to exist. At such moments it is possible that cerebral activity sinks to a minimum. Most of us probably fall several times a day into a fit somewhat like this: The eyes are fixed on vacancy, the sounds of the world melt into confused unity, the attention is dispersed so that the whole body is felt, as it were, at once, and the foreground of consciousness is filled, if by anything, by a sort of solemn sense of surrender to the empty passing of time. In the dim background of our mind we know meanwhile what we ought to be doing: getting up, dressing ourselves, answering the person who has spoken to us, trying to make the next step in our reasoning. But somehow we cannot *start;* the *pensée de derrière la tête* fails to pierce the shell of lethargy that wraps our state about. Every moment we expect the spell to break, for we know no reason why it should continue. But it does continue, pulse after pulse, and we float with it, until —also without reason that we can discover—an energy is given, something—we know not what—enables us to gather ourselves together, we wink our eyes, we shake our heads, the background-ideas become effective, and the wheels of life go round again.

This is the extreme of what is called dispersed attention. Between this extreme and the extreme of concentrated attention, in which absorption in the interest of the moment is so complete that grave bodily injuries may be unfelt, there are intermediate degrees, and these have been studied experimentally. The problem is known as that of

ATTENTION. 219

The Span of Consciousness.—How many objects can we attend to at once when they are not embraced in one conceptual system? Prof. Cattell experimented with combinations of letters exposed to the eye for so short a fraction of a second that attention to them in succession seemed to be ruled out. When the letters formed familiar words, three times as many of them could be named as when their combination was meaningless. If the words formed a sentence, twice as many could be caught as when they had no connection. "The sentence was then apprehended as a whole. If not apprehended thus, almost nothing is apprehended of the several words; but if the sentence as a whole is apprehended, then the words appear very distinct."

A word is a conceptual system in which the letters do not enter consciousness separately, as they do when apprehended alone. A sentence flashed at once upon the eye is such a system relatively to its words. A conceptual system may *mean* many sensible objects, may be translated later into them, but as an actual existent mental state, it does not *consist of* the consciousnesses of these objects. When I think of the word *man* as a whole, for instance, what is in my mind is something different from what is there when I think of the letters *m*, *a*, and *n*, as so many disconnected data.

When data are so disconnected that we have no conception which embraces them together it is much harder to apprehend several of them at once, and the mind tends to let go of one whilst it attends to another. Still, within limits this can be avoided. M. Paulhan has experimented on the matter by declaiming one poem aloud whilst he repeated a different one mentally, or by writing one sentence whilst speaking another, or by performing calculations on paper whilst reciting poetry. He found that "the most favorable condition for the doubling of the mind was its simultaneous application to two heterogeneous operations. Two operations of the same sort, two multiplications, two recitations, or the reciting of one poem and writing of another, render the process more uncertain and difficult."

M. Paulhan compared the time occupied by the same two operations done simultaneously or in succession, and found that there was often a considerable gain of time from doing them simultaneously. For instance:

"I multiply 421 312 212 by 2; the operation takes 6 seconds; the recitation of four verses also takes 6 seconds. But the two operations done at once only take 6 seconds, so that there is no loss of time from combining them."

If, then, by the original question, how many objects can we attend to at once, be meant how many entirely disconnected systems or processes can go on simultaneously, the answer is, *not easily more than one, unless the processes are very habitual; but then two, or even three*, without very much oscillation of the attention. Where, however, the processes are less automatic, as in the story of Julius Cæsar dictating four letters whilst he writes a fifth, there must be a rapid oscillation of the mind from one to the next, and no consequent gain of time.

When the things to be attended to are minute sensations, and when the effort is to be exact in noting them, it is found that attention to one interferes a good deal with the perception of the other. A good deal of fine work has been done in this field by Professor Wundt. He tried to note the exact position on a dial of a rapidly revolving hand, at the moment when a bell struck. Here were two disparate sensations, one of vision, the other of sound, to be noted together. But it was found that in a long and patient research, the eye-impression could seldom or never be noted at the exact moment when the bell actually struck. An earlier or a later point were all that could be seen.

The Varieties of Attention.—Attention may be divided into kinds in various ways. It is either to

a) Objects of sense (sensorial attention); or to

ATTENTION. 221

b) Ideal or represented objects (intellectual attention). It is either

c) Immediate; or

d) Derived: immediate, when the topic or stimulus is interesting in itself, without relation to anything else; derived, when it owes its interest to association with some other immediately interesting thing. What I call derived attention has been named 'apperceptive' attention. Furthermore, Attention may be either

e) Passive, reflex, involuntary, effortless; or

f) Active and voluntary.

Voluntary attention is always derived; we never make an *effort* to attend to an object except for the sake of some *remote* interest which the effort will serve. But both sensorial and intellectual attention may be either passive or voluntary.

In *involuntary attention* of the *immediate sensorial* sort the stimulus is either a sense-impression, very intense, voluminous, or sudden; or it is an *instinctive* stimulus, a perception which, by reason of its nature rather than its mere force, appeals to some one of our congenital impulses and has a directly exciting quality. In the chapter on Instinct we shall see how these stimuli differ from one animal to another, and what most of them are in man: strange things, moving things, wild animals, bright things, pretty things, metallic things, words, blows, blood, etc., etc., etc.

Sensitiveness to immediately exciting sensorial stimuli characterizes the attention of childhood and youth. In mature age we have generally selected those stimuli which are connected with one or more so-called permanent interests, and our attention has grown irresponsive to the rest. But childhood is characterized by great active energy, and has few organized interests by which to meet new impressions and decide whether they are worthy of notice or not, and the consequence is that extreme mobility of the attention with which we are all familiar in children, and which makes of their first lessons such chaotic affairs. Any strong sensation whatever produces accommodation of the organs which perceive it, and absolute oblivion, for the time being, of the task in hand. This reflex and passive character of the attention which, as a French writer says, makes the child seem to belong less to himself than to every object which happens to catch his notice, is the first thing which the teacher must overcome. It never is overcome in some people, whose work, to the end of life, gets done in the interstices of their mind-wandering.

The passive sensorial attention is *derived* when the impression, without being either strong or of an instinctively exciting nature, is connected by previous experience and education with things that are so. These things may be called the *motives* of the attention. The impression draws an interest from them, or perhaps it even fuses into a single complex object with them; the result is that it is brought into the focus of the mind. A faint tap *per se* is not an interesting sound; it may well escape being discriminated from the general rumor of the world. But when it is a signal, as that of a lover on the window-pane, hardly will it go unperceived. Herbart writes:

"How a bit of bad grammar wounds the ear of the purist! How a false note hurts the musician! or an offence against good manners the man of the world! How rapid is progress in a science when its first principles have been so well impressed upon us that we reproduce them mentally with perfect distinctness and ease! How slow and uncertain, on the other hand, is our learning of the principles themselves, when familiarity with the still more elementary percepts connected with the subject has not given us an adequate predisposition!—Apperceptive attention may be plainly observed in very small children when, hearing the speech of their elders, as yet unintelligible to them, they suddenly catch a single known word here and there, and repeat it to themselves; yes! even in the dog who looks round at us when we speak of him and pronounce his name. Not far removed is the talent which mind-wandering school-boys display during the hours of instruction, of noticing every moment in which the teacher tells a story. I remember classes in which, instruction being uninteresting, and discipline relaxed, a buzzing murmur was always to be heard, which invariably stopped for as long a time as an anecdote lasted. How could the boys, since they seemed to hear nothing, notice when the anecdote began? Doubtless most of them always heard something of the teacher's talk; but most of it had no connection with their previous knowledge and occupations, and therefore the separate words no sooner entered their consciousness than they fell out of it again; but, on the other hand, no sooner did the words awaken old thoughts, forming strongly-connected series with which the new impression easily combined, than out of new and old together a total interest resulted which drove the vagrant ideas below the threshold of consciousness, and brought for a while settled attention into their place."

Involuntary intellectual attention is immediate when we follow in thought a train of images exciting or interesting *per se;* derived, when the images are interesting only as means to a remote end, or merely because they are associated with something which makes them dear. The brain-currents may then form so solidly unified a system, and the absorption in their object be so deep, as to banish not only ordinary sensations, but even the severest pain. Pascal, Wesley, Robert Hall, are said to have had this capacity. Dr. Carpenter says of himself that "he has frequently begun a lecture whilst suffering neuralgic pain so severe as to make him apprehend that he would find it impossible to proceed; yet no sooner has he by a determined effort fairly launched himself into the stream of thought, than he has found himself continuously borne along without the least distraction, until the end has come, and the attention has been released; when the pain has recurred with a force that has overmastered all resistance, making him wonder how he could have ever ceased to feel it." *

Voluntary Attention.—Dr. Carpenter speaks of launching himself by a determined *effort*. This effort characterizes what we called *active or voluntary attention*. It is a feeling which everyone knows, but which most people would call quite indescribable. We get it in the sensorial sphere whenever we seek to catch an impression of extreme *faintness*, be it of sight, hearing, taste, smell, or touch; we get it whenever we seek to *discriminate* a sensation merged in a mass of others that are similar; we get it whenever we *resist the attractions* of more potent stimuli and keep our mind occupied with some object that is naturally unimpressive. We get it in the intellectual sphere under exactly similar conditions: as when we strive to sharpen and make distinct an idea which we but vaguely seem to have; or painfully discriminate a shade of meaning from its similars; or resolutely hold fast to a thought so discordant with our impulses that, if left unaided, it would quickly yield place to images of an exciting and impassioned kind. All forms of attentive effort would be exercised at once by one whom we might suppose at a dinner-party resolutely to listen to a neighbor giving him insipid and unwelcome advice in a low voice, whilst all around the guests were loudly laughing and talking about exciting and interesting things.

There is no such thing as voluntary attention sustained for more than a few seconds at a time. What is called sustained voluntary attention is a repetition of successive efforts which bring back the topic to the mind. The topic once brought back, if a congenial one, *develops;* and if its development is interesting it engages the attention passively for a time. Dr. Carpenter, a moment back, described the stream of thought, once entered, as 'bearing him along.'

---

* Mental Physiol., § 124. The oft-cited case of soldiers in battle not perceiving that they are wounded is of an analogous sort.

This passive interest may be short or long. As soon as it flags, the attention is diverted by some irrelevant thing, and then a voluntary effort may bring it back to the topic again; and so on, under favorable conditions, for hours together. During all this time, however, note that it is not an identical *object* in the psychological sense, but a succession of mutually related objects forming an identical *topic* only, upon which the attention is fixed. *No one can possibly attend continuously to an object that does not change.*

Now there are always some objects that for the time being *will not develop*. They simply *go out ;* and to keep the mind upon anything related to them requires such incessantly renewed effort that the most resolute Will ere long gives out and lets its thought follow the more stimulating solicitations after it has withstood them for what length of time it can. There are topics known to every man from which he shies like a frightened horse, and which to get a glimpse of is to shun. Such are his ebbing assets to the spendthrift in full career. But why single out the spendthrift, when to every man actuated by passion the thought of interests which negate the passion can hardly for more than a fleeting instant stay before the mind? It is like 'memento mori' in the heyday of the pride of life. Nature rises at such suggestions, and excludes them from the view:—How long, O healthy reader, can you now continue thinking of your tomb?—In milder instances the difficulty is as great, especially when the brain is fagged. One snatches at any and every passing pretext, no matter how trivial or external, to escape from the odiousness of the matter in hand. I know a person, for example, who will poke the fire, set chairs straight, pick dust-specks from the floor, arrange his table, snatch up the newspaper, take down any book which catches his eye, trim his nails, waste the morning *anyhow*, in short, and all without premeditation,—simply because the only thing he *ought* to attend to is the preparation of a noonday lesson in formal logic which he detests. Anything but *that!*

Once more, the object must change. When it is one of sight, it will actually become invisible; when of hearing, inaudible,—if we attend to it too unmovingly. Helmholtz, who has put his sensorial attention to the severest tests, by using his eyes on objects which in common life are expressly overlooked, makes some interesting remarks on this point in his section on retinal rivalry. The phenomenon called by that name is this, that if we look with each eye upon a different picture (as in the annexed stereoscopic slide), sometimes one picture, sometimes the other, or

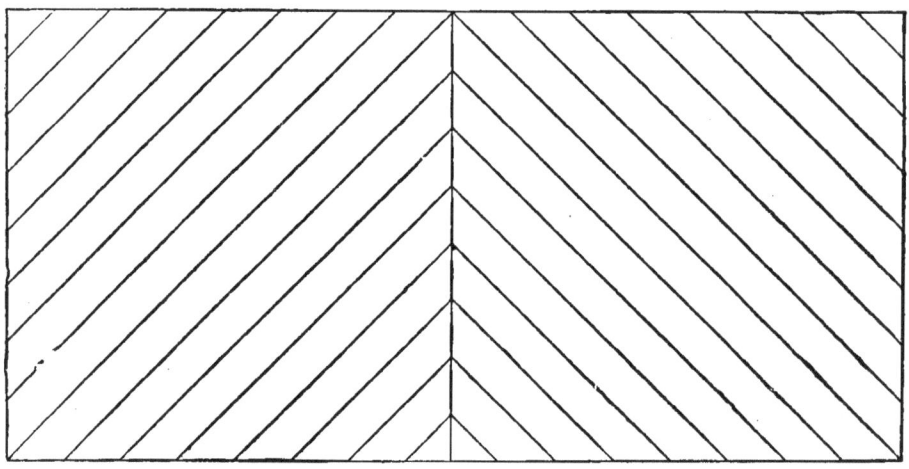

Fig. 54.

parts of both, will come to consciousness, but hardly ever both combined. Helmholtz now says:

"I find that I am able to attend voluntarily, now to one and now to the other system of lines; and that then this system remains visible alone for a certain time, whilst the other completely vanishes. This happens, for example, whenever I try to count the lines first of one and then of the other system. . . . But it is extremely hard to chain the attention down to one of the systems for long, unless we associate with our looking some distinct purpose which keeps the activity of the attention perpetually renewed.

Such a one is counting the lines, comparing their intervals, or the like. An equilibrium of the attention, persistent for any length of time, is under no circumstances attainable. The natural tendency of attention when left to itself is to wander to ever new things; and so soon as the interest of its object is over, so soon as nothing new is to be noticed there, it passes, in spite of our will, to something else. *If we wish to keep it upon one and the same object, we must seek constantly to find out something new about the latter*, especially if other powerful impressions are attracting us away."

These words of Helmholtz are of fundamental importance. And if true of sensorial attention, how much more true are they of the intellectual variety! The *conditio sine quâ non* of sustained attention to a given topic of thought is that we should roll it over and over incessantly and consider different aspects and relations of it in turn. Only in pathological states will a fixed and ever monotonously recurring idea possess the mind.

Genius and Attention.—And now we can see why it is that what is called sustained attention is the easier, the richer in acquisitions and the fresher and more original the mind. In such minds, subjects bud and sprout and grow. At every moment, they please by a new consequence and rivet the attention afresh. But an intellect unfurnished with materials, stagnant, unoriginal, will hardly be likely to consider any subject long. A glance exhausts its possibilities of interest. Geniuses are commonly believed to excel other men in their power of sustained attention. In most of them, it is to be feared, the so-called 'power' is of the passive sort. Their ideas coruscate, every subject branches infinitely before their fertile minds, and so for hours they may be rapt. *But it is their genius making them attentive, not their attention making geniuses of them.* And, when we come down to the root of the matter, we see that they differ from ordinary men less in the character of their attention than in the nature of the objects upon which it is successively bestowed. In the genius, these form a concatenated series, suggesting each other mutually by some rational law. Therefore we call the attention 'sustained' and the topic of meditation for hours 'the same.' In the common man the series is for the most part incoherent, the objects have no rational bond, and we call the attention wandering and unfixed.

It is probable that genius tends actually to prevent a man from acquiring habits of voluntary attention, and that moderate intellectual endowments are the soil in which we may best expect, here as elsewhere, the virtues of the will strictly so called, to thrive. But, whether the attention come by grace of genius or by dint of will, the longer one does attend to a topic the more mastery of it one has. And the faculty of voluntarily bringing back a wandering attention over and over again is the very root of judgment, character, and will. No one is *compos sui* if he have it not. An education which should improve this faculty would be *the* education *par excellence*. But it is easier to define this ideal than to give practical directions for bringing it about. The only general pedagogic maxim bearing on attention is that the more interests the child has in advance in the subject, the better he will attend. Induct him therefore in such a way as to knit each new thing on to some acquisition already there; and if possible awaken curiosity, so that the new thing shall seem to come as an answer, or part of an answer, to a question preëxisting in his mind.

The Physiological Conditions of Attention.—These seem to be the following:

1) *The appropriate cortical centre must be excited ideationally as well as sensorially, before attention to an object can take place.*

2) *The sense-organ must then adapt itself to clearest reception of the object, by the adjustment of its muscular apparatus.*

3) *In all probability a certain afflux of blood to the cortical centre must ensue.*

ATTENTION.

Of this third condition I will say no more, since we have no proof of it in detail, and I state it on the faith of general analogies. Conditions 1) and 2), however, are verifiable; and the best order will be to take the latter first.

The Adaptation of the Sense-organ.—This occurs not only in sensorial but also in intellectual attention to an object.

That it is present when we attend to *sensible* things is obvious. When we look or listen we accommodate our eyes and ears involuntarily, and we turn our head and body as well; when we taste or smell we adjust the tongue, lips, and respiration to the object; in feeling a surface we move the palpatory organ in a suitable way; in all these acts, besides making involuntary muscular contractions of a positive sort, we inhibit others which might interfere with the result—we close the eyes in tasting, suspend the respiration in listening, etc. The result is a more or less massive organic feeling that attention is going on. This organic feeling we usually treat as part of the sense of our *own activity*, although it comes in to us from our organs after they are accommodated. Any object, then, if *immediately* exciting, causes a reflex accommodation of the sense-organ, which has two results—first, the feeling of activity in question; and second, the object's increase in clearness.

But in *intellectual* attention similar feelings of activity occur. Fechner was the first, I believe, to analyze these feelings, and discriminate them from the stronger ones just named. He writes:

" When we transfer the attention from objects of one sense to those of another, we have an indescribable feeling (though at the same time one perfectly determinate, and reproducible at pleasure), of altered *direction* or differently localized tension (*Spannung*). We feel a strain forward in the eyes. one directed sidewise in the ears, increasing with the degree of our attention, and changing according as we look at an object carefully, or listen to something attentively; and we speak accordingly of *straining the attention*. The difference is most plainly felt when the attention oscillates rapidly between eye and ear; and the feeling localizes itself with most decided difference in regard to the various sense-organs, according as we wish to discriminate a thing delicately by touch, taste, or smell.

" But now I have, when I try to vividly recall a picture of memory or fancy, a feeling perfectly analogous to that which I experience when I seek to apprehend a thing keenly by eye or ear; and this analogous feeling is very differently localized. While in sharpest possible attention to real objects (as well as to after-images) the strain is plainly forwards, and (when the attention changes from one sense to another) only alters its direction between the several external sense-organs, leaving the rest of the head free from strain, the case is different in memory or fancy, for here the feeling withdraws entirely from the external sense-organs, and seems rather to take refuge in that part of the head which the brain fills. If I wish, for example, to *recall* a place or person, it will arise before me with vividness, not according as I strain my attention forwards, but rather in proportion as I, so to speak, retract it backwards."

In myself the 'backward retraction' which is felt during attention to ideas of memory, etc., seems to be principally constituted by the feeling of an actual rolling outwards and upwards of the eyeballs, such as occurs in sleep, and is the exact opposite of their behavior when we look at a physical thing.

This accommodation of the sense-organ is not, however, the *essential* process, even in sensorial attention. It is a secondary result which may be prevented from occurring, as certain observations show. Usually, it is true that no object lying in the marginal portions of the field of vision can catch our attention without at the same time 'catching our eye'—that is, fatally provoking such movements of rotation and accommodation as will focus its image on the fovea, or point of greatest sensibility. Practice, however, enables us, *with effort,* to attend to a marginal object whilst keeping the eyes immovable. The object under these circumstances never becomes perfectly distinct —the place of its image on the retina makes distinctness impossible—but (as anyone can satisfy himself by trying) we become more vividly conscious of it than we were before the effort was made. Teachers thus notice the acts of children in the school-room at whom they appear not to be looking. Women in general train their peripheral visual attention more than men. Helmholtz states the fact so strikingly that I will quote his observation in full. He was trying to combine in a single solid percept pairs of stereoscopic pictures illuminated instantaneously by the electric spark. The pictures were in a dark box which the spark from time to time lighted up; and, to keep the eyes from wandering betweenwhiles, a pin-hole was pricked through the middle of each picture, through which the light of the room came, so that each eye had presented to it during the dark intervals a single bright point. With parallel optical axes these points combined into a single image; and the slightest movement of the eyeballs was betrayed by this image at once becoming double. Helmholtz now found that simple linear figures could, when the eyes were thus kept immovable, be perceived as solids at a single flash of the spark. But when the figures were complicated photographs, many successive flashes were required to grasp their totality.

"Now it is interesting," he says, "to find that, although we keep steadily fixating the pin-holes and never allow their combined image to break into two, we can nevertheless, before the spark comes, keep our attention voluntarily turned to any particular portion we please of the dark field, so as then, when the spark comes, to receive an impression only from such parts of the picture as lie in this region. In this respect, then, our attention is quite independent of the position and accommodation of the eyes, and of any known alteration in these organs, and free to direct itself by a conscious and voluntary effort upon any selected portion of a dark and undifferenced field of view. This is one of the most important observations for a future theory of attention." *

The Ideational Excitement of the Centre.—But if the peripheral part of the picture in this experiment be not physically accommodated for, what is meant by its sharing our attention? What happens when we 'distribute' or 'disperse' the latter upon a thing for which we remain unwilling to 'adjust'? This leads us to that second feature in the process, the '*ideational excitement*' of which we spoke. *The effort to attend to the marginal region of the picture consists in nothing more nor less than the effort to form as clear an* IDEA *as is possible of what is there portrayed.* The idea is to come to the help of the sensation and make it more distinct. It may come with effort, and such a mode of coming is the remaining part of what we know as our attention's 'strain' under the circumstances. Let us show how universally present in our acts of attention is this anticipatory thinking of the thing to which we attend. Mr. Lewes's name of *preperception* seems the best possible designation for this imagining of an experience before it occurs.

It must as a matter of course be present when the attention is of the intellectual variety, for the thing attended to then *is* nothing but an idea, an inward reproduction or conception. If then we prove ideal construction of the object to be present in *sensorial* attention, it will be present everywhere. When, however, sensorial attention is at its height, it is impossible to tell how much of the percept comes from without and how much from within; but if we find that the *preparation* we make for it always partly consists of the creation of an imaginary duplicate of the object in the mind, that will be enough to establish the point in dispute.

* Physiol. Optik, p. 741.

In reaction-time experiments, keeping our mind intent upon the motion about to be made shortens the time. This shortening we ascribed in Chap. VIII to the fact that the signal when it comes finds the motor-centre already charged almost to the explosion-point in advance. Expectant attention to a reaction thus goes with sub-excitement of the centre concerned.

Where the impression to be caught is very weak, the way not to miss it is to sharpen our attention for it by preliminary contact with it in a stronger form. Helmholtz says: "If we wish to begin to observe overtones, it is advisable, just before the sound which is to be analyzed, to sound very softly the note of which we are in search.... If you place the resonator which corresponds to a certain overtone, for example g' of the sound c, against your ear, and then make the note c sound, you will hear g' much strengthened by the resonator.... This strengthening by the resonator can be used to make the naked ear attentive to the sound which it is to catch. For when the resonator is gradually removed, the g' grows weaker; but the attention, once directed to it, holds it now more easily fast, and the observer hears the tone g' now in the natural unaltered sound of the note with his unaided ear."

Wundt, commenting on experiences of this sort, says that "The same thing is to be noticed in weak or fugitive visual impressions. Illuminate a drawing by electric sparks separated by considerable intervals, and after the first, and often after the second and third spark, hardly anything will be recognized. But the confused image is held fast in memory; each successive illumination completes it; and so at last we attain to a clearer perception. The primary motive to this inward activity proceeds usually from the outer impression itself. We hear a sound in which, from certain associations, we suspect a certain overtone; the next thing is to recall the overtone in memory; and finally we catch it in the sound we hear. Or perhaps we see some mineral substance we have met before; the impression awakens the memory-image, which again more or less completely melts with the impression itself. . . . Different qualties of impression require disparate adaptations. And we remark that our feeling of the *strain* of our inward attentiveness increases with every increase in the strength of the impressions on whose perception we are intent."

The natural way of conceiving all this is under the symbolic form of a brain-cell played upon from two directions. Whilst the object excites it from without, other brain-cells arouse it from within. *The plenary energy of the brain-cell demands the co-operation of both factors:* not when merely present, but when both present and inwardly imagined, is the object fully attended to and perceived.

A few additional experiences will now be perfectly clear. Helmholtz, for instance, adds this observation concerning the stereoscopic pictures lit by the electric spark. "In pictures," he says, "so simple that it is relatively difficult for me to see them double, I can succeed in seeing them double, even when the illumination is only instantaneous, the moment I strive to *imagine in a lively way how they ought then to look.* The influence of attention is here pure; for all eye-movements are shut out."

Again, writing of retinal rivalry, Helmholtz says:

"It is not a trial of strength between two sensations, but depends on our fixing or failing to fix the attention. Indeed, there is scarcely any phenomenon so well fitted for the study of the causes which are capable of determining the attention. It is not enough to form the conscious intention of seeing first with one eye and then with the other; *we must form as clear a notion as possible of what we expect to see. Then it will actually appear.*"

In Figs. 55 and 56, where the result is ambiguous, we can make the change from one apparent form to the other by imagining strongly in advance the form we wish to see. Similarly in those puzzles where certain lines in a picture form by their combination an object that has no connection with what the picture obviously represents; or indeed in every case where an object is inconspicuous and hard to discern from the background; we may not be able to see it for a long time; but, having once seen it, we can attend to it again whenever we like, on account of the mental dupli-

FIG. 55. FIG. 56.

cate of it which our imagination now bears. In the meaningless French words '*pas de lieu Rhône que nous*,' who can recognize immediately the English 'paddle your own canoe'? But who that has once noticed the identity can fail to have it arrest his attention again? When watching for the distant clock to strike, our mind is so filled with its image that at every moment we think we hear the longed-for or dreaded sound. So of an awaited footstep. Every stir in the wood is for the hunter his game; for the fugitive his pursuers. Every bonnet in the street is momentarily taken by the lover to enshroud the head of his idol. The image in the mind *is* the attention; the preperception is half of the perception of the looked-for thing.

It is for this reason that men have no eyes but for those aspects of things which they have already been taught to discern. Any one of us can notice a phenomenon after it has once been pointed out, which not one in ten thousand could ever have discovered for himself. Even in poetry and the arts, some one has to come and tell us what aspects to single out, and what effects to admire, before our æsthetic nature can 'dilate' to its full extent and never 'with the wrong emotion.' In kindergarten-instruction one of the exercises is to make the children see how many features they can point out in such an object as a flower or a stuffed bird. They readily name the features they know already, such as leaves, tail, bill, feet. But they may look for hours without distinguishing nostrils, claws, scales, etc., until their attention is called to these details; thereafter, however, they see them every time. In short, *the only things which we commonly see are those which we preperceive,* and the only things which we preperceive are those which have been labelled for us, and the labels stamped into our mind. If we lost our stock of labels we should be intellectually lost in the midst of the world.

Educational Corollaries.—First, to *strengthen attention in children* who care nothing for the subject they are studying and let their wits go wool-gathering. The interest here must be 'derived' from something that the teacher associates with the task, a reward or a punishment if nothing less internal comes to mind. If a topic awakens no spontaneous attention it must borrow an interest from elsewhere. But the best interest is internal, and we must always try, in teaching a class, to knit our novelties by rational links on to things of which they already have pre-perceptions. The old and familiar is readily attended to by the mind and helps to hold in turn the new, forming, in Herbartian phraseology, an '*Apperceptionsmasse*' for it. Of course the teacher's talent is best shown by knowing what 'Apperceptionsmasse' to use. Psychology can only lay down the general rule.

Second, take that mind-wandering which at a later age may trouble us *whilst reading or listening to a discourse.* If attention be the reproduction of the sensation from within, the habit of reading not merely with the eye, and of listening not merely with the ear, but of articulating to one's self the words seen or heard, ought to deepen one's attention to the latter. Experience shows that this is the case. I can keep my wandering mind a great deal more closely upon a conversation or a lecture if I actively re-echo to myself the words than if I simply hear them; and I find a number of my students who report benefit from voluntarily adopting a similar course.

Attention and Free Will.—I have spoken as if our attention were wholly determined by neural conditions. I believe that the array of *things* we can attend to is so determined. No object can *catch* our attention except by the neural machinery. But the *amount* of the attention which an object receives after it has caught our mental eye is another question. It often takes effort to keep the mind upon it. We feel that we can make more or less of the effort as we choose. If this feeling be not deceptive, if our effort be a spiritual force, and an indeterminate one, then of course it contributes coequally with the cerebral conditions to the result. Though it *introduce* no new idea, it will deepen and prolong the stay in consciousness of innumerable ideas which else would fade more quickly away. The delay thus gained might not be more than a second in duration—but that second may be *critical;* for in the constant rising and falling of considerations in the mind, where two associated systems of them are nearly in equilibrium it is often a matter of but a second more or less of attention at the outset, whether one system shall gain force to occupy the field and develop itself, and exclude the other, or be excluded itself by the other. When developed, it may make us act; and that act may seal our doom. When we come to the chapter on the Will, we shall see that the whole drama of the voluntary life hinges on the amount of attention, slightly more or slightly less, which rival motor ideas may receive. But the whole feeling of reality, the whole sting and excitement of our voluntary life, depends on our sense that in it things are *really being decided* from one moment to another, and that it is not the dull rattling off of a chain that was forged innumerable ages ago. This appearance, which makes life and history tingle with such a tragic zest, *may* not be an illusion. Effort may be an original force and not a mere effect, and it may be indeterminate in amount. The last word of sober insight here is ignorance, for the forces engaged are too delicate ever to be measured in detail. Psychology, however, as a would-be 'Science,' must, like every other Science, *postulate* complete determinism in its facts, and abstract consequently from the effects of free will, even if such a force exist. I shall do so in this book like other psychologists; well knowing, however, that such a procedure, although a methodical device justified by the subjective need of arranging the facts in a simple and 'scientific' form, does not settle the ultimate truth of the free-will question one way or the other.

CHAPTER XIV.

CONCEPTION.

Different states of mind can mean the same. The function by which we mark off, discriminate, draw a line round, and identify a numerically distinct subject of discourse is called *conception*. It is plain that whenever one and the same mental state thinks of many things, it must be the vehicle of many conceptions. If it has such a multiple conceptual function, it may be called a state of compound conception.

We may conceive realities supposed to be extra-mental, as steam-engine; fictions, as mermaid; or mere *entia rationis*, like difference or nonentity. But whatever we do conceive, our conception is of that and nothing else—nothing else, that is, *instead* of that, though it may be of much else *in addition* to that. Each act of conception results from our attention's having singled out some one part of the mass of matter-for-thought which the world presents, and from our holding fast to it, without confusion. Confusion occurs when we do not know whether a certain object proposed to us is *the same* with one of our meanings or not; so that the conceptual function requires, to be complete, that the thought should not only say 'I mean this,' but also say 'I don't mean that.'

Each conception thus eternally remains what it is, and never can become another. The mind may change its states, and its meanings, at different times; may drop one conception and take up another: but the dropped conception itself can in no intelligible sense be said to *change into* its successor. The paper, a moment ago white, I may now see to be scorched black. But my *conception* 'white' does not change into my *conception* 'black.' On the contrary, it stays alongside of the objective blackness, as a different meaning in my mind, and by so doing lets me judge the blackness as the paper's change. Unless it stayed, I should simply say 'blackness' and know no more. Thus, amid the flux of opinions and of physical things, the world of conceptions, or things intended to be thought about, stands stiff and immutable, like Plato's Realm of Ideas.

Some conceptions are of things, some of events, some of qualities. Any fact, be it thing, event, or quality, may be conceived sufficiently for purposes of identification, if only it be singled out and marked so as to separate it from other things. Simply calling it 'this' or 'that' will suffice. To speak in technical language, a subject may be conceived by its *denotation*, with no *connotation*, or a very minimum of connotation, attached. The essential point is that it should be re-identified by us as that which the talk is about; and no full representation of it is necessary for this, even when it is a fully representable thing.

In this sense, creatures extremely low in the intellectual scale may have conception. All that is required is that they should recognize the same experience again. A polyp would be a conceptual thinker if a feeling of 'Hollo! thingumbob again!' ever flitted through its mind. This sense of sameness is the very keel and backbone of our consciousness. The same matters can be thought of in different states of mind, and some of these states can know that they mean the same matters which the other states meant. In other words, *the mind can always intend, and know when it intends, to think the Same.*

Conceptions of Abstract, of Universal, and of Problematic Objects.—The sense of our meaning is an entirely peculiar element of the thought. It is one of those evanescent and 'transitive' facts of mind which introspection cannot turn round upon, and isolate and hold up for examination, as an entomologist passes round an insect on a pin. In the (somewhat clumsy) terminology I have used, it has to do with the 'fringe' of the object, and is a 'feeling of tendency,' whose neural counterpart is undoubtedly a lot of dawning and dying processes too faint and complex to be traced. (See p. 169.) The geometer, with his one definite figure before him, knows perfectly that his thoughts apply to countless other figures as well, and that although he *sees* lines of a certain special bigness, direction, color, etc., he *means* not one of these details. When I use the word *man* in two different sentences, I may have both times exactly the same sound upon my lips and the same picture in my mental eye, but I may mean, and at the very moment of uttering the word and imagining the picture know that I mean, two entirely different things. Thus when I say: "What a wonderful man Jones is!" I am perfectly aware that I mean by man to exclude Napoleon Bonaparte or Smith. But when I say: "What a wonderful thing Man is!" I am equally well aware that I mean no such exclusion. This added consciousness is an absolutely positive sort of feeling, transforming what would otherwise be mere noise or vision into something *understood ;* and determining the sequel of my thinking, the later words and images, in a perfectly definite way.

No matter how definite and concrete the habitual imagery of a given mind may be, the things represented appear always surrounded by their fringe of relations, and this is as integral a part of the mind's object as the things themselves are. We come, by steps with which everyone is sufficiently familiar, to think of whole classes of things as well as of single specimens; and to think of the special qualities or attributes of things as well as of the complete things—in other words, we come to have *universals* and *abstracts*, as the logicians call them, for our objects. We also come to think of objects which are only *problematic*, or not yet definitely representable, as well as of objects imagined in all their details. An object which is problematic is defined by its relations only. We think of a thing *about* which certain facts must obtain. But we do not yet know how the thing will look when realized—that is, although conceiving it we cannot *imagine* it. We have in the relations, however, enough to individualize our topic and distinguish it from all the other meanings of our mind. Thus, for example, we may conceive of a perpetual-motion machine. Such a machine is a *quæsitum* of a perfectly definite kind,—we can always tell whether the actual machines offered us do or do not agree with what we mean by it. The natural possibility or impossibility of the thing never touches the question of its conceivability in this problematic way. 'Round-square,' again, or 'black-white-thing,' are absolutely definite conceptions; it is a mere accident, as far as conception goes, that they happen to stand for things which nature never shows us, and of which we consequently can make no picture.

The nominalists and conceptualists carry on a great quarrel over the question whether "the mind can frame abstract or universal ideas." Ideas, it should be said, of abstract or universal objects. But truly in comparison with the wonderful fact that our thoughts, however different otherwise, can still be of *the same,* the question whether that same be a single thing, a whole class of things, an abstract quality or something unimaginable, is an insignificant matter of detail. Our meanings are of singulars, particulars, indefinites, problematics, and universals, mixed together in every way. A singular individual is as much *conceived* when he is isolated and identified away from the rest of the world in my mind, as is the most rarefied and universally applicable quality he may possess —*being,* for example, when treated in the same way. From every point of view, the overwhelming and portentous character ascribed to universal conceptions is surprising. Why, from Socrates downwards, philosophers should have vied with each other in scorn of the knowledge of the particular, and in adoration of that of the general, is hard to understand, seeing that the more adorable knowledge ought to be that of the more adorable things, and that the *things* of worth are all concretes and singulars. The only value of universal characters is that they help us, by reasoning, to know new truths about individual things. The restriction of one's meaning, moreover, to an individual thing, probably requires even more complicated brain-processes than its extension to all the instances of a kind; and the mere mystery, as such, of the knowledge, is equally great, whether generals or singulars be the things known. In sum, therefore, the traditional Universal-worship can only be called a bit of perverse sentimentalism, a philosophic 'idol of the cave.'

Nothing can be conceived as the same without being conceived in a novel state of mind. It seems hardly necessary to add this, after what was said on p. 156. Thus, my armchair is one of the things of which I have a conception; I knew it yesterday and recognized it when I looked at it. But if I think of it to-day as the same arm-chair which I looked at yesterday, it is obvious that the very conception of it *as* the same is an additional complication to the thought, whose inward constitution must alter in consequence. In short, it is logically impossible that the same thing should be *known as the same* by two successive copies of the same thought. As a matter of fact, the thoughts by which we know that we mean the same thing are apt to be very different indeed from each other. We think the thing now substantively, now transitively; now in a direct image, now in one symbol, and now in another symbol; but nevertheless we somehow always *do* know which of all possible subjects we have in mind. Introspective psychology must here throw up the sponge; the fluctuations of subjective life are too exquisite to be described by its coarse terms. It must confine itself to bearing witness to the fact that all sorts of different subjective states do form the vehicle by which the same is known; and it must contradict the opposite view.

CHAPTER XV.

DISCRIMINATION.

Discrimination versus Association.—On p. 15 I spoke of the baby's first object being the germ out of which his whole later universe develops by the addition of new parts from without and the discrimination of others within. Experience, in other words, is trained *both* by association and dissociation, and psychology must be writ *both* in synthetic and in analytic terms. Our original sensible totals are, on the one hand, subdivided by discriminative attention, and, on the other, united with other totals,—either through the agency of our own movements, carrying our senses from one part of space to another, or because new objects come successively and replace those by which we were at first impressed. The 'simple impression' of Hume, the 'simple idea' of Locke are abstractions, never realized in experience. Life, from the very first, presents us with concreted objects, vaguely continuous with the rest of the world which envelops them in space and time, and potentially divisible into inward elements and parts. These objects we break asunder and reunite. We must do both for our knowledge of them to grow; and it is hard to say, on the whole, which we do most. But since the elements with which the traditional associationism performs its constructions—'simple sensations,' namely—are all products of discrimination carried to a high pitch, it seems as if we ought to discuss the subject of analytic attention and discrimination first.

Discrimination defined.—The noticing of any *part* whatever of our object is an act of discrimination. Already on p. 218 I have described the manner in which we often spon-

taneously lapse into the undiscriminating state, even with
regard to objects which we have already learned to distinguish. Such anæsthetics as chloroform, nitrous oxide, etc.,
sometimes bring about transient lapses even more total, in
which numerical discrimination especially seems gone; for
one sees light and hears sound, but whether one or many
lights and sounds is quite impossible to tell. Where the
parts of an object have already been discerned, and each
made the object of a special discriminative act, we can
with difficulty feel the object again in its pristine unity;
and so prominent may our consciousness of its composition
be, that we may hardly believe that it ever could have
appeared undivided. But this is an erroneous view, the
undeniable fact being that *any number of impressions,
from any number of sensory sources, falling simultaneously on a mind* WHICH HAS NOT YET EXPERIENCED
THEM SEPARATELY, *will yield a single undivided object to
that mind.* The law is that all things fuse that *can* fuse,
and that nothing separates except what must. What
makes impressions separate is what we have to study in
this chapter.

Conditions which favor **Discrimination.**—I will treat successively of differences:

(1) So far as they are directly *felt;*
(2) So far as they are *inferred;*
(3) So far as they are *singled out in compounds.*

Differences directly felt.—The first condition is that *the
things to be discriminated must* BE *different,* either in time,
place, or quality. In other words, and physiologically
speaking, they must awaken neural processes which are
distinct. But this, as we have just seen, though an indispensable condition, is not a sufficient condition. To begin
with, the several neural processes must be distinct *enough.*
No one can help singling out a black stripe on a white
ground, or feeling the contrast between a bass note and a
high one sounded immediately after it. Discrimination is
here *involuntary.* But where the objective difference is

less, discrimination may require considerable effort of attention to be performed at all.

Secondly, *the sensations excited by the differing objects must not fall simultaneously, but must fall in immediate* SUCCESSION upon the same organ. It is easier to compare successive than simultaneous sounds, easier to compare two weights or two temperatures by testing one after the other with the same hand, than by using both hands and comparing both at once. Similarly it is easier to discriminate shades of light or color by moving the eye from one to the other, so that they successively stimulate the same retinal tract. In testing the local discrimination of the skin, by applying compass-points, it is found that they are felt to touch different spots much more readily when set down one after the other than when both are applied at once. In the latter case they may be two or three inches apart on the back, thighs, etc., and still feel as if they were set down in one spot. Finally, in the case of smell and taste it is well-nigh impossible to compare simultaneous impressions at all. The reason why successive impression so much favors the result seems to be that there is a real *sensation of difference,* aroused by the shock of transition from one perception to another which is unlike the first. This sensation of difference has its own peculiar quality, no matter what the terms may be, between which it obtains. It is, in short, one of those transitive feelings, or feelings of relation, of which I treated in a former place (p. 161); and, when once aroused, its object lingers in the memory along with the substantive terms which precede and follow, and enables our *judgments of comparison* to be made.

Where the difference between the successive sensations is but slight, the transition between them must be made as immediate as possible, and both must be compared *in memory,* in order to get the best results. One cannot judge accurately of the difference between two similar wines whilst the second is still in one's mouth. So of sounds, warmths, etc.—we must get the dying phases of both sensations of the pair we are comparing. Where, however, the difference is strong, this condition is immaterial, and we can then compare a sensation actually felt with another carried in memory only. The longer the interval of time between the sensations, the more uncertain is their discrimination.

The difference, thus immediately felt between two terms, is independent of our ability to say anything *about* either of the terms by itself. I can feel two distinct spots to be touched on my skin, yet not know which is above and which below. I can observe two neighboring musical tones to differ, and still not know which of the two is the higher in pitch. Similarly I may discriminate two neighboring tints, whilst remaining uncertain which is the bluer or the yellower, or *how* either differs from its mate.

I said that in the immediate succession of m upon n the shock of their difference is *felt*. It is felt *repeatedly* when we go back and forth from n to n; and we make a point of getting it thus repeatedly (by alternating our attention at least) whenever the shock is so slight as to be with difficulty perceived. But in addition to being felt at the brief instant of transition, the difference also feels as if incorporated and taken up into the second term, which feels 'different-from-the-first' even while it lasts. It is obvious that the 'second term' of the mind in this case is not bald n, but a very complex object; and that the sequence is not simply first 'm,' then '*difference*,' then 'n'; but first 'm,' then '*difference*,' then '*n-different-from-m*.' The first and third states of mind are substantive, the second transitive. As our brains and minds are actually made, it is impossible to get certain m's and n's in immediate sequence and to keep them *pure*. If kept pure, it would mean that they remained uncompared. With us, inevitably, by a mechanism which we as yet fail to understand, the shock of difference is felt between them, and the second object is not n pure, but *n-as-different-from-m*. The pure idea of n is *never in the mind at all* when m has gone before

Differences inferred.—With such direct perceptions of difference as this, we must not confound those entirely unlike cases in which we *infer* that two things must differ because we know enough *about* each of them taken by itself to warrant our classing them under distinct heads. It often happens, when the interval is long between two experiences, that our judgments are guided, not so much by a positive image or copy of the earlier one, as by our recollection of certain facts about it. Thus I know that the sunshine to-day is less bright than on a certain day last week, because I then said it was quite dazzling, a remark I should not now care to make. Or I know myself to feel livelier now than I did last summer, because I can now psychologize, and then I could not. We are constantly comparing feelings with whose quality our imagination has no sort of *acquaintance* at the time—pleasures, or pains, for example. It is notoriously hard to conjure up in imagination a lively image of either of these classes of feeling. The associationists may prate of an idea of pleasure being a pleasant idea, of an idea of pain being a painful one, but the unsophisticated sense of mankind is against them, agreeing with Homer that the memory of griefs when past may be a joy, and with Dante that there is no greater sorrow than, in misery, to recollect one's happier time.

The 'Singling out' of Elements in a Compound.—It is safe to lay it down as a fundamental principle that *any total impression made on the mind must be unanalyzable so long as its elements have never been experienced apart or in other combinations elsewhere.* The components of an absolutely changeless group of not-elsewhere-occurring attributes could never be discriminated. If all cold things were wet, and all wet things cold; if all hard things pricked our skin, and no other things did so: is it likely that we should discriminate between coldness and wetness, and hardness and pungency, respectively? If all liquids were transparent and no non-liquid were transparent, it would be long before we had separate names for liquidity and transparency. If heat were a function of position above the earth's surface, so that the higher a thing was the hotter it became, one word would serve for hot and high. We have, in fact, a number of sensations whose concomitants are invariably the same, and we find it, accordingly, impossible to analyze them out from the totals in which they are found. The contraction of the diaphragm and the expansion of the lungs, the shortening of certain muscles and the rotation of certain joints, are examples. We learn that the *causes* of such groups of feelings are multiple, and therefore we frame theories about the composition of the feelings themselves, by 'fusion,' 'integration,' 'synthesis,' or what not. But by direct introspection no analysis of the feelings is ever made. A conspicuous case will come to view when we treat of the emotions. Every emotion has its 'expression,' of quick breathing, palpitating heart, flushed face, or the like. The expression gives rise to bodily feelings; and the emotion is thus necessarily and invariably accompanied by these bodily feelings. The consequence is that it is impossible to apprehend it as a spiritual state by itself, or to analyze it away from the lower feelings in question. It is in fact impossible to prove that it exists as a distinct psychic fact. The present writer strongly doubts that it does so exist.

In general, then, if an object affects us simultaneously in a number of ways, *abcd*, we get a peculiar integral impression, which thereafter characterizes to our mind the individuality of that object, and becomes the sign of its presence; and which is only resolved into *a*, *b*, *c*, and *d*, respectively, by the aid of farther experiences. These we now may turn to consider.

If any single quality or constituent, a, of such an object have previously been known by us isolatedly, or have in any other manner already become an object of separate acquaintance on our part, so that we have an image of it, distinct or vague, in our mind, disconnected with *bcd*, *then that constituent a may be analyzed out from the total impression.* Analysis of a thing means separate attention to each of its parts. In Chapter XIII we saw that one condition of attending to a thing was the formation from within of a separate image of that thing, which should, as it were, go out to meet the impression received. Attention being the condition of analysis, and separate imagination being the condition of attention, it follows also that separate imagination is the condition of analysis. *Only such elements as we are acquainted with, and can imagine separately, can be discriminated within a total sense-impression.* The image seems to welcome its own mate from out of the compound, and to separate it from the other constituents; and thus the compound becomes broken for our consciousness into parts.

All the facts cited in Chapter XIII to prove that attention involves inward reproduction prove that discrimination involves it as well. In looking for any object in a room, for a book in a library, for example, we detect it the more readily if, in addition to merely knowing its name, etc., we carry in our mind a distinct image of its appearance. The assafœdita in 'Worcestershire sauce' is not obvious to anyone who has not tasted assafœtida *per se*. In a 'cold' color an artist would never be able to analyze out the pervasive presence of *blue*, unless he had previously made acquaintance with the color blue by itself. All the colors we actually experience are mixtures. Even the purest primaries always come to us with some white. Absolutely pure red or green or violet is never experienced, and so can never be discerned in the so-called primaries with which we have to deal: the latter consequently pass for pure.— The reader will remember how an overtone can only be attended to in the midst of its consorts in the voice of a musical instrument, by sounding it previously alone. The imagination, being then full of it, hears the like of it in the compound tone.

Non-isolable elements may be discriminated, provided

DISCRIMINATION. 251

their concomitants change. Very few elements of reality are experienced by us in absolute isolation. The most that usually happens to a constituent *a* of a compound phenomenon *abcd* is that its *strength* relatively to *bcd* varies from a maximum to a minimum; or that it appears linked with *other* qualities, in other compounds, as *aefg* or *ahik*. Either of these vicissitudes in the mode of our experiencing *a* may, under favorable circumstances, lead us to feel the difference between it and its concomitants, and to single it out—not absolutely, it is true, but approximately—and so to analyze the compound of which it is a part. The act of singling out is then called *abstraction*, and the element disengaged is an *abstract*.

Fluctuation in a quality's intensity is a less efficient aid to our abstracting of it than variety in the combinations in which it appears. *What is associated now with one thing and now with another tends to become dissociated from either, and to grow into an object of abstract contemplation by the mind.* One might call this the *law of dissociation by varying concomitants*. The practical result of this law is that a mind which has once dissociated and abstracted a character by its means can analyze it out of a total whenever it meets with it again.

Dr. Martineau gives a good example of the law: " When a red ivory ball, seen for the first time, has been withdrawn, it will leave a mental representation of itself, in which all that it simultaneously gave us will indistinguishably coexist. Let a white ball succeed to it; now, and not before, will an attribute detach itself, and the *color*, by force of contrast, be shaken out into the foreground. Let the white ball be replaced by an egg, and this new difference will bring the *form* into notice from its previous slumber, and thus that which began by being simply an object cut out from the surrounding scene becomes for us first a *red* object, then a *red round* object, and so on."

Why the repetition of the character in combination with different wholes will cause it thus to break up its adhesion with any one of them, and roll out, as it were, alone upon the table of consciousness, is a little of a mystery, but one which need not be considered here.

Practice improves Discrimination.—Any personal or practical interest in the results to be obtained by distinguishing, makes one's wits amazingly sharp to detect differences. And long training and practice in distinguishing has the same effect as personal interest. Both of these agencies give to small amounts of objective difference the same effectiveness upon the mind that, under other circumstances, only large ones would have.

That 'practice makes perfect' is notorious in the field of motor accomplishments. But motor accomplishments depend in part on sensory discrimination. Billiard-playing, rifle-shooting, tight-rope-dancing demand the most delicate appreciation of minute disparities of sensation, as well as the power to make accurately graduated muscular response thereto. In the purely sensorial field we have the well-known virtuosity displayed by the professional buyers and testers of various kinds of goods. One man will distinguish by taste between the upper and the lower half of a bottle of old Madeira. Another will recognize, by feeling the flour in a barrel, whether the wheat was grown in Iowa or Tennessee. The blind deaf-mute, Laura Bridgman, so improved her touch as to recognize, after a year's interval, the hand of a person who once had shaken hers; and her sister in misfortune, Julia Brace, is said to have been employed in the Hartford Asylum to sort the linen of its multitudinous inmates, after it came from the wash, by her wonderfully educated sense of smell.

The fact is so familiar that few, if any, psychologists have even recognized it as needing explanation. They have seemed to think that practice must, in the nature of things, improve the delicacy of discernment, and have let the matter rest. At most they have said, "Attention accounts for it; we attend more to habitual things, and what we attend to we perceive more minutely." This answer, though true, is too general; but we can say nothing more about the matter here.

CHAPTER XVI.

ASSOCIATION.

The Order of our Ideas.—After discrimination, association! It is obvious that all advance in knowledge must consist of both operations; for in the course of our education, objects at first appearing as wholes are analyzed into parts, and objects appearing separately are brought together and appear as new compound wholes to the mind. Analysis and synthesis are thus the incessantly alternating mental activities, a stroke of the one preparing the way for a stroke of the other, much as, in walking, a man's two legs are alternately brought into use, both being indispensable for any orderly advance.

The manner in which trains of imagery and consideration follow each other through our thinking, the restless flight of one idea before the next, the transitions our minds make between things wide as the poles asunder, transitions which at first sight startle us by their abruptness, but which, when scrutinized closely, often reveal intermediating links of perfect naturalness and propriety—all this magical, imponderable streaming has from time immemorial excited the admiration of all whose attention happened to be caught by its omnipresent mystery. And it has furthermore challenged the race of philosophers to banish something of the mystery by formulating the process in simpler terms. The problem which the philosophers have set themselves is that of ascertaining, between the thoughts which thus appear to sprout one out of the other, *principles of connection* whereby their peculiar succession or coexistence may be explained.

But immediately an ambiguity arises: which sort of

connection is meant ? connection *thought-of*, or connection *between thoughts ?* These are two entirely different things, and only in the case of one of them is there any hope of finding 'principles.' The jungle of connections *thought of* can never be formulated simply. Every conceivable connection may be thought of—of coexistence, succession, resemblance, contrast, contradiction, cause and effect, means and end, genus and species, part and whole, substance and property, early and late, large and small, landlord and tenant, master and servant,—Heaven knows what, for the list is literally inexhaustible. The only simplification which could possibly be aimed at would be the reduction of the relations to a small number of *types*, like those which some authors call the 'categories' of the understanding. According as we followed one category or another we should sweep, from any object with our thought, in this way or in that, to others. Were *this* the sort of connection sought between one moment of our thinking and another, our chapter might end here. For the only summary description of these categories is that they are all thinkable relations, and that the mind proceeds from one object to another by some intelligible path.

Is it determined by any laws? But as a matter of fact, What determines the particular path? Why do we at a given time and place proceed to think of b if we have just thought of a, and at another time and place why do we think, not of b, but of c? Why do we spend years straining after a certain scientific or practical problem, but all in vain—our thought unable to evoke the solution we desire? And why, some day, walking in the street with our attention miles away from that quest, does the answer saunter into our minds as carelessly as if it had never been called for—suggested, possibly, by the flowers on the bonnet of the lady in front of us, or possibly by nothing that we can discover ?

The truth must be admitted that thought works under strange conditions. Pure 'reason' is only one out of a thousand possibilities in the thinking of each of us. Who can count all the silly fancies, the grotesque suppositions, the utterly irrelevant reflections he makes in the course of a day? Who can swear that his prejudices and irrational opinions constitute a less bulky part of his mental furniture than his clarified beliefs? And yet, the *mode of genesis* of the worthy and the worthless in our thinking seems the same.

The laws are cerebral laws. *There seem to be mechanical conditions on which thought depends, and which, to say the least, determine the order in which the objects for her comparisons and selections are presented.* It is a suggestive fact that Locke, and many more recent Continental psychologists, have found themselves obliged to invoke a mechanical process to account for the *aberrations* of thought, the obstructive prepossessions, the frustrations of reason. This they found in the law of habit, or what we now call association by contiguity. But it never occurred to these writers that a process which could go the length of actually producing some ideas and sequences in the mind might safely be trusted to produce others too; and that those habitual associations which further thought may also come from the same mechanical source as those which hinder it. Hartley accordingly suggested habit as a sufficient explanation of the sequence of our thoughts, and in so doing planted himself squarely upon the properly *causal* aspect of the problem, and sought to treat both rational and irrational associations from a single point of view. How does a man come, after having the thought of A, to have the thought of B the next moment? or how does he come to think A and B always together? These were the phenomena which Hartley undertook to explain by cerebral physiology. I believe that he was, in essential respects, on the right track, and I propose simply to revise his conclusions by the aid of distinctions which he did not make.

Objects are associated, not ideas. We shall avoid confusion if we consistently speak as if *association*, so far as the word stands for an *effect, were between* THINGS THOUGHT OF—*as if it were* THINGS, *not ideas, which are associated in the mind.* We shall talk of the association of *objects*, not of the association of *ideas*. And so far as association stands for a *cause*, it is between *processes in the brain*— it is these which, by being associated in certain ways, determine what successive objects shall be thought.

The Elementary Principle.—I shall now try to show that there is no other *elementary* causal law of association than the law of neural habit. All the *materials* of our thought are due to the way in which one elementary process of the cerebral hemispheres tends to excite whatever other elementary process it may have excited at any former time. The number of elementary processes at work, however, and the nature of those which at any time are fully effective in rousing the others, determine the character of the total brain-action, and, as a consequence of this, they determine the object thought of at the time. According as this resultant object is one thing or another, we call it a product of association by contiguity or of association by similarity, or contrast, or whatever other sorts we may have recognized as ultimate. Its *production*, however, is, in each one of these cases, to be explained by a merely quantitative variation in the elementary brain-processes momentarily at work under the law of habit.

My thesis, stated thus briefly, will soon become more clear; and at the same time certain disturbing factors, which coöperate with the law of neural habit, will come to view.

Let us then assume as the basis of all our subsequent reasoning this law: *When two elementary brain-processes have been active together or in immediate succession, one of them, on re-occurring, tends to propagate its excitement into the other.*

But, as a matter of fact, every elementary process has unavoidably found itself at different times excited in conjunction with *many* other processes. Which of these others it shall awaken now becomes a problem. Shall *b* or *c* be aroused next by the present *a*? To answer this, we must make a further postulate, based on the fact of *tension* in nerve-tissue, and on the fact of summation of excitements, each incomplete or latent in itself, into an open resultant (see p. 128). The process *b*, rather than *c*, will awake, if in addition to the vibrating tract *a* some other tract *d* is in a state of sub-excitement, and formerly was excited with *b* alone and not with *a*. In short, we may say:

The amount of activity at any given point in the brain-cortex is the sum of the tendencies of all other points to discharge into it, such tendencies being proportionate (1) *to the number of times the excitement of each other point may have accompanied that of the point in question;* (2) *to the intensity of such excitements;* and (3) *to the absence of any rival point functionally disconnected with the first point, into which the discharges might be diverted.*

Expressing the fundamental law in this most complicated way leads to the greatest ultimate simplification. Let us, for the present, only treat of spontaneous trains of thought and ideation, such as occur in revery or musing. The case of voluntary thinking toward a certain end shall come up later.

Spontaneous Trains of Thought.—Take, to fix our ideas, the two verses from 'Locksley Hall':

"I, the heir of all *the ages* in the foremost files of time,"

and—

"For I doubt not through *the ages* one increasing purpose runs"

Why is it that when we recite from memory one of these lines, and get as far as *the ages*, that portion of the *other* line which follows and, so to speak, sprouts out of *the ages* does not also sprout out of our memory and confuse the sense of our words? Simply because the word that follows *the ages* has its brain-process awakened not simply by the brain-process of *the ages* alone, but by it *plus* the brain processes of all the words preceding *the ages*. The word *ages* at its moment of strongest activity would, *per se*, indifferently discharge into either 'in' or 'one.' So would the previous words (whose tension is momentarily much less strong than that of *ages*) each of them indifferently discharge into either of a large number of other words with which they have been at different times combined. But when the processes of '*I, the heir of all the ages,*' simultaneously vibrate in the brain, the last one of them in a maximal, the others in a fading, phase of excitement, then the strongest line of discharge will be that which they *all alike* tend to take. '*In*' and not '*one*' or any other word will be the next to awaken, for its brain-process has previously vibrated in unison not only with that of *ages*, but with that of all those other words whose activity is dying away. It is a good case of the effectiveness over thought of what we called on p. 168 a 'fringe.'

But if some one of these preceding words—'heir,' for example—had an intensely strong association with some brain-tracts entirely disjoined in experience from the poem of 'Locksley Hall'—if the reciter, for instance, were tremulously awaiting the opening of a will which might make him a millionaire—it is probable that the path of discharge through the words of the poem would be suddenly interrupted at the word 'heir.' His *emotional interest in that word* would be such that its *own special associations would prevail* over the combined ones of the other words. He would, as we say, be abruptly reminded of his personal situation, and the poem would lapse altogether from his thoughts.

The writer of these pages has every year to learn the names of a large number of students who sit in alphabetical order in a lecture-room. He finally learns to call them by name, as they sit in their accustomed places. On meeting one in the street, however, early in the year, the face hardly ever recalls the name, but it may recall the place of its owner in the lecture-room, his neighbors' faces, and consequently his general alphabetical position: and then, usually as the common associate of all these combined data, the student's name surges up in his mind.

A father wishes to show to some guests the progress of his rather dull child in kindergarten-instruction. Holding the knife upright on the table, he says, " What do you call that, my boy ?" "I calls it a *knife*, I does," is the sturdy reply, from which the child cannot be induced to swerve by any alteration in the form of question, until the father, recollecting that in the kindergarten a pencil was used and not a knife, draws a long one from his pocket, holds it in the same way, and then gets the wished-for answer, " I calls it *vertical*." All the concomitants of the kindergarten experience had to recombine their effect before the word ' vertical ' could be reawakened.

Total Recall.—The ideal working of the law of compound association, as Prof. Bain calls it, were it numodified by any extraneous influence, would be such as to keep the mind in a perpetual treadmill of concrete reminiscences from which no detail could be omitted. Suppose, for example, we begin by thinking of a certain dinner-party. The only thing which all the components of the dinner-party could combine to recall would be the first concrete occurrence which ensued upon it. All the details of this occurrence could in turn only combine to awaken the next following occurrence, and so on. If a, b, c, d, e, for instance, be the elementary nerve-tracts excited by the last act of the dinner-party, call this act A, and l, m, n, o, p be those of walking home through the frosty night, which we may call B, then the thought of A must awaken that of B, because a, b, c, d, e will each and all discharge into l through the paths by which their original discharge took place. Similarly they will discharge into m, n, o, and p; and these latter tracts will also each reinforce the other's action because, in the experience B, they have already vibrated in unison. The lines in Fig. 57 symbolize the summation of discharges into each of the components of B, and the consequent strength of the combination of influences by which B in its totality is awakened.

Hamilton first used the word 'redintegration' to designate all association. Such processes as we have just described might in an emphatic sense be termed redintegrations, for they would necessarily lead, if unobstructed, to the reinstatement in thought of the *entire* content of large trains of past experience. From this complete redintegration there could be no escape save through the irruption of some new and strong present impression of the senses, or through the excessive tendency of some one of the elementary brain-tracts to discharge independently into an aberrant quarter of the brain. Such was the tendency of the

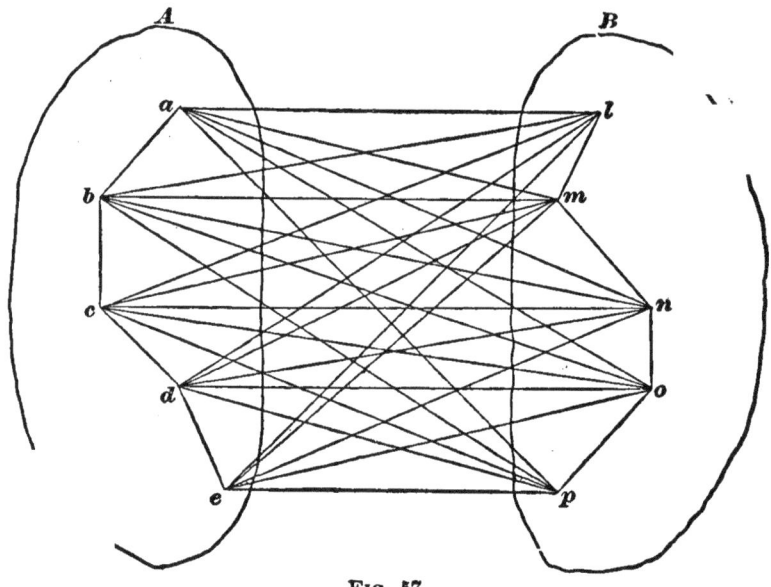

FIG. 57.

word 'heir' in the verse from 'Locksley Hall,' which was our first example. How such tendencies are constituted we shall have soon to inquire with some care. Unless they are present, the panorama of the past, once opened, must unroll itself with fatal literality to the end, unless some outward sound, sight, or touch divert the current of thought.

Let us call this process *impartial redintegration*, or, still better, *total recall*. Whether it ever occurs in an absolutely complete form is doubtful. We all immediately recognize, however, that in some minds there is a much greater tendency than in others for the flow of thought to take this form. Those insufferably garrulous old women, those dry and fanciless beings who spare you no detail, however petty, of the facts they are recounting, and upon the thread of whose narrative all the irrelevant items cluster as pertinaciously as the essential ones, the slaves of literal fact, the stumblers over the smallest abrupt step in thought, are figures known to all of us. Comic literature has made her profit out of them. Juliet's nurse is a classical example. George Eliot's village characters and some of Dickens's minor personages supply excellent instances.

Perhaps as successful a rendering as any of this mental type is the character of Miss Bates in Miss Austen's 'Emma.' Hear how she redintegrates:

"'But where could *you* hear it?' cried Miss Bates. 'Where could you possibly hear it, Mr. Knightley? For it is not five minutes since I received Mrs. Cole's note—no, it cannot be more than five—or at least ten—for I had got my bonnet and spencer on, just ready to come out—I was only gone down to speak to Patty again about the pork—Jane was standing in the passage—were not you, Jane?—for my mother was so afraid that we had not any salting-pan large enough. So I said I would go down and see, and Jane said: "Shall I go down instead? for I think you have a little cold, and Patty has been washing the kitchen." "Oh, my dear," said I—well, and just then came the note. A Miss Hawkins—that's all I know—a Miss Hawkins, of Bath. But, Mr. Knightley, how could you possibly have heard it? for the very moment Mr. Cole told Mrs. Cole of it, she sat down and wrote to me. A Miss Hawkins—'"

Partial Recall.—This case helps us to understand why it is that the ordinary spontaneous flow of our ideas does not follow the law of total recall. *In no revival of a past experience are all the items of our thought equally operative in determining what the next thought shall be. Always some ingredient is prepotent over the rest.* Its special suggestions or associations in this case will often be different from those which it has in common with the whole group of items; and its tendency to awaken these outlying associates will deflect the path of our revery. Just as in the original sensible experience our attention focalized itself upon a few of the impressions of the scene before us, so here in the reproduction of those impressions an equal partiality is shown, and some items are emphasized above the rest. What these items shall be is, in most cases of spontaneous revery, hard to determine beforehand. In subjective terms we say that *the prepotent items are those which appeal most to our* INTEREST.

Expressed in brain-terms, the law of interest will be: *some one brain-process is always prepotent above its concomitants in arousing action elsewhere.*

"Two processes," says Mr. Hodgson, "are constantly going on in redintegration. The one a process of corrosion, melting, decay; the other a process of renewing, arising, becoming. . . . No object of representation remains long before consciousness in the same state, but fades, decays, and becomes indistinct. Those parts of the object, however, which possess an interest resist this tendency to gradual decay of the whole object. . . . This inequality in the object—some parts, the uninteresting, submitting to decay; others, the interesting parts, resisting it—when it has continued for a certain time, ends in becoming a new object."

Only where the interest is diffused equally over all the parts is this law departed from. It will be least obeyed by those minds which have the smallest variety and intensity of interests—those who, by the general flatness and poverty of their æsthetic nature, are kept for ever rotating among the literal sequences of their local and personal history.

Most of us, however, are better organized than this, and our musings pursue an erratic course, swerving continually into some new direction traced by the shifting play of interest as it ever falls on some partial item in each complex representation that is evoked. Thus it so often comes about that we find ourselves thinking at two nearly adjacent moments of things separated by the whole diameter of space and time. Not till we carefully recall each step of our cogitation do we see how naturally we came by Hodgson's law to pass from one to the other. Thus, for instance, after looking at my clock just now (1879), I found myself thinking of a recent resolution in the Senate about our legal-tender notes. The clock called up the image of the man who had repaired its gong. He suggested the jeweller's shop where I had last seen him; that shop, some shirt-studs which I had bought there; they, the value of gold and its recent decline; the latter, the equal value of greenbacks, and this, naturally, the question of how long they were to last, and of the Bayard proposition. Each of these images offered various points of interest. Those which formed the turning-points of my thought are easily assigned. The gong was momentarily the most interesting part of the clock, because, from having begun with a beautiful tone, it had become discordant and aroused disappointment. But for this the clock might have suggested the friend who gave it to me, or any one of a thousand circumstances connected with clocks. The jeweller's shop suggested the studs, because they alone of all its contents were tinged with the egoistic interest of possession. This interest in the studs, their value, made me single out the material as its chief source, etc., to the end. Every reader who will arrest himself at any moment and say, "How came I to be thinking of just this?" will be sure to trace a train of representations linked together by lines of contiguity and points of interest inextricably combined. This is the ordinary process of the association of ideas as it spontaneously goes on in average minds. *We may call it ordinary*, or *mixed, association*, or, if we like better, *partial recall*.

Which Associates come up, in Partial Recall?—Can we determine, now, when a certain portion of the going thought has, by dint of its interest, become so prepotent as to make its own exclusive associates the dominant features of the coming thought—can we, I say, determine *which* of its own associates shall be evoked? For they are many. As Hodgson says:

"The interesting parts of the decaying object are free to combine again with any objects or parts of objects with which at any time they have been combined before. All the former combinations of these parts may come back into consciousness; one must, but which will?"

Mr. Hodgson replies:

"There can be but one answer: that which has been most *habitually* combined with them before. This new object begins at once to form itself in consciousness, and to group its parts round the part still remaining from the former object; part after part comes out and arranges itself in its old position; but scarcely has the process begun, when the original law of interest begins to operate on this new formation, seizes on the interesting parts and impresses them on the attention to the exclusion of the rest, and the whole process is repeated again with endless variety. I venture to propose this as a complete and true account of the whole process of redintegration."

In restricting the discharge from the interesting item into that channel which is simply most *habitual* in the sense of most frequent, Hodgson's account is assuredly imperfect. An image by no means always revives its most frequent associate, although frequency is certainly one of the most potent determinants of revival. If I abruptly utter the word *swallow*, the reader, if by habit an ornithologist, will think of a bird; if a physiologist or a medical specialist in throat-diseases, he will think of deglutition. If I say *date*, he will, if a fruit-merchant or an

Arabian traveller, think of the produce of the palm; if an habitual student of history, figures with A.D. or B.C. before them will rise in his mind. If I say *bed, bath, morning*, his own daily toilet will be invincibly suggested by the combined names of three of its habitual associates. But frequent lines of transition are often set at naught. The sight of a certain book has most frequently awakened in me thoughts of the opinions therein propounded. The idea of suicide has never been connected with the volume. But a moment since, as my eye fell upon it, suicide was the thought that flashed into my mind. Why? Because but yesterday I received a letter informing me that the author's recent death was an act of self-destruction. Thoughts tend, then, to awaken their most recent as well as their most habitual associates. This is a matter of notorious experience, too notorious, in fact, to need illustration. If we have seen our friend this morning, the mention of his name now recalls the circumstances of that interview, rather than any more remote details concerning him. If Shakespeare's plays are mentioned, and we were last night reading 'Richard II.,' vestiges of that play rather than of 'Hamlet' or 'Othello' float through our mind. Excitement of peculiar tracts, or peculiar modes of general excitement in the brain, leave a sort of tenderness or exalted sensibility behind them which takes days to die away. As long as it lasts, those tracts or those modes are liable to have their activities awakened by causes which at other times might leave them in repose. Hence, *recency* in experience is a prime factor in determining revival in thought.*

Vividness in an original experience may also have the same effect as habit or recency in bringing about likeli-

---

* I refer to a recency of a few hours. Mr. Galton found that experiences from boyhood and youth were more likely to be suggested by words seen at random than experiences of later years. See his highly interesting account of experiments in his Inquiries into Human Faculty, pp 191-203

hood of revival. If we have once witnessed an execution, any subsequent conversation or reading about capital punishment will almost certainly suggest images of that particular scene. Thus it is that events lived through only once, and in youth, may come in after-years, by reason of their exciting quality or emotional intensity, to serve as types or instances used by our mind to illustrate any and every occurring topic whose interest is most remotely pertinent to theirs. If a man in his boyhood once talked with Napoleon, any mention of great men or historical events, battles or thrones, or the whirligig of fortune, or islands in the ocean, will be apt to draw to his lips the incidents of that one memorable interview. If the word *tooth* now suddenly appears on the page before the reader's eye, there are fifty chances out of a hundred that, if he gives it time to awaken any image, it will be an image of some operation of dentistry in which he has been the sufferer. Daily he has touched his teeth and masticated with them; this very morning he brushed, used, and picked them; but the rarer and remoter associations arise more promptly because they were so much more intense.

A fourth factor in tracing the course of reproduction is *congruity in emotional tone* between the reproduced idea and our mood. The same objects do not recall the same associates when we are cheerful as when we are melancholy. Nothing, in fact, is more striking than our inability to keep up trains of joyous imagery when we are depressed in spirits. Storm, darkness, war, images of disease, poverty, perishing, and dread afflict unremittingly the imaginations of melancholiacs. And those of sanguine temperament, when their spirits are high, find it impossible to give any permanence to evil forebodings or to gloomy thoughts. In an instant the train of association dances off to flowers and sunshine, and images of spring and hope. The records of Arctic or African travel perused in one mood awaken no thoughts but those of horror at the malignity of Nature; read at another time they suggest only enthusiastic reflections on the indomitable power and pluck of man. Few novels so overflow with joyous animal spirits as 'The Three Guardsmen' of Dumas. Yet it may awaken in the mind of a reader depressed with sea-sickness (as the writer can personally testify) a most woful consciousness of the cruelty and carnage of which heroes like Athos, Porthos, and Aramis make themselves guilty.

Habit, recency, vividness, and emotional congruity are, then, all reasons why one representation rather than another should be awakened by the interesting portion of a departing thought. We may say with truth that *in the majority of cases the coming representation will have been either habitual, recent, or vivid, and will be congruous*. If all these qualities unite in any one absent associate, we may predict almost infallibly that that associate of the going object will form an important ingredient in the object which comes next. In spite of the fact, however, that the succession of representations is thus redeemed from perfect indeterminism and limited to a few classes whose characteristic quality is fixed by the nature of our past experience, it must still be confessed that an immense number of terms in the linked chain of our representations fall outside of all assignable rule. To take the instance of the clock given on page 263. Why did the jeweller's shop suggest the shirt-studs rather than a chain which I had bought there more recently, which had cost more, and whose sentimental associations were much more interesting? Any reader's experience will easily furnish similar instances. So we must admit that to a certain extent, even in those forms of ordinary mixed association which lie nearest to impartial redintegration, *which* associate of the interesting item shall emerge must be called largely a matter of accident—accident, that is, for our intelligence. No doubt it is determined by cerebral causes, but they are too subtle and shifting for our analysis.

Focalized Recall, or Association by Similarity.—In partial or mixed association we have all along supposed the interesting portion of the disappearing thought to be of considerable extent, and to be sufficiently complex to constitute by itself a concrete object. Sir William Hamilton relates, for instance, that after thinking of Ben Lomond he found himself thinking of the Prussian system of education, and discovered that the links of association were a German gentleman whom he had met on Ben Lomond, Germany, etc. The interesting part of Ben Lomond as he had experienced it, the part operative in determining the train of his ideas, was the complex image of a particular man. But now let us suppose that the interested attention refines itself still further and accentuates a portion of the passing object, so small as to be no longer the image of a concrete thing, but only of an abstract quality or property. Let us moreover suppose that the part thus accentuated persists in consciousness (or, in cerebral terms, has its brain-process continue) after the other portions of the object have faded. *This small surviving portion will then surround itself with its own associates* after the fashion we have already seen, and the relation between the new thought's object and the object of the faded thought will be a *relation of similarity.* The pair of thoughts will form an instance of what is called '*association by similarity.*'

The similars which are here associated, or of which the first is followed by the second in the mind, are seen to be *compounds*. Experience proves that this is always the case. *There is no tendency on the part of* SIMPLE *'ideas,' attributes, or qualities to remind us of their like.* The thought of one shade of blue does not summon up that of another shade of blue, etc., unless indeed we have in mind some general purpose of nomenclature or comparison which requires a review of several blue tints.

Now two compound things are similar when some one quality or group of qualities is shared alike by both, although as regards their other qualities they may have nothing in common. The moon is similar to a gas-jet, it is also similar to a foot-ball; but a gas-jet and a foot-ball are not similar to each other. When we affirm the similarity of two compound things, we should always say *in what respect it obtains*. Moon and gas-jet are similar in respect of luminosity, and nothing else; moon and foot-ball in respect of rotundity, and nothing else. Foot-ball and gas-jet are in no respect similar—that is, they possess no common point, no identical attribute. *Similarity, in compounds, is partial identity*. When the *same* attribute appears in two phenomena, though it be their only common property, the two phenomena are similar in so far forth. To return now to our associated representations. If the thought of the moon is succeeded by the thought of a foot-ball, and that by the thought of one of Mr. X's railroads, it is because the attribute rotundity in the moon broke away from all the rest and surrounded itself with an entirely new set of companions—elasticity, leathery integument, swift mobility in obedience to human caprice, etc.; and because the last-named attribute in the foot-ball in turn broke away from its companions, and, itself persisting, surrounded itself with such new attributes as make up the notions of a 'railroad king,' of a rising and falling stock-market, and the like.

The gradual passage from total to focalized, through what we have called ordinary partial, recall may be sym-

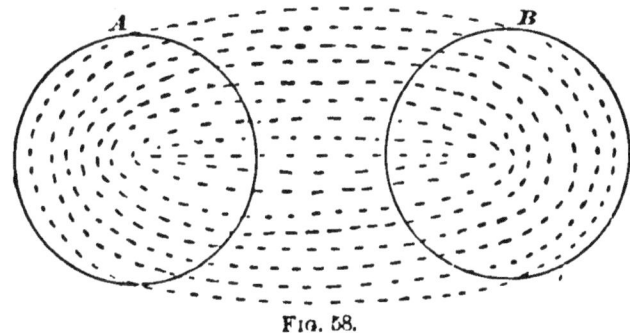

Fig. 58.

bolized by diagrams. Fig. 58 is total, Fig. 59 is partial, and Fig. 60 focalized, recall. *A* in each is the passing,

B the coming, thought. In 'total recall,' all parts of A are equally operative in calling up B. In 'partial recall,' most parts of A are inert. The part M alone breaks out and awakens B. In similar association or 'focalized recall,' the part M is much smaller than in the previous case,

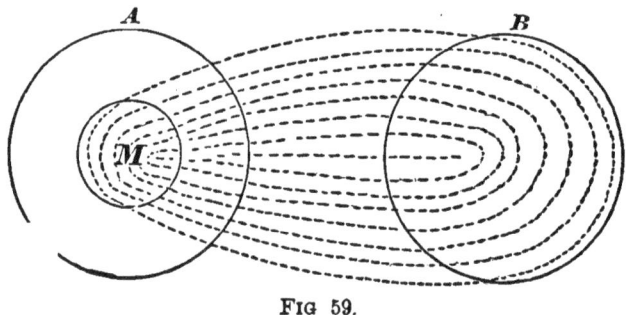

FIG 59.

and after awakening its new set of associates, instead of fading out itself, it continues persistently active along with them, forming an identical part in the two ideas, and making these, *pro tanto*, resemble each other.*

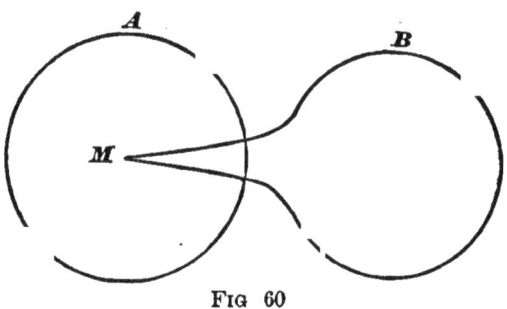

FIG 60

Why a single portion of the passing thought should break out from its concert with the rest and act, as we say, on its own hook, why the other parts should become inert, are mysteries which we can ascertain but not explain.

---

* Miss M. W. Calkins (Philosophical Review, I. 389, 1892) points out that the persistent feature of the going thought, on which the association in cases of similarity hinges, is by no means always so slight as to warrant the term 'focalized.' "If the sight of the whole breakfast-room be followed by the visual image of yesterday's

ASSOCIATION.

Possibly a minuter insight into the laws of neural action will some day clear the matter up ; possibly neural laws will not suffice, and we shall need to invoke a dynamic reaction of the consciousness itself. But into this we cannot enter now.

Voluntary Trains of Thought.—Hitherto we have assumed the process of suggestion of one object by another to be spontaneous. The train of imagery wanders at its own sweet will, now trudging in sober grooves of habit, now with a hop, skip, and jump, darting across the whole field of time and space. This is revery, or musing; but great segments of the flux of our ideas consist of something very different from this. They are guided by a distinct purpose or conscious interest; and the course of our ideas is then called *voluntary*.

Physiologically considered, we must suppose that a purpose means the persistent activity of certain rather definite brain-processes throughout the whole course of thought. Our most usual cogitations are not pure reveries, absolute driftings, but revolve about some central interest or topic to which most of the images are relevant, and towards which we return promptly after occasional digressions.

---

breakfast-table, with the same setting and in the same surroundings, the association is practically total," and yet the case is one of similarity. For Miss Calkins, accordingly, the more important distinction is that between what she calls *desistent* and *persistent* association. In 'desistent' association all parts of the going thought fade out and are replaced. In 'persistent' association some of them remain, and form a bond of similarity between the mind's successive objects; but only where this bond is extremely delicate (as in the case of an abstract relation or quality) is there need to call the persistent process 'focalized.' I must concede the justice of Miss Calkins's criticism, and think her new pair of terms a useful contribution. Wundt's division of associations into the two classes of *external* and *internal* is congruent with Miss Calkins's division. Things associated internally must have some element in common ; and Miss Calkins's word 'persistent' suggests how this may cerebrally come to pass. 'Desistent,' on the other hand, suggests the process by which the successive ideas become external to each other or preserve no inner tie.

This interest is subserved by the persistently active brain-tracts we have supposed. In the mixed associations which we have hitherto studied, the parts of each object which form the pivots on which our thoughts successively turn have their interest largely determined by their connection with some *general interest* which for the time has seized upon the mind. If we call Z the brain-tract of general interest, then, if the object abc turns up, and b has more associations with Z than have either a or c, b will become the object's interesting, pivotal portion, and will call up its own associates exclusively. For the energy of b's brain-tract will be augmented by Z's activity,—an activity which, from lack of previous connection between Z and a and Z and c, does not influence a or c. If, for instance, I think of Paris whilst I am *hungry*, I shall not improbably find that its *restaurants* have become the pivot of my thought, etc., etc.

Problems.—But in the theoretic as well as in the practical life there are interests of a more acute sort, taking the form of definite images of some achievement which we desire to effect. The train of ideas arising under the influence of such an interest constitutes usually the thought of the *means* by which the end shall be attained. If the end by its simple presence does not instantaneously suggest the means, the search for the latter becomes a *problem;* and the discovery of the means forms a new sort of end, of an entirely peculiar nature—an end, namely, which we intensely desire before we have attained it, but of the nature of which, even whilst most strongly craving it, we have no distinct imagination whatever (compare pp. 241-2).

The same thing occurs whenever we seek to recall something forgotten, or to state the reason for a judgment which we have made intuitively. The desire strains and presses in a direction which it feels to be right, but towards a point which it is unable to see. In short, the *absence of an item* is a determinant of our representations quite as positive as its presence can ever be. The gap becomes no mere void, but what is called an *aching* void. If we try to explain in terms of brain-action how a thought which only potentially exists can yet be effective, we seem driven to believe that the brain-tract thereof must actually be excited, but only in a minimal and sub-conscious way. Try, for instance, to symbolize what goes on in a man who is racking his brains to remember a thought which occurred to him last week. The associates of the thought are there, many of them at least, but they refuse to awaken the thought itself. We cannot suppose that they do not irradiate *at all* into its brain-tract, because his mind quivers on the very edge of its recovery. Its actual rhythm sounds in his ears; the words seem on the imminent point of following, but fail (see p. 165). Now the only difference between the effort to recall things forgotten and the search after the means to a given end is that the latter have not, whilst the former have, already formed a part of our experience. If we first study *the mode of recalling a thing forgotten*, we can take up with better understanding the voluntary quest of the unknown.

Their Solution.—The forgotten thing is felt by us as a gap in the midst of certain other things. We possess a dim idea of where we were and what we were about when it last occurred to us. We recollect the general subject to which it pertains. But all these details refuse to shoot together into a solid whole, for the lack of the missing thing, so we keep running over them in our mind, dissatisfied, craving something more. From each detail there radiate lines of association forming so many tentative guesses. Many of these are immediately seen to be irrelevant, are therefore void of interest, and lapse immediately from consciousness. Others are associated with the other details present, and with the missing thought as well. When *these* surge up, we have a peculiar feeling that we are 'warm,' as the children say when they play hide and seek; and such associates as these we clutch at and keep before the attention. Thus we recollect successively that when we last were considering the matter in question we were at the dinner-table; then that our friend J. D. was there; then that the subject talked about was so and so; finally, that the thought came *à propos* of a certain anecdote, and then that it had something to do with a French quotation. Now all these added associates *arise independently of the will*, by the spontaneous processes we know so well. *All that the will does is to emphasize and linger over those which seem pertinent, and ignore the rest.* Through this hovering of the attention in the neighborhood of the desired object, the accumulation of associates becomes so great that the combined tensions of their neural processes break through the bar, and the nervous wave pours into the tract which has so long been awaiting its advent. And as the expectant, sub-conscious

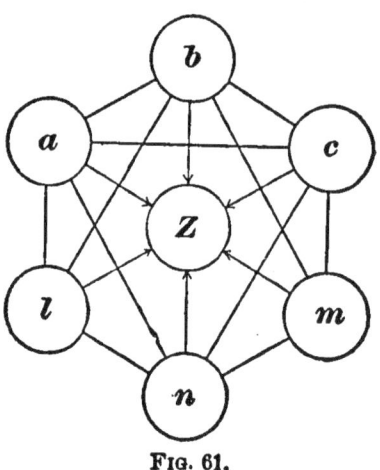

FIG. 61.

itching, so to speak, bursts into the fulness of vivid feeling, the mind finds an inexpressible relief.

The whole process can be rudely symbolized in a diagram. Call the forgotten thing Z, the first facts with which we felt it was related a, b, and c, and the details finally operative in calling it up l, m, and n. Each circle will then stand for the brain-process principally concerned in the thought of the fact lettered within it. The activity in Z will at first be a mere tension; but as the activities in a, b, and c little by little irradiate into l, m, and n, and as all these processes are somehow connected with Z, their combined irradiations upon Z, represented by the centripetal arrows, succeed in rousing Z also to full activity.

Turn now to the case of finding the unknown means to a distinctly conceived end. The end here stands in the place of a, b, c, in the diagram. It is the starting-point of the irradiations of suggestion; and here, as in that case, what the voluntary attention does is only to dismiss some of the suggestions as irrelevant, and hold fast to others which are felt to be more pertinent—let these be symbolized by l, m, n. These latter at last accumulate sufficiently to discharge all together into Z, the excitement of which process is, in the mental sphere, equivalent to the solution of our problem. The only difference between this and the previous case is that in this one there need be no original sub-excitement in Z, coöperating from the very first. In the solving of a problem, all that we are aware of in advance seems to be its *relations*. It must be a cause, or it must be an effect, or it must contain an attribute, or it must be a means, or what not. We know, in short, a lot *about* it, whilst as yet we have no *acquaintance* with it. Our perception that one of the objects which turn up is, at last, our *quæsitum*, is due to our recognition that its relations are identical with those we had in mind, and this may be a rather slow act of judgment. Every one knows that an object may be for some time present to his mind before its relations to other matters are perceived. Just so the relations may be there before the object is.

From the guessing of newspaper enigmas to the plotting of the policy of an empire there is no other process than this. We must trust to the laws of cerebral nature to present us spontaneously with the appropriate idea, but we must know it for the right one when it comes.

It is foreign to my purpose here to enter into any detailed analysis of the different classes of mental pursuit. In a scientific research we get perhaps as rich an example as can be found. The inquirer starts with a fact of which he seeks the reason, or with an hypothesis of which he seeks the proof. In either case he keeps turning the matter incessantly in his mind until, by the arousal of associate upon associate, some habitual, some similar, one arises which he recognizes to suit his need. This, however, may take years. No rules can be given by which the investigator may proceed straight to his result; but both here and in the case of reminiscence the accumulation of helps in the way of associations may advance more rapidly by the use of certain routine methods. In striving to recall a thought, for example, we may of set purpose run through the successive classes of circumstance with which it may possibly have been connected, trusting that when the right member of the class has turned up it will help the thought's revival. Thus we may run through all the *places* in which we may have had it. We may run through the *persons* whom we remember to have conversed with, or we may call up successively all the *books* we have lately been reading. If we are trying to remember a person we may run through a list of streets or of professions. Some item out of the lists thus methodically gone over will very likely be associated with the fact we are in need of, and may suggest it or help to do so. And yet the item might never have arisen without such systematic procedure. In scientific research this accumulation of associates has been methodized by Mill under the title of 'The Four Methods of Experimental Inquiry.' By the 'method of agreement,' by that of 'difference,' by those of 'residues' and 'concomitant variations' (which cannot here be more nearly defined), we make certain lists of cases; and by ruminating these lists in our minds the cause we seek will be more likely to emerge. But the final stroke of discovery is only prepared, not effected, by them. The brain-tracts must, of their own accord, shoot the right way at last, or we shall still grope in darkness. That in some brains the tracts *do* shoot the right way much oftener than in others, and that we cannot tell why,—these are ultimate facts to which we must never close our eyes. Even in forming our lists of instances according to Mill's methods, we are at the mercy of the spontaneous workings of Similarity in our brain. How are a number of facts, resembling the one whose cause we seek, to be brought together in a list unless one will rapidly suggest another through association by similarity?

Similarity no Elementary Law.—Such is the analysis I propose, first of the three main types of spontaneous, and then of voluntary, trains of thought. It will be observed that the *object called up may bear any logical relation whatever to the one which suggested it.* The law requires only that one condition should be fulfilled. The fading object must be due to a brain-process some of whose elements awaken through habit some of the elements of the brain-process of the object which comes to view. This awakening is the causal agency in the kind of association called Similarity, as in any other sort. The similarity *itself* between the objects has no causal agency in carrying us from one to the other. It is but a result—the effect of the usual causal agent when this happens to work in a certain way. Ordinary writers talk as if the similarity of the objects were itself an agent, coördinate with habit, and independent of it, and like it able to push objects before the mind. This is quite unintelligible. The similarity of two things does not exist till both things are there—it is meaningless to talk of it as an *agent of production* of anything, whether in the physical or the psychical realms. It is a relation which the mind perceives after the fact, just as it may perceive the relations of superiority, of distance, of causality, of container and content, of substance and accident, or of contrast, between an object and some second object which the associative machinery calls up.

Conclusion.—To sum up, then, we see that *the difference between the three kinds of association reduces itself to a simple difference in the amount of that portion of the nerve-tract supporting the going thought which is operative in calling up the thought which comes.* But the *modus operandi* of this active part is the same, be it large or be it small. The items constituting the coming object waken in every instance because their nerve-tracts once were excited continuously with those of the going object or its operative part. This ultimate physiological law of habit among the neural elements is what *runs* the train. The direction of its course and the form of its transitions are due to the unknown conditions by which in some brains action tends to focalize itself in small spots, while in others it fills patiently its broad bed. What these differing conditions are, it seems impossible to guess. Whatever they are, they are what separate the man of genius from the prosaic creature of habit and routine thinking. In the chapter on Reasoning we shall need to recur again to this point. I trust that the student will now feel that the way to a deeper understanding of the order of our ideas lies in the direction of cerebral physiology. The *elementary* process of revival can be nothing but the law of habit. Truly the day is distant when physiologists shall actually trace from cell-group to cell-group the irradiations which we have hypothetically invoked. Probably it will never arrive. The schematism we have used is, moreover, taken immediately from the analysis of objects into their elementary parts, and only extended by analogy to the brain. And yet it is only as incorporated in the brain that such a schematism can represent anything *causal*. This is, to my mind, the conclusive reason for saying that the order of *presentation of the mind's materials* is due to cerebral physiology alone.

The law of accidental prepotency of certain processes over others falls also within the sphere of cerebral probabilities. Granting such instability as the brain-tissue requires, certain points must always discharge more quickly and strongly than others; and this prepotency would shift its place from moment to moment by accidental causes, giving us a perfect mechanical diagram of the capricious play of similar association in the most gifted mind. A study of dreams confirms this view. The usual abundance of paths of irradiation seems, in the dormant brain, reduced. A few only are pervious, and the most fantastic sequences occur because the currents run—'like sparks in burnt-up paper'—wherever the nutrition of the moment creates an opening, but nowhere else.

The *effects of interested attention and volition* remain. These activities seem to hold fast to certain elements and, by emphasizing them and dwelling on them, to make their associates the only ones which are evoked. *This* is the point at which an anti-mechanical psychology must, if anywhere, make its stand in dealing with association. Everything else is pretty certainly due to cerebral laws. My own opinion on the question of active attention and spiritual spontaneity is expressed elsewhere (see p. 237). But even though there be a mental spontaneity, it can certainly not create ideas or summon them *ex abrupto*. Its power is limited to *selecting* amongst those which the associative machinery introduces. If it can emphasize, reinforce, or protract for half a second either one of these, it can do all that the most eager advocate of free will need demand; for it then decides the direction of the *next* associations by making them hinge upon the emphasized term; and determining in this wise the course of the man's thinking, it also determines his acts.

CHAPTER XVII.

THE SENSE OF TIME.

The sensible present has duration. Let any one try, I will not say to arrest, but to notice or attend to, the *present* moment of time. One of the most baffling experiences occurs. Where is it, this present? It has melted in our grasp, fled ere we could touch it, gone in the instant of becoming. As a poet, quoted by Mr. Hodgson, says,

"Le moment où je parle est déjà loin de moi,"

and it is only as entering into the living and moving organization of a much wider tract of time that the strict present is apprehended at all. It is, in fact, an altogether ideal abstraction, not only never realized in sense, but probably never even conceived of by those unaccustomed to philosophic meditation. Reflection leads us to the conclusion that it *must* exist, but that it *does* exist can never be a fact of our immediate experience. The only fact of our immediate experience is what has been well called 'the specious' present, a sort of saddle-back of time with a certain length of its own, on which we sit perched, and from which we look in two directions into time. The unit of composition of our perception of time is a *duration*, with a bow and a stern, as it were—a rearward- and a forward-looking end. It is only as parts of this *duration-block* that the relation of *succession* of one end to the other is perceived. We do not first feel one end and then feel the other after it, and from the perception of the succession infer an interval of time between, but we seem to feel the interval of time as a whole, with its two ends embedded in it. The experience is from the outset a synthetic datum, not a simple one; and to sensible perception its elements are inseparable, although attention looking back may easily decompose the experience, and distinguish its beginning from its end.

The moment we pass beyond a very few seconds our consciousness of duration ceases to be an immediate perception and becomes a construction more or less symbolic. To realize even an hour, we must count 'now! now! now! now!' indefinitely. Each 'now' is the feeling of a separate *bit* of time, and the exact sum of the bits never makes a clear impression on our mind. The *longest bit of duration* which we can apprehend at once so as to discriminate it from longer and shorter bits of time would seem (from experiments made for another purpose in Wundt's laboratory) to be about 12 seconds. *The shortest interval* which we can feel as time at all would seem to be $\frac{1}{500}$ of a second. That is, Exner recognized two electric sparks to be successive when the second followed the first at that interval.

We have no sense for empty time. Let one sit with closed eyes and, abstracting entirely from the outer world, attend exclusively to the passage of time, like one who wakes, as the poet says, "to hear time flowing in the middle of the night, and all things moving to a day of doom." There seems under such circumstances as these no variety in the material content of our thought, and what we notice appears, if anything, to be the pure series of durations budding, as it were, and growing beneath our indrawn gaze. Is this really so or not? The question is important; for, if the experience be what it roughly seems, we have a sort of special sense for pure time—a sense to which empty duration is an adequate stimulus; while if it be an illusion, it must be that our perception of time's flight, in the experiences quoted, is due to the *filling* of the time, and to our *memory* of a content which it had a moment previous, and which we feel to agree or disagree with its content now.

It takes but a small exertion of introspection to show that the latter alternative is the true one, and that *we can no more perceive a duration than we can perceive an extension, devoid of all sensible content.* Just as with closed eyes we see a dark visual field in which a curdling play of obscurest luminosity is always going on; so, be we never so abstracted from distinct outward impressions, we are always inwardly immersed in what Wundt has somewhere called the twilight of our general consciousness. Our heart-beats, our breathing, the pulses of our attention, fragments of words or sentences that pass through our imagination, are what people this dim habitat. Now, all these processes are rhythmical, and are apprehended by us, as they occur, in their totality; the breathing and pulses of attention, as coherent successions, each with its rise and fall; the heart-beats similarly, only relatively far more brief; the words not separately, but in connected groups. In short, empty our minds as we may, some form of *changing process* remains for us to feel, and cannot be expelled. And along with the sense of the process and its rhythm goes the sense of the length of time it lasts. Awareness of *change* is thus the condition on which our perception of time's flow depends; but there exists no reason to suppose that empty time's own changes are sufficient for the awareness of change to be aroused. The change must be of some concrete sort.

Appreciation of Longer Durations.—In the experience of watching empty time flow—'empty' to be taken hereafter in the relative sense just set forth—we tell it off in pulses. We say 'now! now! now!' or we count 'more! more! more!' as we feel it bud. This composition out of units of duration is called the law of time's *discrete flow.* The discreteness is, however, merely due to the fact that our successive acts of *recognition* or *apperception* of *what* it is are discrete. The sensation is as continuous as any sensation can be. All continuous sensations are *named* in beats. We notice that a certain finite 'more' of them is passing or already past. To adopt Hodgson's image, the sensation is the measuring-tape, the perception the dividing-engine which stamps its length. As we listen to a steady sound, we *take it in* in discrete pulses of recognition, calling it successively 'the same! the same! the same!' The case stands no otherwise with time.

After a small number of beats our impression of the amount we have told off becomes quite vague. Our only way of knowing it accurately is by counting, or noticing the clock, or through some other symbolic conception. When the times exceed hours or days, the conception is absolutely symbolic. We think of the amount we mean either solely as a *name,* or by running over a few salient *dates* therein, with no pretence of imagining the full durations that lie between them. No one has anything like a *perception* of the greater length of the time between now and the first century than of that between now and the tenth. To an historian, it is true, the longer interval will suggest a host of additional dates and events, and so appear a more *multitudinous* thing. And for the same reason most people will think they directly perceive the length of the past fortnight to exceed that of the past week. But there is properly no comparative time-*intuition* in these cases at all. It is but dates and events representing time, their abundance symbolizing its length. I am sure that this is so, even where the times compared are no more than an hour or so in length. It is the same with spaces of many miles, which we always compare with each other by the numbers that measure them.

From this we pass naturally to speak of certain familiar variations in our estimation of lengths of time. *In general, a time filled with varied and interesting experiences seems short in passing, but long as we look back. On the other hand, a tract of time empty of experiences seems long in passing, but in retrospect short.* A week of travel and sight-seeing may subtend an angle more like three weeks in the memory; and a month of sickness yields hardly more memories than a day. The length in retrospect depends obviously on the multitudinousness of the memories which the time affords. Many objects, events, changes, many subdivisions, immediately widen the view as we look back. Emptiness, monotony, familiarity, make it shrivel up.

The same space of time seems shorter as we grow older— that is, the days, the months, and the years do so; whether the hours do so is doubtful, and the minutes and seconds to all appearance remain about the same. An old man probably does not *feel* his past life to be any longer than he did when he was a boy, though it may be a dozen times as long. In most men all the events of manhood's years are of such familiar *sorts* that the individual impressions do not last. At the same time more and more of the earlier events get forgotten, the result being that no greater multitude of distinct objects remains in the memory.

So much for the apparent shortening of tracts of time in *retrospect*. They shorten *in passing* whenever we are so fully occupied with their content as not to note the actual time itself. A day full of excitement, with no pause, is said to pass ' ere we know it.' On the contrary, a day full of waiting, of unsatisfied desire for change, will seem a small eternity. *Tædium, ennui, Langweile, boredom,* are words for which, probably, every language known to man has its equivalent. It comes about whenever, from the relative emptiness of content of a tract of time, we grow attentive to the passage of the time itself. Expecting, and being ready for, a new impression to succeed; when it fails to come, we get an empty time instead of it; and such experiences, ceaselessly renewed, make us most formidably aware of the extent of the mere time itself. Close your eyes and simply wait to hear somebody tell you that a minute has elapsed, and the full length of your leisure with it seems incredible. You engulf yourself into its bowels as into those of that interminable first week of an ocean voyage, and find yourself wondering that history can have overcome many such periods in its course. All because you attend so closely to the mere feeling of the time *per se*, and because your attention to that is susceptible of such fine-grained successive subdivision. The *odiousness* of the whole experience comes from its insipidity; for *stimulation* is the indispensable requisite for pleasure in an experience, and the feeling of bare time is the least stimulating experience we can have. The sensation of tedium is a *protest*, says Volkmann, against the entire present.

The feeling of past time **is a** present feeling. In reflecting on the *modus operandi* of our consciousness of time, we are at first tempted to suppose it the easiest thing in the world to understand. Our inner states succeed each other. They know themselves as they are; then of course, we say, they must know their own succession. But this philosophy is too crude; for between the mind's own changes *being* successive, and *knowing their own succession*, lies as broad a chasm as between the object and subject of any case of cognition in the world. *A succession of feelings, in and of itself, is not a feeling of succession. And since, to our successive feelings, a feeling of their succession is added, that must be treated as an additional fact requiring its own special elucidation*, which this talk about the feelings knowing their time-relations as a matter of course leaves all untouched.

If we represent the actual time-stream of our thinking by an horizontal line, the thought *of* the stream or of any segment of its length, past, present, or to come, might be figured in a perpendicular raised upon the horizontal at a certain point. The length of this perpendicular stands for a certain object or content, which in this case is the time thought of at the actual moment of the stream upon which the perpendicular is raised.

There is thus a sort of *perspective projection* of past objects upon present consciousness, similar to that of wide landscapes upon a camera-screen.

And since we saw a while ago that our maximum distinct *perception* of duration hardly covers more than a dozen seconds (while our maximum vague perception is probably not more than that of a minute or so), we must suppose that *this amount of duration is pictured fairly steadily in each passing instant of consciousness* by virtue of some fairly constant feature in the brain-process to which the consciousness is tied. *This feature of the brain-process, whatever it be, must be the cause of our perceiving the fact of time at all.* The duration thus steadily perceived is hardly more than the 'specious present,' as it was called a few pages back. Its *content* is in a constant flux, events dawning into its forward end as fast as they fade out of its rearward one, and each of them changing its time-coefficient from 'not yet,' or 'not quite yet,' to 'just gone,' or 'gone,' as it passes by. Meanwhile, the specious present, the intuited duration, stands permanent, like the rainbow on the waterfall, with its own quality unchanged by the events that stream through it. Each of these, as it slips out, retains the power of being reproduced; and when reproduced, is reproduced with the duration and neighbors which it originally had. Please observe, however, that the reproduction of an event, *after* it has once completely dropped out of the rearward end of the specious present, is an entirely different psychic fact from its direct perception in the specious present as a thing immediately past. A creature might be entirely devoid of *reproductive* memory, and yet have the time-sense; but the latter would be limited, in his case, to the few seconds immediately passing by. In the next chapter, assuming the sense of time as given, we will turn to the analysis of what happens in reproductive memory, the recall of *dated* things.

CHAPTER XVIII.

MEMORY.

Analysis of the Phenomenon of Memory.—Memory proper, or secondary memory as it might be styled, is the knowledge of a former state of mind after it has already once dropped from consciousness; or rather *it is the knowledge of an event, or fact,* of which meantime we have not been thinking, *with the additional consciousness that we have thought or experienced it before.*

The first element which such a knowledge involves would seem to be the revival in the mind of an image or copy of the original event. And it is an assumption made by many writers that such revival of an image is all that is needed to constitute the memory of the original occurrence. But such a revival is obviously not a *memory*, whatever else it may be; it is simply a duplicate, a second event, having absolutely no connection with the first event except that it happens to resemble it. The clock strikes to-day; it struck yesterday; and may strike a million times ere it wears out. The rain pours through the gutter this week; it did so last week; and will do so *in sæcula sæculorum*. But does the present clock-stroke become aware of the past ones, or the present stream recollect the past stream, because they repeat and resemble them? Assuredly not. And let it not be said that this is because clock-strokes and gutters are physical and not psychical objects; for psychical objects (sensations, for example) simply recurring in successive editions will remember each other *on that account* no more than clock-strokes do. No memory is involved in the mere fact of recurrence. The successive editions of a feeling are so many independent events, each snug in its own skin. Yesterday's feeling is dead and buried; and the presence of to-day's is no reason why it should resuscitate along with to-day's. A farther condition is required before the present image can be held to stand for a *past original*.

That condition is that the fact imaged be *expressly referred to the past*, thought as *in the past*. But how can we think a thing as in the past, except by thinking of the past together with the thing, and of the relation of the two? And how can we think of the past? In the chapter on Time-perception we have seen that our intuitive or immediate consciousness of pastness hardly carries us more than a few seconds backward of the present instant of time. Remoter dates are conceived, not perceived; known symbolically by names, such as 'last week,' '1850'; or thought of by events which happened in them, as the year in which we attended such a school, or met with such a loss. So that if we wish to think of a particular past epoch, we must think of a name or other symbol, or else of certain concrete events, associated therewithal. Both must be thought of, to think the past epoch adequately. And to 'refer' any special fact to the past epoch is to think that fact *with* the names and events which characterize its date, to think it, in short, with a lot of contiguous associates.

But even this would not be memory. Memory requires more than mere dating of a fact in the past. It must be dated in *my* past. In other words, I must think that I directly experienced its occurrence. It must have that 'warmth and intimacy' which were so often spoken of in the chapter on the Self, as characterizing all experiences 'appropriated' by the thinker as his own.

A general feeling of the past direction in time, then, a particular date conceived as lying along that direction, and defined by its name or phenomenal contents, an event imagined as located therein, and owned as part of my experience,—such are the elements of every object of memory.

Retention and Recall.—Such being the phenomenon of memory, or the analysis of its object, can we see how it comes to pass? can we lay bare its causes?

Its complete exercise presupposes two things:
1) The *retention* of the remembered fact; and
2) Its *reminiscence, recollection, reproduction,* or *recall.*

Now *the cause both of retention and of recollection is the law of habit in the nervous system, working as it does in the 'association of ideas.'*

Association explains Recall.—Associationists have long explained *recollection* by association. James Mill gives an account of it which I am unable to improve upon, unless it might be by translating his word 'idea' into 'thing thought of,' or 'object.'

"There is," he says, "a state of mind familiar to all men, in which we are said to remember. In this state it is certain we have not in the mind the idea which we are trying to have in it. How is it, then, that we proceed, in the course of our endeavor, to procure its introduction into the mind? If we have not the idea itself, we have certain ideas connected with it. We run over those ideas, one after another, in hopes that some one of them will suggest the idea we are in quest of; and if any one of them does, it is always one so connected with it as to call it up in the way of association. I meet an old acquaintance, whose name I do not remember, and wish to recollect. I run over a number of names, in hopes that some of them may be associated with the idea of the individual. I think of all the circumstances in which I have seen him engaged; the time when I knew him, the persons along with whom I knew him, the things he did, or the things he suffered; and if I chance upon any idea with which the name is associated, then immediately I have the recollection; if not, my pursuit of it is vain. There is another set of cases, very familiar, but affording very important evidence on the subject. It frequently happens that there are matters which we desire not to forget. What is the contrivance to which we have recourse for preserving the memory —that is, for making sure that it will be called into existence when it is our wish that it should? All men invariably employ the same expedient. They endeavor to form an association between the idea of the thing to be remembered and some sensation, or some idea, which they know beforehand will occur at or near the time when they wish the remembrance to be in their minds. If this association is formed and the association or idea with which it has been formed occurs, the sensation, or idea, calls up the remembrance, and the object of him who formed the association is attained. To use a vulgar instance: a man receives a commission from his friend, and, that he may not forget it, ties a knot in his handkerchief. How is this fact to be explained? First of all, the idea of the commission is associated with the making of the knot. Next, the handkerchief is a thing which it is known beforehand will be frequently seen, and of course at no great distance of time from the occasion on which the memory is desired. The handkerchief being seen, the knot is seen, and this sensation recalls the idea of the commission, between which and itself the association had been purposely formed."

In short, we make search in our memory for a forgotten idea, just as we rummage our house for a lost object. In both cases we visit what seems to us the probable *neighborhood* of that which we miss. We turn over the things under which, or within which, or alongside of which, it may possibly be; and if it lies near them, it soon comes to view. But these matters, in the case of a mental object sought, are nothing but its *associates*. The machinery of recall is thus the same as the machinery of association, and the machinery of association, as we know, is nothing but the elementary law of habit in the nerve-centres.

It also explains retention. And this same law of habit is the machinery of retention also. Retention means *liability* to recall, and it means nothing more than such liability. The only proof of there being retention is that recall actually takes place. The retention of an experience is, in short, but another name for the *possibility* of thinking it again, or the *tendency* to think it again, with its past surroundings. Whatever accidental cue may turn this tendency into an actuality, the permanent *ground* of the tendency itself lies in the organized neural paths by which the cue calls up the memorable experience, the past associates, the sense that the self was there, the belief that it all really happened, etc., as previously described. When the recollection is of the 'ready' sort, the resuscitation takes place the instant the cue arises; when it is slow, resuscitation comes after delay. But be the recall prompt or slow, the condition which makes it possible at all (or, in other words, the 'retention' of the experience) is neither more nor less than the brain-paths which *associate* the experience with the occasion and cue of the recall. *When slumbering, these paths are the condition of retention; when active, they are the condition of recall.*

Brain-scheme.—A simple scheme will now make the whole cause of memory plain. Let n be a past event, o its 'setting' (concomitants, date, self present, warmth and intimacy, etc., etc., as already set forth), and m some present thought or fact which may appropriately become the occasion of its recall. Let the nerve-centres, active in the thought of m, n, and o, be represented by M, N, and O, respectively; then the *existence*

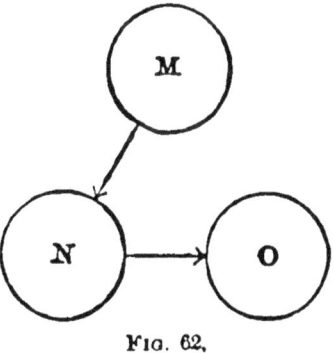

Fig. 62.

of the *paths* symbolized by the lines between M and N and N and O will be the fact indicated by the phrase 'retention of the event n in the memory,' and the *excitement* of the brain along these paths will be the condition of the event n's actual recall. The *retention* of n, it will be observed, is no mysterious storing up of an 'idea' in an unconscious state. It is not a fact of the mental order at all. It is a purely physical phenomenon, a morphological feature, the presence of these 'paths,' namely, in the finest recesses of the brain's tissue. The recall or recollection, on the other hand, is a *psycho-physical* phenomenon, with both a bodily and a mental side. The bodily side is the excitement of the paths in question; the mental side is the conscious representation of the past occurrence, and the belief that we experienced it before.

The only hypothesis, in short, to which the facts of inward experience give countenance is that *the brain-tracts excited by the event proper, and those excited in its recall, are in part* DIFFERENT *from each other*. If we could revive the past event without any associates we should exclude the possibility of memory, and simply dream that we were undergoing the experience as if for the first time. Wherever, in fact, the recalled event does appear without a definite setting, it is hard to distinguish it from a mere creation of fancy. But in proportion as its image lingers and recalls associates which gradually become more definite, it grows more and more distinctly into a remembered thing. For example, I enter a friend's room and see on the wall a painting. At first I have the strange, wondering consciousness, 'Surely I have seen that before,' but when or how does not become clear. There only clings to the picture a sort of penumbra of familiarity,—when suddenly I exclaim: "I have it! It is a copy of part of one of the Fra Angelicos in the Florentine Academy—I recollect it there." Only when the image of the Academy arises does the picture become remembered, as well as seen.

The Conditions of Goodness in Memory.—The remembered fact being n, then, the path N—O is what arouses for n its setting when it *is* recalled, and makes it other than a mere imagination. The path M—N, on the other hand, gives the cue or occasion of its being recalled at all. *Memory being thus altogether conditioned on brain-paths, its excellence in a given individual will depend partly on the* NUMBER *and partly on the* PERSISTENCE *of these paths.*

The persistence or permanence of the paths is a physiological property of the brain-tissue of the individual, whilst their number is altogether due to the facts of his mental experience. Let the quality of permanence in the paths be called the native tenacity, or physiological retentiveness. This tenacity differs enormously from infancy to old age, and from one person to another. Some minds are like wax under a seal—no impression, however disconnected with others, is wiped out. Others, like a jelly, vibrate to every touch, but under usual conditions retain no permanent mark. These latter minds, before they can recollect a fact, must weave it into their permanent stores of knowledge. They have no *desultory* memory. Those persons, on the contrary who retain names, dates and addresses, anecdotes, gossip, poetry, quotations, and all sorts of miscellaneous facts, without an effort, have desultory memory in a high degree, and certainly owe it to the unusual tenacity of their brain-substance for any path once formed therein. No one probably was ever effective on a voluminous scale without a high degree of this physiological retentiveness. In the practical as in the theoretic life, the man whose acquisitions *stick* is the man who is always achieving and advancing, whilst his neighbors, spending most of their time in relearning what they once knew but have forgotten, simply hold their own. A Charlemagne, a Luther, a Leibnitz, a Walter Scott, any example, in short, of your quarto or folio editions of mankind, must needs have amazing retentiveness of the purely physiological sort. Men without this retentiveness may excel in the *quality* of their work at this point or at that, but will never do such mighty sums of it, or be influential contemporaneously on such a scale.

But there comes a time of life for all of us when we can do no more than hold our own in the way of acquisitions, when the old paths fade as fast as the new ones form in our brain, and when we forget in a week quite as much as we can learn in the same space of time. This equilibrium may last many, many years. In extreme old age it is upset in the reverse direction, and forgetting prevails over acquisition, or rather there is no acquisition. Brain-paths are so transient that in the course of a few minutes of conversation the same question is asked and its answer forgotten half a dozen times. Then the superior tenacity of the paths formed in childhood becomes manifest: the dotard will retrace the facts of his earlier years after he has lost all those of later date.

So much for the permanence of the paths. Now for their number.

It is obvious that the more there are of such paths as M—N in the brain, and the more of such possible cues or occasions for the recall of n in the mind, the prompter and surer, on the whole, the memory of n will be, the more frequently one will be reminded of it, the more avenues of approach to it one will possess. In mental terms, *the more other facts a fact is associated with in the mind, the better possession of it our memory retains.* Each of its associates bceomes a hook to which it hangs, a means to fish it up by when sunk beneath the surface. Together, they form a network of attachments by which it is woven into the entire tissue of our thought. The 'secret of a good memory' is thus the secret of forming diverse and multiple associations with every fact we care to retain. But this forming of associations with a fact, what is it but *thinking about* the fact as much as possible? Briefly, then, of two men with the same outward experiences and the same amount of mere native tenacity, *the one who* THINKS *over his experiences most, and weaves them into systematic relations with each other, will be the one with the best memory.* We see examples of this on every hand. Most men have a good memory for facts connected with their own pursuits. The college athlete who remains a dunce at his books will astonish you by his knowledge of men's 'records' in various feats and games, and will be a walking dictionary of sporting statistics. The reason is that he is constantly going over these things in his mind, and comparing and making series of them. They form for him not so many odd facts, but a concept-system—so they stick. So the merchant remembers prices, the politician other politicians' speeches and votes, with a copiousness which amazes outsiders, but which the amount of thinking they bestow on these subjects easily explains. The great memory for facts which a Darwin and a Spencer reveal in their books is not incompatible with the possession on their part of a brain with only a middling degree of physiological retentiveness. Let a man early in life set himself the task of verifying such a theory as that of evolution, and facts will soon cluster and cling to him like grapes to their stem. Their relations to the theory will hold them fast; and the more of these the mind is able to discern, the greater the erudition will become. Meanwhile the theorist may have little, if any, desultory memory. Unutilizable facts may be unnoted by him and forgotten as soon as heard. An ignorance almost as encyclopædic as his erudition may coexist with the latter, and hide, as it were, in the interstices of its web. Those who have had much to do with scholars and *savants* will readily think of examples of the class of mind I mean.

In a system, every fact is connected with every other by some thought-relation. The consequence is that every fact is retained by the combined suggestive power of all the other facts in the system, and forgetfulness is well-nigh impossible.

The reason **why** cramming is **such** a **bad** mode of **study** is now made clear. I mean by cramming that way of preparing for examinations by committing 'points' to memory during a few hours or days of intense application immediately preceding the final ordeal, little or no work having been performed during the previous course of the term. Things learned thus in a few hours, on one occasion, for one purpose, cannot possibly have formed many associations with other things in the mind. Their brain-processes are led into by few paths, and are relatively little liable to be awakened again. Speedy oblivion is the almost inevitable fate of all that is committed to memory in this simple way. Whereas, on the contrary, the same materials taken in gradually, day after day, recurring in different contexts, considered in various relations, associated with other external incidents, and repeatedly reflected on, grow into such a system, form such connections with the rest of the mind's fabric, lie open to so many paths of approach, that they remain permanent possessions. This is the *intellectual* reason why habits of continuous application should be enforced in educational establishments. Of course there is no moral turpitude in cramming. Did it lead to the desired end of secure learning, it were infinitely the best method of study. But it does not; and students themselves should understand the reason why.

One's native retentiveness is unchangeable. It will now appear clear that *all improvement of the memory lies in the line of* ELABORATING THE ASSOCIATES *of each of the several things to be remembered. No amount of culture would seem capable of modifying a man's* GENERAL *retentiveness.* This is a physiological quality, given once for all with his organization, and which he can never hope to change. It differs no doubt in disease and health; and it is a fact of observation that it is better in fresh and vigorous hours than when we are fagged or ill. We may say, then, that a man's native tenacity will fluctuate somewhat with his hygiene, and that whatever is good for his tone of health will also be good for his memory. We may even say that whatever amount of intellectual exercise is bracing to the general tone and nutrition of the brain will also be profitable to the general retentiveness. But more than this we cannot say; and this, it is obvious, is far less than most people believe.

It is, in fact, commonly thought that certain exercises, systematically repeated, will strengthen, not only a man's remembrance of the particular facts used in the exercises, but his faculty for remembering facts at large. And a plausible case is always made out by saying that practice in learning words by heart makes it easier to learn new words in the same way. If this be true, then what I have just said is false, and the whole doctrine of memory as due to 'paths' must be revised. But I am disposed to think the alleged fact untrue. I have carefully questioned several mature actors on the point, and all have denied that the practice of learning parts has made any such difference as is alleged. What it has done for them is to improve their power of *studying* a part systematically. Their mind is now full of precedents in the way of intonation, emphasis, gesticulation; the new words awaken distinct suggestions and decisions; are caught up, in fact, into a preexisting network, like the merchant's prices, or the athlete's store of 'records,' and are recollected easier, although the mere native tenacity is not a whit improved, and is usually, in fact, impaired by age. It is a case of better remembering by better *thinking*. Similarly when schoolboys improve by practice in ease of learning by heart, the improvement will, I am sure, be always found to reside in the *mode of study of the particular piece* (due to the greater interest, the greater suggestiveness, the generic similarity with other pieces, the more sustained attention, etc., etc.), and not at all to any enhancement of the brute retentive power.

The error I speak of pervades an otherwise useful and judicious book, 'How to Strengthen the Memory,' by Dr. M. C. Holbrook of New York. The author fails to distinguish between the general physiological retentiveness and the retention of particular things, and talks as if both must be benefited by the same means.

"I am now treating," he says, "a case of loss of memory in a person advanced in years, who did not know that his memory had failed most remarkably till I told him of it. He is making vigorous efforts to bring it back again, and with partial success. The method pursued is to spend two hours daily, one in the morning and one in the evening, in exercising this faculty. The patient is instructed to give the closest attention to all that he learns, so that it shall be impressed on his mind clearly. He is asked to recall every evening all the facts and experiences of the day, and again the next morning. Every name heard is written down and impressed on his mind clearly, and an effort made to recall it at intervals. Ten names from among public men are ordered to be committed to memory every week. A verse of poetry is to be learned, also a verse from the Bible, daily. He is asked to remember the number of the page in any book where any interesting fact is recorded. These and other methods are slowly resuscitating a failing memory."

I find it very hard to believe that the memory of the poor old gentleman is a bit the better for all this torture except in respect of the particular facts thus wrought into it, and other matters that may have been connected therewithal.

Improving the Memory.—All improvement of memory consists, then, in the improvement of one's *habitual methods of recording facts*. Methods have been divided into the mechanical, the ingenious, and the judicious.

The *mechanical methods* consist in the intensification, prolongation, and *repetition* of the impression to be remembered. The modern method of teaching children to read by blackboard work, in which each word is impressed by the fourfold channel of eye, ear, voice, and hand, is an example of an improved mechanical method of memorizing.

Judicious methods of remembering things are nothing but logical ways of conceiving them and working them into rational systems, classifying them, analyzing them into parts, etc., etc. All the sciences are such methods.

Of *ingenious methods* many have been invented, under the name of technical memories. By means of these systems it is often possible to retain entirely disconnected facts, lists of names, numbers, and so forth, so multitudinous as to be entirely unrememberable in a natural way.

The method consists usually in a framework learned mechanically, of which the mind is supposed to remain in secure and permanent possession. Then, whatever is to be remembered is deliberately associated by some fanciful analogy or connection with some part of this framework, and this connection thenceforward helps its recall. The best known and most used of these devices is the figure-alphabet. To remember numbers, e.g., a figure-alphabet is first formed, in which each numerical digit is represented by one or more letters. The number is then translated into such letters as will best make a word, if possible a word suggestive of the object to which the number belongs. The word will then be remembered when the numbers alone might be forgotten.* The recent system of Loisette is a method, much less mechanical, of weaving the thing into associations which may aid its recall.

Recognition.—If, however, a phenomenon be met with too often, and with too great a variety of contexts, although its image is retained and reproduced with correspondingly great facility, it fails to come up with any one particular setting, and the projection of it backwards to a particular past date consequently does not come about. We *recognize* but do not *remember* it—its associates form too confused a cloud. A similar result comes about when a definite setting is only nascently aroused. We then feel that we have seen the object already, but when or where we cannot say, though we may seem to ourselves to be on the brink of saying it. That nascent cerebral excitations can thus affect consciousness is obvious from what happens when we seek to remember a name. It tingles, it trembles on the verge, but does not come. Just such a tingling and trembling of unre-

---

* A common figure-alphabet is this:

1	2	3	4	5	6	7	8	9	0
t	n	m	r	l	sh	g	f	b	s
d					j	k	v	p	c
					ch	c			z
					g	qu			

covered associates is the penumbra of recognition that may surround any experience and make it seem familiar, though we know not why.

There is a curious experience which everyone seems to have had—the feeling that the present moment in its completeness has been experienced before—we were saying just this thing, in just this place, to just these people, etc. This 'sense of preëxistence' has been treated as a great mystery and occasioned much speculation. Dr. Wigan considered it due to a dissociation of the action of the two hemispheres, one of them becoming conscious a little later than the other, but both of the same fact. I must confess that the quality of mystery seems to me here a little strained. I have over and over again in my own case succeeded in resolving the phenomenon into a case of memory, so indistinct that whilst some past circumstances are presented again, the others are not. The dissimilar portions of the past do not arise completely enough at first for the date to be identified. All we get is the present scene with a general suggestion of pastness about it. That faithful observer, Prof. Lazarus, interprets the phenomenon in the same way; and it is noteworthy that just as soon as the past context grows complete and distinct the emotion of weirdness fades from the experience.

Forgetting.—In the practical use of our intellect, forgetting is as important a function as remembering. 'Total recall' (see p. 261) we saw to be comparatively rare in association. If we remembered everything, we should on most occasions be as ill off as if we remembered nothing. It would take as long for us to recall a space of time as it took the original time to elapse, and we should never get ahead with our thinking. All recollected times undergo, accordingly, what M. Ribot calls foreshortening; and this foreshortening is due to the omission of an enormous number of the facts which filled them. "We thus reach the paradoxical result," says M. Ribot, "that one condition of remembering is that we should forget Without totally forgetting a prodigious number of states of consciousness, and momentarily forgetting a large number, we could not remember at all. Oblivion, except in certain cases, is thus no malady of memory, but a condition of its health and its life."

Pathological Conditions.—Hypnotic subjects as a rule forget all that has happened in their trance. But in a succeeding trance they will often remember the events of a past one. This is like what happens in those cases of 'double personality' in which no recollection of one of the lives is to be found in the other. The sensibility in these cases often differs from one of the alternate personalities to another, the patient being often anæsthetic in certain respects in one of the secondary states. Now the memory may come and go with the sensibility. M. Pierre Janet proved in various ways that what his patients forgot when anæsthetic they remembered when the sensibility returned. For instance, he restored their tactile sense temporarily by means of electric currents, passes, etc., and then made them handle various objects, such as keys and pencils, or make particular movements, like the sign of the cross. The moment the anæsthesia returned they found it impossible to recollect the objects or the acts. 'They had had nothing in their hands, they had done nothing,' etc. The next day, however, sensibility being again restored by similar processes, they remembered perfectly the circumstance, and told what they had handled or done.

All these pathological facts are showing us that the sphere of possible recollection may be wider than we think, and that in certain matters apparent oblivion is no proof against possible recall under other conditions. They give no countenance, however, to the extravagant opinion that absolutely no part of our experience can be forgotten.

CHAPTER XIX.

IMAGINATION.

What it is.—*Sensations, once experienced, modify the nervous organism, so that copies of them arise again in the mind after the original outward stimulus is gone.* No mental copy, however, can arise in the mind, of any kind of sensation which has never been directly excited from without.

The blind may dream of sights, the deaf of sounds, for years after they have lost their vision or hearing; but the man *born* deaf can never be made to imagine what sound is like, nor can the man *born* blind ever have a mental vision. In Locke's words, already quoted, " the mind can frame unto itself no one new simple idea." The originals of them all must have been given from without. Fantasy, or Imagination, are the names given to the faculty of reproducing copies of originals once felt. The imagination is called 'reproductive' when the copies are literal; 'productive' when elements from different originals are recombined so as to make new wholes.

When represented with surroundings concrete enough to constitute a *date*, these pictures, when they revive, form *recollections*. We have just studied the machinery of recollection. When the mental pictures are of data freely combined, and reproducing no past combination exactly, we have acts of imagination properly so called.

Men differ in visual imagination. Our ideas or images of past sensible experiences may be either distinct and adequate or dim, blurred, and incomplete. It is likely that the different degrees in which different men are able to make them sharp and complete has had something to do with keeping up such philosophic disputes as that of **Berkeley** with Locke over abstract ideas. Locke had spoken of our possessing 'the general idea of a triangle' which "must be neither oblique nor rectangle, neither equilateral, equicrural, nor scalenon, but all and none of these at once." Berkeley says: "If any man has the faculty of framing in his mind such an idea of a triangle as is here described, it is in vain to pretend to dispute him out of it, nor would I go about it. All I desire is that the reader would fully and certainly inform himself whether *he* has such an idea or no."

Until very recent years it was supposed by philosophers that there was a typical human mind which all individual minds were like, and that propositions of universal validity could be laid down about such faculties as 'the Imagination.' Lately, however, a mass of revelations have poured in which make us see how false a view this is. There are imaginations, not 'the Imagination,' and they must be studied in detail.

Mr. Galton in 1880 began a statistical inquiry which may be said to have made an era in descriptive psychology. He addressed a circular to large numbers of persons asking them to describe the image in their mind's eye of their breakfast-table on a given morning. The variations were found to be enormous; and, strange to say, it appeared that eminent scientific men on the average had less visualizing power than younger and more insignificant persons.

The reader will find details in Mr. Galton's 'Inquiries into Human Faculty,' pp. 83-114. I have myself for many years collected from each and all of my psychology-students descriptions of their own visual imagination; and found (together with some curious idiosyncrasies) corroboration of all the variations which Mr. Galton reports. As examples, I subjoin extracts from two cases near the ends of the scale. The writers are first cousins, grandsons of a distinguished man of science. The one who is a good visualizer says:

" This morning's breakfast-table is both dim and bright;

it is dim if I try to think of it when my eyes are open upon any object; it is perfectly clear and bright if I think of it with my eyes closed.—All the objects are clear at once, yet when I confine my attention to any one object it becomes far more distinct.—I have more power to recall color than any other one thing: if, for example, I were to recall a plate decorated with flowers I could reproduce in a drawing the exact tone, etc. The color of anything that was on the table is perfectly vivid.—There is very little limitation to the extent of my images: I can see all four sides of a room, I can see all four sides of two, three, four, even more rooms with such distinctness that if you should ask me what was in any particular place in any one, or ask me to count the chairs, etc., I could do it without the least hesitation.—The more I learn by heart the more clearly do I see images of my pages. Even before I can recite the lines I see them so that I could give them very slowly word for word, but my mind is so occupied in looking at my printed image that I have no idea of what I am saying, of the sense of it, etc. When I first found myself doing this I used to think it was merely because I knew the lines imperfectly; but I have quite convinced myself that I really do see an image. The strongest proof that such is really the fact is, I think, the following:

"I can look down the mentally seen page and see the words that *commence* all the lines, and from any one of these words I can continue the line. I find this much easier to do if the words begin in a straight line than if there are breaks. Example:

>   *Étant fait* . . . . .
>   *Tous* . . . . .
>   *A des* . . . . . .
>   *Que fit* . . . . . .
>   *Céres* . . . . .
>   *Avec* . . . . . .
>   *Un fleur* . . . . .
>   *Comme* . . . . .
>   (La Fontaine 8. iv.)"

The poor visualizer says:

"My ability to form mental images seems, from what I have studied of other people's images, to be defective and somewhat peculiar. The process by which I seem to remember any particular event is not by a series of distinct images, but a sort of panorama, the faintest impressions of which are perceptible through a thick fog.—I cannot shut my eyes and get a distinct image of anyone, although I used to be able to a few years ago, and the faculty seems to have gradually slipped away.—In my most vivid dreams, where the events appear like the most real facts, I am often troubled with a dimness of sight which causes the images to appear indistinct.—To come to the question of the breakfast-table, there is nothing definite about it. Everything is vague. I cannot say *what* I see. I could not possibly count the chairs, but I happen to know that there are ten. I see nothing in detail.—The chief thing is a general impression that I cannot tell exactly what I do see. The coloring is about the same, as far as I can recall it, only very much washed out. Perhaps the only color I can see at all distinctly is that of the table-cloth, and I could probably see the color of the wall-paper if I could remember what color it was."

A person whose visual imagination is strong finds it hard to understand how those who are without the faculty can think at all. *Some people undoubtedly have no visual images at all worthy of the name*, and instead of *seeing* their breakfast-table, they tell you that they *remember* it or *know* what was on it. The 'mind-stuff' of which this 'knowing' is made seems to be verbal images exclusively. But if the words 'coffee,' 'bacon,' 'mullins,' and 'eggs' lead a man to speak to his cook, to pay his bills, and to take measures for the morrow's meal exactly as visual and gustatory memories would, why are they not, for all practical intents and purposes, as good a kind of material in which to think ? In fact, we may suspect them to be for most purposes better than terms with a richer imaginative coloring. The scheme of relationship and the conclusion being the essential things in thinking, that kind of mindstuff which is handiest will be the best for the purpose. Now words, uttered or unexpressed, are the handiest mental elements we have. Not only are they very *rapidly* revivable, but they are revivable as actual sensations more easily than any other items of our experience. Did they not possess some such advantage as this, it would hardly be the case that the older men are and the more effective as thinkers, the more, as a rule, they have lost their visualizing power, as Mr. Galton found to be the case with members of the Royal Society.

Images of Sounds.—These also differ in individuals. Those who think by preference in auditory images are called *audiles* by Mr. Galton. *This type*, says M. Binet, *"appears to be rarer than the visual.* Persons of this type imagine what they think of in the language of sound. In order to remember a lesson they impress upon their mind, not the look of the page, but the sound of the words. They reason, as well as remember, by ear. In performing a mental addition they repeat verbally the names of the figures, and add, as it were, the sounds, without any thought of the graphic signs. Imagination also takes the auditory form. 'When I write a scene,' said Legouvé to Scribe, 'I *hear;* but you *see*. In each phrase which I write, the voice of the personage who speaks strikes my ear. *Vous, qui êtes le théâtre même,* your actors walk, gesticulate before your eyes; I am a *listener*, you a *spectator.*'—'Nothing more true,' said Scribe; 'do you know where I am when I write a piece? In the middle of the parterre.' It is clear that the *pure audile*, seeking to develop only a single one of his faculties, may, like the pure visualizer, perform astounding feats of memory— Mozart, for example, noting from memory the *Miserere* of the Sistine Chapel after two hearings; the deaf Beethoven, composing and inwardly repeating his enormous symphonies. On the other hand, the man of auditory type, like the visual, is exposed to serious dangers; for if he lose his auditory images, he is without resource and breaks down completely."

Images of Muscular Sensations.—Professor Stricker of Vienna, who seems to be a 'motile' or to have this form of imagination developed in unusual strength, has given a careful analysis of his own case. His recollections both of his own movements and of those of other things are accompanied invariably by distinct muscular feelings in those parts of his body which would naturally be used in effecting or in following the movement. In thinking of a soldier marching, for example, it is as if he were helping the image to march by marching himself in his rear. And if he suppresses this sympathetic feeling in his own legs and concentrates all his attention on the imagined soldier, the latter becomes, as it were, paralyzed. In general his imagined movements, of whatsoever objects, seem paralyzed, the moment no feelings of movement either in his own eyes or in his own limbs accompany them. The movements of articulate speech play a predominant part in his mental life. "When, after my experimental work," he says, "I proceed to its description, as a rule I reproduce in the first instance only words which I had already associated with the perception of the various details of the observation whilst the latter was going on. For speech plays in all my observing so important a part that I ordinarily clothe phenomena in words as fast as I observe them."

Most persons, on being asked *in what sort of terms they imagine words*, will say, 'In terms of hearing.' It is not until their attention is expressly drawn to the point that they find it difficult to say whether auditory images or motor images connected with the organs of articulation predominate. A good way of bringing the difficulty to consciousness is that proposed by Stricker: Partly open your mouth and then imagine any word with labials or dentals in it, such as 'bubble,' 'toddle.' Is your image under these conditions distinct? To most people the image is at first 'thick,' as the sound of the word would be if they tried to pronounce it with the lips parted. Many can never imagine the words clearly with the mouth open; others succeed after a few preliminary trials. The experiment proves how dependent our verbal imagination is on actual feelings in lips, tongue, throat, larynx, etc. Prof. Bain says that "a *suppressed articulation is in fact the material of our recollection,* the intellectual manifestation, the *idea* of speech." In persons whose auditory imagination is weak, the articulatory image does indeed seem to constitute the whole material for verbal thought. Professor Stricker says that in his own case no auditory image enters into the words of which he thinks.

Images of Touch.—These are very strong in some people. The most vivid touch-images come when we ourselves barely escape local injury, or when we see another injured. The place may then actually tingle with the imaginary sensation—perhaps not altogether imaginary, since goose-flesh, paling or reddening, and other evidences of actual muscular contraction in the spot, may result.

"An educated man," says Herr G. H. Meyer, "told me once that on entering his house one day he received a shock from crushing the finger of one of his little children in the door. At the moment of his fright he felt a violent pain in the corresponding finger of his own body, and this pain abode with him three days."

The imagination of a blind deaf-mute like Laura Bridgman must be confined entirely to tactile and motor material. *All blind persons must belong to the 'tactile' and 'motile' types* of the French authors. When the young man whose cataracts were removed by Dr. Franz was shown different geometric figures, he said he " had not been able to form from them the idea of a square and a disk until he perceived a sensation of what he saw in the points of his fingers, as if he really touched the objects."

Pathological Differences.—The study of Aphasia (see p. 114) has of late years shown how unexpectedly individuals

differ in the use of their imagination. In some the habitual
'thought-stuff,' if one may so call it, is visual; in others
it is auditory, articulatory, or motor; in most, perhaps, it
is evenly mixed. These are the "indifferents" of Charcot.
The same local cerebral injury must needs work different
practical results in persons who differ in this way. In
one what is thrown out of gear is a much-used brain-
tract; in the other an unimportant region is affected. A
particularly instructive case was published by Charcot in
1883. The patient was a merchant, an exceedingly accomplished man, but a visualizer of the most exclusive type.
Owing to some intra-cerebral accident he suddenly lost all
his visual images, and with them much of his intellectual
power, without any other perversion of faculty. He soon
discovered that he could carry on his affairs by using his
memory in an altogether new way, and described clearly
the difference between his two conditions. "Every time
he returns to A., from which place business often calls him,
he seems to himself as if entering a strange city. He
views the monuments, houses, and streets with the same
surprise as if he saw them for the first time. When asked
to describe the principal public place of the town, he answered, 'I know that it is there, but it is impossible to
imagine it, and I can tell you nothing about it.'"

He can no more remember his wife and children's face
than he can remember A. Even after being with them
some time they seem unusual to him. He forgets his own
face, and once spoke to his image in a mirror, taking it for
a stranger. He complains of his loss of feeling for colors.
" My wife has black hair, this I know; but I can no more
recall its color than I can her person and features." This
visual amnesia extends to objects dating from his childhood's years—paternal mansion, etc., forgotten. No other
disturbances but this loss of visual images. Now when he
seeks something in his correspondence, he must rummage
among the letters like other men, until he meets the passage. He can recall only the first few verses of the Iliad,

and must *grope* to recite H omer, Virgil, and Horace. Figures which he adds he must now whisper to himself. He realizes clearly that he must help his memory out with auditory images, which he does with effort. *The words and expressions which he recalls seem now to echo in his ear, an altogether novel sensation for him.* If he wishes to learn by heart anything, a series of phrases for example, he must *read them several times aloud,* so as to impress his ear. When later he repeats the thing in question, the sensation of inward hearing which precedes articulation rises up in his mind. This feeling was formerly unknown to him.

Such a man would have suffered relatively little inconvenience if his images for hearing had been those suddenly destroyed.

The Neural Process in Imagination.—Most medical writers assume that the cerebral activity on which imagination depends occupies a different *seat* from that subserving sensation. It is, however, a simpler interpretation of the facts to suppose that *the same nerve-tracts are concerned in the two processes.* Our mental images are aroused always by way of association; some previous idea or sensation must have 'suggested' them. Association is surely due to currents from one cortical centre to another. Now all we need suppose is that these intra-cortical currents are unable to produce in the cells the strong explosions which currents from the sense-organs occasion, to account for the subjective difference between images and sensations, without supposing any difference in their local seat. To the strong degree of explosion corresponds the character of 'vividness' or sensible presence, in the object of thought; to the weak degree, that of 'faintness' or outward unreality.

If we admit that sensation and imagination are due to the activity of the same parts of the cortex, we can see a very good teleological reason why they should correspond to discrete kinds of process in these centres, and why the process which gives the sense that the object is really there ought normally to be arousable only by currents entering from the periphery and not by currents from the neighboring cortical parts. We can see, in short, why *the sensational process* OUGHT TO *be discontinuous with all normal ideational processes, however intense.* For, as Dr. Münsterberg justly observes, " Were there not this peculiar arrangement we should not distinguish reality and fantasy, our conduct would not be accommodated to the facts about us, but would be inappropriate and senseless, and we could not keep ourselves alive."

Sometimes, by exception, the deeper sort of explosion may take place from intra-cortical excitement alone. In the sense of hearing, sensation and imagination *are* hard to discriminate where the sensation is so weak as to be just perceptible. At night, hearing a very faint striking of the hour by a far-off clock, our imagination reproduces both rhythm and sound, and it is often difficult to tell which was the last real stroke. So of a baby crying in a distant part of the house, we are uncertain whether we still hear it, or only imagine the sound. Certain violin-players take advantage of this in diminuendo terminations. After the pianissimo has been reached they continue to bow as if still playing, but are careful not to touch the strings. The listener hears in imagination a degree of sound fainter than the pianissimo. *Hallucinations*, whether of sight or hearing, are another case in point, to be touched on in the next chapter. I may mention as a fact still unexplained that several observers (Herr G. H. Meyer, M. Ch. Féré, Professor Scott of Ann Arbor, and Mr. T. C. Smith, one of my students) have noticed negative after-images of objects which they had been imagining with the mind's eye. It is as if the retina itself were locally fatigued by the act.

CHAPTER XX.

PERCEPTION.

Perception and Sensation compared.—A pure sensation we saw above, p. 12, to be an abstraction never realized in adult life. Anything which affects our sense-organs does also more than that: it arouses processes in the hemispheres which are partly due to the organization of that organ by past experiences, and the results of which in consciousness are described as ideas which the sensation suggests. The first of these ideas is that of the *thing* to which the sensible quality belongs. *The consciousness of particular material things present to sense* is nowadays called *perception*. The consciousness of such things may be more or less complete; it may be of the mere name of the thing and its other essential attributes, or it may be of the thing's various remoter relations. It is impossible to draw any sharp line of distinction between the barer and the richer consciousness, because the moment we get beyond the first crude sensation all our consciousness is of what is *suggested*, and the various suggestions shade gradually into each other, being one and all products of the same psychological machinery of association. In the directer consciousness fewer, in the remoter more, associative processes are brought into play.

Sensational and reproductive brain-processes combined, then, are what give us the content of our perceptions. Every concrete particular material thing is a conflux of sensible qualities, with which we have become acquainted at various times. Some of these qualities, since they are more constant, interesting, or practically important, we regard as essential constituents of the thing. In a general way, such are the tangible shape, size, mass, etc. Other properties, being more fluctuating, we regard as more or less accidental or inessential. We call the former qualities the reality, the latter its appearances. Thus, I hear a sound, and say 'a horse-car'; but the sound is not the horse-car, it is one of the horse-car's least important manifestations. The real horse-car is a feelable, or at most a feelable and visible, thing which in my imagination the sound calls up. So when I get, as now, a brown eye-picture with lines not parallel, and with angles unlike, and call it my big solid rectangular walnut library-table, that picture is not the table. It is not even like the table as the table is for vision, when rightly seen. It is a distorted perspective view of three of the sides of what I mentally *perceive* (more or less) in its totality and undistorted shape. The back of the table, its square corners, its size, its heaviness, are features of which I am conscious when I look, almost as I am conscious of its name. The suggestion of the name is of course due to mere custom. But no less is that of the back, the size, weight, squareness, etc.

Nature, as Reid says, is frugal in her operations, and will not be at the expense of a particular instinct to give us that knowledge which experience and habit will soon produce. Reproduced attributes tied together with presently felt attributes in the unity of a *thing* with a name, these are the materials out of which my actually perceived table is made. Infants must go through a long education of the eye and ear before they can perceive the realities which adults perceive. *Every perception is an acquired perception.*

The Perceptive State of Mind is not a Compound.—There is no reason, however, for supposing that this involves a 'fusion' of separate sensations and ideas. The thing perceived is the object of a unique state of thought; due no doubt in part to sensational, and in part to ideational currents, but in no wise 'containing' psychically the identical 'sensations' and images which these currents would severally have aroused if the others were not simultaneously there. .We can often directly notice a sensible difference in the consciousness, between the latter case and the former. The sensible quality changes under our very eye. Take the already-quoted catch, *Pas de lieu Rhône que nous:* one may read this over and over again without recognizing the sounds to be identical with those of the words *paddle your own canoe.* As the English associations arise, the sound itself appears to change. Verbal sounds are usually perceived with their meaning at the moment of being heard. Sometimes, however, the associative irradiations are inhibited for a few moments (the mind being preoccupied with other thoughts), whilst the words linger on the ear as mere echoes of acoustic sensation. Then, usually, their interpretation suddenly occurs. But at that moment one may often surprise a change in the very *feel* of the word. Our own language would sound very different to us if we heard it without understanding, as we hear a foreign tongue. Rises and falls of voice, odd sibilants and other consonants, would fall on our ear in a way of which we can now form no notion. Frenchmen say that English sounds to them like the *gazouillement des oiseaux*—an impression which it certainly makes on no native ear. Many of us English would describe the sound of Russian in similar terms. All of us are conscious of the strong inflections of voice and explosives and gutturals of German speech in a way in which no German can be conscious of them.

This is probably the reason why, if we look at an isolated printed word and repeat it long enough, it ends by assuming an entirely unnatural aspect. Let the reader try this with any word on this page. He will soon begin to wonder if it can possibly be the word he has been using, all his life with that meaning. It stares at him from the paper like a glass eye, with no speculation in it. Its body is indeed there, but its soul is fled. It is reduced, by this new way of attending to it, to its sensational nudity We never before attended to it in this way, but habitually got it clad with its meaning the moment we caught sight of it, and rapidly passed from it to the other words of the phrase. We apprehended it, in short, with a cloud of associates, and thus perceiving it, we felt it quite otherwise than as we feel it now divested and alone.

Another well-known change is when we look at a landscape with our head upside-down. Perception is to a certain extent baffled by this manœuvre; gradations of distance and other space-determinations are made uncertain; the reproductive or associative processes, in short, decline; and, simultaneously with their diminution, the colors grow richer and more varied, and the contrasts of light and shade more marked. The same thing occurs when we turn a painting bottom-upward. We lose much of its meaning, but, to compensate for the loss, we feel more freshly the value of the mere tints and shadings, and become aware of any lack of purely sensible harmony or balance which they may show. Just so, if we lie on the floor and look up at the mouth of a person talking behind us. His lower lip here takes the habitual place of the upper one upon our retina, and seems animated by the most extraordinary and unnatural mobility, a mobility which now strikes us because (the associative processes being disturbed by the unaccustomed point of view) we get it as a naked sensation and not as part of a familiar object perceived.

Once more, then, we find ourselves driven to admit that when qualities of an object impress our sense and we thereupon perceive the object, the pure sensation as such of those qualities does not still exist inside of the perception and form a constituent thereof. The pure sensation is one thing and the perception another, and neither can take place at the same time with the other, because their cerebral conditions are not the same. They may *resemble* each other, but in no respect are they identical states of mind.

Perception is of Definite and Probable Things.—The chief cerebral conditions of perception are old paths of association radiating from the sense-impression. If a certain impression be strongly associated with the attributes of a certain thing, that thing is almost sure to be perceived when we get the impression. Examples of such things would be familiar people, places, etc., which we recognize and name at a glance. But *where the impression is associated with more than one reality*, so that either of two discrepant sets of residual properties may arise, the perception is doubtful and vacillating, and *the most that can then be said of it is that it will be of a* PROBABLE *thing,* of the thing which would most usually have given us that sensation.

In these ambiguous cases it is interesting to note that perception is rarely abortive ; *some* perception takes place. The two discrepant sets of associates do not neutralize each other or mix and make a blur. What we more commonly get is first one object in its completeness, and then the other in its completeness. In other words, *all brain-processes are such as give rise to what we may call* FIGURED *consciousness.* If paths are shot-through at all, they are shot-through in consistent systems, and occasion thoughts of definite objects, not mere hodge-podges of elements. Even where the brain's functions are half thrown out of gear, as in aphasia or dropping asleep, this law of figured consciousness holds good. A person who suddenly gets sleepy whilst reading aloud will read wrong; but instead of emitting a mere broth of syllables, he will make such mistakes as to read 'supper-time' instead of 'sovereign,' 'overthrow' instead of 'opposite,' or indeed utter entirely imaginary phrases, composed of several definite words, instead of phrases of the book. So in aphasia: where the disease is mild the patient's mistakes consist in using entire wrong words instead of right ones. It is only in grave lesions that he becomes quite inarticulate. These facts show how subtle is the associative link; how delicate yet how strong that connection among brain-paths which makes any number of them, once excited together, thereafter tend to vibrate as a systematic whole. A small group of elements, '*this*,' common to two systems, *A* and *B*, may touch off *A* or *B* according as accident decides the next step (see Fig. 63). If it happen that a single point leading from '*this*' to *B* is momentarily a little more pervious than any leading from '*this*' to *A*, then that little advantage will upset the equilibrium in favor of the entire system *B*. The currents will sweep first through that point

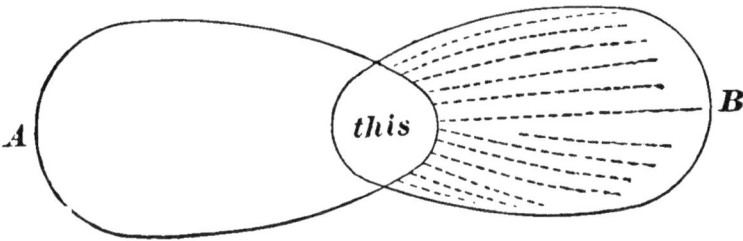

FIG. 63

and thence into all the paths of *B*, each increment of advance making *A* more and more impossible. The thoughts correlated with *A* and *B*, in such a case, will have objects different, though similar. The similarity will, however, consist in some very limited feature if the 'this' be small. *Thus the faintest sensations will give rise to the perception of definite things if only they resemble those which the things are wont to arouse.*

Illusions.—Let us now, for brevity's sake, treat *A* and B in Fig. 63 as if they stood for objects instead of brain-processes. And let us furthermore suppose that *A* and *B* are, both of them, objects which might probably excite the sensation which I have called '*this*,' but that on the present occasion *A* and not *B* is the one which actually does so. If, then, on this occasion '*this*' suggests *A* and not *B*, the result is a *correct perception*. But if, on the contrary, 'this' suggests *B* and not *A*, the result is a *false perception*, or, as it is technically called, an *illusion*. But the *process* is the same, whether the perception be true or false.

Note that in every illusion what is false is what is inferred, not what is immediately given. The 'this,' if it were felt by itself alone, would be all right; it only becomes misleading by what it suggests. If it is a sensation of sight, it may suggest a tactile object, for example, which later tactile experiences prove to be not there. *The so-called 'fallacy of the senses,' of which the ancient sceptics made so much account, is not fallacy of the senses proper, but rather of the intellect, which interprets wrongly what the senses give.**

So much premised, let us look a little closer at these illusions. They are due to two main causes. *The wrong object is perceived either because*

1) *Although not on this occasion the real cause, it is yet the habitual, inveterate, or most probable cause of 'this';* or because

2) *The mind is temporarily full of the thought of that object, and therefore 'this' is peculiarly prone to suggest it at this moment.*

I will give briefly a number of examples under each head. The first head is the more important, because it includes a number of constant illusions to which all men are subject, and which can only be dispelled by much experience.

Illusions of the First Type.—One of the oldest instances dates from Aristotle. Cross two fingers and roll a pea, penholder, or other small object between them. It will seem double. Professor Croom Robertson has given the clearest analysis of this illusion. He observes that if the object be brought into

FIG. 64.

---

* In Mind, IX. 206, M. Binet points out the fact that what is fallaciously inferred is always an object of some other sense than the 'this.' 'Optical illusions' are generally errors of touch and muscular sensibility, and the fallaciously perceived object and the experiences which correct it are both tactile in these cases.

contact first with the forefinger and next with the second finger, the two contacts seem to come in at different points of space. The forefinger-touch seems higher, though the finger is really lower; the second-finger-touch seems lower, though the finger is really higher. " We perceive the contacts as double because we refer them to two distinct parts of space." The touched sides of the two fingers are normally not together in space, and customarily never do touch one thing; the one thing which now touches them, therefore, seems in two places, i.e. seems two things.

There is a whole batch of illusions which come from optical sensations interpreted by us in accordance with our usual rule, although they are now produced by an unusual object. The *stereoscope* is an example. The eyes see a picture apiece, and the two pictures are a little disparate, the one seen by the right eye being a view of the object taken from a point slightly to the right of that from which the left eye's picture is taken. Pictures thrown on the two eyes by solid objects present this sort of disparity, so that we react on the sensation in our usual way, and perceive a solid. If the pictures be exchanged we perceive a hollow mould of the object, for a hollow mould would cast just such disparate pictures as these. Wheatstone's instrument, the *pseudoscope*, allows us to look at solid objects and see with each eye the other eye's picture. We then perceive the solid object hollow, *if it be an object which might probably be hollow*, but not otherwise. Thus the perceptive process is true to its law, which is *always to react on the sensation in a determinate and figured fashion if possible, and in as probable a fashion as the case admits*. A human face, e.g., never appears hollow to the pseudoscope, for to couple faces and hollowness violates all our habits. For the same reason it is very easy to make an intaglio cast of a face, or the painted inside of a pasteboard mask, look convex, instead of concave as they are.

Curious illusions of movement in objects occur whenever the eyeballs move without our intending it. We have learned in an earlier chapter (p. 72) that the original visual feeling of movement is produced by any image passing over the retina. Originally, however, this sensation is definitely referred neither to the object nor to the eyes. Such definite reference grows up later, and obeys certain simple laws. For one thing, we believe *objects* to move whenever we get the retinal movement-feeling, but think our *eyes* are still. This gives rise to an illusion when, after whirling on our heel, we stand still; for then objects appear to continue whirling in the same direction in which, a moment previous, our body actually whirled. The reason is that our *eyes* are animated, under these conditions, by an involuntary *nystagmus* or oscillation in their orbits, which may easily be observed in anyone with vertigo after whirling. As these movements are unconscious, the retinal movement-feelings which they occasion are naturally referred to the objects seen. The whole phenomenon fades out after a few seconds. And it ceases if we voluntarily fix our eyes upon a given point.

There is an illusion of movement of the opposite sort, with which every one is familiar at *railway stations*. Habitually, when we ourselves move forward, our entire field of view glides backward over our retina. When our movement is due to that of the windowed carriage, car, or boat in which we sit, all stationary objects visible through the window give us a sensation of gliding in the opposite direction. Hence, whenever we get this sensation, of a window with *all* objects visible through it moving in one direction, we react upon it in our customary way, and perceive a stationary field of view, over which the window, and we ourselves inside of it, are passing by a motion of our own. Consequently when another train comes alongside of ours in a station, and fills the entire window, and, after standing still awhile, begins to glide away, we judge that it is *our* train which is moving, and that the other train is still. If, however, we catch a glimpse of any part of the station through the windows, or between the cars, of the other train, the illusion of our own movement instantly disappears, and we perceive the other train to be the one in motion. This, again, is but making the usual and probable inference from our sensation.

Another illusion due to movement is explained by Helmholtz. Most wayside objects, houses, trees, etc., look small when seen from the windows of a swift train. This is because we perceive them in the first instance unduly near. And we perceive them unduly near because of their extraordinarily rapid parallactic flight backwards. When we ourselves move forward all objects glide backwards, as aforesaid; but the nearer they are, the more rapid is this apparent translocation. Relative rapidity of passage backwards is thus so familiarly associated with nearness that when we feel it we perceive nearness. But with a given size of retinal image the nearer an object is, the smaller do we judge its actual size to be. Hence in the train, the faster we go, the nearer do the trees and houses seem; and the nearer they seem, the smaller (with that size of retinal image) must they look.

The feelings of our eyes' convergence, of their accommodation, the size of the retinal image, etc., may give rise to illusions about the size and distance of objects, which also belong to this first type.

Illusions of the Second Type.—In this type we perceive a wrong object because our mind is full of the thought of it at the time, and any sensation which is in the least degree connected with it touches off, as it were, a train already laid, and gives us a sense that the object is really before us Here is a familiar example:

"If a sportsman, while shooting woodcock in cover. sees a bird about the size and color of a woodcock get up and fly through the foliage, not having time to see more than that it is a bird of such a size and color, he immediately supplies by inference the other qualities of a woodcock, and is afterwards disgusted to find that he has shot a thrush. I have done so myself, and could hardly believe that the thrush was the bird I fired at, so complete was my mental supplement to my visual perception." *

As with game, so with enemies, ghosts, and the like. Anyone waiting in a dark place and expecting or fearing strongly a certain object will interpret any abrupt sensation to mean that object's presence. The boy playing 'I spy,' the criminal skulking from his pursuers, the superstitious person hurrying through the woods or past the churchyard at midnight, the man lost in the woods, the girl who tremulously has made an evening appointment with her swain, all are subject to illusions of sight and sound which make their hearts beat till they are dispelled. Twenty times a day the lover, perambulating the streets with his preoccupied fancy, will think he perceives his idol's bonnet before him.

The Proof-reader's Illusion.—I remember one night in Boston, whilst waiting for a 'Mount Auburn' car to bring me to Cambridge, reading most distinctly that name upon the signboard of a car on which (as I afterwards learned) 'North Avenue' was painted. The illusion was so vivid that I could hardly believe my eyes had deceived me. All reading is more or less performed in this way.

"Practised novel- or newspaper-readers could not possibly get on so fast if they had to see accurately every single letter of every word in order to perceive the words. More than half of the words come out of their mind, and hardly half from the printed page. Were this not so, did we perceive each letter by itself, typographic errors in well-known words would never be overlooked. Children, whose ideas are not yet ready enough to perceive words at a glance, read them wrong if they are printed wrong, that is, right according to the way of printing. In a foreign language, although it may be printed with the same letters, we read by so much the more slowly as we do not understand, or are unable promptly to perceive, the words. But we notice

---

* Romanes, Mental Evolution in Animals, p. 324.

misprints all the more readily. For this reason Latin and Greek, and still better Hebrew, works are more correctly printed, because the proofs are better corrected, than in German works. Of two friends of mine, one knew much Hebrew, the other little; the latter, however, gave instruction in Hebrew in a gymnasium; and when he called the other to help correct his pupils' exercises, it turned out that he could find out all sorts of little errors better than his friend, because the latter's perception of the words as totals was too swift." *

Testimony to personal identity is proverbially fallacious for similar reasons. A man has witnessed a rapid crime or accident, and carries away his mental image. Later he is confronted by a prisoner whom he forthwith perceives in the light of that image, and recognizes or 'identifies' as the criminal, although he may never have been near the spot. Similarly at the so-called 'materializing séances' which fraudulent mediums give: in a dark room a man sees a gauze-robed figure who in a whisper tells him she is the spirit of his sister, mether, wife, or child, and falls upon his neck. The darkness, the previous forms, and the expectancy have so filled his mind with premonitory images that it is no wonder he perceives what is suggested. These fraudulent 'séances' would furnish most precious documents to the psychology of perception, if they could only be satisfactorily inquired into. In the hypnotic trance any suggested object is sensibly perceived. In certain subjects this happens more or less completely after waking from the trance. It would seem that under favorable conditions a somewhat similar susceptibility to sug-

---

* M. Lazarus: Das Leben d. Seele (1857), II. p. 32. In the ordinary hearing of speech half the words we seem to hear are supplied out of our own head. A language with which we are familiar is understood even when spoken in low tones and far off. An unfamiliar language is unintelligible under these conditions. The 'ideas' for interpreting the sounds by not being ready-made in our minds, as they are in our familiar mother-tongue, do not start up at so faint a cue.

gestion may exist in certain persons who are not otherwise entranced at all.

This suggestibility obtains in all the senses, although high authorities have doubted this power of imagination to falsify present impressions of sense. Everyone must be able to give instances from the smell-sense. When we have paid the faithless plumber for pretending to mend our drains, the intellect inhibits the nose from perceiving the same unaltered odor, until perhaps several days go by. As regards the ventilation or heating of rooms, we are apt to feel for some time as we think we ought to feel. If we believe the ventilator is shut, we feel the room close. On discovering it open, the oppression disappears.

It is the same with touch. Everyone must have felt the sensible quality change under his hand, as sudden contact with something moist or hairy, in the dark, awoke a shock of disgust or fear which faded into calm recognition of some familiar object. Even so small a thing as a crumb of potato on the table-cloth, which we pick up, thinking it a crumb of bread, feels horrible for a few moments to our fancy, and different from what it is.

In the sense of hearing, similar mistakes abound. Everyone must recall some experience in which sounds have altered their character as soon as the intellect referred them to a different source. The other day a friend was sitting in my room, when the clock, which has a rich low chime, began to strike. "Hollo!" said he, "hear that hand-organ in the garden," and was surprised at finding the real source of the sound. I have had myself a striking illusion of the sort. Sitting reading, late one night, I suddenly heard a most formidable noise proceeding from the upper part of the house, which it seemed to fill. It ceased, and in a moment renewed itself. I went into the hall to listen, but it came no more. Resuming my seat in the room, however, there it was again, low, mighty, alarming, like a rising flood or the *avant-courier* of an awful gale. It came from all space. Quite startled, I again went into the hall, but it had already ceased once more. On returning a second time to the room, I discovered that it was nothing but the breathing of a little Scotch terrier which lay asleep on the floor. The noteworthy thing is that as soon as I recognized what it was, I was compelled to think it a different sound, and could not then hear it as I had heard it a moment before.

The sense of sight is pregnant with illusions of both the types considered. No sense gives such fluctuating impressions of the same object as sight does. With no sense are we so apt to treat the sensations immediately given as mere signs; with none is the invocation from memory of a *thing*, and the consequent perception of the latter, so immediate. The 'thing' which we perceive always resembles, as we shall hereafter see, the object of some absent sensation, usually another optical figure which in our mind has come to be a standard bit of reality; and it is this incessant reduction of our immediately given optical objects to more standard and 'real' forms which has led some authors into the mistake of thinking that our optical sensations are originally and natively of no particular form at all.

Of accidental and occasional illusions of sight many amusing examples might be given. One will suffice. It is a reminiscence of my own. I was lying in my berth in a steamer listening to the sailors 'at their devotions with the holystones' outside; when, on turning my eyes to the window, I perceived with perfect distinctness that the chief-engineer of the vessel had entered my state-room, and was standing looking through the window at the men at work upon the guards. Surprised at his intrusion, and also at his intentness and immobility, I remained watching him and wondering how long he would stand thus. At last I spoke; but getting no reply, sat up in my berth, and then saw that what I had taken for the engineer was my own cap and coat hanging on a peg beside the window. The illusion was complete; the engineer was a peculiar-looking man; and I saw him unmistakably; but after the illusion had vanished I found it hard voluntarily to make the cap and coat look like him at all.

'**Apperception.**'—In Germany since Herbart's time psychology has always had a great deal to say about a process called *Apperception*. The incoming ideas or sensations are said to be 'apperceived' by 'masses' of ideas already in the mind. It is plain that the process we have been describing as perception is, at this rate, an apperceptive process. So are all recognition, classing, and naming; and passing beyond these simplest suggestions, all farther thoughts about our percepts are apperceptive processes as well. I have myself not used the word apperception, because it has carried very different meanings in the history of philosophy, and 'psychic reaction,' 'interpretation,' 'conception,' 'assimilation,' 'elaboration,' or simply 'thought,' are perfect synonyms for its Herbartian meaning, widely taken. It is, moreover, hardly worth while to pretend to analyze the so-called apperceptive performances beyond the first or perceptive stage, because their variations and degrees are literally innumerable. 'Apperception' is a name for the sum total of the effects of what we have studied as association; and it is obvious that the things which a given experience will suggest to a man depend on what Mr. Lewes calls his entire psychostatical conditions, his nature and stock of ideas, or, in other words, his character, habits, memory, education, previous experience, and momentary mood. We gain no insight into what really occurs either in the mind or in the brain by calling all these things the 'apperceiving mass,' though of course this may upon occasion be convenient. On the whole I am inclined to think Mr. Lewes's term of 'assimilation' the most fruitful one yet used.

The 'apperceiving mass' is treated by the Germans as the active factor, the apperceived sensation as the passive one; the sensation being usually modified by the ideas in the mind. Out of the interaction of the two, cognition is produced. But as Steinthal remarks, the apperceiving mass is itself often modified by the sensation. To quote him: "Although the *a priori* moment commonly shows itself to be the more powerful, apperception-processes can perfectly well occur in which the new observation transforms or enriches the apperceiving group of ideas. A child who hitherto has seen none but four-cornered tables apperceives a round one as a table; but by this the apperceiving mass ('table') is enriched. To his previous knowledge of tables comes this new feature that they need not be four-cornered, but may be round. In the history of science it has happened often enough that some discovery, at the same time that it was apperceived, i.e. brought into connection with the system of our knowledge, transformed the whole system. In principle, however, we must maintain that, although either factor is both active and passive, the *a priori* factor is almost always the more active of the two." *

Genius and Old-fogyism.—This account of Steinthal's brings out very clearly the *difference between our psychological conceptions and what are called concepts in logic.* In logic a concept is unalterable; but what are popularly called our 'conceptions of things' alter by being used. The aim of 'Science' is to attain conceptions so adequate and exact that we shall never need to change them. There is an everlasting struggle in every mind between the tendeney to keep unchanged, and the tendency to renovate, its ideas. Our education is a ceaseless compromise between the conservative and the progressive factors. Every new experience must be disposed of under *some* old head. The great point is to find the head which has to be least altered to take it in. Certain Polynesian natives, seeing horses for the first time, called them pigs, that being the nearest head. My child of two played for a week with the first orange that was given him, calling it a 'ball.' He

---

* Einleitung in die Psychologie u. Sprachwissenschaft (1881), p. 171.

called the first whole eggs he saw 'potatoes,' having been accustomed to see his 'eggs' broken into a glass, and his potatoes without the skin. A folding pocket-corkscrew he unhesitatingly called 'bad-scissors.' Hardly any one of us can make new heads easily when fresh experiences come. Most of us grow more and more enslaved to the stock conceptions with which we have once become familiar, and less and less capable of assimilating impressions in any but the old ways. Old-fogyism, in short, is the inevitable terminus to which life sweeps us on. Objects which violate our established habits of 'apperception' are simply not taken account of at all; or, if on some occasion we are forced by dint of argument to admit their existence, twenty-four hours later the admission is as if it were not, and every trace of the unassimilable truth has vanished from our thought. Genius, in truth, means little more than the faculty of perceiving in an unhabitual way.

On the other hand, nothing is more congenial, from babyhood to the end of life, than to be able to assimilate the new to the old, to meet each threatening violator or burster of our well-known series of concepts, as it comes in, see through its unwontedness, and ticket it off as an old friend in disguise. This victorious assimilation of the new is in fact the type of all intellectual pleasure. The lust for it is scientific curiosity. The relation of the new to the old, before the assimilation is performed, is wonder. We feel neither curiosity nor wonder concerning things so far beyond us that we have no concepts to refer them to or standards by which to measure them.* The Fuegians, in

---

* The great maxim in pedagogy is to knit every new piece of knowledge on to a preëxisting curiosity—i.e., to assimilate its matter in some way to what is already known. Hence the advantage of "comparing all that is far off and foreign to something that is near home, of making the unknown plain by the example of the known, and of connecting all the instruction with the personal experience of the pupil. . . . If the teacher is to explain the distance of the sun from the earth, let him ask . . . 'If anyone there in the sun fired

Darwin's voyage, wondered at the small boats, but took the big ship as a 'matter of course.' Only what we partly know already inspires us with a desire to know more. The more elaborate textile fabrics, the vaster works in metal, to most of us are like the air, the water, and the ground, absolute existences which awaken no ideas. It is a matter of course that an engraving or a copper-plate inscription should possess that degree of beauty. But if we are shown a *pen*-drawing of equal perfection, our personal sympathy with the difficulty of the task makes us immediately wonder at the skill. The old lady admiring the Academician's picture says to him: " And is it really all done *by hand?*"

The Physiological Process in Perception.—Enough has now been said to prove the general law of perception, which is this: that *whilst part of what we perceive comes through our senses from the object before us, another part* (and it may be the larger part) *always comes out of our own mind.*

At bottom this is but a case of the general fact that our nerve-centres are organs for reacting on sense-impressions, and that our hemispheres, in particular, are given us that records of our past private experience may coöperate in the reaction. Of course such a general statement is vague. If we try to put an exact meaning into it, what we find most natural to believe is that the *brain reacts* by paths which the previous experiences have worn, *and which make us perceive the probable thing,* i.e., the thing by which on the previous occasions the reaction was most frequently aroused. The reaction of the hemispheres consists in the lighting up of a certain system of paths by

---

off a cannon straight at you, what should you do?' 'Get out of the way,' would be the answer. 'No need of that,' the teacher might reply. 'You may quietly go to sleep in your room, and get up again, you may wait till your confirmation-day, you may learn a trade, and grow as old as I am,—*then* only will the cannon-ball be getting near, *then* you may jump to one side! See, so great as that is the sun's distance!'" (K. Lange, Ueber Apperception, 1879, p. 76.)

the current entering from the outer world. What corre‹ sponds to this mentally is a certain special pulse of thought, the thought, namely, of that most probable object. Farther than this in the analysis we can hardly go.

Hallucinations.—Between normal perception and illusion we have seen that there is no break, the *process* being identically the same in both. The last illusions we considered might fairly be called hallucinations. We must now consider the false perceptions more commonly called by that name. In ordinary parlance hallucination is held to differ from illusion in that, whilst there is an object really there in illusion, *in hallucination there is no objective stimulus at all.* We shall presently see that this supposed absence of objective stimulus in hallucination is a mistake, and that hallucinations are often only *extremes* of the perceptive process, in which the secondary cerebral reaction is out of all normal proportion to the peripheral stimulus which occasions the activity. Hallucinations usually appear abruptly and have the character of being forced upon the subject. But they possess various degrees of apparent *objectivity*. One mistake *in limine* must be guarded against. They are often talked of as *images* projected outwards by mistake. But where an hallucination is complete, it is much more than a mental image. *An hallucination, subjectively considered, is a sensation, as good and true a sensation as if there were a real object there.* The object happens not to be there, that is all.

The milder degrees of hallucination have been designated as *pseudo-hallucinations*. Pseudo-hallucinations and hallucinations have been sharply distinguished from each other only within a few years. From ordinary images of memory and fancy, pseudo-hallucinations differ in being much more vivid, minute, detailed, steady, abrupt, and spontaneous, in the sense that all feeling of our own activity in producing them is lacking. Dr. Kandinsky had a patient who, after taking opium or haschisch, had abun‧ dant pseudo-hallucinations and hallucinations. As he also had strong visualizing power and was an educated physician, the three sorts of phenomena could be easily compared. Although projected outwards (usually not farther than the limit of distinctest vision, a foot or so), the pseudo-hallucinations *lacked the character of objective reality* which the hallucinations possessed, but, unlike the pictures of imagination, it was almost impossible to produce them at will. Most of the 'voices' which people hear (whether they give rise to delusions or not) are pseudo-hallucinations. They are described as '*inner*' voices, although their character is entirely unlike the inner speech of the subjcet with himself. I know several persons who hear such inner voices making unforeseen remarks whenever they grow quiet and listen for them. They are a very common incident of delusional insanity, and may at last grow into vivid or completely exteriorized hallucinations. The latter are comparatively frequent occurrences in sporadic form; and certain individuals are liable to have them often. From the results of the 'Census of Hallucinations,' which was begun by Edmund Gurney, it would appear that, roughly speaking, one person at least in every ten is likely to have had a vivid hallucination at some time in his life. The following case from a healthy person will give an idea of what these hallucinations are:

"When a girl of eighteen, I was one evening engaged in a very painful discussion with an elderly person. My distress was so great that I took up a thick ivory knitting-needle that was lying on the mantelpiece of the parlor and broke it into small pieces as I talked. In the midst of the discussion I was very wishful to know the opinion of a brother with whom I had an unusually close relationship. I turned round and saw him sitting at the farther side of a centre-table, with his arms folded (an unusual position with him), but, to my dismay, I perceived from the sarcastic expression of his mouth that he was not in sympathy with me, was not 'taking my side,' as I should then have expressed it. The surprise cooled me, and the discussion was dropped.

"Some minutes after, having occasion to speak to my brother, I turned towards him, but he was gone. I inquired when he left the room, and was told that he had not been in it, which I did not believe, thinking that he had come in for a minute and had gone out without being noticed. About an hour and a half afterwards he appeared, and convinced me, with some trouble, that he had never been near the house that evening. He is still alive and well."

The hallucinations of fever-delirium are a mixture of pseudo-hallucination, true hallucination, and illusion. Those of opium, haschish, and belladonna resemble them in this respect. The commonest hallucination of all is that of hearing one's own name called aloud. Nearly one half of the sporadic cases which I have collected are of this sort.

Hallucination and Illusion.—Hallucinations are easily produced by verbal suggestion in hypnotic subjects. Thus, point to a dot on a sheet of paper, and call it 'General Grant's photograph,' and your subject will see a photograph of the General there instead of the dot. The dot gives objectivity to the appearance, and the suggested notion of the General gives it form. Then magnify the dot by a lens; double it by a prism or by nudging the eyeball; reflect it in a mirror; turn it upside-down; or wipe it out; and the subject will tell you that the 'photograph' has been enlarged, doubled, reflected, turned about, or made to disappear. In M. Binet's language, the dot is the outward *point de repère* which is needed to give objectivity to your suggestion, and without which the latter will only produce an inner image in the subject's mind. M. Binet has shown that such a peripheral *point de repère* is used in an enormous number, not only of hypnotic hallucinations, but of hallucinations of the insane. These latter are often *unilateral;* that is, the patient hears the voices always on one side of him, or sees the figure only when a certain one of his eyes is open. In many of these cases it has been distinctly proved that a morbid irritation in the internal ear, or an opacity in the humors of the eye, was the starting point of the current which the patient's diseased acoustic or optical centres clothed with their peculiar products in the way of ideas. *Hallucinations produced in this way are 'illusions'*; and *M. Binet's theory, that all hallucinations must start in the periphery, may be called an attempt to reduce hallucination and illusion to one physiological type*, the type, namely, to which normal perception belongs. In every case, according to M. Binet, whether of perception, of hallucination, or of illusion, we get the sensational vividness by means of a current from the peripheral nerves. It may be a mere trace of a current. But that trace is enough to kindle the maximal process of disintegration in the cells (cf. p. 310), and to give to the object perceived the character of *externality*. What the *nature* of the object shall be will depend wholly on the particular system of paths in which the process is kindled. Part of the thing in all cases comes from the sense organ, the rest is furnished by the mind. But we cannot by introspection distinguish between these parts; and our only formula for the result is that the brain has *reacted on* the impression in the resulting way.

M. Binet's theory accounts indeed for a multitude of cases, but certainly not for all. The prism does not always double the false appearance, nor does the latter always disappear when the eyes are closed. For Binet, an abnormally or exclusively active part of the cortex gives the *nature* of what shall appear, whilst a peripheral sense-organ alone can give the *intensity* sufficient to make it appear projected into real space. But since this intensity is after all but a matter of degree, one does not see why, under rare conditions, the degree in question *might* not be attained by inner causes exclusively. In that case we should have certain hallucinations centrally initiated, as well as the peripherally initiated hallucinations which are the only sort that M. Binet's theory allows. *It seems probable on the whole, therefore, that centrally initiated hallucinations can exist.* How often they do exist is another question. The existence of hallucinations which affect more than one sense is an argument for central initiation. For, grant that the thing seen may have its starting point in the outer world, the voice which it is heard to utter must be due to an influence from the visual region, i.e. must be of central origin.

Sporadic cases of hallucination, visiting people only once in a lifetime (which seem to be a quite frequent type), are on any theory hard to understand in detail. They are often extraordinarily complete ; and the fact that many of them are reported as *veridical,* that is, as coinciding with real events, such as accidents, deaths, etc., of the persons seen, is an additional complication of the phenomenon. The first really scientific study of hallucination in all its possible bearings, on the basis of a large mass of empirical material, was begun by Mr. Edmund Gurney and is continned by other members of the Society for Psychical Research; and the 'Census' is now being applied to several countries under the auspices of the International Congress of Experimental Psychology. It is to be hoped that out of these combined labors something solid will eventually grow. The facts shade off into the phenomena of motor automatism, trance, etc.; and nothing but a wide comparative study can give really instructive results.*

---

* The writer of the present work is Agent of the Census for America, and will thankfully receive accounts of cases of hallucination of vision, hearing, etc., of which the reader may have knowledge.

CHAPTER XXI.

THE PERCEPTION OF SPACE.

As adult thinkers we have a definite and apparently instantaneous knowledge of the sizes, shapes, and distances of the things amongst which we live and move; and we have moreover a practically definite notion of the whole great infinite continuum of real space in which the world swings and in which all these things are located. Nevertheless it seems obvious that the baby's world is vague and confused in all these respects. How does our definite knowledge of space grow up? This is one of the quarrelsome problems in psychology. This chapter must be so brief that there will be no room for the polemic and historic aspects of the subject, and I will state simply and dogmatically the conclusions which seem most plausible to me.

The quality of voluminousness exists in all sensations, just as intensity does. We call the reverberations of a thunder-storm more voluminous than the squeaking of a slate-pencil; the entrance into a warm bath gives our skin a more massive feeling than the prick of a pin; a little neuralgic pain, fine as a cobweb, in the face, seems less extensive than the heavy soreness of a boil or the vast discomfort of a colic or a lumbago; and a solitary star looks smaller than the noonday sky. Muscular sensations and semicircular-canal sensations have volume. Smells and tastes are not without it; and sensations from our inward organs have it in a marked degree.

Repletion and emptiness, suffocation, palpitation, headache, are examples of this, and certainly not less spatial is the consciousness we have of our general bodily condition in nausea, fever, heavy drowsiness, and fatigue. Our entire cubic content seems then sensibly manifest to us as such, and feels much larger than any local pulsation, pressure, or discomfort. Skin and retina are, however, the organs in which the space-element plays the most active part. Not only does the maximal vastness yielded by the retina surpass that yielded by any other organ, but the intricacy with which our attention can subdivide this vastness and perceive it to be composed of lesser portions simultaneously coexisting alongside of each other is without a parallel elsewhere. The ear gives a greater vastness than the skin, but is considerably less able to subdivide it. The *vastness, moreover, is as great in one direction as in another.* Its dimensions are so vague that in it there is no question as yet of surface as opposed to depth; 'volume' being the best short name for the sensation in question.

Sensations of different orders are roughly comparable with each other as to their volumes. Persons born blind are said to be surprised at the largeness with which objects appear to them when their sight is restored. Franz says of his patient cured of cataract: "He saw everything much larger than he had supposed from the idea obtained by his sense of touch. Moving, and especially living, objects appeared very large." Loud sounds have a certain enormousness of feeling. 'Glowing' bodies as Hering says, give us a perception "which seems *roomy* (*raumhaft*) in comparison with that of strictly surface-color. A glowing iron looks luminous through and through, and so does a flame." The interior of one's mouth-cavity feels larger when explored by the tongue than when looked at. The crater of a newly-extracted tooth, and the movements of a loose tooth in its socket, feel quite monstrous. A midge buzzing against the drum of the ear will often seem as big as a butterfly. The pressure of the air in the tympanic cavity upon the membrane gives an astonishingly large sensation.

The voluminousness of the feeling seems to bear very little relation to the size of the organ that yields it. The ear and eye are comparatively minute organs, yet they give us feelings of great volume. The same lack of exact proportion between size of feeling and size of organ affected obtains within the limits of particular sensory organs. An object appears smaller on the lateral portions of the retina than it does on the fovea, as may be easily verified by holding the two forefingers parallel and a couple of inches apart, and transferring the gaze of one eye from one to the other. Then the finger not directly looked at will appear to shrink. On the skin, if two points kept equidistant (blunted compass- or scissors-points, for example) be drawn along so as really to describe a pair of parallel lines, the lines will appear farther apart in some spots than in others. If, for example, we draw them across the face, the person experimented upon will feel as if they began to diverge near the mouth and to include it in a well-marked ellipse.

FIG 65 (after Weber).
The dotted lines give the real course of the points, the continuous lines the course as felt.

NOW MY FIRST THESIS IS THAT THIS EXTENSITY, *discernible in each and every sensation, though more developed in some than in others*, IS THE ORIGINAL SENSATION OF SPACE, out of which all the exact knowledge about space that we afterwards come to have is woven by processes of discrimination, association, and selection.

The Construction of Real Space.—To the babe who first opens his senses upon the world, though the experience is one of vastness or extensity, it is of an extensity within which no definite divisions, directions, sizes, or distances are yet marked out. Potentially, the room in which the child is born is subdivisible into a multitude of parts, fixed or movable, which at any given moment of time have definite relations to each other and to his person. Poten tially, too, this room taken as a whole can be prolonged in various directions by the addition to it of those farther lying spaces which constitute the outer world. But actu ally the further spaces are unfelt, and the subdivisions are undiscriminated, by the babe; the chief part of whose edu cation during his first year of life consists in his becoming acquainted with them and recognizing and identifying them in detail. This process may be called that of the *con struction of real space*, as a newly apprehended object, out of the original chaotic experiences of vastness. It consists of several subordinate processes:

First, the total object of vision or of feeling at any time *must have smaller objects definitely discriminated within it;*

Secondly, *objects seen or tasted must be identified with objects felt, heard*, etc., and *vice versa*, so that *the same 'thing'* may come to be recognized, although apprehended in such widely differing ways;

Third, the total extent felt at any time must be conceived as *definitely located in the midst of the surrounding extents of which the world consists;*

Fourth, these objects *must appear arranged in definite order* in the so-called three dimensions; and

Fifth, their relative sizes must be perceived—in other words, *they must be measured*.

Let us take these processes in regular order.

1) **Subdivision or Discrimination.** — Concerning this there is not much to be added to what was set forth in Chapter XV. Moving parts, sharp parts, brightly colored parts of the total field of perception 'catch the attention' and are then discerned as special objects surrounded by the remainder of the field of view or touch. That when

such objects are discerned apart they should appear as thus surrounded, must be set down as an ultimate fact of our sensibility of which no farther account can be given. Later, as one partial object of this sort after another has become familiar and identifiable, the attention can be caught by more than one at once. We then see or feel a number of distinct objects alongside of each other in the general extended field. The 'alongsideness' is in the first instance vague—it may not carry with it the sense of definite directions or distances—and it too must be regarded as an ultimate fact of our sensibility.

2) **Coalescence of Different Sensations into the Same 'Thing.'**—When two senses are impressed simultaneously we tend to identify their objects as *one thing*. When a conductor is brought near the skin, the snap heard, the spark seen, and the sting felt, are all located together and believed to be different aspects of one entity, the 'electric discharge.' The space of the seen object fuses with the space of the heard object and with that of the felt object by an ultimate law of our consciousness, which is that we simplify, unify, and identify as much as we possibly can. *Whatever sensible data can be attended to together we locate together. Their several extents seem one extent. The place at which each appears is held to be the same with the place at which the others appear.* This is the first and great 'act' by which our world gets spatially arranged.

In this *coalescence in a 'thing,'* one of the coalescing sensations is held to *be* the thing, the other sensations are taken for its more or less accidental *properties*, or modes of appearance. The sensation chosen to be essentially the thing is the most constant and practically important of the lot; most often it is hardness or weight. But the hardness or weight is never without tactile bulk; and as we can always see something in our hand when we feel something there, we equate the bulk felt with the bulk seen, and thenceforward this common bulk is also apt to figure as of the essence of the 'thing.' Frequently a shape so figures, sometimes a temperature, a taste, etc.; but for the most part temperature, smell, sound, color, or whatever other phenomena may vividly impress us simultaneously with the bulk felt or seen, figure among the accidents. Smell and sound impress us, it is true, when we neither see nor touch the thing; but they are strongest when we see or touch, so we locate the *source* of these properties within the touched or seen space, whilst the properties themselves we regard as overflowing in a weakened form into the spaces filled by other things. *In all this, it will be observed, the sense-data whose spaces coalesce into one are yielded by different sense-organs.* Such data have no tendency to displace each other from consciousness, but can be attended to together all at once. Often indeed they vary concomitantly and reach a maximum together. We may be sure, therefore, that the general rule of our mind is to locate IN *each other* all sensations which are associated in simultaneous experience and do not interfere with each other's perception.

3) **The Sense of the Surrounding World.**—*Different impressions on the same sense-organ* do interfere with each other's perception and cannot well be attended to at once. Hence *we do not locate them in each other's spaces, but arrange them in a serial order of exteriority, each alongside of the rest, in a space larger than that which any one sensation brings.* We can usually recover anything lost from our sight by moving our eyes back in its direction; and it is through these constant changes that every field of seen things comes at last to be thought of as always having a fringe of *other things possible to be seen* spreading in all directions round about it. Meanwhile the movements concomitantly with which the various fields alternate are also felt and remembered; and gradually (through association) this and that movement come in our thought to suggest this or that extent of fresh objects introduced. Gradually, too, since the objects vary indefinitely in kind, we abstract from their several natures and think separately

of their mere extents, of which extents the various movements remain as the only constant introducers and associates. More and more, therefore, do we think of movement and seen extent as mutually involving each other, until at last we may get to regard them as synonymous; and, empty space then meaning for us mere *room for movement*, we may, if we are psychologists, readily but erroneously assign to the 'muscular sense' the chief rôle in perceiving extensiveness at all.

4) **The Serial Order of Locations.**—The muscular sense *has* much to do with defining the *order of position* of things seen, felt, or heard. We look at a point; another point upon the retina's margin catches our attention, and in an instant we turn the fovea upon it, letting its image successively fall upon all the points of the intervening retinal line. The line thus traced so rapidly by the second point is itself a visual object, with the first and second point at its respective ends. It *separates* the points, which become *located by its length* with reference to each other. If a third point catch the attention, more peripheral still than the second point, then a still greater movement of the eyeball and a continuation of the line will result, the second point now appearing *between* the first and third. Every moment of our life, peripherally-lying objects are drawing lines like this between themselves and other objects which they displace from our attention as we bring them to the centre of our field of view. Each peripheral retinal point comes in this way to *suggest* a line at the end of which it lies, a line which a possible movement will trace; and even the motionless field of vision ends at last by signifying a system of positions brought out by possible movements between its centre and all peripheral parts.

It is the same with our skin and joints. By moving our hand over objects we trace lines of direction, and new impressions arise at their ends. The 'lines' are sometimes on the articular surfaces, sometimes on the skin as well; in either case they give a definite order of arrangement to the successive objects between which they intervene. Similarly with sounds and smells. With our heads in a certain position, a certain sound or a certain smell is most distinct. Turning our head makes this experience fainter and brings another sound, or another smell, to its maximum. The two sounds or smells are thus separated by the movement located at its ends, the movement itself being realized as a sweep through space whose value is given partly by the semicircular-canal feeling, partly by the articular cartilages of the neck, and partly by the impressions produced upon the eye.

By such general principles of action as these everything looked at, felt, smelt, or heard comes to be located in a more or less definite position relatively to other collateral things either actually presented or only imagined as possibly there. I say 'collateral' things, for I prefer not to complicate the account just yet with any special consideration of the 'third dimension,' distance, or depth, as it has been called.

5) **The Measurement of Things in Terms of Each Other.**—Here the first thing that seems evident is that we have no *immediate* power of comparing together with any accuracy the extents revealed by different sensations. Our mouth-cavity feels indeed to the tongue larger than it feels to the finger or eye, our lips feel larger than a surface equal to them on our thigh. So much comparison is immediate; but it is vague; and for anything exact we must resort to other help.

The great agent in comparing the extent felt by one sensory surface with that felt by another is superposition—superposition of one surface upon another, and superposition of one outer thing upon many surfaces.

Two surfaces of skin superposed on each other are felt simultaneously, and by the law laid down on p. 339 are judged to occupy an identical place. Similarly of our hand, when seen and felt at the same time by its resident sensibility.

In these identifications and reductions of the many to the one it must be noticed that *when the resident sensations of largeness of two opposed surfaces conflict, one of the sensations is chosen as the true standard and the other treated as illusory.* *Thus an empty tooth-socket is believed to be* really smaller than the finger-tip which it will not admit, although it may *feel* larger; and in general it may be said that the hand, as the almost exclusive organ of palpation, gives its own magnitude to the other parts, instead of having its size determined by them.

But even though exploration of one surface by another were impossible, *we could always measure our various surfaces against each other by applying the same extended object first to one and then to another.* We might of course at first suppose that the object itself waxed and waned as it glided from one place to another (cf. above, Fig. 65); but the principle of simplifying as much as possible our world would soon drive us out of that assumption into the easier one that objects as a rule keep their sizes, and that most of our sensations are affected by errors for which a constant allowance must be made.

In the retina there is no reason to suppose that the bignesses of two impressions (lines or blotches) falling on different regions are at first felt to stand in any exact mutual ratio. But if the impressions come from the *same object*, then we might judge their sizes to be just the same. This, however, only when the relation of the object to the eye is believed to be on the whole unchanged. When the object, by moving, changes its relations to the eye, the sensation excited by its image even on the same retinal region becomes so fluctuating that we end by ascribing no absolute import whatever to the retinal space-feeling which at any moment we may receive. So complete does this overlooking of retinal magnitude become that it is next to impossible to compare the visual magnitudes of objects at different distances without making the experiment of superposition. We cannot say beforehand how much of a distant house or tree our finger will cover. The various answers to the familiar question, How large is the moon? —answers which vary from a cartwheel to a wafer—illustrate this most strikingly. The hardest part of the training of a young draughtsman is his learning to feel directly the retinal (i.e. primitively sensible) magnitudes which the different objects in the field of view subtend. To do this he must recover what Ruskin calls the 'innocence of the eye'—that is, a sort of childish perception of stains of color merely as such, without consciousness of what they mean.

With the rest of us this innocence is lost. *Out of all the visual magnitudes of each known object we have selected one as the 'real' one to think of, and degraded all the others to serve as its signs.* This real magnitude is determined by æsthetic and practical interests. It is that which we get when the object is at the distance most propitious for exact visual discrimination of its details. This is the distance at which we hold anything we are examining. Farther than this we see it too small, nearer too large. And the larger and the smaller feeling vanish in the act of suggesting this one, their more important *meaning*. As I look along the dining-table I overlook the fact that the farther plates and glasses *feel* so much smaller than my own, for I *know* that they are all equal in size; and the feeling of them, which is a present sensation, is eclipsed in the glare of the knowledge, which is a merely imagined one.

It is the same with shape as with size. Almost all the visible shapes of things are what we call perspective 'distortions.' Square table-tops constantly present two acute and two obtuse angles; circles drawn on our wall-papers, our carpets, or on sheets of paper, usually show like ellipses; parallels approach as they recede; human bodies are foreshortened; and the transitions from one to another of these altering forms are infinite and continual. Out of the flux, however, one phase always stands prominent. It is the **form** the object **has** when we see it easiest and best: **and** that is when our eyes and the object both are in what may be called *the normal position*. In this position our head is upright and our optic axes either parallel or symmetrically convergent; the plane of the object is perpendicular to the visual plane; and if the object is one containing many lines, it is turned so as to make them, as far as possible, either parallel or perpendicular to the visual plane. In this situation it is that we compare all shapes with each other; here every exact measurement and every decision is made.

Most sensations are signs to us of other sensations **whose space-value is held to be more real.** *The thing as it would appear to the eye if it were in the normal position* is what we *think of* whenever we get one of the other optical views. Only as represented in the normal position do we believe we see the object as it *is;* elsewhere, only as it seems. Experience and custom soon teach us, however, that the seeming appearance passes into the real one by continuous gradations. They teach us, moreover, that seeming and being may be strangely interchanged. Now a real circle may slide into a seeming ellipse; now an ellipse may, by sliding in the same direction, become a seeming circle; now a rectangular cross grows slant-legged; now a slant-legged one grows rectangular.

Almost any form in oblique vision may be thus a derivative of almost any other in 'primary' vision; and we must learn, when we get one of the former appearances, to translate it into the appropriate one of the latter class; we must learn of what optical 'reality' it is one of the optical signs. Having learned this, we do but obey that law of economy or simplification which dominates our whole psychic life, when we think exclusively of the 'reality' and ignore as much as our consciousness will let us the 'sign' by which we came to apprehend it. The signs of each probable real thing being multiple and the thing itself one and fixed, we gain the same mental relief by abandoning the former for the latter that we do when we abandon mental images, with all their fluctuating characters, for the definite and unchangeable *names* which they suggest. The selection of the several 'normal' appearances from out of the jungle of our optical experiences, to serve as the real sights of which we shall think, has thus some analogy to the habit of thinking in words, in that by both we substitute terms few and fixed for terms manifold and vague.

If an optical sensation can thus be a mere sign to recall another sensation of the same sense, judged more real, *a fortiori* can sensations of one sense be signs of realities which are objects of another. Smells and tastes make us believe the *visible* cologne-bottle, strawberry, or cheese to be there. Sights suggest objects of touch, touches suggest objects of sight, etc. In all this substitution and suggestive recall the only law that holds good is that in general the most *interesting* of the sensations which the 'thing' can give us is held to represent its real nature most truly. It is a case of the selective activity mentioned on p. 170 ff.

The Third Dimension or Distance.—This service of sensations as mere signs, to be ignored when they have evoked the other sensations which are their significates, was noticed first by Berkeley in his new theory of vision. He dwelt particularly on the fact that the signs were not *natural* signs, but properties of the object merely *associated by experience* with the more real aspects of it which they recall. The tangible 'feel' of a thing, and the 'look' of it to the eye, have absolutely no point in common, said Berkeley; and if I think of the look of it when I get the feel, or think of the feel when I get the look, that is merely due to the fact that I have on so many previous occasions had the two sensations at once. When we open our eyes, for example, we think we see how far off the object is. But this feeling of distance, according to Berkeley, cannot possibly be a retinal sensation, for a point in outer space can only impress our retina by the single dot which it projects 'in the fund of the eye,' and this dot is the same for *all* distances. Distance from the eye, Berkeley considered not to be an optical object at all, but an object of

THE PERCEPTION OF SPACE. 347

touch, of which we have optical signs of various sorts, such as the image's apparent magnitude, its 'faintness' or 'confusion,' and the 'strain' of accommodation and convergence. By distance being an object of 'touch,' Berkeley meant that our notion of it consists in ideas of the amount of muscular movement of arm or legs which would be required to place our hand upon the object. Most authors have agreed with Berkeley that creatures unable to move either their eyes or limbs would have no notion whatever of distance or the third dimension.

This opinion seems to me unjustifiable. I cannot get over the fact that all our sensations are of *volume*, and that the primitive field of view (however imperfectly distance may be discriminated or measured in it) cannot be of something *flat*, as these authors unanimously maintain. Nor can I get over the fact that distance, when I see it, is a genuinely *optical feeling*, even though I be at a loss to assign any one physiological process in the organ of vision to the varying degrees of which the variations of the feeling uniformly correspond. It is awakened by all the optical signs which Berkeley mentioned, and by more besides, such as Wheatstone's binocular disparity, and by the parallax which follows on slightly moving the head. When awakened, however, it seems optical, and not heterogeneous with the other two dimensions of the visual field.

The mutual equivalencies of the distance-dimension with the up-and-down and right-to-left dimensions of the field of view can easily be settled without resorting to experiences of touch. A being reduced to a single eyeball would perceive the same tridimensional world which we do, if he had our intellectual powers. For the *same moving things*, by alternately covering different parts of his retina, would determine the mutual equivalencies of the first two dimensions of the field of view; and by exciting the physiological cause of his perception of depth in various degrees, they would establish a scale of equivalency between the first two and the third.

First of all, one of the sensations given by the object would be chosen to represent its 'real' size and shape, in accordance with the principles so lately laid down. One sensation would measure the 'thing' present, and the 'thing' would measure the other sensations—the peripheral parts of the retina would be equated with the central by receiving the image of the same object. This needs no elucidation in case the object does not change its distance or its front. But suppose, to take a more complicated case, that the object is a stick, seen first in its whole length, and then rotated round one of its ends; let this fixed end be the one near the eye. In this movement the stick's image will grow progressively shorter; its farther end will appear less and less separated laterally from its fixed near end; soon it will be screened by the latter, and then reappear on the opposite side, the image there finally resuming its original length. Suppose this movement to become a familiar experience; the mind will presumably react upon it after its usual fashion (which is that of unifying all data which it is in any way possible to unify), and consider it the movement of a constant object rather than the transformation of a fluctuating one. Now, the *sensation of depth* which it receives during the experience is awakened more by the far than by the near end of the object. But how much depth? What shall measure its amount? Why, at the moment the far end is about to be eclipsed, the difference of its distance from the near end's distance must be judged equal to the stick's whole length; but that length has already been seen and measured by a certain visual sensation of breadth. *So we find that given amounts of the visual depth-feeling become signs of given amounts of the visual breadth-feeling, depth becoming equated with breadth. The measurement of distance is, as Berkeley truly said, a result of suggestion and experience. But visual experience alone is adequate to produce it, and this he erroneously denied.*

The Part played by the Intellect in Space-perception.— But although Berkeley was wrong in his assertion that out of optical experience alone no perception of distance can be evolved, he gave a great impetus to psychology by showing how originally incoherent and incommensurable in respect of their extensiveness our different sensations are, and how our actually so rapid space-perceptions are almost altogether acquired by education. Touch-space is one world; sight-space is another world. The two worlds have no essential or intrinsic congruence, and only through the 'association of ideas' do we know what a seen object signifies in terms of touch. Persons with congenital cataracts relieved by surgical aid, whose world until the operation has been a world of tangibles exclusively, are ludicrously unable at first to name any of the objects which newly fall upon their eye. "It might very well be *a horse*," said the latest patient of this sort of whom we have an account, when a 10-litre bottle was held up a foot from his face.* Neither do such patients have any accurate notion in motor terms of the relative distances of things from their eyes. All such confusions very quickly disappear with practice, and the novel optical sensations translate themselves into the familiar language of touch. The facts do not prove in the least that the optical sensations are not *spatial*, but only that it needs a subtler sense for analogy than most people have, to discern the *same* spatial aspects and relations in them which previously-known tactile and motor experiences have yielded.

Conclusion.— To sum up, the whole history of space-perception is explicable if we admit on the one hand sensations with certain amounts of extensity native to them, and on the other the ordinary powers of discrimination, selection, and association in the mind's dealings with them. The fluctuating import of many of our optical

---

* Cf. Raehlmann in Zeitschrift für Psychol. und Physiol. der Sinnesorgane, II. 79.

sensations, the same sensation being so ambiguous as regards size, shape, locality, and the like, has led many to believe that such attributes as these could not possibly be the result of sensation at all, but must come from some higher power of intuition, synthesis, or whatever it might be called. But the fact that a present sensation can at any time become the sign of a represented one judged to be more real, sufficiently accounts for all the phenomena without the need of supposing that the quality of extensity is created out of non-extensive experiences by a super-sensational faculty of the mind.

CHAPTER XXII.

REASONING.

What Reasoning is.—We talk of man being the rational animal; and the traditional intellectualist philosophy has always made a great point of treating the brutes as wholly irrational creatures. Nevertheless, it is by no means easy to decide just what is meant by reason, or how the peculiar thinking process called reasoning differs from other thought-sequences which may lead to similar results.

Much of our thinking consists of trains of images suggested one by another, of a sort of spontaneous revery of which it seems likely enough that the higher brutes should be capable. This sort of thinking leads nevertheless to rational conclusions, both practical and theoretical. The links between the terms are either 'contiguity' or 'similarity,' and with a mixture of both these things we can hardly be very incoherent. As a rule, in this sort of irresponsible thinking, the terms which fall to be coupled together are empirical concretes, not abstractions. A sunset may call up the vessel's deck from which I saw one last summer, the companions of my voyage, my arrival into port, etc.; or it may make me think of solar myths, of Hercules' and Hector's funeral pyres, of Homer and whether he could write, of the Greek alphabet, etc. If habitual contiguities predominate, we have a prosaic mind; if rare contiguities, or similarities, have free play, we call the person fanciful, poetic, or witty. But the thought as a rule is of matters taken in their entirety. Having been thinking of one, we find later that we are thinking of another, to which we have been lifted along, we hardly know how. If an abstract quality figures in the procession, it arrests our attention but for a moment, and fades into something else; and is never very abstract. Thus, in thinking of the sun-myths, we may have a gleam of admiration at the gracefulness of the primitive human mind, or a moment of disgust at the narrowness of modern interpreters. But, in the main, we think less of qualities than of concrete things, real or possible, just as we may experience them.

Our thought here may be rational, but it is not *reasoned*, is not reasoning in the strict sense of the term. In reasoning, although our results may be thought of as concrete things, they are *not suggested immediately by other concrete things*, as in the trains of simply associative thought. They are linked to the concretes which precede them by intermediate steps, and these steps are formed by *abstract general characters* articulately denoted and expressly analyzed out. A thing inferred by reasoning need neither have been an habitual associate of the datum from which we infer it, nor need it be similar to it. It may be a thing entirely unknown to our previous experience, something which no simple association of concretes could ever have evoked. The great difference, in fact, between that simpler kind of rational thinking which consists in the concrete objects of past experience merely suggesting each other, and reasoning distinctively so called, is this: that whilst the empirical thinking is only reproductive, reasoning is productive. An empirical, or 'rule-of-thumb,' thinker can deduce nothing from data with whose behavior and associates in the concrete he is unfamiliar. But put a reasoner amongst a set of concrete objects which he has neither seen nor heard of before, and with a little time, if he is a good reasoner, he will make such inferences from them as will quite atone for his ignorance. Reasoning helps us out of unprecedented situations—situations for which all our common associative wisdom, all the 'education' which we share in common with the beasts, leaves us without resource.

REASONING. 353

Exact Definition of it.—*Let us make this ability to deal with novel data the technical differentia of reasoning.* This will sufficiently mark it out from common associative thinking, and will immediately enable us to say just what peculiarity it contains.

It contains analysis and abstraction. Whereas the merely empirical thinker stares at a fact in its entirety, and remains helpless, or gets 'stuck,' if it suggests no concomitant or similar, the reasoner breaks it up and notices some one of its separate attributes. This attribute he takes to be the essential part of the whole fact before him. This attribute has properties or consequences which the fact until then was not known to have, but which, now that it is noticed to contain the attribute, it must have.

Call the fact or concrete datum S;
    the essential attribute M;
    the attribute's property P.

Then the reasoned inference of P from S cannot be made without M's intermediation. The 'essence' M is thus that third or middle term in the reasoning which a moment ago was pronounced essential. *For his original concrete S the reasoner substitutes its abstract property M.* What is true of M, what is coupled with M, thereupon holds true of S, is coupled with S. As M is properly one of the *parts* of the entire S, *reasoning may then be very well defined as the substitution of parts and their implications or consequences for wholes.* And the art of the reasoner will consist of two stages:

First, *sagacity*, or the ability to discover what part, M, lies embedded in the whole S which is before him;

Second, *learning*, or the ability to recall promptly M's consequences, concomitants, or implications.

If we glance at the ordinary syllogism—

$$M \text{ is } P;$$
$$S \text{ is } M;$$
$$\therefore S \text{ is } P$$

—we see that the second or minor premise, the 'subsumption' as it is sometimes called, is the one requiring the sagacity; the first or major the one requiring the fertility, or fulness of learning. Usually the learning is more apt to be ready than the sagacity, the ability to seize fresh aspects in concrete things being rarer than the ability to learn old rules; so that, in most actual cases of reasoning, the minor premise, or the way of conceiving the subject, is the one that makes the novel step in thought. This is, to be sure, not always the case; for the fact that M carries P with it may also be unfamiliar and now formulated for the first time.

The perception that S is M is a *mode of conceiving S*. The statement that M is P is an *abstract or general proposition*. A word about both is necessary.

What is meant by a Mode of Conceiving.—When we conceive of S merely as M (of vermilion merely as a mercury-compound, for example), we neglect all the other attributes which it may have, and attend exclusively to this one. We mutilate the fulness of S's reality. Every reality has an infinity of aspects or properties. Even so simple a fact as a line which you trace in the air may be considered in respect to its form, its length, its direction, and its location. When we reach more complex facts, the number of ways in which we may regard them is literally endless. Vermilion is not only a mercury-compound, it is vividly red, heavy, and expensive, it comes from China, and so on, *ad infinitum*. All objects are well-springs of properties, which are only little by little developed to our knowledge, and it is truly said that to know one thing thoroughly would be to know the whole universe. Mediately or immediately, that one thing is related to everything else; and to know *all* about it, all its relations need be known. But each relation forms one of its attributes, one angle by which some one may conceive it, and while so conceiving it may ignore the rest of it. A man is such a complex fact. But out of the complexity all that an army commissary picks out as important for his purposes is his property of eating so many pounds a day; the general, of marching so many miles; the chair-maker, of having such a shape; the orator, of responding to such and such feelings; the theatre-manager, of being willing to pay just such a price, and no more, for an evening's amusement. Each of these persons singles out the particular side of the entire man which has a bearing on *his* concerns, and not till this side is distinctly and separately conceived can the proper practical conclusions *for that reasoner* be drawn; and when they are drawn the man's other attributes may be ignored.

All ways of conceiving a concrete fact, if they are true ways at all, are equally true ways. *There is no property* ABSOLUTELY *essential to any one thing.* The same property which figures as the essence of a thing on one occasion becomes a very inessential feature upon another. Now that I am writing, it is essential that I conceive my paper as a surface for inscription. If I failed to do that, I should have to stop my work. But if I wished to light a fire, and no other materials were by, the essential way of conceiving the paper would be as combustible material; and I need then have no thought of any of its other destinations. It is really *all* that it is: a combustible, a writing surface, a thin thing, a hydrocarbonaceous thing, a thing eight inches one way and ten another, a thing just one furlong east of a certain stone in my neighbor's field, an American thing, etc., etc., *ad infinitum.* Whichever one of these aspects of its being I temporarily class it under makes me unjust to the other aspects. But as I always am classing it under one aspect or another, I am always unjust, always partial, always exclusive. My excuse is necessity—the necessity which my finite and practical nature lays upon me. My thinking is first and last and always for the sake of my doing, and I can only do one thing at a time. A God who is supposed to drive the whole universe abreast may also be supposed, without detriment to his activity, to see all parts of it at once and without emphasis. But were our human attention so to disperse itself, we should simply stare vacantly at things at large and forfeit our opportunity of doing any particular act. Mr. Warner, in his Adirondack story, shot a bear by aiming, not at his eye or heart, but 'at him generally.' But we cannot aim 'generally' at the universe; or if we do, we miss our game. Our scope is narrow, and we must attack things piecemeal, ignoring the solid fulness in which the elements of Nature exist, and stringing one after another of them together in a serial way, to suit our little interests as they change from hour to hour. In this, the partiality of one moment is partly atoned for by the different sort of partiality of the next. To me now, writing these words, emphasis and selection seem to be the essence of the human mind. In other chapters other qualities have seemed, and will again seem, more important parts of psychology.

Men are so ingrainedly partial that, for common-sense and scholasticism (which is only common-sense grown articulate), the notion that there is no one quality genuinely, absolutely, and exclusively essential to anything is almost unthinkable. "A thing's essence makes it *what* it is. Without an exclusive essence it would be nothing in particular, would be quite nameless, we could not say it was this rather than that. What you write on, for example,— why talk of its being combustible, rectangular, and the like, when you know that these are mere accidents, and that what it really is, and was made to be, is just *paper* and nothing else?" The reader is pretty sure to make some such comment as this. But he is himself merely insisting on an aspect of the thing which suits his own petty purpose, that of *naming* the thing; or else on an aspect which suits the manufacturer's purpose, that of *producing an article for which there is a vulgar demand.* Meanwhile the reality overflows these purposes at every pore. Our usual purpose with it, our commonest title for it, and the properties which this title suggests, have in reality nothing sacramental. They characterize *us* more than they characterize the thing. But we are so stuck in our prejudices, so petrified intellectually, that to our vulgarest names, with their suggestions, we ascribe an eternal and exclusive worth. The thing must be, essentially, what the vulgarest name connotes; what less usual names connote, it can be only in an 'accidental' and relatively unreal sense.*

Locke undermined the fallacy. But none of his successors, so far as I know, have radically escaped it, or seen that *the only meaning of essence is teleological, and that classification and conception are purely teleological weapons of the mind*. The essence of a thing is that one of its properties which is so *important for my interests* that in comparison with it I may neglect the rest. Amongst those other things which have this important property I class it, after this property I name it, as a thing endowed with this property I conceive it; and whilst so classing, naming, and conceiving it, all other truth about it becomes to me as naught. The properties which are important vary from man to man and from hour to hour. Hence divers appellations and conceptions for the same thing. But many objects of daily use—as paper ink, butter, overcoat—have properties of such constant unwavering importance, and have such stereotyped names, that we end by believing that to conceive them in those ways is to conceive them in the only true way. Those are no truer ways of conceiving

---

* Readers brought up on Popular Science may think that the molecular structure of things is their real essence in an absolute sense, and that water is H-O-H more deeply and truly than it is a solvent of sugar or a slaker of thirst. Not a whit! It is *all* of these things with equal reality, and the only reason why *for the chemist* it is H-O-H primarily, and only secondarily the other things, is that *for his purpose* of laboratory analysis and synthesis, and inclusion in the science which treats of compositions and decompositions, the H-O-H aspect of it is the more important one to bear in mind

them than any others; they are only more frequently serviceable ways to us.

Reasoning is always for a subjective interest. To revert now to our symbolic representation of the reasoning process:

$$\frac{\begin{array}{c} M \text{ is } P \\ S \text{ is } M \end{array}}{S \text{ is } P}$$

M is discerned and picked out for the time being to be the essence of the concrete fact, phenomenon, or reality, S. But M in this world of ours is inevitably conjoined with P; so that P is the next thing that we may expect to find conjoined with the fact S. We may conclude or infer P, through the intermediation of the M which our sagacity began by discerning, when S came before it, to be the essence of the case.

Now note that if P have any value or importance for us, M was a very good character for our sagacity to pounce upon and abstract. If, on the contrary, P were of no importance, some other character than M would have been a better essence for us to conceive of S by. Psychologically, as a rule, P overshadows the process from the start. We are *seeking* P, or something like P. But the bare totality of S does not yield it to our gaze; and casting about for some point in S to take hold of which will lead us to P, we hit, if we are sagacious, upon M, because M happens to be just the character which is knit up with P. Had we wished Q instead of P, and were N a property of S conjoined with Q, we ought to have ignored M, noticed N, and conceived of S as a sort of N exclusively.

Reasoning is always to attain some particular conclusion, or to gratify some special curiosity. It not only breaks up the datum placed before it and conceives it abstractly; it must conceive it *rightly* too; and conceiving it rightly means conceiving it by that one particular abstract character which leads to the one sort of conclusion which it is the reasoner's temporary interest to attain.

The *results* of reasoning may be hit upon by accident. The stereoscope was actually a result of reasoning; it is conceivable, however, that a man playing with pictures and mirrors might accidentally have hit upon it. Cats have been known to open doors by pulling latches, etc. But no cat, if the latch got out of order, could open the door again, unless some new accident of random fumbling taught her to associate some new total movement with the total phenomenon of the closed door. A reasoning man, however would open the door by first analyzing the hindrance. He would ascertain what particular feature of the door was wrong. The lever, e.g., does not raise the latch sufficiently from its slot—case of insufficient elevation: raise door bodily on hinges! Or door sticks at bottom by friction against sill: raise it bodily up! Now it is obvious that a child or an idiot might without this reasoning learn the *rule* for opening that particular door. I remember a clock which the maid-servant had discovered would not go unless it were supported so as to tilt slightly forwards. She had stumbled on this method after many weeks of groping. The reason of the stoppage was the friction of the pendulum-bob against the back of the clock-case, a reason which an educated man would have analyzed out in five minutes. I have a student's lamp of which the flame vibrates most unpleasantly unless the chimney be raised about a sixteenth of an inch. I learned the remedy after much torment by accident, and now always keep the chimney up with a small wedge. But my procedure is a mere association of two totals, diseased object and remedy. One learned in pneumatics could have abstracted the *cause* of the disease, and thence inferred the remedy immediately. By many measurements of triangles one might find their area always equal to their height multiplied by half their base, and one might formulate an empirical law to that effect. But a reasoner saves himself all this trouble by seeing that it is the essence (*pro hac vice*) of a triangle to be the half of a parallelogram whose area is the height into the entire base.

To see this he must invent additional lines; and the geometer must often draw such to get at the essential property he may require in a figure. The essence consists in some *relation of the figure to the new lines,* a relation not obvious at all until they are put in. The geometer's genius lies in the imagining of the new lines, and his sagacity in the perceiving of the relation.

Thus, there are two great points in reasoning. *First, an extracted character is taken as equivalent to the entire datum from which it comes; and,*

Second, the character thus taken suggests a certain consequence more obviously than it was suggested by the total datum as it originally came. Take these points again, successively.

1) Suppose I say, when offered a piece of cloth, "I won't buy that; it looks as if it would fade," meaning merely that something about it suggests the idea of fading to my mind,—my judgment, though possibly correct, is not reasoned, but purely empirical; but if I can say that into the color there enters a certain dye which I know to be chemically unstable, and that *therefore* the color will fade, my judgment is reasoned. The notion of the dye, which is one of the parts of the cloth, is the connecting link between the latter and the notion of fading. So, again, an uneducated man will expect from past experience to see a piece of ice melt if placed near the fire, and the tip of his finger look coarse if he view it through a convex glass. In neither of these cases could the result be anticipated without full previous acquaintance with the entire phenomenon. It is not a result of reasoning.

But a man who should conceive heat as a mode of motion, and liquefaction as identical with increased motion of molecules; who should know that curved surfaces bend light-rays in special ways, and that the apparent size of anything is connected with the amount of the 'bend' of its light-rays as they enter the eye,—such a man would make the right inferences for all these objects, even though he had never in his life had any concrete experience of them: and he would do this because the ideas which we have above supposed him to possess would mediate in his mind between the phenomena he starts with and the conclusions he draws. But these ideas are all mere extracted portions or circumstances. The motions which form heat, the bending of the light-waves, are, it is true, excessively recondite ingredients; the hidden pendulum I spoke of above is less so; and the sticking of a door on its sill in the earlier example would hardly be so at all. But each and all agree in this, that they bear a *more evident relation* to the conclusion than did the facts in their immediate totality.

2) And now to prove the second point: Why are the couplings, consequences, and implications of extracts more evident and obvious than those of entire phenomena? For two reasons.

First, the extracted characters are more general than the concretes, and the connections they may have are, therefore, more familiar to us, having been more often met in our experience. Think of heat as motion, and whatever is true of motion will be true of heat; but we have had a hundred experiences of motion for every one of heat. Think of the rays passing through this lens as bending towards the perpendicular, and you substitute for the comparatively unfamiliar lens the very familiar notion of a particular change in direction of a line, of which notion every day brings us countless examples.

The other reason why the relations of the extracted characters are so evident is that their properties are so *few*, compared with the properties of the whole, from which we derived them. In every concrete fact the characters and their consequences are so inexhaustibly numerous that we may lose our way among them before noticing the particular consequence it behooves us to draw. But, if we are lucky enough to single out the proper character, we take in, as it were, by a single glance all its possible consequences. Thus the character of scraping the sill has very few suggestions, prominent among which is the suggestion that the scraping will cease if we raise the door; whilst the entire refractory door suggests an enormous number of notions to the mind. Such examples may seem trivial, but they contain the essence of the most refined and transcendental theorizing. The reason why physics grows more deductive the more the fundamental properties it assumes are of a mathematical sort, such as molecular mass or wave-length, is that the immediate consequences of these notions are so few that we can survey them all at once, and promptly pick out those which concern us.

Sagacity.—To reason, then, we must be able to extract characters,—not *any* characters, but the right characters for our conclusion. If we extract the wrong character, it will not lead to that conclusion. Here, then, is the difficulty: *How are characters extracted, and why does it require the advent of a genius in many cases before the fitting character is brought to light?* Why cannot anybody reason as well as anybody else? Why does it need a Newton to notice the law of the squares, a Darwin to notice the survival of the fittest? To answer these questions we must begin a new research, and see how our insight into facts naturally grows.

All our knowledge at first is vague. When we say that a thing is vague, we mean that it has no subdivisions *ab intra*, nor precise limitations *ab extra;* but still all the forms of thought may apply to it. It may have unity, reality, externality, extent, and what not—*thinghood*, in a word, but thinghood only as a whole. In this vague way, probably, does the room appear to the babe who first begins to be conscious of it as something other than his moving nurse. It has no subdivisions in his mind, unless, perhaps, the window is able to attract his separate notice. In this vague way, certainly, does every entirely new experience appear to the adult. A library, a museum, a machine-shop, are mere confused wholes to the uninstructed, but the machinist, the antiquary, and the bookworm perhaps hardly notice the whole at all, so eager are they to pounce upon the details. Familiarity has in them bred discrimination. Such vague terms as 'grass,' 'mould,' and 'meat' do not exist for the botanist or the anatomist. They know too much about grasses, moulds, and muscles. A certain person said to Charles Kingsley, who was showing him the dissection of a caterpillar, with its exquisite viscera, "Why, I thought it was nothing but skin and squash!" A layman present at a shipwreck, a battle, or a fire is helpless. Discrimination has been so little awakened in him by experience that his consciousness leaves no single point of the complex situation accented and standing out for him to begin to act upon. But the sailor, the fireman, and the general know directly at what corner to take up the business. They 'see into the situation'—that is, they analyze it—with their first glance. It is full of delicately differenced ingredients which their education has little by little brought to their consciousness, but of which the novice gains no clear idea.

How this power of analysis was brought about we saw in our chapters on Discrimination and Attention. We dissociate the elements of originally vague totals by attending to them or noticing them alternately, of course. But what determines which element we shall attend to first? There are two immediate and obvious answers: first, our practical or instinctive interests; and second, our æsthetic interests. The dog singles out of any situation its smells, and the horse its sounds, because they may reveal facts of practical moment, and are instinctively exciting to these several creatures. The infant notices the candle-flame or the window, and ignores the rest of the room, because those objects give him a vivid pleasure. So, the country boy dissociates the blackberry, the chestnut, and the wintergreen, from the vague mass of other shrubs and trees, for their practical uses, and the savage is delighted with the beads, the bits of looking-glass, brought by an exploring vessel, and gives no heed to the features of the vessel itself, which is too much beyond his sphere. These æsthetic and practical interests, then, are the weightiest factors in making particular ingredients stand out in high relief. What they lay their accent on, that we notice; but what they are in themselves we cannot say. We must content ourselves here with simply accepting them as irreducible ultimate factors in determining the way our knowledge grows.

Now, a creature which has few instinctive impulses, or interests practical or æsthetic, will dissociate few characters, and will, at best, have limited reasoning powers; whilst one whose interests are very varied will reason much better. Man, by his immensely varied instincts, practical wants, and æsthetic feelings, to which every sense contributes, would, by dint of these alone, be sure to dissociate vastly more characters than any other animal; and accordingly we find that the lowest savages reason incomparably better than the highest brutes. The diverse interests lead, too, to a diversification of experiences, whose accumulation becomes a condition for the play of that *law of dissociation by varying concomitants* of which I treated on p. 251.

The Help given by Association by Similarity.—It is probable, also, that man's *superior association by similarity* has much to do with those discriminations of character on which his higher flights of reasoning are based. As this latter is an important matter, and as little or nothing was said of it in the chapter on Discrimination, it behooves me to dwell a little upon it here.

What does the reader do when he wishes to see in what the precise likeness or difference of two objects lies? He transfers his attention as rapidly as possible, backwards and forwards, from one to the other. The rapid alteration in consciousness shakes out, as it were, the points of difference or agreement, which would have slumbered forever unnoticed if the consciousness of the objects compared had occurred at widely distant periods of time. What does the scientific man do who searches for the reason or law embedded in a phenomenon? He deliberately accumulates all the instances he can find which have any analogy to that phenomenon; and, by simultaneously filling his mind with them all, he frequently succeeds in detaching from the collection the peculiarity which he was unable to formulate in one alone; even though that one had been preceded in his former experience by all of those with which he now at once confronts it. These examples show that the mere general fact of having occurred at some time in one's experience, with varying concomitants, is not by itself a sufficient reason for a character to be dissociated now. We need something more; we need that the varying concomitants should in all their variety be brought into consciousness *at once.* Not till then will the character in question escape from its adhesion to each and all of them and stand alone. This will immediately be recognized by those who have read Mill's Logic as the ground of Utility in his famous 'four methods of experimental inquiry,' the methods of agreement, of difference, of residues, and of concomitant variations. Each of these gives a list of analogous instances out of the midst of which a sought-for character may roll and strike the mind.

Now it is obvious that any mind in which association by similarity is highly developed is a mind which will spontaneously form lists of instances like this. Take a present fact A, with a character m in it. The mind may fail at first to notice this character m at all. But if A calls up C, D, E, and F,—these being phenomena which resemble A in possessing m, but which may not have entered for months into the experience of the animal who now experiences A, why, plainly, such association performs the part of the reader's deliberately rapid comparison referred to above, and of the systematic consideration of like cases by the scientific investigator, and may lead to the noticing of m in an abstract way. Certainly this is obvious; and no conclusion is left to us but to assert that, after the few most powerful practical and æsthetic interests, our chief help towards noticing those special characters of phenomena which, when once possessed and named, are used as reasons, class names, essences, or middle terms, *is this association by similarity.* Without it, indeed, the deliberate procedure of the scientific man would be impossible: he could never collect his analogous instances. But it operates of itself in highly-gifted minds without any deliberation, spontaneously collecting analogous instances, uniting in a moment what in nature the whole breadth of space and time keeps separate, and so permitting a perception of identical points in the midst of different circumstances, which minds governed wholly by the law of contiguity could never begin to attain.

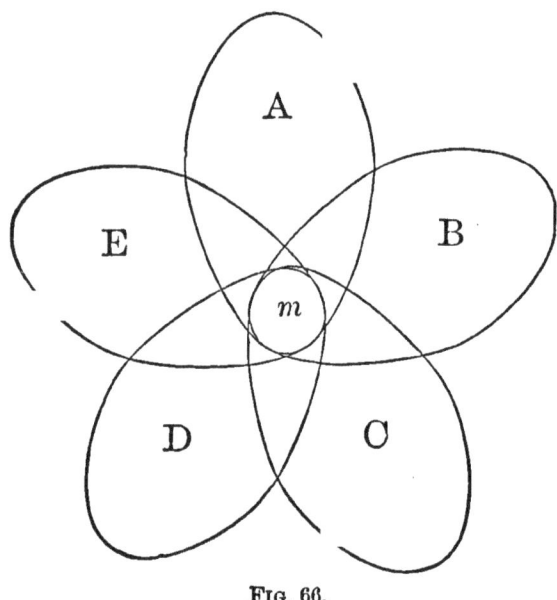

FIG. 66.

Figure 66 shows this. If m, in the present representation A, calls up B, C, D, and E, which are similar to A in possessing it, and calls them up in rapid succession, then m, being associated almost simultaneously with such varying concomitants, will 'roll out' and attract our separate notice.

If so much is clear to the reader, he will be willing to admit that the mind *in which this mode of association most prevails* will, from its better opportunity of extricating characters, be the one most prone to reasoned thinking; whilst, on the other hand, a mind in which we do not detect reasoned thinking will probably be one in which association by contiguity holds almost exclusive sway.

Geniuses are, by common consent, considered to differ from ordinary minds by an unusual development of association by similarity. One of Professor Bain's best strokes of work is the exhibition of this truth. It applies to geniuses in the line of reasoning as well as in other lines.

The Reasoning Powers of Brutes.—As the genius is to the vulgarian, so the vulgar human mind is to the intelligence of a brute. Compared with men, it is probable that brutes neither attend to abstract characters, nor have associations by similarity. Their thoughts probably pass from one concrete object to its habitual concrete successor far more uniformly than is the case with us. In other words, their associations of ideas are almost exclusively by contiguity. So far, however, as any brute might think by abstract characters instead of by the association of concretes, he would have to be admitted to be a reasoner in the true human sense. How far this may take place is quite uncertain. Certain it is that the more intelligent brutes *obey* abstract characters, whether they mentally single them out as such or not. They act upon things according to their *class*. This involves some sort of emphasizing, if not abstracting, of the class-essence by the animal's mind. A concrete individual with none of his characters emphasized is one thing; a sharply conceived attribute marked off from everything else by a name is another. But between no analysis of a concrete, and complete analysis; no abstraction of an embedded character, and complete abstraction, every possible intermediary grade must lie. And some of these grades ought to have names, for they are certainly represented in the mind. Dr. Romanes has proposed the name *recept*, and Prof. Lloyd Morgan the name *construct*, for the idea of a vaguely abstracted and generalized object-class. A definite abstraction is called an *isolate* by the latter author. Neither *construct* nor *recept* seems to me a felicitous word; but poor as both are, they form a distinct addition to psychology, so I give them here. Would such a word as *influent* sound better than *recept* in the following passage from Romanes?

" Water-fowl adopt a somewhat different mode of alighting upon land, or even upon ice, from that which they adopt when alighting upon water; and those kinds which dive from a height (such as terns and gannets) never do so upon land or upon ice. These facts prove that the animals have one recept answering to a solid surface, and another answering to a fluid. Similarly a man will not dive from a height over hard ground or over ice, nor will he jump into water in the same way as he jumps upon dry land. In other words, like the water-fowl he has two distinct recepts, one of which answers to solid ground, and the other to an unresisting fluid. But unlike the water-fowl he is able to bestow upon each of these recepts a name, and thus to raise them both to the level of concepts. So far as the practical purposes of locomotion are concerned, it is of course immaterial whether or not he thus raises his recepts into concepts; but . . . for many other purposes it is of the highest importance that he is able to do this." *

A certain well-bred retriever of whom I know never bit his birds. But one day having to bring two birds at once, which, though unable to fly, were 'alive and kicking,' he deliberately gave one a bite which killed it, took the other one still alive to his master, and then returned for the first. It is impossible not to believe that some such abstract thoughts as 'alive—get away—must kill,' . . . etc., passed in rapid succession through this dog's mind, whatever the

---

* Mental Evolution in Man, p. 74.

sensible imagery may have been with which they were blended. Such practical obedience to the special aspects of things which may be important involves the essence of reasoning. But the characters whose presence impress brutes are very few, being only those which are directly connected with their most instinctive interests. They never extract characters for the mere fun of the thing, as men do. One is tempted to explain this as the result in them of an almost entire absence of such association by similarity as characterizes the human mind. A thing may remind a brute of its full similars, but not of things to which it is but slightly similar; and all that dissociation by varying concomitants, which in man is based so largely on association by similarity, hardly seems to take place at all in the infra-human mind. One total object suggests another total object, and the lower mammals find themselves acting with propriety, they know not why. The great, the fundamental, defect of their minds seems to be the inability of their groups of ideas to break across in unaccustomed places. They are enslaved to routine, to cut-and-dried thinking; and if the most prosaic of human beings could be transported into his dog's soul, he would be appalled at the utter absence of fancy which there reigns. Thoughts would not be found to call up their similars, but only their habitual successors. Sunsets would not suggest heroes' deaths, but supper-time. This is why man is the only metaphysical animal. To wonder why the universe should be as it is presupposes the notion of its being different, and a brute, who never reduces the actual to fluidity by breaking up its literal sequences in his imagination, can never form such a notion. He takes the world simply for granted, and never wonders at it at all.

CHAPTER XXIII.

CONSCIOUSNESS AND MOVEMENT.

All consciousness is motor. The reader will not have forgotten, in the jungle of purely inward processes and products through which the last chapters have borne him, that the final result of them all must be some form of bodily activity due to the escape of the central excitement through outgoing nerves. The whole neural organism, it will be remembered, is, physiologically considered, but a machine for converting stimuli into reactions; and the intellectual part of our life is knit up with but the middle or 'central' part of the machine's operations. We now go on to consider the final or emergent operations, the bodily activities, and the forms of consciousness consequent thereupon.

Every impression which impinges on the incoming nerves produces some discharge down the outgoing ones, whether we be aware of it or not. Using sweeping terms and ignoring exceptions, *we might say that every possible feeling produces a movement, and that the movement is a movement of the entire organism, and of each and all its parts*. What happens patently when an explosion or a flash of lightning startles us, or when we are tickled, happens latently with every sensation which we receive. The only reason why we do not feel the startle or tickle in the case of insignificant sensations is partly its very small amount, partly our obtuseness. Professor Bain many years ago gave the name of the Law of Diffusion to this phenomenon of general discharge, and expressed it thus: "According as an impression is accompanied with Feeling, the aroused currents diffuse themselves over the brain leading to a general agitation of the moving organs, as well as affecting the viscera."

There are probably no exceptions to the diffusion of every impression through the *nerve-centres*. The *effect* of a new wave through the centres may, however, often be to interfere with processes already going on there; and the outward consequence of such interference may be the checking of bodily activities in process of occurrence. When this happens it probably is like the siphoning of certain channels by currents flowing through others; as when, in walking, we suddenly stand still because a sound, sight, smell, or thought catches our attention. But there are cases of arrest of peripheral activity which depend, not on inhibition of centres, but on stimulation of centres which discharge outgoing currents of an inbibitory sort. Whenever we are startled, for example, our heart momentarily stops or slows its beating, and then palpitates with accelerated speed. The brief arrest is due to an outgoing current down the pneumogastric nerve. This nerve, when stimulated, stops or slows the heartbeats, and this particular effect of startling fails to occur if the nerve be cut.

In general, however, the stimulating effects of a sense-impression preponderate over the inhibiting effects, so that we may roughly say, as we began by saying, that the wave of discharge produces an activity in all parts of the body. The task of tracing out *all* the effects of any one incoming sensation has not yet been performed by physiologists. Recent years have, however, begun to enlarge our information; and we have now experimental proof that the heartbeats, the arterial pressure, the respiration, the sweat-glands, the pupil, the bladder, bowels, and uterus, as well as the voluntary muscles, may have their tone and degree of contraction altered even by the most insignificant sensorial stimuli. In short, *a process set up anywhere in the centres reverberates everywhere, and in some way or other affects the organism throughout, making its activities either greater or less.* It is as if the nerve-central mass were like a good conductor charged with electricity, of which the tension cannot be changed at all without changing it everywhere at once.

Herr Schneider has tried to show, by an ingenious zoölogical review, that all the *special* movements which highly evolved animals make are differentiated from the two originally simple movements of contraction and expansion in which the entire body of simple organisms takes part. The tendency to contract is the source of all the self-protective impulses and reactions which are later developed, including that of flight. The tendency to expand splits up, on the contrary, into the impulses and instincts of an aggressive kind, feeding, fighting, sexual intercourse, etc. I cite this as a sort of evolutionary reason to add to the mechanical *a priori* reason why there *ought* to be the diffusive wave which *a posteriori* instances show to exist.

I shall now proceed to a detailed study of the more important classes of movement consequent upon cerebro-mental change. They may be enumerated as—
1) Expressions of Emotion;
2) Instinctive or Impulsive Performances; and
3) Voluntary Deeds;

and each shall have a chapter to itself.

CHAPTER XXIV.

EMOTION.

Emotions compared with Instincts.—An emotion is a tendency to feel, and an instinct is a tendency to act, characteristically, when in presence of a certain object in the environment. But the emotions also have their bodily 'expression,' which may involve strong muscular activity (as in fear or anger, for example); and it becomes a little hard in many cases to separate the description of the 'emotional' condition from that of the 'instinctive' reaction which one and the same object may provoke. Shall *fear* be described in the chapter on Instincts or in that on Emotions? Where shall one describe *curiosity, emulation,* and the like? The answer is quite arbitrary from the scientific point of view, and practical convenience may decide. As inner mental conditions, emotions are quite indescribable. Description, moreover, would be superfluous, for the reader knows already how they feel. Their relations to the objects which prompt them and to the reactions which they provoke are all that one can put down in a book.

Every object that excites an instinct excites an emotion as well. The only distinction one may draw is that the reaction called emotional terminates in the subject's own body, whilst the reaction called instinctive is apt to go farther and enter into practical relations with the exciting object. In both instinct and emotion the mere memory or imagination of the object may suffice to liberate the excitement. One may even get angrier in thinking over one's insult than one was in receiving it; and melt more over a mother who is dead than one ever did when she was living. In the rest of the chapter I shall use the word *object* of emotion indifferently to mean one which is physically present or one which is merely thought of.

The varieties of emotion are innumerable. *Anger, fear, love, hate, joy, grief, shame, pride*, and their varieties, may be called the *coarser* emotions, being coupled as they are with relatively strong bodily reverberations. The *subtler* emotions are the moral, intellectual, and æsthetic feelings, and their bodily reaction is usually much less strong. The mere description of the objects, circumstances, and varieties of the different species of emotion may go to any length. Their internal shadings merge endlessly into each other, and have been partly commemorated in language, as, for example, by such synonyms as hatred, antipathy, animosity, resentment, dislike, aversion, malice, spite, revenge, abhorrence, etc., etc. Dictionaries of synonyms have discriminated them, as well as text-books of psychology—in fact, many German psychological text-books *are* nothing but dictionaries of synonyms when it comes to the chapter on Emotion. But there are limits to the profitable elaboration of the obvious, and the result of all this flux is that the merely descriptive literature of the subject, from Descartes downwards, is one of the most tedious parts of psychology. And not only is it tedious, but you feel that its subdivisions are to a great extent either fictitious or unimportant, and that its pretences to accuracy are a sham. But unfortunately there is little psychological writing about the emotions which is not merely descriptive. As emotions are described in novels, they interest us, for we are made to share them. We have grown acquainted with the concrete objects and emergencies which call them forth, and any knowing touch of introspection which may grace the page meets with a quick and feeling response. Confessedly literary works of aphoristic philosophy also flash lights into our emotional life, and give us a fitful delight. But as far as the 'scientific psychology' of the emotions goes, I may have been surfeited by too much reading of classic works on the subject, but I should as lief read verbal descriptions of the shapes of the rocks on a New Hampshire farm as toil through them again. They give one nowhere a central point of view, or a deductive or generative principle. They distinguish and refine and specify *in infinitum* without ever getting on to another logical level. Whereas the beauty of all truly scientific work is to get to ever deeper levels. Is there no way out from this level of individual description in the case of the emotions? I believe there is a way out, if one will only take it.

The Cause of their Varieties.—The trouble with the emotions in psychology is that they are regarded too much as absolutely individual things. So long as they are set down as so many eternal and sacred psychic entities, like the old immutable species in natural history, so long all that *can* be done with them is reverently to catalogue their separate characters, points, and effects. But if we regard them as products of more general causes (as 'species' are now regarded as products of heredity and variation), the mere distinguishing and cataloguing becomes of subsidiary importance. Having the goose which lays the golden eggs, the description of each egg already laid is a minor matter. I will devote the next few pages to setting forth one very general cause of our emotional feeling, limiting myself in the first instance to what may be called the *coarser* emotions.

The feeling, in the coarser emotions, results from the **bodily expression**. Our natural way of thinking about these coarser emotions is that the mental perception of some fact excites the mental affection called the emotion, and that this latter state of mind gives rise to the bodily expression. My theory, on the contrary, is that *the bodily changes follow directly the perception of the exciting fact, and that our feeling of the same changes as they occur* is *the emotion*. Common-sense says, we lose our fortune, are sorry and weep, we meet a bear, are frightened and run;

we are insulted by a rival, are angry and strike. The hypothesis here to be defended says that this order of sequence is incorrect, that the one mental state is not immediately induced by the other, that the bodily manifestations must first be interposed between, and that the more rational statement is that we feel sorry because we cry, angry because we strike, afraid because we tremble, and not that we cry, strike, or tremble because we are sorry, angry, or fearful, as the case may be. Without the bodily states following on the perception, the latter would be purely cognitive in form, pale, colorless, destitute of emotional warmth. We might then see the bear and judge it best to run, receive the insult and deem it right to strike, but we should not actually *feel* afraid or angry.

Stated in this crude way, the hypothesis is pretty sure to meet with immediate disbelief. And yet neither many nor far-fetched considerations are required to mitigate its paradoxical character, and possibly to produce conviction of its truth.

To begin with, *particular perceptions certainly do produce wide-spread bodily effects by a sort of immediate physical influence, antecedent to the arousal of an emotion or emotional idea.* In listening to poetry, drama, or heroic narrative we are often surprised at the cutaneous shiver which like a sudden wave flows over us, and at the heart-swelling and the lachrymal effusion that unexpectedly catch us at intervals. In hearing music the same is even more strikingly true. If we abruptly see a dark moving form in the woods, our heart stops beating, and we catch our breath instantly and before any articulate idea of danger can arise. If our friend goes near to the edge of a precipice, we get the well-known feeling of 'all-overishness,' and we shrink back, although we positively *know* him to be safe, and have no distinct imagination of his fall. The writer well remembers his astonishment, when a boy of seven or eight, at fainting when he saw a horse bled. The blood was in a bucket, with a stick in it, and, if memory does not deceive him, he stirred it round and saw it drip from the stick with no feeling save that of childish curiosity. Suddenly the world grew black before his eyes, his ears began to buzz, and he knew no more. He had never heard of the sight of blood producing faintness or sickness, and he had so little repugnance to it, and so little apprehension of any other sort of danger from it, that even at that tender age, as he well remembers, he could not help wondering how the mere physical presence of a pailful of crimson fluid could occasion in him such formidable bodily effects.

The best proof that the immediate cause of emotion is a physical effect on the nerves is furnished by *those pathological cases in which the emotion is objectless*. One of the chief merits, in fact, of the view which I propose seems to be that we can so easily formulate by its means pathological cases and normal cases under a common scheme. In every asylum we find examples of absolutely unmotived fear, anger, melancholy, or conceit; and others of an equally unmotived apathy which persists in spite of the best of outward reasons why it should give way. In the former cases we must suppose the nervous machinery to be so 'labile' in some one emotional direction that almost every stimulus (however inappropriate) causes it to upset in that way, and to engender the particular complex of feelings of which the psychic body of the emotion consists. Thus, to take one special instance, if inability to draw deep breath, fluttering of the heart, and that peculiar epigastric change felt as 'precordial anxiety,' with an irresistible tendency to take a somewhat crouching attitude and to sit still, and with perhaps other visceral processes not now known, all spontaneously occur together in a certain person, his feeling of their combination *is* the emotion of dread, and he is the victim of what is known as morbid fear. A friend who has had occasional attacks of this most distressing of all maladies tells me that in his case the whole drama seems to centre about the region of the heart and respiratory apparatus, that his main effort during the attacks is to get control of his inspirations and to slow his heart, and that the moment he attains to breathing deeply and to holding himself erect, the dread, *ipso facto,* seems to depart.

The emotion here is nothing but the feeling of a bodily state, and it has a purely bodily cause.

The next thing to be noticed is this, that *every one of the bodily changes, whatsoever it be, is* FELT, *acutely or obscurely, the moment it occurs.* If the reader has never paid attention to this matter, he will be both interested and astonished to learn how many different local bodily feelings he can detect in himself as characteristic of his various emotional moods. It would be perhaps too much to expect him to arrest the tide of any strong gust of passion for the sake of any such curious analysis as this; but he can observe more tranquil states, and that may be assumed here to be true of the greater which is shown to be true of the less. Our whole cubic capacity is sensibly alive; and each morsel of it contributes its pulsations of feeling, dim or sharp, pleasant, painful, or dubious, to that sense of personality that every one of us unfailingly carries with him. It is surprising what little items give accent to these complexes of sensibility. When worried by any slight trouble, one may find that the focus of one's bodily consciousness is the contraction, often quite inconsiderable, of the eyes and brows. When momentarily embarrassed, it is something in the pharynx that compels either a swallow, a clearing of the throat, or a slight cough; and so on for as many more instances as might be named. The various permutations of which these organic changes are susceptible make it abstractly possible that no shade of emotion should be without a bodily reverberation as unique, when taken in its totality, as is the mental mood itself. The immense number of parts modified is what makes it so difficult for us to reproduce in cold blood the total and integral expression of any one emotion. We may catch the trick with the voluntary muscles, but fail with the skin, glands, heart, and other viscera. Just as an artificially imitated sneeze lacks something of the reality, so the attempt to imitate grief or enthusiasm in the absence of its normal instigating cause is apt to be rather 'hollow.'

I now proceed to urge the vital point of my whole theory, which is this: *If we fancy some strong emotion, and then try to abstract from our consciousness of it all the feelings of its bodily symptoms, we find we have nothing left behind,* no 'mind-stuff' out of which the emotion can be constituted, and that a cold and neutral state of intellectual perception is all that remains. It is true that, although most people, when asked, say that their introspection verifies this statement, some persist in saying theirs does not. Many cannot be made to understand the question. When you beg them to imagine away every feeling of laughter and of tendency to laugh from their consciousness of the ludicrousness of an object, and then to tell you what the feeling of its ludicrousness would be like, whether it be anything more than the perception that the object belongs to the class 'funny,' they persist in replying that the thing proposed is a physical impossibility, and that they always *must* laugh if they see a funny object. Of course the task proposed is not the practical one of seeing a ludicrous object and annihilating one's tendency to laugh. It is the purely speculative one of subtracting certain elements of feeling from an emotional state supposed to exist in its fulness, and saying what the residual elements are. I cannot help thinking that all who rightly apprehend this problem will agree with the proposition above laid down. What kind of an emotion of fear would be left if the feeling neither of quickened heart-beats nor of shallow breathing, neither of trembling lips nor of weakened limbs, neither of goose-flesh nor of visceral stirrings, were present, it is quite impossible for me to think. Can one fancy the state of rage and picture no ebullition in the chest, no flushing of the face, no dilatation of the nostrils, no clenching of the teeth, no impulse to vigorous action, but in their stead limp muscles, calm breathing, and a placid face? The present writer, for one, certainly cannot. The rage is as completely evaporated as the sensation of its so-called manifestations, and the only thing that can possibly be supposed to take its place is some cold-blooded and dispassionate judicial sentence, confined entirely to the intellectual realm, to the effect that a certain person or persons merit chastisement for their sins. In like manner of grief: what would it be without its tears, its sobs, its suffocation of the heart, its pang in the breast-bone? A feelingless cognition that certain circumstances are deplorable, and nothing more. Every passion in turn tells the same story. A disembodied human emotion is a sheer nonentity. I do not say that it is a contradiction in the nature of things, or that pure spirits are necessarily condemned to cold intellectual lives; but I say that for *us* emotion dissociated from all bodily feeling is inconceivable. The more closely I scrutinize my states, the more persuaded I become that whatever 'coarse' affections and passions I have are in very truth constituted by, and made up of, those bodily changes which we ordinarily call their expression or consequence; and the more it seems to me that, if I were to become corporeally anæsthetic, I should be excluded from the life of the affections, harsh and tender alike, and drag out an existence of merely cognitive or intellectual form. Such an existence, although it seems to have been the ideal of ancient sages, is too apathetic to be keenly sought after by those born after the revival of the worship of sensibility, a few generations ago.

Let not this view be called materialistic. It is neither more nor less materialistic than any other view which says that our emotions are conditioned by nervous processes. No reader of this book is likely to rebel against such a saying so long as it is expressed in general terms; and if any one still finds materialism in the thesis now defended, that must be because of the special processes invoked

They are *sensational* processes, processes due to inward currents set up by physical happenings. Such processes have, it is true, always been regarded by the platonizers in psychology as having something peculiarly base about them. But our emotions must always be *inwardly* what they are, whatever be the physiological ground of their apparition. If they are deep, pure, worthy, spiritual facts on any conceivable theory of their physiological source, they remain no less deep, pure, spiritual, and worthy of regard on this present sensational theory. They carry their own inner measure of worth with them; and it is just as logical to use the present theory of the emotions for proving that sensational processes need not be vile and material, as to use their vileness and materiality as a proof that such a theory cannot be true.

This view explains the great variability of emotion. If such a theory is true, then each emotion is the resultant of a sum of elements, and each element is caused by a physiological process of a sort already well known. The elements are all organic changes, and each of them is the reflex effect of the exciting object. Definite questions now immediately arise—questions very different from those which were the only possible ones without this view. Those were questions of classification: "Which are the proper genera of emotion, and which the species under each?"—or of description: "By what expression is each emotion characterized?" The questions now are *causal:* just what changes does this object and what changes does that object excite?" and "How come they to excite these particular changes and not others?" We step from a superficial to a deep order of inquiry. Classification and description are the lowest stage of science. They sink into the background the moment questions of causation are formulated, and remain important only so far as they facilitate our answering these. Now the moment an emotion is causally accounted for, as the arousal by an object of a lot of reflex acts which are forthwith felt, *we immediately* see why there is no limit to the number of possible different emotions which may exist, and why the emotions of different individuals may vary indefinitely, both as to their constitution and as to the objects which call them forth. For there is nothing sacramental or eternally fixed in reflex action. Any sort of reflex effect is possible, and reflexes actually vary indefinitely, as we know.

In short, *any classification of the emotions is seen to be as true and as 'natural' as any other*, if it only serves some purpose; and such a question as "What is the 'real' or 'typical' expression of anger, or fear?" is seen to have no objective meaning at all. Instead of it we now have the question as to how any given 'expression' of anger or fear may have come to exist; and that is a real question of physiological mechanics on the one hand, and of history on the other, which (like all real questions) is in essence answerable, although the answer may be hard to find. On a later page I shall mention the attempts to answer it which have been made.

A Corollary verified.—If our theory be true, a necessary corollary of it ought to be this: that any voluntary and cold-blooded arousal of the so-called manifestations of a special emotion should give us the emotion itself. Now within the limits in which it can be verified, experience corroborates rather than disproves this inference. Everyone knows how panic is increased by flight, and how the giving way to the symptoms of grief or anger increases those passions themselves. Each fit of sobbing makes the sorrow more acute, and calls forth another fit stronger still, until at last repose only ensues with lassitude and with the apparent exhaustion of the machinery. In rage, it is notorious how we 'work ourselves up' to a climax by repeated outbreaks of expression. Refuse to express a passion, and it dies. Count ten before venting your anger, and its occasion seems ridiculous. Whistling to keep up courage is no mere figure of speech. On the other hand, sit all day in a moping posture, sigh, and reply to everything with a dismal voice, and your melancholy lingers. There is no more valuable precept in moral education than this, as all who have experience know: if we wish to conquer undesirable emotional tendencies in ourselves, we must assiduously, and in the first instance cold-bloodedly, go through the *outward movements* of those contrary dispositions which we prefer to cultivate. The reward of persistency will infallibly come, in the fading out of the sullenness or depression, and the advent of real cheerfulness and kindliness in their stead. Smooth the brow, brighten the eye, contract the dorsal rather than the ventral aspect of the frame, and speak in a major key, pass the genial compliment, and your heart must be frigid indeed if it do not gradually thaw!

Against this it is to be said that many actors who perfectly mimic the outward appearances of emotion in face, gait, and voice declare that they feel no emotion at all. Others, however, according to Mr. Wm. Archer, who has made a very instructive statistical inquiry among them, say that the emotion of the part masters them whenever they play it well. The explanation for the discrepancy amongst actors is probably simple. The *visceral and organic* part of the expression can be suppressed in some men, but not in others, and on this it must be that the chief part of the felt emotion depends. Those actors who feel the emotion are probably unable, those who are inwardly cold are probably able, to affect the dissociation in a complete way.

An Objection replied to.—It may be objected to the general theory which I maintain that stopping the expression of an emotion often makes it worse. The funniness becomes quite excruciating when we are forbidden by the situation to laugh, and anger pent in by fear turns into tenfold hate. Expressing either emotion freely, however, gives relief.

This objection is more specious than real. *During* the expression the emotion is always felt. *After* it, the centres having normally discharged themselves. we feel it no more. But where the facial part of the discharge is suppressed the thoracic and visceral may be all the more violent and persistent, as in suppressed laughter; or the original emotion may be changed, by the combination of the provoking object with the restraining pressure, into *another emotion altogether,* in which different and possibly profounder organic disturbance occurs. If I would kill my enemy but dare not, my emotion is surely altogether other than that which would possess me if I let my anger explode.—On the whole, therefore this objection has no weight.

The Subtler Emotions.—In the æsthetic emotions the bodily reverberation and the feeling may both be faint. A connoisseur is apt to judge a work of art dryly and intellectually, and with no bodily thrill. On the other hand, works of art may arouse intense emotion; and whenever they do so, the experience is completely covered by the terms of our theory. Our theory requires that *incoming currents* be the basis of emotion. But, whether secondary organic reverberations be or be not aroused by it, the perception of a work of art (music, decoration, etc.) is always in the first instance at any rate an affair of incoming currents. The work itself is an object of sensation; and, the perception of an object of sensation being a 'coarse' or vivid experience, what pleasure goes with it will partake of the 'coarse' or vivid form.

That there may be subtle pleasure too, I do not deny. In other words, there may be purely cerebral emotion, independent of all currents from outside. Such feelings as moral satisfaction, thankfulness, curiosity, relief at getting a problem solved, may be of this sort. But the thinness and paleness of these feelings, when unmixed with bodily effects, is in very striking contrast to the coarser emotions. In all sentimental and impressionable people the bodily effects mix in: the voice breaks and the eyes moisten when the moral truth is felt, etc. Wherever there is anything like *rapture,* however intellectual its ground, we find these secondary processes ensue. Unless we actually laugh at the neatness of the demonstration or witticism; unless we thrill at the case of justice, or tingle at the act of magnanimity, our state of mind can hardly be called emotional at all. It is in fact a mere intellectual perception of how certain things are to be called—neat, right, witty, generous, and the like. Such a judicial state of mind as this is to be classed among cognitive rather than among emotional acts.

Description of Fear.—For the reasons given on p. 374, I will append no inventory or classification of emotions or description of their symptoms. The reader has practically almost all the facts in his own hand. As an example, however, of the best sort of descriptive work on the symptoms, I will quote Darwin's account of them in fear.

"Fear is often preceded by astonishment, and is so far akin to it that both lead to the senses of sight and hearing being instantly aroused. In both cases the eyes and mouth are widely opened and the eyebrows raised. The frightened man at first stands like a statue, motionless and breathless, or crouches down as if instinctively to escape observation. The heart beats quickly and violently, so that it palpitates or knocks against the ribs; but it is very doubtful if it then works more efficiently than usual, so as to send a greater supply of blood to all parts of the body; for the skin instantly becomes pale as during incipient faintness. This paleness of the surface, however, is probably in large part, or is exclusively, due to the vaso-motor centre being affected in such a manner as to cause the contraction of the small arteries of the skin. That the skin is much affected under the sense of great fear, we see in the marvellous manner in which perspiration immediately exudes from it. This exudation is all the more remarkable, as the surface is then cold, and hence the term, a cold sweat; whereas the sudorific glands are properly excited into action when the surface is heated. The hairs also on the skin stand erect, and the superficial muscles shiver.

In connection with the disturbed action of the heart the breathing is hurried.. The salivary glands act imperfectly; the mouth becomes dry and is often opened and shut. I have also noticed that under slight fear there is strong tendency to yawn. One of the best marked symptoms is the trembling of all the muscles of the body; and this is often first seen in the lips. From this cause, and from the dryness of the mouth, the voice becomes husky or indistinct or may altogether fail. ' *Obstupui steteruntque comœ, et vox faucibus hæsit.*' . . . As fear increases into an agony of terror, we behold, as under all violent emotions, diversified results. The heart beats wildly or must fail to act and faintness ensue; there is a death-like pallor; the breathing is labored; the wings of the nostrils are widely dilated; there is a gasping and convulsive motion of the lips, a tremor on the hollow cheek, a gulping and catching of the throat; the uncovered and protruding eyeballs are fixed on the object of terror; or they may roll restlessly from side to side, *huc illuc volens oculos totumque pererrat.* The pupils are said to be enormously dilated. All the muscles of the body may become rigid or may be thrown into convulsive movements. The hands are alternately clenched and opened, often with a twitching movement. The arms may be protruded as if to avert some dreadful danger, or may be thrown wildly over the head. The Rev. Mr. Hagenauer has seen this latter action in a terrified Australian. In other cases there is a sudden and uncontrollable tendency to headlong flight; and so strong is this that the boldest soldiers may be seized with a sudden panic."*

ᘐ Genesis of the Emotional Reactions.—How come the various objects which excite emotion to produce such special and different bodily effects? This question was not asked till quite recently, but already some interesting suggestions towards answering it have been made.

Some movements of expression can be accounted for as

---
* Origin of the Emotions (N Y. ed.), p. 292

weakened repetitions of movements which formerly (when they were stronger) *were of utility to the subject.* Others are similarly weakened repetitions of movements which under other conditions were *physiologically necessary concomitants of the useful movements.* Of the latter reactions the respiratory disturbances in anger and fear might be taken as examples—organic reminiscences, as it were, reverberations in imagination of the blowings of the man making a series of combative efforts, of the pantings of one in precipitate flight. Such at least is a suggestion made by Mr. Spencer which has found approval. And he also was the first, so far as I know, to suggest that other movements in anger and fear could be explained by the nascent excitation of formerly useful acts.

"To have in a slight degree," he says, "such psychical states as accompany the reception of wounds, and are experienced during flight, is to be in a state of what we call fear. And to have in a slight degree such psychical states as the processes of catching, killing, and eating imply, is to have the desires to catch, kill, and eat. That the propensities to the acts are nothing else than nascent excitations of the psychical state involved in the acts, is proved by the natural language of the propensities. Fear, when strong, expresses itself in cries, in efforts to escape, in palpitations, in tremblings; and these are just the manifestations that go along with an actual suffering of the evil feared. The destructive passion is shown in a general tension of the muscular system, in gnashing of teeth and protrusion of the claws, in dilated eyes and nostrils in growls; and these are weaker forms of the actions that accompany the killing of prey. To such objective evidences every one can add subjective evidences. Everyone can testify that the psychical state called fear consists of mental representations of certain painful results; and that the one called anger consists of mental representations of the actions and impressions which would occur while inflicting some kind of pain."

The principle of *revival, in weakened form, of reactions useful in more violent dealings with the object inspiring the emotion,* has found many applications. So slight a symptom as the snarl or sneer, the one-sided uncovering of the upper teeth, is accounted for by Darwin as a survival from the time when our ancestors had large canines, and unfleshed them (as dogs now do) for attack. Similarly the raising of the eyebrows in outward attention, the opening of the mouth in astonishment, come, according to the same author, from the utility of these movements in extreme cases. The raising of the eyebrows goes with the opening of the eye for better vision; the opening of the mouth with the intensest listening, and with the rapid catching of the breath which precedes muscular effort. The distention of the nostrils in anger is interpreted by Spencer as an echo of the way in which our ancestors had to breathe when, during combat, their "mouth was filled up by a part of an antagonist's body that had been seized" (!). The trembling of fear is supposed by Mantegazza to be for the sake of warming the blood (!). The reddening of the face and neck is called by Wundt a compensatory arrangement for relieving the brain of the blood-pressure which the simultaneous excitement of the heart brings with it. The effusion of tears is explained both by this author and by Darwin to be a blood-withdrawing agency of a similar sort. The contraction of the muscles around the eyes, of which the primitive use is to protect those organs from being too much gorged with blood during the screaming fits of infancy, survives in adult life in the shape of the frown, which instantly comes over the brow when anything difficult or displeasing presents itself either to thought or action.

"As the habit of contracting the brows has been followed by infants during innumerable generations, at the commencement of every crying or screaming fit," says Darwin, "it has become firmly associated with the incipient sense of something distressing or disagreeable. Hence, under similar circumstances, it would be apt to be continued during maturity, although never then developed, into a crying fit. Screaming or weeping begins to be voluntarily restrained at an early period of life, whereas frowning is hardly ever restrained at any age."

Another principle, to which Darwin perhaps barely does sufficient justice, may be called the principle of *reacting similarly to analogous-feeling stimuli*. There is a whole vocabulary of descriptive adjectives common to impressions belonging to different sensible spheres—experiences of all classes are *sweet*, impressions of all classes *rich* or *solid*, sensations of all classes *sharp*. Wundt and Piderit accordingly explain many of our most expressive reactions upon moral causes as symbolic gustatory movements. As soon as any experience arises which has an affinity with the feeling of sweet, or bitter, or sour, the same movements are executed which would result from the taste in point. "All the states of mind which language designates by the metaphors bitter, harsh, sweet, combine themselves, therefore, with the corresponding mimetic movements of the mouth." Certainly the emotions of disgust and satisfaction do express themselves in this mimetic way. Disgust is an incipent regurgitation or retching, limiting its expression often to the grimace of the lips and nose; satisfaction goes with a sucking smile, or tasting motion of the lips. The ordinary gesture of negation—among us, moving the head about its axis from side to side—is a reaction originally used by babies to keep disagreeables from getting into their mouth, and may be observed in perfection in any nursery. It is now evoked where the stimulus is only an unwelcome idea. Similarly the nod forward in affirmation is after the analogy of taking food into the mouth. The connection of the expression of moral or social disdain or dislike, especially in women, with movements having a perfectly definite original olfactory function, is too obvious for comment. Winking is the effect of any threatening surprise, not only of what puts the eyes in danger; and a momentary aversion of the eyes is very apt to be one's first symptom of response to an unexpectedly unwelcome proposition.—These may suffice as examples of movements expressive from analogy.

But if certain of our emotional reactions can be explained by the two principles invoked—and the reader will himself have felt how conjectural and fallible in some of the instances the explanation is—there remain many reaotions which cannot so be explained at all, and these we must write down for the present as purely idiopathic effects of the stimulus. Amongst them are the effects on the viscera and internal glands, the dryness of the mouth and diarrhœa and nausea of fear, the liver-disturbances which sometimes produce jaundice after excessive rage, the urinary secretion of sanguine excitement, and the bladder-contraction of apprehension, the gaping of expectancy, the 'lump in the throat' of grief, the tickling there and the swallowing of embarrassment, the 'precordial anxiety' of dread, the changes in the pupil, the various sweatings of the skin, cold or hot, local or general, and its flushings, together with other symptoms which probably exist but are too hidden to have been noticed or named. Trembling, which is found in many excitements besides that of terror, is, *pace* Mr. Spencer and Sig. Mantegazza, quite pathological. So are terror's other strong symptoms: they are harmful to the creature who presents them. In an organism as complex as the nervous system there must be many *incidental* reactions which would never themselves have been evolved independently, for any utility they might possess. Sea-sickness, ticklishness, shyness, the love of music, of the various intoxicants, nay, the entire æsthetic life of man, must be traced to this accidental origin. It would be foolish to suppose that none of the reactions called emotional could have arisen in this *quasi*-accidental way.

CHAPTER XXV.

INSTINCT.

Its Definition.—*Instinct is usually defined as the faculty of acting in such a way as to produce certain ends, without foresight of the ends, and without previous education in the performance.* Instincts are the functional correlatives of structure. With the presence of a certain organ goes, one may say, almost always a native aptitude for its use.

The actions we call instinctive all conform to the general reflex type; they are called forth by determinate sensory stimuli in contact with the animal's body, or at a distance in his environment. The cat runs after the mouse, runs or shows fight before the dog, avoids falling from walls and trees, shuns fire and water, etc., not because he has any notion either of life or of death, or of self, or of preservation. He has probably attained to no one of these conceptions in such a way as to react definitely upon it. He acts in each case separately, and simply because he cannot help it; being so framed that when that particular running thing called a mouse appears in his field of vision he *must* pursue; that when that particular barking and obstreperous thing called a dog appears there he *must* retire, if at a distance, and scratch if close by; that he *must* withdraw his feet from water and his face from flame, etc. His nervous system is to a great extent a preorganized bundle of such reactions—they are as fatal as sneezing, and as exactly correlated to their special excitants as it is to its own. Although the naturalist may, for his own convenience, class these reactions under general heads, he must not forget that in the animal it is a particular sensation or perception or image which calls them forth.

At first this view astounds us by the enormous number of special adjustments it supposes animals to possess ready-made in anticipation of the outer things among which they are to dwell. *Can* mutual dependence be so intricate and go so far? Is each thing born fitted to particular other things, and to them exclusively, as locks are fitted to their keys? Undoubtedly this must be believed to be so. Each nook and cranny of creation, down to our very skin and entrails, has its living inhabitants, with organs suited to the place, to devour and digest the food it harbors and to meet the dangers it conceals; and the minuteness of adaptation thus shown in the way of *structure* knows no bounds. Even so are there no bounds to the minuteness of adaptation in the way of *conduct* which the several inhabitants display.

The older writings on instinct are ineffectual wastes of words, because their authors never came down to this definite and simple point of view, but smothered everything in vague wonder at the clairvoyant and prophetic power of the animals—so superior to anything in man—and at the beneficence of God in endowing them with such a gift. But God's beneficence endows them, first of all, with a nervous system; and, turning our attention to this, makes instinct immediately appear neither more nor less wonderful than all the other facts of life.

Every instinct is an impulse. Whether we shall call such impulses as blushing, sneezing, coughing, smiling, or dodging, or keeping time to music, instincts or not, is a mere matter of terminology. The process is the same throughout. In his delightfully fresh and interesting work, 'Der Thierische Wille,' Herr G. H. Schneider subdivides impulses (*Triebe*) into sensation-impulses, perception-impulses, and idea-impulses. To crouch from cold is a sensation-impulse; to turn and follow, if we see people running one way, is a perception-impulse; to cast about for cover, if it begins to blow and rain, is an imagination-impulse. A single complex instinctive action may involve successively the awakening of impulses of all three classes. Thus a hungry lion starts to *seek* prey by the awakening in him of imagination coupled with desire; he begins to *stalk* it when, on eye, ear, or nostril, he gets an impression of its presence at a certain distance; he *springs* upon it, either when the booty takes alarm and flees, or when the distance is sufficiently reduced; he proceeds to *tear* and *devour* it the moment he gets a sensation of its contact with his claws and fangs. Seeking, stalking, springing, and devouring are just so many different kinds of muscular contraction, and neither kind is called forth by the stimulus appropriate to the other.

Now, why do the various animals do what seem to us such strange things, in the presence of such outlandish stimuli? Why does the hen, for example, submit herself to the tedium of incubating such a fearfully uninteresting set of objects as a nestful of eggs, unless she have some sort of a prophetic inkling of the result? The only answer is *ad hominem*. We can only interpret the instincts of brutes by what we know of instincts in ourselves. Why do men always lie down, when they can, on soft beds rather than on hard floors? Why do they sit round the stove on a cold day? Why, in a room, do they place themselves, ninety-nine times out of a hundred, with their faces towards its middle rather than to the wall? Why do they prefer saddle of mutton and champagne to hard-tack and ditch-water? Why does the maiden interest the youth so that everything about her seems more important and significant than anything else in the world? Nothing more can be said than that these are human ways, and that every creature *likes* its own ways, and takes to the following them as a matter of course. Science may come and consider these ways, and find that most of them are useful. But it is not for the sake of their utility that they are followed, but because at the moment of following them we feel that that is the only appropriate and natural thing to do. Not one man in a billion, when taking his dinner, ever thinks of utility. He eats because the food tastes good and makes him want more. If you ask him *why* he should want to eat more of what tastes like that, instead of revering you as a philosopher he will probably laugh at you for a fool. The connection between the savory sensation and the act it awakens is for him absolute and *selbstverständlich,* an '*a priori* synthesis' of the most perfect sort, needing no proof but its own evidence. It takes, in short, what Berkeley calls a mind debauched by learning to carry the process of making the natural seem strange, so far as to ask for the *why* of any instinctive human act. To the metaphysician alone can such questions occur as: Why do we smile, when pleased, and not scowl? Why are we unable to talk to a crowd as we talk to a single friend? Why does a particular maiden turn our wits so upside-down? The common man can only say, " *Of course* we smile, *of course* our heart palpitates at the sight of the crowd, *of course* we love the maiden, that beautiful soul clad in that perfect form, so palpably and flagrantly made from all eternity to be loved!"

And so, probably, does each animal feel about the particular things it tends to do in presence of particular objects. They, too, are *a priori* syntheses. To the lion it is the lioness which is made to be loved; to the bear, the she-bear. To the broody hen the notion would probably seem monstrous that there should be a creature in the world to whom a nestful of eggs was not the utterly fascinating and precious and never-to-be-too-much-sat-upon object which it is to her.

Thus we may be sure that, however mysterious some animals' instincts may appear to us, our instincts will appear no less mysterious to them. And we may conclude that, to the animal which obeys it, every impulse and every step of every instinct shines with its own sufficient light, and seems at the moment the only eternally right and proper thing to do. It is done for its own sake exclusively. What voluptuous thrill may not shake a fly, when she at last discovers the one particular leaf, or carrion, or bit of dung, that out of all the world can stimulate her ovipositor to its discharge? Does not the discharge then seem to her the only fitting thing? And need she care or know anything about the future maggot and its food?

Instincts are **not always** blind or invariable. Nothing is commoner than the remark that man differs from lower creatures by the almost total absence of instincts, and the assumption of their work in him by 'reason.' A fruitless discussion might be waged on this point by two theorizers who were careful not to define their terms. We must of course avoid a quarrel about words, and the facts of the case are really tolerably plain. Man has a far greater variety of *impulses* than any lower animal; and any one of these impulses, taken in itself, is as 'blind' as the lowest instinct can be; but, owing to man's memory, power of reflection, and power of inference, they come each one to be felt by him, after he has once yielded to them and experienced their results, in connection with a *foresight* of those results. In this condition an impulse acted out may be said to be acted out, in part at least, *for the sake* of its results. It is obvious that *every instinctive act, in an animal with memory, must cease to be 'blind' after being once repeated*, and must be accompanied with foresight of its 'end' just so far as that end may have fallen under the animal's cognizance. An insect that lays her eggs in a place where she never sees them hatched must always do so 'blindly'; but a hen who has already hatched a brood can hardly be assumed to sit with perfect 'blindness' on her second nest. Some expectation of consequences must in every case like this be aroused; and this expectation, according as it is that of something desired or of something disliked, must necessarily either re-enforce or inhibit the mere impulse. The hen's idea of the chickens would probably encourage her to sit; a rat's memory, on the other hand, of a former escape from a trap would neutralize his impulse to take bait from anything that reminded him of that trap. If a boy sees a fat hop‹ ping-toad, he probably has incontinently an impulse (especially if with other boys) to smash the creature with a stone, which impulse we may suppose him blindly to obey. But something in the expression of the dying toad's clasped hands suggests the meanness of the act, or reminds him of sayings he has heard about the sufferings of animals being like his own; so that, when next he is tempted by a toad, an idea arises which, far from spurring him again to the torment, prompts kindly actions, and may even make him the toad's champion against less reflecting boys.

It is plain, then, that, *no matter how well endowed an animal may originally be in the way of instincts, his resultant actions will be much modified if the instincts combine with experience,* if in addition to impulses he have memories, associations, inferences, and expectations, on any considerable scale. An object O, on which he has an instinctive impulse to react in the manner A, would *directly* provoke him to that reaction. But O has meantime become for him a *sign* of the nearness of P, on which he has an equally strong impulse to react in the manner B, quite unlike A. So that when he meets O, the immediate impulse A and the remote impulse B struggle in his breast for the mastery. The fatality and uniformity said to be characteristic of instinctive actions will be so little manifest that one might be tempted to deny to him altogether the possession of any instinct about the object O. Yet how false this judgment would be! The instinct about O is there; only by the complication of the associative machinery it has come into conflict with another instinct about P.

Here we immediately reap the good fruits of our simple physiological conception of what an instinct is. If it be a mere excito-motor impulse, due to the preëxistence of a certain 'reflex arc' in the nerve-centres of the creature, of course it must follow the law of all such reflex arcs. One liability of such arcs is to have their activity 'inhibited' by other processes going on at the same time. It makes no difference whether the arc be organized at birth, or ripen spontaneously later, or be due to acquired habit; it must take its chances with all the other arcs, and sometimes succeed, and sometimes fail, in drafting off the currents through itself. The mystical view of an instinct would make it invariable. The physiological view would require it to show occasional irregularities in any animal in whom the number of separate instincts, and the possible entrance of the same stimulus into several of them, were great. And such irregularities are what every superior animal's instincts do show in abundance.

Wherever the mind is elevated enough to discriminate; wherever several distinct sensory elements must combine to discharge the reflex arc; wherever, instead of plumping into action instantly at the first rough intimation of what *sort* of a thing is there, the agent waits to see which *one* of its kind it is and what the *circumstances* are of its appearance; wherever different individuals and different circumstances can impel him in different ways; wherever these are the conditions—we have a masking of the elementary constitution of the instinctive life. The whole story of our dealings with the lower wild animals is the history of our taking advantage of the way in which they judge of everything by its mere label, as it were, so as to ensnare or kill them. Nature, in them, has left matters in this rough way, and made them act *always* in the manner which would be *oftenest* right. There are more worms unattached to hooks than impaled upon them; therefore, on the whole, says Nature to her fishy children, bite at *every* worm and take your chances. But as her children get higher, and their lives more precious, she reduces the risks. Since what seems to be the same object may be now a genuine food and now a bait; since in gregarious species each individual may prove to be either the friend or the rival, according to the circumstances, of another;

since any entirely unknown object may be fraught with weal or woe, *Nature implants contrary impulses to act on many classes of things*, and leaves it to slight alterations in the conditions of the individual case to decide which impulse shall carry the day. Thus, greediness and suspicion, curiosity and timidity, coyness and desire, bashfulness and vanity, sociability and pugnacity, seem to shoot over into each other as quickly, and to remain in as unstable an equilibrium, in the higher birds and mammals as in man. All are impulses, congenital, blind at first, and productive of motor reactions of a rigorously determinate sort. *Each one of them then is an instinct*, as instincts are commonly defined. But they contradict each other—'experience' in each particular opportunity of application usually deciding the issue. *The animal that exhibits them loses the 'instinctive' demeanor* and appears to lead a life of hesitation and choice, an intellectual life; *not, however, because he has no instincts—rather because he has so many that they block each other's path.*

Thus we may confidently say that however uncertain man's reactions upon his environment may sometimes seem in comparison with those of lower mammals, the uncertainty is probably not due to their possession of any principles of action which he lacks. *On the contrary, man possesses all the impulses that they have, and a great many more besides.* In other words, there is no material antagonism between instinct and reason. Reason, *per se*, can inhibit no impulses; the only thing that can neutralize an impulse is an impulse the other way. Reason may, however, make an *inference which will excite the imagination so as to let loose* the impulse the other way; and thus, though the animal richest in reason is also the animal richest in instinctive impulses too, he never seems the fatal automaton which a *merely* instinctive animal must be.

Two Principles of Non-uniformity.—Instincts may be masked in the mature animal's life by two other causes. These are:

a. The *inhibition of instincts by habits;* and
b. The *transitoriness of instincts.*

a. The law of inhibition of instincts by habits is this: *When objects of a certain class elicit from an animal a certain sort of reaction, it often happens that the animal becomes partial to the first specimen of the class on which it has reacted, and will not afterward react on any other specimen.*

The selection of a particular hole to live in, of a particular mate, of a particular feeding-ground, a particular variety of diet, a particular anything, in short, out of a possible multitude, is a very wide-spread tendency among animals, even those low down in the scale. The limpet will return to the same sticking-place in its rock, and the lobster to its favorite nook on the sea-bottom. The rabbit will deposit its dung in the same corner; the bird makes its nest on the same bough. But each of these preferences carries with it an insensibility to *other* opportunities and occasions—an insensibility which can only be described physiologically as an inhibition of new impulses by the habit of old ones already formed. The possession of homes and wives of our own makes us strangely insensible to the charms of those of other people. Few of us are adventurous in the matter of food; in fact, most of us think there is something disgusting in a bill of fare to which we are unused. Strangers, we are apt to think, cannot be worth knowing, especially if they come from distant cities, etc. The original impulse which got us homes, wives, dietaries, and friends at all, seems to exhaust itself in its first achievements and to leave no surplus energy for reacting on new cases. And so it comes about that, witnessing this torpor, an observer of mankind might say that no *instinctive* propensity toward certain objects existed at all. It existed, but it existed *miscellaneously,* or as an instinct pure and simple, only before habit was formed. A habit, once grafted on an instinctive tendency, restricts the range of the tendency itself, and keeps us from reacting on any but the habitual object, although other objects might just as well have been chosen had they been the first-comers.

Another sort of arrest of instinct by habit is where the same class of objects awakens contrary instinctive impulses. Here the impulse first followed toward a given individual of the class is apt to keep him from ever awakening the opposite impulse in us. In fact, the whole class may be protected by this individual specimen from the application to it of the other impulse. Animals, for example, awaken in a child the opposite impulses of fearing and fondling. But if a child, in his first attempts to pat a dog, gets snapped at or bitten, so that the impulse of fear is strongly aroused, it may be that for years to come no dog will excite in him the impulse to fondle again. On the other hand, the greatest natural enemies, if carefully introduced to each other when young and guided at the outset by superior authority, settle down into those 'happy families' of friends which we see in our menageries. Young animals, immediately after birth, have no instinct of fear, but show their dependence by allowing themselves to be freely handled. Later, however, they grow 'wild,' and, if left to themselves, will not let man approach them. I am told by farmers in the Adirondack wilderness that it is a very serious matter if a cow wanders off and calves in the woods and is not found for a week or more. The calf, by that time, is as wild and almost as fleet as a deer, and hard to capture without violence. But calves rarely show any wildness to the men who have been in contact with them during the first days of their life, when the instinct to attach themselves is uppermost, nor do they dread strangers as they would if brought up wild.

Chickens give a curious illustration of the same law. Mr. Spalding's wonderful article on instinct shall supply us with the facts. These little creatures show opposite instincts of attachment and fear, either of which may be aroused by the same object, man. If a chick is born in the absence of the hen, it " will follow any moving object.

And when guided by sight alone, they seem to have no more disposition to follow a hen than to follow a duck or a human being. Unreflecting lookers-on, when they saw chickens a day old running after me," says Mr. Spalding, " and older ones following me for miles, and answering to my whistle, imagined that I must have some occult power over the creatures: whereas I had simply allowed them to follow me from the first. There is the instinct to follow; and the ear, prior to experience, attaches them to the right object." *

But if a man presents himself for the first time when the instinct of *fear* is strong, the phenomena are altogether reversed. Mr. Spalding kept three chickens hooded until they were nearly four days old, and thus describes their behavior:

" Each of them, on being unhooded, evinced the greatest terror to me, dashing off in the opposite direction whenever I sought to approach it. The table on which they were unhooded stood before a window, and each in its turn beat against the window like a wild bird. One of them darted behind some books, and, squeezing itself into a corner, remained cowering for a length of time. We might guess at the meaning of this strange and exceptional wildness; but the odd fact is enough for my present purpose. Whatever might have been the meaning of this marked change in their mental constitution—had they been unhooded on the previous day they would have run to me instead of from me—it could not have been the effect of experience; it must have resulted wholly from changes in their own organizations." †

Their case was precisely analogous to that of the Adirondack calves. The two opposite instincts relative to the same object ripen in succession. If the first one engenders a habit, that habit will inhibit the application of the second

---

* Spalding, Macmillan's Magazine, Feb. 1873, p. 287.
† *Ibid.*, p. 289.

instinct to that object. All animals are tame during the earliest phase of their infancy. Habits formed then limit the effects of whatever instincts of wildness may later be evolved.

b. This leads us to the **law of transitoriness,** which is this: *Many instincts ripen at a certain age and then fade away.* A consequence of this law is that if, during the time of such an instinct's vivacity, objects adequate to arouse it are met with, a *habit* of acting on them is formed, which remains when the original instinct has passed away; but that if no such objects are met with, then no habit will be formed; and, later on in life, when the animal meets the objects, he will altogether fail to react, as at the earlier epoch he would instinctively have done.

No doubt such a law is restricted. Some instincts are far less transient than others—those connected with feeding and 'self-preservation' may hardly be transient at all,—and some, after fading out for a time, recur as strong as ever; e.g., the instincts of pairing and rearing young. The law, however, though not absolute, is certainly very widespread, and a few examples will illustrate just what it means.

In the chickens and calves above mentioned it is obvious that the instinct to follow and become attached fades out after a few days, and that the instinct of flight then take its place, the conduct of the creature toward man being decided by the formation or non-formation of a certain habit during those days. The transiency of the chicken's instinct to follow is also proved by its conduct toward the hen. Mr. Spalding kept some chickens shut up till they were comparatively old, and, speaking of these, he says:

"A chicken that has not heard the call of the mother until eight or ten days old then hears it as if it heard it not. I regret to find that on this point my notes are not so full as I could wish, or as they might have been. There is, however, an account of one chicken that could not be returned to the mother when ten days old. The hen followed it, and tried to entice it in every way; still, it continually left her and ran to the house or to any person of whom it caught sight. This it persisted in doing, though beaten back with a small branch dozens of times, and, indeed, cruelly maltreated. It was also placed under the mother at night, but it again left her in the morning."

The instinct of sucking is ripe in all mammals at birth, and leads to that habit of taking the breast which, in the human infant, may be prolonged by daily exercise long beyond its usual term of a year or a year and a half. But the instinct itself is transient, in the sense that if, for any reason, the child be fed by spoon during the first few days of its life and not put to the breast, it may be no easy matter after that to make it suck at all. So of calves. If their mother die, or be dry, or refuse to let them suck for a day or two, so that they are fed by hand, it becomes hard to get them to suck at all when a new nurse is provided. The ease with which sucking creatures are weaned, by simply breaking the habit and giving them food in a new way, shows that the instinct, purely as such, must be entirely extinct.

Assuredly the simple fact that instincts are transient, and that the effect of later ones may be altered by the habits which earlier ones have left behind, is a far more philosophical explanation than the notion of an instinctive constitution vaguely 'deranged' or 'thrown out of gear.'

I have observed a Scotch terrier, born on the floor of a stable in December, and transferred six weeks later to a carpeted house, make, when he was less than four months old, a very elaborate pretence of burying things, such as gloves, etc., with which he had played till he was tired. He scratched the carpet with his forefeet, dropped the object from his mouth upon the spot, then scratched all about it, and finally went away and let it lie. Of course, the act was entirely useless. I saw him perform it at that age some four or five times, and never again in his life.

The conditions were not present to fix a habit which should last when the prompting instinct died away. But suppose meat instead of a glove, earth instead of a carpet, hunger-pangs instead of a fresh supper a few hours later, and it is easy to see how this dog might have got into a habit of burying superfluous food, which might have lasted all his life. Who can swear that the strictly instinctive part of the food-burying propensity in the wild *Canidæ* may not be as short-lived as it was in this terrier?

Leaving lower animals aside, and turning to human instincts, we see the law of transiency corroborated on the widest scale by the alternation of different interests and passions as human life goes on. With the child, life is all play and fairy-tales and learning the external properties of 'things'; with the youth, it is bodily exercises of a more systematic sort, novels of the real world, boon-fellowship and song, friendship and love, nature, travel and adventure, science and philosophy; with the man, ambition and policy, acquisitiveness, responsibility to others, and the selfish zest of the battle of life. If a boy grows up alone at the age of games and sports, and learns neither to play ball, nor row, nor sail, nor ride, nor skate, nor fish, nor shoot, probably he will be sedentary to the end of his days; and, though the best of opportunities be afforded him for learning these things later, it is a hundred to one but he will pass them by and shrink back from the effort of taking those necessary first steps the prospect of which, at an earlier age, would have filled him with eager delight. The sexual passion expires after a protracted reign; but it is well known that its peculiar manifestations in a given individual depend almost entirely on the habits he may form during the early period of its activity. Exposure to bad company then makes him a loose liver all his days; chastity kept at first makes the same easy later on. In all pedagogy the great thing is to strike the iron while hot, and to seize the wave of the pupil's interest in each successive subject before its ebb has come, so that knowledge may be got and a habit of skill acquired—a headway of interest, in short, secured, on which afterward the individual may float. There is a happy moment for fixing skill in drawing, for making boys collectors in natural history, and presently dissectors and botanists; then for initiating them into the harmonies of mechanics and the wonders of physical and chemical law. Later, introspective psychology and the metaphysical and religious mysteries take their turn; and, last of all, the drama of human affairs and worldly wisdom in the widest sense of the term. In each of us a saturation-point is soon reached in all these things; the impetus of our purely intellectual zeal expires, and unless the topic be one associated with some urgent personal need that keeps our wits constantly whetted about it, we settle into an equilibrium, and live on what we learned when our interest was fresh and instinctive, without adding to the store. Outside of their own business, the ideas gained by men before they are twenty-five are practically the only ideas they shall have in their lives. They *cannot* get anything new. Disinterested curiosity is past, the mental grooves and channels set, the power of assimilation gone. If by chance we ever do learn anything about some entirely new topic, we are afflicted with a strange sense of insecurity, and we fear to advance a resolute opinion. But with things learned in the plastic days of instinctive curiosity we never lose entirely our sense of being at home. There remains a kinship, a sentiment of intimate acquaintance, which, even when we know we have failed to keep abreast of the subject, flatters us with a sense of power over it, and makes us feel not altogether out of the pale.

Whatever individual exceptions to this might be cited are of the sort that 'prove the rule.'

To detect the moment of the instinctive readiness for the subject is, then, the first duty of every educator. As for the pupils, it would probably lead to a more earnest temper on the part of college students if they had less belief in their unlimited future intellectual potentialities, and could be brought to realize that whatever physics and political economy and philosophy they are now acquiring are, for better or worse, the physics and political economy and philosophy that will have to serve them to the end.

Enumeration of Instincts in Man.—Professor Preyer, in his careful little work, 'Die Seele des Kindes,' says "instinctive acts are in man few in number, and, apart from those connected with the sexual passion, difficult to recognize after early youth is past." And he adds, "so much the more attention should we pay to the instinctive movements of new-born babies, sucklings, and small children." That instinctive acts should be easiest *recognized* in childhood would be a very natural effect of our principles of transitoriness, and of the restrictive influence of habits once acquired; but they are far indeed from being 'few in number' in man. Professor Preyer divides the movements of infants into *impulsive, reflex,* and *instinctive.* By impulsive movements he means *random* movements of limbs, body, and voice, with no aim, and before perception is aroused. Among the first reflex movements are crying on contact with the air, *sneezing, snuffling, snoring, coughing, sighing, sobbing, gagging, vomiting, hiccuping, starting, moving the limbs when touched, and sucking.* To these may now be added *hanging by the hands* (see *Nineteenth Century,* Nov. 1891). Later on come *biting, clasping objects,* and *carrying them to the mouth, sitting up, standing, creeping,* and *walking.* It is probable that the centres for executing these three latter acts ripen spontaneously, just as those for flight have been proved to do in birds, and that the appearance of *learning* to stand and walk, by trial and failure, is due to the exercise beginning in most children before the centres are ripe. Children vary enormously in the rate and manner in which they learn to walk. With the first impulses to *imitation,* those to significant *vocalization* are born. *Emulation* rapidly ensues, with *pugnacity* in its train. *Fear* of definite objects comes in early, *sympathy* much later, though on the instinct (or emotion?—see p. 373) of sympathy so much in human life depends. *Shyness* and *sociability, play, curiosity, acquisitiveness,* all begin very early in life. The *hunting instinct, modesty, love,* the *parental instinct,* etc., come later. By the age of 15 or 16 the whole array of human instincts is complete. It will be observed that *no other mammal, not even the monkey, shows so large a list.* In a perfectly-rounded development every one of these instincts would start a habit toward certain objects and inhibit a habit towards certain others. Usually this is the case; but, in the one-sided development of civilized life, it happens that the timely age goes by in a sort of starvation of objects, and the individual then grows up with gaps in his psychic constitution which future experiences can never fill. Compare the accomplished gentleman with the poor artisan or tradesman of a city: during the adolescence of the former, objects appropriate to his growing interests, bodily and mental, were offered as fast as the interests awoke, and, as a consequence, he is armed and equipped at every angle to meet the world. Sport came to the rescue and completed his education where real things were lacking. He has tasted of the essence of every side of human life, being sailor, hunter, athlete, scholar, fighter, talker, dandy, man of affairs, etc., all in one. Over the city poor boy's youth no such golden opportunities were hung, and in his manhood no desires for most of them exist. Fortunate it is for him if gaps are the only anomalies his instinctive life presents; perversions are too often the fruit of his unnatural bringing-up.

Description of Fear.—In order to treat at least one instinct at greater length, I will take the instance of *fear.*

Fear is a reaction aroused by the same objects that arouse ferocity. The antagonism of the two is an interesting study in instinctive dynamics. We both fear, and wish to kill, anything that may kill us; and the question which of the two impulses we shall follow is usually decided by some one of those collateral circumstances of the particular case, to be moved by which is the mark of superior mental natures. Of course this introduces uncertainty into the reaction; but it is an uncertainty found in the higher brutes as well as in men, and ought not to be taken as proof that we are less instinctive than they. Fear has bodily expressions of an extremely energetic kind, and stands, beside lust and anger, as one of the three most exciting emotions of which our nature is susceptible. The progress from brute to man is characterized by nothing so much as by the decrease in frequency of proper occasions for fear. In civilized life, in particular, it has at last become possible for large numbers of people to pass from the cradle to the grave without ever having had a pang of genuine fear. Many of us need an attack of mental disease to teach us the meaning of the word. Hence the possibility of so much blindly optimistic philosophy and religion. The atrocities of life become 'like a tale of little meaning though the words are strong'; we doubt if anything like *us* ever really was within the tiger's jaws, and conclude that the horrors we hear of are but a sort of painted tapestry for the chambers in which we lie so comfortably at peace with ourselves and with the world.

Be this as it may, fear is a genuine instinct, and one of the earliest shown by the human child. *Noises* seem especially to call it forth. Most noises from the outer world, to a child bred in the house, have no exact significance. They are simply startling. To quote a good observer, M. Perez:

" Children between three and ten months are less often alarmed by visual than by auditory impressions. In cats, from the fifteenth day, the contrary is the case. A child, three and a half months old, in the midst of the turmoil of a conflagration, in presence of the devouring flames and ruined walls, showed neither astonishment nor fear, but smiled at the woman who was taking care of him, while his parents were busy. The noise, however, of the trumpet of the firemen, who were approaching, and that of the wheels of the engine, made him start and cry. At this age I have never yet seen an infant startled at a flash of lightning, even when intense; but I have seen many of them alarmed at the voice of the thunder. . . . Thus fear comes rather by the ears than by the eyes, to the child without experience." *

The effect of noise in heightening any terror we may feel in adult years is very marked. The *howling* of the storm, whether on sea or land, is a principal cause of our anxiety when exposed to it. The writer has been interested in noticing in his own person, while lying in bed, and kept awake by the wind outside, how invariably each loud gust of it arrested momentarily his heart. A dog attacking us is much more dreadful by reason of the noises he makes.

Strange men, and *strange animals*, either large or small, excite fear, but especially men or animals advancing toward us in a threatening way. This is entirely instinctive and antecedent to experience. Some children will cry with terror at their very first sight of a cat or dog, and it will often be impossible for weeks to make them touch it. Others will wish to fondle it almost immediately. Certain kinds of 'vermin,' especially spiders and snakes, seem to excite a fear unusually difficult to overcome. It is impossible to say how much of this difference is instinctive and how much the result of stories heard about these creatures. That the fear of 'vermin' ripens gradually seemed to me to be proved in a child of my own to whom I gave a live frog once, at the age of six to eight months, and again when he was a year and a half old. The first time, he seized it promptly, and holding it in spite of its struggling, at last got its head into his mouth. He then let

---

* Psychologie de l'Enfant, p. 72.

it crawl up his breast, and get upon his face, without showing alarm. But the second time, although he had seen no frog and heard no story about a frog betweenwhiles, it was almost impossible to induce him to touch it. Another child, a year old, eagerly took some very large spiders into his hand. At present he is afraid, but has been exposed meanwhile to the teachings of the nursery. One of my children from her birth upwards saw daily the pet pug-dog of the house, and never betrayed the slightest fear until she was (if I recollect rightly) about eight months old. Then the instinct suddenly seemed to develop, and with such intensity that familiarity had no mitigating effect. She screamed whenever the dog entered the room, and for many months remained afraid to touch him. It is needless to say that no change in the pug's unfailingly friendly conduct had anything to do with this change of feeling in the child Two of my children were afraid, when babies, of *fur:* Richet reports a similar observation.

Preyer tells of a young child screaming with fear on being carried near to the *sea*. The great source of terror to infancy is solitude. The teleology of this is obvious, as is also that of the infant's expression of dismay—the never-failing cry—on waking up and finding himself alone.

Black things, and especially *dark places*, holes, caverns, etc., arouse a peculiarly gruesome fear. This fear, as well as that of solitude, of being 'lost,' are explained after a fashion by ancestral experience. Says Schneider:

"It is a fact that men, especially in childhood, fear to go into a dark cavern or a gloomy wood. This feeling of fear arises, to be sure, partly from the fact that we easily suspect that dangerous beasts may lurk in these localities —a suspicion due to stories we have heard and read. But, on the other hand, it is quite sure that this fear at a certain perception is also directly inherited. Children who have been carefully guarded from all ghost-stories are nevertheless terrified and cry if led into a dark place, especially if sounds are made there. Even an adult can easily observe that an uncomfortable timidity steals over him in a lonely wood at night, although he may have the fixed conviction that not the slightest danger is near.

" This feeling of fear occurs in many men even in their own house after dark, although it is much stronger in a dark cavern or forest. The fact of such instinctive fear is easily explicable when we consider that our savage ancestors through innumerable generations were accustomed to meet with dangerous beasts in caverns, especially bears, and were for the most part attacked by such beasts during the night and in the woods, and that thus an inseparable association between the perceptions of darkness, caverns, woods, and fear took place, and was inherited." *

High places cause fear of a peculiarly sickening sort, though here, again, individuals differ enormously. The utterly blind instinctive character of the motor impulses here is shown by the fact that they are almost always entirely unreasonable, but that reason is powerless to suppress them. That they are a mere incidental peculiarity of the nervous system, like liability to sea-sickness, or love of music, with no teleological significance, seems more than probable. The fear in question varies so much from one person to another, and its detrimental effects are so much more obvious than its uses, that it is hard to see how it could be a selected instinct. Man is anatomically one of the best fitted of animals for climbing about high places. The best psychical complement to this equipment would seem to be a ' level head ' when there, not a dread of going there at all. In fact, the teleology of fear, beyond a certain point, is more than dubious. A certain amount of timidity obviously adapts us to the world we live in, but the *fear-paroxysm* is surely altogether harmful to him who is its prey.

---

* Der Menschliche Wille, p. 224.

Fear of the supernatural is one variety of fear. It is difficult to assign any normal object for this fear, unless it were a genuine ghost. But, in spite of psychical-research societies, science has not yet adopted ghosts; so we can only say that certain *ideas* of supernatural agency, associated with real circumstances, produce a peculiar kind of horror. This horror is probably explicable as the result of a combination of simpler horrors. To bring the ghostly terror to its maximum, many usual elements of the dreadful must combine, such as loneliness, darkness, inexplicable sounds, especially of a dismal character, moving figures half discerned (or, if discerned, of dreadful aspect), and a vertiginous baffling of the expectation. This last element, which is *intellectual*, is very important. It produces a strange emotional 'curdle' in our blood to see a process with which we are familiar deliberately taking an unwonted course. Anyone's heart would stop beating if he perceived his chair sliding unassisted across the floor. The lower animals appear to be sensitive to the mysteriously exceptional as well as ourselves. My friend Professor W. K. Brooks told me of his large and noble dog being frightened into a sort of epileptic fit by a bone being drawn across the floor by a thread which the dog did not see. Darwin and Romanes have given similar experiences. The idea of the supernatural involves that the usual should be set at naught. In the witch and hobgoblin supernatural, other elements still of fear are brought in—caverns, slime and ooze, vermin, corpses, and the like. A human corpse seems normally to produce an instinctive dread, which is no doubt somewhat due to its mysteriousness, and which familiarity rapidly dispels. But, in view of the fact that cadaveric, reptilian, and underground horrors play so specific and constant a part in many nightmares and forms of delirium, it seems not altogether unwise to ask whether these forms of dreadful circumstance may not at a former period have been more normal objects of the environment than now. The ordinary cock-sure evolutionist ought to have no difficulty in explaining these terrors, and the scenery that provokes them, as relapses into the consciousness of the cave-men, a consciousness usually overlaid in us by experiences of more recent date.

There are certain other pathological fears, and certain peculiarities in the expression of ordinary fear, which might receive an explanatory light from ancestral conditions, even infra-human ones. In ordinary fear, one may either run, or remain semi-paralyzed. The latter condition reminds us of the so-called death-shamming instinct shown by many animals. Dr. Lindsay, in his work 'Mind in Animals,' says this must require great self-command in those that practise it. But it is really no feigning of death at all, and requires no self-command. It is simply a terror-paralysis which has been so useful as to become hereditary. The beast of prey does not think the motionless bird, insect, or crustacean dead. He simply fails to notice them at all; because his senses, like ours, are much more strongly excited by a moving object than by a still one. It is the same instinct which leads a boy playing 'I spy' to hold his very breath when the seeker is near, and which makes the beast of prey himself in many cases motionlessly lie in wait for his victim or silently 'stalk' it, by stealthy advances alternated with periods of immobility. It is the opposite of the instinct which makes us jump up and down and move our arms when we wish to attract the notice of someone passing far away, and makes the shipwrecked sailor upon the raft where he is floating frantically wave a cloth when a distant sail appears. Now, may not the statue-like, crouching immobility of some melancholiacs, insane with general anxiety and fear of everything, be in some way connected with this old instinct? They can give no *reason* for their fear to move; but immobility makes them feel safer and more comfortable. Is not this the mental state of the 'feigning' animal?

Again, take the strange symptom which has been described of late years by the rather absurd name of *agoraphobia*. The patient is seized with palpitation and terror at the sight of any open place or broad street which he has to cross alone. He trembles, his knees bend, he may even faint at the idea. Where he has sufficient self-command he sometimes accomplishes the object by keeping safe under the lee of a vehicle going across, or joining himself to a knot of other people. But usually he slinks round the sides of the square, hugging the houses as closely as he can. This emotion has no utility in a civilized man, but when we notice the chronic agoraphobia of our domestic cats, and see the tenacious way in which many wild animals, especially rodents, cling to cover, and only venture on a dash across the open as a desperate measure—even then making for every stone or bunch of weeds which may give a momentary shelter—when we see this we are strongly tempted to ask whether such an odd kind of fear in us be not due to the accidental resurrection, through disease, of a sort of instinct which may in some of our remote ancestors have had a permanent and on the whole a useful part to play?

CHAPTER XXVI.

WILL.

Voluntary Acts.—Desire, wish, will, are states of mind which everyone knows, and which no definition can make plainer. We desire to feel, to have, to do, all sorts of things which at the moment are not felt, had, or done. If with the desire there goes a sense that attainment is not possible, we simply *wish;* but if we believe that the end is in our power, we *will* that the desired feeling, having, or doing shall be real; and real it presently becomes, either immediately upon the willing or after certain preliminaries have been fulfilled.

The only ends which follow *immediately* upon our willing seem to be movements of our own bodies. Whatever *feelings* and *havings* we may will to get come in as results of preliminary movements which we make for the purpose. This fact is too familiar to need illustration; so that we may start with the proposition that the only *direct* outward effects of our will are bodily movements. The mechanism of production of these voluntary movements is what befalls us to study now.

They are secondary performances. The movements we have studied hitherto have been automatic and reflex, and (on the first occasion of their performance, at any rate) unforeseen by the agent. The movements to the study of which we now address ourselves, being desired and intended beforehand, are of course done with full prevision of what they are to be. It follows from this that *voluntary movements must be secondary, not primary, functions of our organism.* This is the first point to understand in the psychology of Volition. Reflex, instinctive, and emotional movements are all primary performances. The nerve-centres are so organized that certain stimuli pull the trigger of certain explosive parts; and a creature going through one of these explosions for the first time undergoes an entirely novel experience. The other day I was standing at a railroad station with a little child, when an express-train went thundering by. The child, who was near the edge of the platform, started, winked, had his breath'ng convulsed, turned pale, burst out crying, and ran frantically towards me and hid his face. I have no doubt that this youngster was almost as much astonished by his own behavior as he was by the train, and more than I was, who stood by. Of course if such a reaction has many times occurred we learn what to expect of ourselves, and can then foresee our conduct, even though it remain as involuntary and uncontrollable as it was before. But if, in voluntary action properly so called, the act must be foreseen, it follows that no creature not endowed with prophetic power can perform an act voluntarily for the first time. Well, we are no more endowed with prophetic vision of what movements lie in our power than we are endowed with prophetic vision of what sensations we are capable of receiving. As we must wait for the sensations to be given us, so we must wait for the movements to be performed involuntarily, before we can frame ideas of what either of these things are. We learn all our possibilities by the way of experience. When a particular movement, having once occurred in a random, reflex, or involuntary way, has left an image of itself in the memory, then the movement can be desired again, and deliberately willed. But it is impossible to see how it could be willed before.

A supply of ideas of the various movements that are possible, left in the memory by experiences of their involuntary performance, is thus the first prerequisite of the voluntary life.

Two Kinds of Ideas of Movement.—Now these ideas may be either *resident* or *remote*. That is, they may be of the movement as it feels, when taking place, in the moving parts; or they may be of the movement as it feels in some other part of the body which it affects (strokes, presses, scratches, etc.), or as it sounds, or as it looks. The resident sensations in the parts that move have been called *kinæsthetic* feelings, the memories of them are kinæsthetic ideas. It is by these kinæsthetic sensations that we are made conscious of *passive movements*—movements communicated to our limbs by others. If you lie with closed eyes, and another person noiselessly places your arm or leg in any arbitrarily chosen attitude, you receive a feeling of what attitude it is, and can reproduce it yourself in the arm or leg of the opposite side. Similarly a man waked suddenly from sleep in the dark is aware of how he finds himself lying. At least this is what happens in normal cases. But when the feelings of passive movement as well as all the other feelings of a limb are lost, we get such results as are given in the following account by Prof. A. Strumpell of his wonderful anæsthetic boy, whose only sources of feeling were the right eye and the left ear: *

" Passive movements could be imprinted on all the extremities to the greatest extent, without attracting the patient's notice. Only in violent forced hyperextension of the joints, especially of the knees, there arose a dull vague feeling of strain, but this was seldom precisely localized. We have often, after bandaging the eyes of the patient, carried him about the room, laid him on a table, given to his arms and legs the most fantastic and apparently the most inconvenient attitudes without his having a suspicion of it. The expression of astonishment in his face, when all at once the removal of the handkerchief revealed his situation, is indescribable in words. Only when his head was made to hang away down he immediately spoke of dizziness, but could not assign its ground. Later he sometimes inferred from the sounds

---

* Deutsches Archiv f. Klin. Medicin, xxii. 821.

connected with the manipulation that something special was being done with him. . . . He had no feelings of muscular fatigue. If, with his eyes shut, we told him to raise his arm and to keep it up, he did so without trouble. After one or two minutes, however, the arm began to tremble and sink without his being aware of it. He asserted still his ability to keep it up. . . . Passively holding still his fingers did not affect him. He thought constantly that he opened and shut his hand, whereas it was really fixed."

No third kind of idea is called for. We need, then, when we perform a movement, either a kinæsthetic or a remote idea of which special movement it is to be. In addition to this it has often been supposed that we need an *idea of the amount of innervation* required for the muscular contraction. The discharge from the motor centre into the motor nerve is supposed to give a sensation *sui generis*, opposed to all our other sensations. These accompany incoming currents, whilst that, it is said, accompanies an outgoing current, and no movement is supposed to be totally defined in our mind, unless an anticipation of this feeling enter into our idea. The movement's degree of strength, and the effort required to perform it, are supposed to be specially revealed by the feeling of innervation. Many authors deny that this feeling exists, and the proofs given of its existence are certainly insufficient.

The various degrees of 'effort' actually felt in making the same movement against different resistances are all accounted for by the incoming feelings from our chest, jaws, abdomen, and other parts sympathetically contracted whenever the effort is great. There is no need of a consciousness of the amount of outgoing current required. If anything be obvious to introspection, it is that the degree of strength put forth is completely revealed to us by incoming feelings from the muscles themselves and their insertions, from the vicinity of the joints, and from the general fixation of the larynx, chest, face, and body.

When a certain degree of energy of contraction rather than another is thought of by us, this complex aggregate of afferent feelings, forming the material of our thought, renders absolutely precise and distinctive our mental image of the exact strength of movement to be made, and the exact amount of resistance to be overcome.

Let the reader try to direct his will towards a particular movement, and then notice what *constituted* the direction of the will. Was it anything over and above the notion of the different feelings to which the movement when effected would give rise? If we abstract from these feelings, will any sign, principle, or means of orientation be left by which the will may innervate the proper muscles with the right intensity, and not go astray into the wrong ones? Strip off these images anticipative of the results of the motion, and so far from leaving us with a complete assortment of directions into which our will may launch itself, you leave our consciousness in an absolute and total vacuum. If I will to write *Peter* rather than *Paul*, it is the thought of certain digital sensations, of certain alphabetic sounds, of certain appearances on the paper, and of no others, which immediately precedes the motion of my pen. If I will to utter the word *Paul* rather than *Peter*, it is the thought of my voice falling on my ear, and of certain muscular feelings in my tongue, lips, and larynx, which guide the utterance. All these are incoming feelings. and between the thought of them, by which the act is mentally specified with all possible completeness, and the act itself, there is no room for any third order of mental phenomenon.

There is indeed the *fiat*, the element of consent, or resolve that the act shall ensue. This, doubtless, to the reader's mind, as to my own, constitutes the essence of the voluntariness of the act. This *fiat* will be treated of in detail further on. It may be entirely neglected here, for it is a constant coefficient, affecting all voluntary actions alike, and incapable of serving to distinguish them. No one will pretend that its quality varies according as the right arm, for example, or the left is used.

An anticipatory image, then, of the sensorial consequences of a movement, plus (on certain occasions) the fiat that these consequences shall become actual, is the only psychic state which introspection lets us discern as the forerunner of our voluntary acts. There is no coercive evidence of any feeling attached to the efferent discharge.

The entire content and material of our consciousness—consciousness of movement, as of all things else—seems thus to be of peripheral origin, and to come to us in the first instance through the peripheral nerves.

The Motor-cue.—Let us call the last idea which in the mind precedes the motor discharge the 'motor-cue.' Now do 'resident' images form the only motor-cue, or will 'remote' ones equally suffice?

There can be no doubt whatever that the cue may be an image either of the resident or of the remote kind. Although, at the outset of our learning a movement, it would seem that the resident feelings must come strongly before consciousness, later this need not be the case. The rule, in fact, would seem to be that they tend to lapse more and more from consciousness, and that the more practised we become in a movement, the more 'remote' do the ideas become which form its mental cue. What we are *interested* in is what sticks in our consciousness; everything else we get rid of as quickly as we can. Our resident feelings of movement have no substantive interest for us at all, as a rule. What interest us are the ends which the movement is to attain. Such an end is generally a remote sensation, an impression which the movement produces on the eye or ear, or sometimes on the skin, nose, or palate. Now let the idea of such an end associate itself definitely with the right discharge, and the thought of the innervation's *resident* effects will become as great an encumbrance as we have already concluded that the feeling of the innervation itself is. The mind does not need it; the end alone is enough.

The idea of the end, then, tends more and more to make itself all-sufficient. Or, at any rate, if the kinæsthetic ideas are called up at all, they are so swamped in the vivid kinæsthetic feelings by which they are immediately overtaken that we have no time to be aware of their separate existence. As I write, I have no anticipation, as a thing distinct from my sensation, of either the look or the digital feel of the letters which flow from my pen. The words chime on my mental *ear*, as it were, before I write them, but not on my mental eye or hand. This comes from the rapidity with which the movements follow on their mental cue. An end consented to as soon as conceived innervates directly the centre of the first movement of the chain which leads to its accomplishment, and then the whole chain rattles off *quasi*-reflexly, as was described on pp. 115–6.

The reader will certainly recognize this to be true in all fluent and unhesitating voluntary acts. The only special fiat there is at the outset of the performance. A man says to himself, " I must change my clothes," and involuntarily he has taken off his coat, and his fingers are at work in their accustomed manner on his waistcoat-buttons, etc.; or we say, " I must go downstairs," and ere we know it we have risen, walked, and turned the handle of the door;— all through the idea of an end coupled with a series of guiding sensations which successively arise. It would seem indeed that we fail of accuracy and certainty in our attainment of the end whenever we are preoccupied with the way in which the movement will feel. We walk a beam the better the less we think of the position of our feet upon it. We pitch or catch, we shoot or chop the better the less tactile and muscular (the less resident), and the more exclusively optical (the more remote), our consciousness is. Keep your *eye* on the place aimed at, and your hand will fetch it; think of your hand, and you will very likely

miss your aim. Dr. Southard found that he could touch
a spot with a pencil-point more accurately with a visual
than with a tactile mental cue. In the former case he
looked at a small object and closed his eyes before trying to touch it. In the latter case he *placed* it with closed
eyes, and then after removing his hand tried to touch it
again. The average error with touch (when the results
were most favorable) was 17.13 mm. With sight it was
only 12.37 mm.—All these are plain results of introspection
and observation. By what neural machinery they are
made possible we do not know.

In Chapter XIX we saw how enormously individuals
differ in respect to their mental imagery. In the type of
imagination called *tactile* by the French authors, it is
probable that the kinæsthetic ideas are more prominent
than in my account. We must not expect too great a
uniformity in individual accounts, nor wrangle overmuch
as to which one 'truly' represents the process.

I trust that I have now made clear what that 'idea of
a movement' is which must precede it in order that it be
voluntary. It is not the thought of the innervation which
the movement requires. It is the anticipation of the
movement's sensible effects, resident or remote, and sometimes very remote indeed. Such anticipations, to say the
least, determine *what* our movements shall be. I have
spoken all along as if they also might determine *that* they
shall be. This, no doubt, has disconcerted many readers,
for it certainly seems as if a special fiat, or consent to the
movement, were required in addition to the mere conception of it, in many cases of volition; and this fiat I have
altogether left out of my account. This leads us to the
next point in our discussion.

Ideo-motor Action.—The question is this: *Is the bare
idea of a movement's sensible effects its sufficient motor-cue,
or must there be an additional mental antecedent, in the
shape of a fiat, decision, consent, volitional mandate, or*

other synonymous phenomenon of consciousness, before the movement can follow?

I answer: Sometimes the bare idea is sufficient, but sometimes an additional conscious element, in the shape of a fiat, mandate, or express consent, has to intervene and precede the movement. The cases without a fiat constitute the more fundamental, because the more simple, variety. The others involve a special complication, which must be fully discussed at the proper time. For the present let us turn to *ideo-motor action*, as it has been termed, or the sequence of movement upon the mere thought of it, without a special fiat, as the type of the process of volition.

Wherever a movement *unhesitatingly and immediately* follows upon the idea of it, we have ideo-motor action. We are then aware of nothing between the conception and the execution. All sorts of neuro-muscular processes come between, of course, but we know absolutely nothing of them. We think the act, and it is done; and that is all that introspection tells us of the matter. Dr. Carpenter, who first used, I believe, the name of ideo-motor action, placed it, if I mistake not, among the curiosities of our mental life. The truth is that it is no curiosity, but simply the normal process stripped of disguise. Whilst talking I become conscious of a pin on the floor, or of some dust on my sleeve. Without interrupting the conversation I brush away the dust or pick up the pin. I make no express resolve, but the mere perception of the object and the fleeting notion of the act seem of themselves to bring the latter about. Similarly, I sit at table after dinner and find myself from time to time taking nuts or raisins out of the dish and eating them. My dinner properly is over, and in the heat of the conversation I am hardly aware of what I do; but the perception of the fruit, and the fleeting notion that I may eat it, seem fatally to bring the act about. There is certainly no express fiat here; any more than there is in all those habitual goings and comings and rearrangements of ourselves which fill every hour of the day, and which incoming sensations instigate so immediately that it is often difficult to decide whether not to call them reflex rather than voluntary acts. As Lotze says:

"We see in writing or piano-playing a great number of very complicated movements following quickly one upon the other, the instigative representations of which remained scarcely a second in consciousness, certainly not long enough to awaken any other volition than the general one of resigning one's self without reserve to the passing over of representation into action. All the acts of our daily life happen in this wise: Our standing up, walking, talking, all this never demands a distinct impulse of the will, but is adequately brought about by the pure flux of thought." *

In all this the determining condition of the unhesitating and resistless sequence of the act seems to be *the absence of any conflicting notion in the mind.* Either there is nothing else at all in the mind, or what is there does not conflict. We know what it is to get out of bed on a freezing morning in a room without a fire, and how the very vital principle within us protests against the ordeal. Probably most persons have lain on certain mornings for an hour at a time unable to brace themselves to the resolve. We think how late we shall be, how the duties of the day will suffer; we say, "I *must* get up, this is ignominious," etc.; but still the warm couch feels too delicious, the cold outside too cruel, and resolutions faints away and postpones itself again and again just as it seemed on the verge of bursting the resistance and passing over into the decisive act. Now how do we *ever* get up under such circumstances? If I may generalize from my own experience, we more often than not get up without any struggle or decision at all. We suddenly find that we *have* got up. A fortunate lapse of consciousness occurs; we forget both

---

* Medicinische Psychologie, p. 293.

the warmth and the cold; we fall into some revery connected with the day's life, in the course of which the idea flashes across us, "Hollo! I must lie here no longer"—an idea which at that lucky instant awakens no contradictory or paralyzing suggestions, and consequently produces immediately its appropriate motor effects. It was our acute consciousness of both the warmth and the cold during the period of struggle, which paralyzed our activity then and kept our idea of rising in the condition of *wish* and not of *will*. The moment these inhibitory ideas ceased, the original idea exerted its effects.

This case seems to me to contain in miniature form the data for an entire psychology of volition. It was in fact through meditating on the phenomenon in my own person that I first became convinced of the truth of the doctrine which these pages present, and which I need here illustrate by no farther examples. The reason why that doctrine is not a self-evident truth is that we have so many ideas which *do not* result in action. But it will be seen that in every such case, without exception, that is because other ideas simultaneously present rob them of their impulsive power. But even here, and when a movement is inhibited from *completely* taking place by contrary ideas, it will *incipiently* take place. To quote Lotze once more:

"The spectator accompanies the throwing of a billiard-ball, or the thrust of the swordsman, with slight movements of his arm; the untaught narrator tells his story with many gesticulations; the reader while absorbed in the perusal of a battle-scene feels a slight tension run through his muscular system, keeping time as it were with the actions he is reading of. These results become the more marked the more we are absorbed in thinking of the movements which suggest them; they grow fainter exactly in proportion as a complex consciousness, under the dominion of a crowd of other representations, withstands the passing over of mental contemplation into outward action."

The 'willing-game,' the exhibitions of so-called 'mind-reading,' or more properly muscle-reading, which have lately grown so fashionable, are based on this incipient obedience of muscular contraction to idea, even when the deliberate intention is that no contraction shall occur.

We may then lay it down for certain that *every representation of a movement awakens in some degree the actual movement which is its object; and awakens it in a maximum degree whenever it is not kept from so doing by an antagonistic representation present simultaneously to the mind.*

The express fiat, or act of mental consent to the movement, comes in when the neutralization of the antagonistic and inhibitory idea is required. But that there is no express fiat needed when the conditions are simple, the reader ought now to be convinced. Lest, however, he should still share the common prejudice that voluntary action without 'exertion of will-power' is Hamlet with the prince's part left out, I will make a few farther remarks. The first point to start from, in understanding voluntary action and the possible occurrence of it with no fiat or express resolve, is the fact that consciousness is *in its very nature impulsive.* We do not first have a sensation or thought, and then have to *add* something dynamic to it to get a movement. Every pulse of feeling which we have is the correlate of some neural activity that is already on its way to instigate a movement. Our sensations and thoughts are but cross-sections, as it were, of currents whose essential consequence is motion, and which have no sooner run in at one nerve than they are ready to run out by another. The popular notion that consciousness is not essentially a forerunner of activity, but that the latter must result from some superadded 'will-force,' is a very natural inference from those special cases in which we think of an act for an indefinite length of time without the action taking place. These cases, however, are not the norm; they are cases of inhibition by antagonistic thoughts. When the blocking is released we feel as if an inward spring were let loose, and this is the additional impulse or *fiat* upon which the act effectively succeeds. We shall study anon the blocking and its release. Our higher thought is full of it. But where there is no blocking, there is naturally no hiatus between the thought-process and the motor discharge. *Movement is the natural immediate effect of the process of feeling, irrespective of what the quality of the feeling may be. It is so in reflex action, it is so in emotional expression, it is so in the voluntary life.* Ideo-motor action is thus no paradox, to be softened or explained away. It obeys the type of all conscious action, and from it one must start to explain the sort of action in which a special fiat is involved.

It may be remarked in passing, that the inhibition of a movement no more involves an express effort or command than its execution does. Either of them *may* require it. But in all simple and ordinary cases, just as the bare presence of one idea prompts a movement, so the bare presence of another idea will prevent its taking place. Try to feel as if you were crooking your finger, whilst keeping it straight. In a minute it will fairly tingle with the imaginary change of position; yet it will not sensibly move, because *its not really moving* is also a part of what you have in mind. Drop *this* idea, think purely and simply of the movement, and nothing else, and, presto! it takes place with no effort at all.

A waking man's behavior is thus at all times the resultant of two opposing neural forces. With unimaginable fineness some currents among the cells and fibres of his brain are playing on his motor nerves, whilst other currents, as unimaginably fine, are playing on the first currents, damming or helping them, altering their direction or their speed. The upshot of it all is, that whilst the currents must always end by being drained off through *some* motor nerves, they are drained off sometimes through one set and sometimes through another; and sometimes they keep each other in equilibrium so long that a superficial observer may think they are not drained off at all. Such an observer must remember, however, that from the physiological point of view a gesture, an expression of the brow, or an expulsion of the breath are movements as much as an act of locomotion is. A king's breath slays as well as an assassin's blow; and the outpouring of those currents which the magic imponderable streaming of our ideas accompanies need not always be of an explosive or otherwise physically conspicuous kind.

Action after Deliberation.—We are now in a position to describe *what happens in deliberate action*, or when the mind has many objects before it, related to each other in antagonistic or in favorable ways. One of these objects of its thought may be an act. By itself this would prompt a movement; some of the additional objects or considerations, however, block the motor discharge, whilst others, on the contrary, solicit it to take place. The result is that peculiar feeling of inward unrest known as *indecision*. Fortunately it is too familiar to need description, for to describe it would be impossible. As long as it lasts, with the various objects before the attention, we are said to *deliberate*; and when finally the original suggestion either prevails and makes the movement take place, or gets definitively quenched by its antagonists, we are said to *decide*, or to *utter our voluntary fiat*, in favor of one or the other course. The reinforcing and inhibiting objects meanwhile are termed the *reasons* or *motives* by which the decision is brought about.

The process of deliberation contains endless degrees of complication. At every moment of it our consciousness is of an extremely complex thing, namely, the whole set of motives and their conflict. Of this complicated object, the totality of which is realized more or less dimly all the while by consciousness, certain parts stand out more or less sharply at one moment in the foreground, and at another moment other parts, in consequence of the oscillations of our attention, and of the 'associative' flow of our ideas. But no matter how sharp the foreground-reasons may be, or how imminently close to bursting through the dam and carrying the motor consequences their own way, the background, however dimly felt, is always there as a fringe (p. 163); and its presence (so long as the indecision actually lasts) serves as an effective check upon the irrevocable discharge. The deliberation may last for weeks or months, occupying at intervals the mind. The motives which yesterday seemed full of urgency and blood and life to-day feel strangely weak and pale and dead. But as little to-day as to-morrow is the question finally resolved. Something tells us that all this is provisional; that the weakened reasons will wax strong again, and the stronger weaken; that equilibrium is unreached; that testing our reasons, not obeying them, is still the order of the day, and that we must wait awhile, patiently or impatiently, until our mind is made up 'for good and all.' This inclining first to one, then to another future, both of which we represent as possible, resembles the oscillations to and fro of a material body within the limits of its elasticity. There is inward strain, but no outward rupture. And this condition, plainly enough, is susceptible of indefinite continuance, as well in the physical mass as in the mind. If the elasticity give way, however, if the dam ever do break, and the currents burst the crust, vacillation is over and decision is irrevocably there.

The decision may come in either of many modes. I will try briefly to sketch the most characteristic types of it, merely warning the reader that this is only an introspective account of symptoms and phenomena, and that all questions of causal agency, whether neural or spiritual, are relegated to a later page.

Five Chief Types of Decision.—Turning now to the form of the decision itself, we may distinguish five chief types. *The first may be called the reasonable type.* It is that of those cases in which the arguments for and against a given course seem gradually and almost insensibly to settle themselves in the mind and to end by leaving a clear balance in favor of one alternative, which alternative we then adopt without effort or constraint. Until this rational balancing of the books is consummated we have a calm feeling that the evidence is not yet all in, and this keeps action in suspense. But some day we wake with the sense that we see the matter rightly, that no new light will be thrown on it by farther delay, and that it had better be settled *now*. In this easy transition from doubt to assurance we seem to ourselves almost passive; the 'reasons' which decide us appearing to flow in from the nature of things, and to owe nothing to our will. We have, however, a perfect sense of being *free*, in that we are devoid of any feeling of coercion. The conclusive reason for the decision in these cases usually is the discovery that we can refer the case to a *class* upon which we are accustomed to act unhesitatingly in a certain stereotyped way. It may be said in general that a great part of every deliberation consists in the turning over of all the possible modes of *conceiving* the doing or not doing of the act in point. The moment we hit upon a conception which lets us apply some principle of action which is a fixed and stable part of our Ego, our state of doubt is at an end. Persons of authority, who have to make many decisions in the day, carry with them a set of heads of classification, each bearing its volitional consequence, and under these they seek as far as possible to range each new emergency as it occurs. It is where the emergency belongs to a species without precedent, to which consequently no cut-and-dried maxim will apply, that we feel most at a loss, and are distressed at the indeterminateness of our task. As soon, however, as we see our way to a familiar classification, we are at ease again. *In action as in reasoning, then, the great thing is the quest of the right conception.* The concrete dilemmas do not come to us with labels gummed upon their backs. We may name them by many names. The wise man is he who succeeds in finding the name which suits the needs of the particular occasion best (p. 357 ff.). A 'reasonable' character is one who has a store of stable and worthy ends, and who does not decide about an action till he has calmly ascertained whether it be ministerial or detrimental to any one of these.

In the next two types of decision, the final fiat occurs before the evidence is all 'in.' It often happens that no paramount and authoritative reason for either course will come. Either seems a good, and there is no umpire to decide which should yield its place to the other. We grow tired of long hesitation and inconclusiveness, and the hour may come when we feel that even a bad decision is better than no decision at all. Under these conditions it will often happen that some accidental circumstance, supervening at a particular movement upon our mental weariness, will upset the balance in the direction of one of the alternatives, to which then we feel ourselves committed, although an opposite accident at the same time might have produced the opposite result.

In the *second type* our feeling is to a great extent that of letting ourselves drift with a certain indifferent acquiescence in a direction accidentally determined *from without*, with the conviction that, after all, we might as well stand by this course as by the other, and that things are in any event sure to turn out sufficiently right.

In the third type the determination seems equally accidental, but it comes from within, and not from without. It often happens, when the absence of imperative principle is perplexing and suspense distracting, that we find ourselves acting, as it were, automatically, and as if by a spontaneous discharge of our nerves, in the direction of one of the horns of the dilemma. But so exciting is this sense of motion after our intolerable pent-up state that we eagerly throw ourselves into it. 'Forward now!' we inwardly cry, 'though the heavens fall.' This reckless and exultant espousal of an energy so little premeditated by us that we feel rather like passive spectators cheering on the display of some extraneous force than like voluntary agents is a type of decision too abrupt and tumultuous to occur often in humdrum and cool-blooded natures. But it is probably frequent in persons of strong emotional endowment and unstable or vacillating character. And in men of the world-shaking type, the Napoleons, Luthers, etc., in whom tenacious passion combines with ebullient activity, when by any chance the passion's outlet has been dammed by scruples or apprehensions, the resolution is probably often of this catastrophic kind. The flood breaks quite unexpectedly through the dam. That it should so often do so is quite sufficient to account for the tendency of these characters to a fatalistic mood of mind. And the fatalistic mood itself is sure to reinforce the strength of the energy just started on its exciting path of discharge.

There is a *fourth form* of decision, which often ends deliberation as suddenly as the third form does. It comes when, in consequence of some outer experience or some inexplicable inward change, *we suddenly pass from the easy and careless to the sober and strenuous mood*, or possibly the other way. The whole scale of values of our motives and impulses then undergoes a change like that which a change of the observer's level produces on a view. The most sobering possible agents are objects of grief and fear. When one of these affects us, all 'light fantastic' notions lose their motive power, all solemn ones find theirs multiplied many-fold. The consequence is an instant abandonment of the more trivial projects with which we had been dallying, and an instant practical acceptance of the more grim and earnest alternative which till then could not extort our mind's consent. All those 'changes of heart,' 'awakenings of conscience,' etc., which make new men of so many of us may be classed under this head. The character abruptly rises to another 'level,' and deliberation comes to an immediate end.

In the *fifth and final type* of decision, the feeling that

the evidence is all in, and that reason has balanced the books, may be either present or absent. But in either case we feel, in deciding, as if we ourselves by our own wilful act inclined the beam: in the former case by adding our living effort to the weight of the logical reason which, taken alone, seems powerless to make the act discharge; in the latter by a kind of creative contribution of something instead of a reason which does a reason's work. The slow dead heave of the will that is felt in these instances makes of them a class altogether different subjectively from all the four preceding classes. What the heave of the will betokens metaphysically, what the effort might lead us to infer about a will-power distinct from motives, are not matters that concern us yet. Subjectively and phenomenally, the *feeling of effort*, absent from the former decisions, accompanies these. Whether it be the dreary resignation for the sake of austere and naked duty of all sorts of rich mundane delights; or whether it be the heavy resolve that of two mutually exclusive trains of future fact, both sweet and good and with no strictly objective or imperative principle of choice between them, one shall forevermore become impossible, while the other shall become reality; it is a desolate and acrid sort of act, an entrance into a lonesome moral wilderness. If examined closely, its chief difference from the former cases appears to be that in those cases the mind at the moment of deciding on the triumphant alternative dropped the other one wholly or nearly out of sight, whereas here both alternatives are steadily held in view, and in the very act of murdering the vanquished possibility the chooser realizes how much in that instant he is making himself lose. It is deliberately driving a thorn into one's flesh; and the sense of *inward effort* with which the act is accompanied is an element which sets this fifth type of decision in strong contrast with the previous four varieties, and makes of it an altogether peculiar sort of mental phenomenon. The immense majority of human decisions are decisions without effort. In comparatively few of them, in most people, does effort accompany the final act. We are, I think, misled into supposing that effort is more frequent than it is by the fact that *during deliberation* we so often have a feeling of how great an effort it would take to make a decision *now*. Later, after the decision has made itself with ease, we recollect this and erroneously suppose the effort also to have been made then.

The existence of the effort as a phenomenal fact in our consciousness cannot of course be doubted or denied. Its significance, on the other hand, is a matter about which the gravest difference of opinion prevails. Questions as momentous as that of the very existence of spiritual causality, as vast as that of universal predestination or freewill, depend on its interpretation. It therefore becomes essential that we study with some care the conditions under which the feeling of volitional effort is found.

The Feeling of Effort.—When I said, awhile back, that *consciousness* (or the neural process which goes with it) *is in its very nature impulsive*, I should have added the proviso that *it must be sufficiently intense*. Now there are remarkable differences in the power of different sorts of consciousness to excite movement. The intensity of some feelings is practically apt to be below the discharging point, whilst that of others is apt to be above it. By practically apt, I mean apt under ordinary circumstances. These circumstances may be habitual inhibitions, like that comfortable feeling of the *dolce far niente* which gives to each and all of us a certain dose of laziness only to be overcome by the acuteness of the impulsive spur; or they may consist in the native inertia, or internal resistance, of the motor centres themselves, making explosion impossible until a certain inward tension has been reached and overpassed. These conditions may vary from one person to another, and in the same person from time to time. The neural inertia may wax or wane, and the habitual inhibitions dwindle or augment. The intensity of particul* thought-processes and stimulations may also change independently, and particular paths of association grow more pervious or less so. There thus result great possibilities of alteration in the actual impulsive efficacy of particular motives compared with others. It is where the normally less efficacious motive becomes more efficacious, and the normally more efficacious one less so, that actions ordinarily effortless, or abstinences ordinarily easy, either become impossible, or are effected (if at all) by the expenditure of effort. A little more description will make it plainer what these cases are.

Healthiness of Will.—*There is a certain normal ratio in the impulsive power of different mental objects, which characterizes what may be called ordinary healthiness oj will*, and which is departed from only at exceptional times or by exceptional individuals. The states of mind which normally possess the most impulsive quality are either those which represent objects of passion, appetite, or emotion—objects of instinctive reaction, in short; or they are feelings or ideas of pleasure or of pain; or ideas which for any reason we have grown accustomed to obey, so that the habit of reacting on them is ingrained; or finally, in comparison with ideas of remoter objects, they are ideas of objects present or near in space and time. Compared with these various objects, all far-off considerations, all highly abstract conceptions, unaccustomed reasons, and motives foreign to the instinctive history of the race, have little or no impulsive power. They prevail, when they ever do prevail, *with effort; and the normal*, as distinguished from the pathological, *sphere of effort is thus found wherever non-instinctive motives to behavior must be reinforced so as to rule the day.*

Healthiness of will moreover requires a certain amount of complication in the process which precedes the fiat or the act. Each stimulus or idea, at the same time that it wakens its own impulse, must also arouse other ideas along with *their* characteristic impulses, and action must finally follow, neither too slowly nor too rapidly, as the resultant of all the forces thus engaged. Even when the decision is pretty prompt, the normal thing is thus a sort of preliminary survey of the field and a vision of which course is best before the fiat comes. And where the will is healthy, *the vision must be right* (i.e., the motives must be on the whole in a normal or not too unusual ratio to each other), *and the action must obey the vision's lead.*

Unhealthiness of will may thus come about in many ways. The action may follow the stimulus or idea too rapidly, leaving no time for the arousal of restraining associates—*we then have a precipitate will*. Or, although the associates may come, the ratio which the impulsive and inhibitive forces normally bear to each other may be distorted, and we then have *a will which is perverse*. The perversity, in turn, may be due to either of many causes—too much intensity, or too little, here; too much or too little inertia there; or elsewhere too much or too little inhibitory power. *If we compare the outward symptoms of perversity together, they fall into two groups*, in one of which normal actions are impossible, and in the other abnormal ones are irrepressible. Briefly, *we may call them respectively the obstructed and the explosive will.*

It must be kept in mind, however, that since the resultant action is always due to the *ratio* between the obstructive and the explosive forces which are present, we never can tell by the mere outward symptoms to what *elementary* cause the perversion of a man's will may be due, whether to an increase of one component or a diminution of the other. One may grow explosive as readily by losing the usual brakes as by getting up more of the impulsive steam; and one may find things impossible as well through the enfeeblement of the original desire as through the advent of new lions in the path. As Dr. Clouston says, "the driver may be so weak that he cannot control well-broken horses, or the horses may be so hard-mouthed that no driver can pull them up."

The Explosive Will. (1. From Defective Inhibition.— There is a normal type of character, for example, in which impulses seem to discharge so promptly into movements that inhibitions get no time to arise. These are the 'daredevil' and 'mercurial' temperaments, overflowing with animation and fizzling with talk, which are so common in the Slavic and Celtic races, and with which the coldblooded and long-headed English character forms so marked a contrast. Simian these people seem to us, whilst we seem to them reptilian. It is quite impossible to judge, as between an obstructed and an explosive individual, which has the greater sum of vital energy. An explosive Italian with good perception and intellect will cut a figure as a perfectly tremendous fellow, on an inward capital that could be tucked away inside of an obstructed Yankee and hardly let you know that it was there. He will be the king of his company, sing the songs and make the speeches, lead the parties, carry out the practical jokes, kiss the girls, fight the men, and, if need be, lead the forlorn hopes and enterprises, so that an onlooker would think he has more life in his little finger than can exist in the whole body of a correct judicious fellow. But the judicious fellow all the while may have all these possibilities and more besides, ready to break out in the same or even a more violent way, if only the brakes were taken off. It is the absence of scruples, of consequences, of considerations, the extraordinary simplification of each moment's mental outlook, that gives to the explosive individual such motor energy and ease; it need not be the greater intensity of any of his passions, motives, or thoughts. As mental evolution goes on, the complexity of human consciousness grows ever greater, and with it the multiplication of the inhibitions to which every impulse is exposed. How much freedom of discourse we English folk lose because we feel obliged always to speak the truth! This predominance of inhibition has a bad as well as a good side; and if a man's impulses are in the main orderly as well as prompt, if he has courage to accept their consequences, and intellect to lead them to a successful end, he is all the better for his hair-trigger organization, and for not being 'sicklied o'er with the pale cast of thought.' Many of the most successful military and revolutionary characters in history have belonged to this simple but quick-witted impulsive type. Problems come much harder to reflective and inhibitive minds. They can, it is true, solve much vaster problems; and they can avoid many a mistake to which the men of impulse are exposed. But when the latter do not make mistakes, or when they are always able to retrieve them, theirs is one of the most engaging and indispensable of human types.

In infancy, and in certain conditions of exhaustion, as well as in peculiar pathological states, the inhibitory power may fail to arrest the explosions of the impulsive discharge. We have then an explosive temperament temporarily realized in an individual who at other times may be of a relatively obstructed type. In other persons, again, hysterics, epileptics, criminals of the neurotic class called *dégénérés* by French authors, there is such a native feebleness in the mental machinery that before the inhibitory ideas can arise the impulsive ones have already discharged into act. In persons healthy-willed by nature bad habits can bring about this condition, especially in relation to particular sorts of impulse. Ask half the common drunkards you know why it is that they fall so often a prey to temptation, and they will say that most of the time they cannot tell. It is a sort of vertigo with them. Their nervous centres have become a sluice-way pathologically unlocked by every passing conception of a bottle and a glass. They do not thirst for the beverage; the taste of it may even appear repugnant; and they perfectly foresee the morrow's remorse. But when they think of the liquor or see it, they find themselves preparing to drink, and do not stop themselves: and more than this they cannot say. Similarly a man may lead a life of incessant love-making or sexual indulgence, though what spurs him thereto seems to be trivial suggestions and notions of possibility rather than any real solid strength of passion or desire. Such characters are too flimsy even to be bad in any deep sense of the word. The paths of natural (or it may be unnatural) impulse are so pervious in them that the slightest rise in the level of innervation produces an overflow. It is the condition recognized in pathology as 'irritable weakness.' The phase known as nascency or latency is so short in the excitement of the neural tissues that there is no opportunity for strain or tension to accumulate within them; and the consequence is that with all the agitation and activity, the amount of real feeling engaged may be very small. The hysterical temperament is the playground *par excellence* of this unstable equilibrium. One of these subjects will be filled with what seems the most genuine and settled aversion to a certain line of conduct, and the very next *instant* follow the stirring of temptation and plunge in it up to the neck.

2.) **From Exaggerated Impulsion.**—Disorderly and impulsive conduct may, on the other hand, come about where the neural tissues preserve their proper inward tone, and where the inhibitory power is normal or even unusually great. In such cases *the strength of the impulsive idea is preternaturally exalted*, and what would be for most people the passing suggestion of a possibility becomes a gnawing, craving urgency to act. Works on insanity are full of examples of these morbid insistent ideas, in obstinately struggling against which the unfortunate victim's soul often sweats with agony ere at last it gets swept away.

The craving for drink in real dipsomaniacs, or for opium or chloral in those subjugated, is of a strength of which normal persons can form no conception. "Were a keg of rum in one corner of a room and were a cannon constantly discharging balls between me and it, I could not refrain from passing before that cannon in order to get the rum;" "If a bottle of brandy stood at one hand and the pit of hell yawned at the other, and I were convinced that I should be pushed in as sure as I took one glass, I could not refrain:" such statements abound in dipsomaniacs' mouths. Dr. Mussey of Cincinnati relates this case:

"A few years ago a tippler was put into an almshouse in this State. Within a few days he had devised various expedients to procure rum, but failed. At length, however, he hit upon one which was successful. He went into the wood-yard of the establishment, placed one hand upon the block, and with an axe in the other struck it off at a single blow. With the stump raised and streaming he ran into the house and cried, 'Get some rum! get some rum! My hand is off!' In the confusion and bustle of the occasion a bowl of rum was brought, into which he plunged the bleeding member of his body, then raising the bowl to his mouth, drank freely, and exultingly exclaimed, 'Now I am satisfied.' Dr. J. E. Turner tells of a man who, while under treatment for inebriety, during four weeks secretly drank the alcohol from six jars containing morbid specimens. On asking him why he had committed this loathsome act, he replied: 'Sir, it is as impossible for me to control this diseased appetite as it is for me to control the pulsations of my heart.'"

Often the insistent idea is of a trivial sort, but it may wear the patient's life out. His hands feel dirty, they must be washed. He *knows* they are not dirty; yet to get rid of the teasing idea he washes them. The idea, however, returns in a moment, and the unfortunate victim, who is not in the least deluded *intellectually*, will end by spending the whole day at the wash-stand. Or his clothes are not 'rightly' put on; and to banish the thought he takes them off and puts them on again, till his toilet consumes two or three hours of time. Most people have the potentiality of this disease. To few has it not happened to conceive, after getting into bed, that they **may** have forgotten to lock the front door, or to turn out the entry gas. And **few** of us have not on some occasion got up to repeat the performance, less because we believed in the reality of its omission than because only so could we banish the worrying doubt and get to sleep.

The Obstructed Will.—In striking contrast with the cases in which inhibition is insufficient or impulsion in excess are those in which impulsion is insufficient or inhibition in excess. We all know the condition described on p. 218, in which the mind for a few moments seems to lose its focussing power and to be unable to rally its attention to any determinate thing. At such times we sit blankly staring and do nothing. The objects of consciousness fail to touch the quick or break the skin. They are there, but do not reach the level of effectiveness. This state of non-efficacious presence is the normal condition of *some* objects, in all of us. Great fatigue or exhaustion may make it the condition of almost all objects; and an apathy resembling that then brought about is recognized in asylums under the name of *abulia* as a symptom of mental disease. The healthy state of the will requires, as aforesaid, both that vision should be right, and that action should obey its lead. But in the morbid condition in question the vision may be wholly unaffected, and the intellect clear, and yet the act either fails to follow or follows in some other way.

" *Video meliora proboque, deteriora sequor* " is the classic expression of this latter condition of mind. The moral tragedy of human life comes almost wholly from the fact that the link is ruptured which normally should hold between vision of the truth and action, and that this pungent sense of effective reality will not attach to certain ideas. Men do not differ so much in their more feelings and conceptions. Their notions of possibility and their ideals are not as far apart as might be argued from their differing fates. No class of them have better sentiments or feel more constantly the difference between the higher and the lower path in life than the hopeless failures, the sentimentalists, the drunkards, the schemers, the 'deadbeats,' whose life is one long contradiction between knowledge and action, and who, with full command of theory, never get to holding their limp characters erect. No one eats of the fruit of the tree of knowledge as they do; as far as moral insight goes, in comparison with them, the orderly and prosperous philistines whom they scandalize are sucking babes. And yet their moral knowledge, always there grumbling and rumbling in the background,—discerning, commenting, protesting, longing, half resolving, —never wholly resolves, never gets its voice out of the minor into the major key, or its speech out of the subjunctive into the imperative mood, never breaks the spell, never takes the helm into its hands. In such characters as Rousseau and Restif it would seem as if the lower motives had all the impulsive efficacy in their hands. Like trains with the right of way, they retain exclusive possession of the track. The more ideal motives exist alongside of them in profusion, but they never get switched on, and the man's conduct is no more influenced by them than an express train is influenced by a wayfarer standing by the roadside and calling to be taken aboard. They are an inert accompaniment to the end of time; and the consciousness of inward hollowness that accrues from habitually seeing the better only to do the worse, is one of the saddest feelings one can bear with him through this vale of tears.

Effort feels like an original force. We now see at one view when it is that effort complicates volition. It does so whenever a rarer and more ideal impulse is called upon to neutralize others of a more instinctive and habitual kind; it does so whenever strongly explosive tendencies are checked, or strongly obstructive conditions overcome. The *âme bien née*, the child of the sunshine, at whose birth the fairies made their gifts, does not need much of it in his life. The hero and the neurotic subject, on the other hand, do. Now our spontaneous way of conceiving the effort, under all these circumstances, is as an active force adding its strength to that of the motives which ultimately prevail. When outer forces impinge upon a body, we say that the resultant motion is in the line of least resistance, or of greatest traction. But it is a curious fact that our spontaneous language never speaks of volition with effort in this way. Of course if we proceed *a priori* and define the line of least resistance as the line that is followed, the physical law must also hold good in the mental sphere. But we *feel*, in all hard cases of volition, as if the line taken, when the rarer and more ideal motives prevail, were the line of greater resistance, and as if the line of coarser motivation were the more pervious and easy one, even at the very moment when we refuse to follow it. He who under the surgeon's knife represses cries of pain, or he who exposes himself to social obloquy for duty's sake, feels as if he were following the line of greatest temporary resistance. He speaks of conquering and overcoming his impulses and temptations.

But the sluggard, the drunkard, the coward, never talk of their conduct in that way, or say they resist their energy, overcome their sobriety, conquer their courage, and so forth. If in general we class all springs of action as propensities on the one hand and ideals on the other, the sensualist never says of his behavior that it results from a victory over his ideals, but the moralist always speaks of his as a victory over his propensities. The sensualist uses terms of inactivity, says he forgets his ideals, is deaf to duty, and so forth; which terms seem to imply that the ideal motives *per se* can be annulled without energy or effort, and that the strongest mere traction lies in the line of the propensities. The ideal impulse appears, in comparison with this, a still small voice which must be artificially reinforced to prevail. Effort is what reinforces it, making things seem as if, while the force of propensity were essentially a fixed quantity, the ideal force might be of various amount. But what determines the amount of the effort when, by its aid, an ideal motive becomes victorious over a great sensual resistance? The very greatness of the resistance itself. If the sensual propensity is small, the effort is small. The latter is *made great* by the presence of a great antagonist to overcome. And if a brief definition of ideal or moral action were required, none could be given which would better fit the appearances than this: *It is action in the line of the greatest resistance.*

The facts may be most briefly symbolized thus, P standing for the propensity, I for the ideal impulse, and E for the effort:

$$I \textit{ per se} < P.$$
$$I + E > P.$$

In other words, if E adds itself to I, P immediately offers the least resistance, and motion occurs in spite of it.

But the E does not seem to form an integral part of the I. It appears adventitious and indeterminate in advance. We can make more or less as we please, and *if* we make enough we can convert the greatest mental resistance into the least. Such, at least, is the impression which the facts spontaneously produce upon us. But we will not discuss the truth of this impression at present; let us rather continue our descriptive detail.

Pleasure and Pain as Springs of Action.—Objects and thoughts of objects start our action, but the pleasures and pains which action brings modify its course and regulate it; and later the thoughts of the pleasures and the pains acquire themselves impulsive and inhibitive power. Not that the thought of a pleasure need be itself a pleasure, usually it is the reverse—*nessun maggior dolore*—as Dante says—and not that the thought of pain need be a pain, for, as Homer says, "griefs are often afterwards an entertainment." But as present pleasures are tremendous reinforcers, and present pains tremendous inhibitors of whatever action leads to them, so the thoughts of pleasures and pains take rank amongst the thoughts which have most impulsive and inhibitive power. The precise relation which these thoughts hold to other thoughts is thus a matter demanding some attention.

If a movement feels agreeable, we repeat and repeat it as long as the pleasure lasts. If it hurts us, our muscular contractions at the instant stop. So complete is the inhibition in this latter case that it is almost impossible for a man to cut or mutilate himself slowly and deliberately— his hand invincibly refusing to bring on the pain. And there are many pleasures which, when once we have begun to taste them, make it all but obligatory to keep up the activity to which they are due. So widespread and searching is this influence of pleasures and pains upon our movements that a premature philosophy has decided that these are our only spurs to action, and that wherever they seem to be absent, it is only because they are so far on among the 'remoter' images that prompt the action that they are overlooked.

This is a great mistake, however. Important as is the influence of pleasures and pains upon our movements, they are far from being our only stimuli. With the manifestations of instinct and emotional expression, for example, they have absolutely nothing to do. Who smiles for the pleasure of the smiling, or frowns for the pleasure of the frown? Who blushes to escape the discomfort of not blushing? Or who in anger, grief, or fear is actuated to the movements which he makes by the pleasures which they yield? In all these cases the movements are discharged fatally by the *vis a tergo* which the stimulus exerts upon a nervous system framed to respond in just that way. The objects of our rage, love, or terror, the occasions of our tears and smiles, whether they be present to our senses, or whether they be merely represented in idea, have this peculiar sort of impulsive power. The *impulsive quality* of mental states is an attribute behind which we cannot go. Some states of mind have more of it than others, some have it in this direction and some in that. Feelings of pleasure and pain have it, and perceptions and imaginations of fact have it, but neither have it exclusively or peculiarly. It is of the essence of all consciousness (or of the neural process which underlies it) to instigate movement of some sort. That with one creature and object it should be of one sort, with others of another sort, is a problem for evolutionary history to explain. However the actual impulsions may have arisen, they must now be described as they exist; and those persons obey a curiously narrow teleological superstition who think themselves bound to interpret them in every instance as effects of the secret solicitancy of pleasure and repugnancy of pain. If the thought of pleasure can impel to action, surely other thoughts may. Experience only can decide which thoughts do. The chapters on Instinct and Emotion have shown us that their name is legion; and with this verdict we ought to remain contented, and not seek an illusory simplification at the cost of half the facts.

If in these our *first* acts pleasures and pains bear no part, as little do they bear in our last acts, or those artificially acquired performances which have become habitual. All the daily routine of life, our dressing and undressing, the coming and going from our work or carrying through of its various operations, is utterly without mental reference to pleasure and pain, except under rarely realized conditions. It is ideo-motor action. As I do not breathe for the pleasure of the breathing, but simply find that I *am* breathing, so I do not write for the pleasure of the writing, but simply because I have once begun, and being in a state of intellectual excitement which keeps venting itself in that way, find that I *am* writing still. Who will pretend that when he idly fingers his knife-handle at the table, it is for the sake of any pleasure which it gives him, or pain which he thereby avoids? We do all these things because at the moment we cannot help it; our nervous systems are so shaped that they overflow in just that way; and for many of our idle or purely 'nervous' and fidgety performances we can assign absolutely no *reason* at all.

Or what shall be said of a shy and unsociable man who receives point-blank an invitation to a small party? The thing is to him an abomination; but your presence exerts a compulsion on him, he can think of no excuse, and so says yes, cursing himself the while for what he does. He is unusually *sui compos* who does not every week of his life fall into some such blundering act as this. Such instances of *voluntas invita* show not only that our acts cannot all be conceived as effects of represented pleasure, but that they cannot even be classed as cases of represented *good*. The class 'goods' contains many more generally influential motives to action than the class 'pleasants.' But almost as little as under the form of pleasures do our acts invariably appear to us under the form of *goods*. All diseased impulses and pathological fixed ideas are instances to the contrary. It is the very badness of the act that gives it then its vertiginous fascination. Remove the prohibition, and the attraction stops. In my university days a student threw himself from an upper entry window of one of the college buildings and was nearly killed. Another student, a friend of my own, had to pass the window daily in coming and going from his room, and experienced a dreadful temptation to imitate the deed. Being a Catholic, he told his director, who said, 'All right! if you must, you must,' and added, 'Go ahead and do it,' thereby instantly quenching his desire. This director knew how to minister to a mind diseased. But we need not go to minds diseased for examples of the occasional tempting-power of simple badness and unpleasantness as such. Every one who has a wound or hurt anywhere, a sore tooth, e.g., will ever and anon press it just to bring out the pain. If we are near a new sort of stink, we must sniff it again inst to verify once more how bad it is

This very day I have been repeating over and over to myself a verbal jingle whose mawkish silliness was the secret of its haunting power. I loathed yet could not banish it.

What holds attention determines action. If one must have a single name for the condition upon which the impulsive and inhibitive quality of objects depends, one had better call it their *interest*. 'The interesting' is a title which covers not only the pleasant and the painful, but also the morbidly fascinating, the tediously haunting, and even the simply habitual, inasmuch as the attention usually travels on habitual lines, and what-we-attend-to and what-interests-us are synonymous terms. It seems as if we ought to look for the secret of an idea's impulsiveness, not in any peculiar relations which it may have with paths of motor discharge,—for *all* ideas have relations with some such paths,—but rather in a preliminary phenomenon, the *urgency, namely, with which it is able to compel attention and dominate in consciousness.* Let it once so dominate, let no other ideas succeed in displacing it, and whatever motor effects belong to it by nature will inevitably occur —its impulsion, in short, will be given to boot, and will manifest itself as a matter of course. This is what we have seen in instinct, in emotion, in common ideo-motor action, in hypnotic suggestion, in morbid impulsion, and in *voluntas invita,*—the impelling idea is simply the one which possesses the attention. It is the same where pleasure and pain are the motor spurs—they drive other thoughts from consciousness at the same time that they instigate their own characteristic 'volitional' effects. And this is also what happens at the moment of the *fiat*, in all the five types of 'decision' which we have described. In short, one does not see any case in which the steadfast occupancy of consciousness does not appear to be the prime condition of impulsive power. It is still more obviously the prime condition of inhibitive power. What checks our impulses is the mere thinking of reasons to the contrary—it is their bare presence to the mind which gives the veto, and makes acts, otherwise seductive, impossible to perform. If we could only *forget* our scruples, our doubts, our fears, what exultant energy we should for a while display!

Will is a relation between the mind and its 'ideas.' In closing in, therefore, after all these preliminaries, upon the more *intimate* nature of the volitional process, we find ourselves driven more and more exclusively to consider the conditions which make ideas prevail in the mind. With the prevalence, once there as a fact, of the motive idea, the *psychology* of volition properly stops. The movements which ensue are exclusively physiological phenomena, following according to physiological laws upon the neural events to which the idea corresponds. The *willing* terminates with the prevalence of the idea; and whether the act then follows or not is a matter quite immaterial, so far as the willing itself goes. I will to write, and the act follows. I will to sneeze, and it does not. I will that the distant table slide over the floor towards me; it also does not. My willing representation can no more instigate my sneezing-centre than it can instigate the table to activity. But in both cases it is as true and good willing as it was when I willed to write. In a word, volition is a psychic or moral fact pure and simple, and is absolutely completed when the stable state of the idea is there. The supervention of motion is a supernumerary phenomenon depending on executive ganglia whose function lies outside the mind. If the ganglia work duly, the act occurs perfectly. If they work, but work wrongly, we have St. Vitus's dance, locomotor ataxy, motor aphasia, or minor degrees of awkwardness. If they don't work at all, tho act fails altogether, and we say the man is paralyzed. He may make a tremendous effort, and contract the other muscles of the body, but the paralyzed limb fails to move. In all these cases, however, the volition considered as a psychic process is intact

Volitional effort is effort of attention. We thus find that *we reach the heart of our inquiry into volition when we ask by what process it is that the thought of any given action comes to prevail stably in the mind.* Where thoughts prevail without effort, we have sufficiently studied in the several chapters on Sensation, Association, and Attention, the laws of their advent before consciousness and of their stay. We shall not go over that ground again, for we know that interest and association are the words, let their worth be what it may, on which our explanations must perforce rely. Where, on the other hand, the prevalence of the thought is accompanied by the phenomenon of effort, the case is much less clear. Already in the chapter on Attention we postponed the final consideration of voluntary attention with effort to a later place. We have now brought things to a point at which we see that attention with effort is all that any case of volition implies. *The essential achievement of the will, in short, when it is most 'voluntary,' is to attend to a difficult object and hold it fast before the mind.* The so-doing *is* the *fiat;* and it is a mere physiological incident that when the object is thus attended to, immediate motor consequences should ensue.

Effort of attention is thus the essential phenomenon of will.* Every reader must know by his own experience

---

* This *volitional* effort pure and simple must be carefully distinguished from the *muscular* effort with which it is usually confounded. The latter consists of all those peripheral feelings to which a muscular 'exertion' may give rise. These feelings, whenever they are massive and the body is not 'fresh,' are rather disagreeable, especially when accompanied by stopped breath, congested head, bruised skin of fingers, toes, or shoulders, and strained joints. And it is only *as thus disagreeable* that the mind must make its *volitional* effort in stably representing their reality and consequently bringing it about. That they happen to be made real by muscular activity is a purely accidental circumstance. There are instances where the fiat demands great volitional effort though the muscular exertion be insignificant, e.g. the getting out of bed and bathing one's self on a cold morning. Again, a soldier standing still to be fired at expects disagreeable senthat this is so, for every reader must have felt some fiery passion's grasp. What constitutes the difficulty for a man laboring under an unwise passion of acting as if the passion were wise? Certainly there is no physical difficulty. It is as easy physically to avoid a fight as to begin one, to pocket one's money as to squander it on one's cupidities, to walk away from as towards a coquette's door. The difficulty is mental: it is that of getting the idea of the wise action to stay before our mind at all. When any strong emotional state whatever is upon us, the tendency is for no images but such as are congruous with it to come up. If others by chance offer themselves, they are instantly smothered and crowded out. If we be joyous, we cannot keep thinking of those uncertainties and risks of failure which abound upon our path; if lugubrious, we cannot think of new triumphs, travels, loves, and joys; nor if vengeful, of our oppressor's community of nature with ourselves. The cooling advice which we get from others when the fever-fit is on us is the most jarring and exasperating thing in life. Reply we cannot, so we get angry; for by a sort of self-preserving instinct which our passion has, it feels that these chill objects, if they once but gain a lodgment, will work and work until they have frozen the very vital spark from out of all our mood and brought our airy castles in ruin to the ground. Such is the inevitable effect of reasonable ideas over others—*if they can once get a quiet hearing;* and passion's cue accordingly is always and everywhere to prevent their still small voice from being heard at all. " Let me not think of that! Don't speak to me of that!" This is the sudden cry of all those who in a passion perceive some sobering considerations about to check them in mid-career. There is something so icy in this cold-water bath, something which seems so hostile to

---

sations from his muscular passivity. The action of his will, in sustaining the expectation, is identical with that required for a painful muscular effort. What is hard for both is *facing an idea as real.*

the movement of our life, so purely negative, in Reason, when she lays her corpse-like finger on our heart and says, "Halt! give up! leave off! go back! sit down!" that it is no wonder that to most men the steadying influence seems, for the time being, a very minister of death.

The strong-willed man, however, is the man who hears the still small voice unflinchingly, and who, when the death-bringing consideration comes, looks at its face, consents to its presence, clings to it, affirms it, and holds it fast, in spite of the host of exciting mental images which rise in revolt against it and would expel it from the mind. Sustained in this way by a resolute effort of attention, the difficult object erelong begins to call up its own congeners and associates and ends by changing the disposition of the man's consciousness altogether. And with his consciousness his action changes, for the new object, once stably in possession of the field of his thoughts, infallibly produces its own motor effects. The difficulty lies in the gaining possession of that field. Though the spontaneous drift of thought is all the other way, the attention must be kept strained on that one object until at last it *grows,* so as to maintain itself before the mind with ease. This strain of the attention is the fundamental act of will. And the will's work is in most cases practically ended when the bare presence to our thought of the naturally unwelcome object has been secured. For the mysterious tie between the thought and the motor centres next comes into play, and, in a way which we cannot even guess at, the obedience of the bodily organs follows as a matter of course.

In all this one sees how the immediate point of application of the volitional effort lies exclusively in the mental world. The whole drama is a mental drama. The whole difficulty is a mental difficulty, a difficulty with an ideal object of our thought. It is, in one word, an *idea* to which our will applies itself, an idea which if we let it go would slip away, but which we will not let go. *Consent to the idea's undivided presence, this is effort's sole achieve-*

ment. Its only function is to get this feeling of consent into the mind. And for this there is but one way. The idea to be consented to must be kept from flickering and going out. It must be held steadily before the mind until it *fills* the mind. Such filling of the mind by an idea, with its congruous associates, *is* consent to the idea and to the fact which the idea represents. If the idea be that, or include that, of a bodily movement of our own, then we call the consent thus laboriously gained a motor volition. For Nature here 'backs' us instantaneously and follows up our inward willingness by outward changes on her own part. She does this in no other instance. Pity she should not have been more generous, nor made a world whose other parts were as immediately subject to our will!

On page 430, in describing the 'reasonable type' of decision, it was said that it usually came when the right conception of the case was found. Where, however, the right conception is an anti-impulsive one, the whole intellectual ingenuity of the man usually goes to work to crowd it out of sight, and to find for the emergency names by the help of which the dispositions of the moment may sound sanctified, and sloth or passion may reign unchecked. How many excuses does the drunkard find when each new temptation comes! It is a new brand of liquor which the interests of intellectual culture in such matters oblige him to test; moreover it is poured out and it is sin to waste it; also others are drinking and it would be churlishness to refuse. Or it is but to enable him to sleep, or just to get through this job of work; or it isn't drinking, it is because he feels so cold; or it is Christmas-day; or it is a means of stimulating him to make a more powerful resolution in favor of abstinence than any he has hitherto made; or it is just this once, and once doesn't count, etc., etc., *ad libitum*—it is, in fact, anything you like except *being a drunkard. That* is the conception that will not stay before the poor soul's attention. But if he once gets able to pick out that way of conceiving, from all the other possible ways of conceiving the various opportunities which occur, if through thick and thin he holds to it that this is being a drunkard and is nothing else, he is not likely to remain one long. The effort by which he succeeds in keeping the right *name* unwaveringly present to his mind proves to be his saving moral act.

Everywhere, then, the function of the effort is the same: to keep affirming and adopting a thought which, if left to itself, would slip away. It may be cold and flat when the spontaneous mental drift is towards excitement, or great and arduous when the spontaneous drift is towards repose. In the one case the effort has to inhibit an explosive, in the other to arouse an obstructed will. The exhausted sailor on a wreck has a will which is obstructed. One of his ideas is that of his sore hands, of the nameless exhaustion of his whole frame which the act of farther pumping involves, and of the deliciousness of sinking into sleep. The other is that of the hungry sea ingulfing him. "Rather the aching toil!" he says; and it becomes reality then, in spite of the inhibiting influence of the relatively luxurious sensations which he gets from lying still. Often again it may be the thought of sleep and what leads to it which is the hard one to keep before the mind. If a patient afflicted with insomnia can only control the whirling chase of his ideas so far as to think of *nothing at all* (which can be done), or so far as to imagine one letter after another of a verse of Scripture or poetry spelt slowly and monotonously out, it is almost certain that here, too, specific bodily effects will follow, and that sleep will come. The trouble is to keep the mind upon a train of objects naturally so insipid. *To sustain a representation, to think*, is, in short, the only moral act, for the impulsive and the obstructed, for sane and lunatics alike. Most maniacs know their thoughts to be crazy, but find them too pressing to be withstood. Compared with them the sane truths are so deadly sober, so cadaverous, that the lunatic cannot bear to look them in the face and say,

"Let these alone be my reality!" But with sufficient effort, as Dr. Wigan says, "Such a man can for a time *wind himself up*, as it were, and determine that the notions of the disordered brain shall not be manifested. Many instances are on record similar to that told by Pinel, where an inmate of the Bicêtre, having stood a long cross-examination, and' given every mark of restored reason, signed his name to the paper authorizing his discharge 'Jesus Christ,' and then went off into all the vagaries connected with that delusion. In the phraseology of the gentleman whose case is related in an early part of this [Wigan's] work he had 'held himself tight' during the examination in order to attain his object; this once accomplished he 'let himself down' again, and, if even *conscious* of his delusion, could not control it. I have observed with such persons that it requires a considerable time to wind themselves up to the pitch of complete self-control, that the effort is a painful tension of the mind. ... When thrown off their guard by any accidental remark or worn out by the length of the examination, they *let themselves go,* and cannot gather themselves up again without preparation."

To sum it all up in a word, *the terminus of the psychological process in volition, the point to which the will is directly applied, is always an idea.* There are at all times *some* ideas from which we shy away like frightened horses the moment we get a glimpse of their forbidding profile upon the threshold of our thought. *The only resistance which our will can possibly experience is the resistance which such an idea offers to being attended to at all.* To attend to it is the volitional act, and the only inward volitional act which we ever perform.

The Question of 'Free-will.'—As was remarked on p. 443, in the experience of effort we feel as if we might make more or less than we actually at any moment are making.

The effort appears, in other words, not as a fixed reaction on our part which the object that resists us necessarily calls forth, but as what the mathematicians call an 'independent variable' amongst the fixed data of the case, our motives, character, etc. If it be really so, if the amount of our effort is not a determinate function of those other data, then, in common parlance, *our wills are free.* If, on the contrary, the amount of effort be a fixed function, so that whatever object at any time fills our consciousness was from eternity bound to fill it then and there, and compel from us the exact effort, neither more nor less, which we bestow upon it,—then our wills are not free, and all our acts are foreordained. *The question of fact in the free-will controversy is thus extremely simple. It relates solely to the amount of effort of attention which we can at any time put forth.* Are the duration and intensity of this effort fixed functions of the object, or are they not? Now, as I just said, it *seems* as if we might exert more or less in any given case. When a man has let his thoughts go for days and weeks until at last they culminate in some particularly dirty or cowardly or cruel act, it is hard to persuade him, in the midst of his remorse, that he might not have reined them in; hard to make him believe that this whole goodly universe (which his act so jars upon) required and exacted it of him at that fatal moment, and from eternity made aught else impossible. But, on the other hand, there is the certainty that all his *effortless* volitions are resultants of interests and associations whose strength and sequence are mechanically determined by the structure of that physical mass, his brain; and the general continuity of things and the monistic conception of the world may lead one irresistibly to postulate that a little fact like effort can form no real exception to the overwhelming reign of deterministic law. Even in effortless volition we have the consciousness of the alternative being also possible. This is surely a delusion here; why is it not a delusion everywhere?

The fact is that the question of free-will is insoluble on strictly psychologic grounds. After a certain amount of effort of attention has been given to an idea, it is manifestly impossible to tell whether either more or less of it *might* have been given or not. To tell that, we should have to ascend to the antecedents of the effort, and defining them with mathematical exactitude, prove, by laws of which we have not at present even an inkling, that the only amount of sequent effort which could *possibly* comport with them was the precise amount that actually came. Such measurements, whether of psychic or of neural quantities, and such deductive reasonings as this method of proof implies, will surely be forever beyond human reach. No serious psychologist or physiologist will venture even to suggest a notion of how they might be practically made. Had one no motives drawn from elsewhere to make one partial to either solution, one might easily leave the matter undecided. But a psychologist cannot be expected to be thus impartial, having a great motive in favor of determinism. He wants to build a *Science;* and a Science is a system of fixed relations. Wherever there are independent variables, there Science stops. So far, then, as our volitions may be independent variables, a scientific psychology must ignore that fact, and treat of them only so far as they are fixed functions. In other words, she must deal with the *general laws* of volition exclusively; with the impulsive and inbibitory character of ideas; with the nature of their appeals to the attention; with the conditions under which effort may arise, etc.; but not with the precise amounts of effort, for these, if our wills be free, are impossible to compute. She thus abstracts from free-will, without necessarily denying its existence. Practically, however, such abstraction is not distinguished from rejection; and most actual psychologists have no hesitation in denying that free-will exists.

For ourselves, we can hand the free-will controversy over to metaphysics. Psychology will surely never grow refined enough to discover, in the case of any individual's decision, a discrepancy between her scientific calculations and the **fact. Her prevision** will never foretell, whether **the effort** be completely predestinate or not, the way in which each individual emergency is resolved. Psychology will be psychology, and Science science, as much as ever (as much and no more) in this world, whether free-will be true in it or not.

We can thus ignore the free-will question in psychology. As we said on p. 452, the operation of free effort, if it existed, could only be to hold some one ideal object, or part of an object, a little longer or a little more intensely before the mind. Amongst the alternatives which present themselves as *genuine possibles*, it would thus make one effective. And although such quickening of one idea might be morally and historically momentous, yet, if considered *dynamically*, it would be an operation amongst those physiological infinitesimals which an actual science must forever neglect.

Ethical Importance of the Phenomenon of Effort.—But whilst eliminating the question about the amount of our effort as one which psychology will never have a practical call to decide, I must say one word about the extraordinarily intimate and important character which the phenomenon of effort assumes in our own eyes as individual men. Of course we measure ourselves by many standards. Our strength and our intelligence, our wealth and even our good luck, are things which warm our heart and make us feel ourselves a match for life. But deeper than all such things, and able to suffice unto itself without them, is the sense of the amount of effort which we can put forth. Those are, after all, but effects, products, and reflections of the outer world within. But the effort seems to belong to an altogether different realm, as if it were the substantive thing which we *are*, and those were but externals which we *carry*. If the 'searching of our heart and reins' be the purpose of this human drama, then what is sought seems to be what effort we can make. He who can make none is but a shadow; he who can make much is a hero. The huge world that girdles us about puts all sorts of questions to us, and tests us in all sorts of ways. Some of the tests we meet by actions that are easy, and some of the questions we answer in articulately formulated words. But the deepest question that is ever asked admits of no reply but the dumb turning of the will and tightening of our heart-strings as we say, " *Yes, I will even have it so!*" When a dreadful object is presented, or when life as a whole turns up its dark abysses to our view, then the worthless ones among us lose their hold on the situation altogether, and either escape from its difficulties by averting their attention, or if they cannot do that, collapse into yielding masses of plaintiveness and fear. The effort required for facing and consenting to such objects is beyond their power to make. But the heroic mind does differently. To it, too, the objects are sinister and dreadful, unwelcome, incompatible with wished-for things. But it can face them if necessary, without for that losing its hold upon the rest of life. The world thus finds in the heroic man its worthy match and mate; and the effort which he is able to put forth to hold himself erect and keep his heart unshaken is the direct measure of his worth and function in the game of human life. He can *stand* this Universe. He can meet it and keep up his faith in it in presence of those same features which lay his weaker brethren low. He can still find a zest in it, not by ' ostrich-like forgetfulness,' but by pure inward willingness to face it with those deterrent objects there. And hereby he makes himself one of the masters and the lords of life. He must be counted with henceforth; he forms a part of human destiny. Neither in the theoretic nor in the practical sphere do we care for, or go for help to, those who have no head for risks, or sense for living on the perilous edge. Our religious life lies more, our practical life lies less, than it used to, on the perilous edge. But just as our courage is so often a reflex of another's courage, so our faith is apt to be a faith in some one else's faith. We draw new life from the heroic example. The prophet has drunk more deeply than anyone of the cup of bitterness, but his countenance is so unshaken and he speaks such mighty words of cheer that his will becomes our will, and our life is kindled at his own.

Thus not only our morality but our religion, so far as the latter is deliberate, depend on the effort which we can make. *"Will you or won't you have it so?"* is the most probing question we are ever asked; we are asked it every hour of the day, and about the largest as well as the smallest, the most theoretical as well as the most practical, things. We answer by *consents or non-consents* and not by words. What wonder that these dumb responses should seem our deepest organs of communication with the nature of things! What wonder if the effort demanded by them be the measure of our worth as men! What wonder if the amount which we accord of it were the one strictly underived and original contribution which we make to the world!

EPILOGUE.

PSYCHOLOGY AND PHILOSOPHY.

What the Word Metaphysics means.—In the last chapter we handed the question of free-will over to 'metaphysics.' It would indeed have been hasty to settle the question absolutely, inside the limits of psychology. Let psychology frankly admit that *for her scientific purposes* determinism may be *claimed*, and no one can find fault. If, then, it turn out later that the claim has only a relative purpose, and may be crossed by counter-claims, the readjustment can be made. Now ethics makes a counter-claim; and the present writer, for one, has no hesitation in regarding her claim as the stronger, and in assuming that our wills are 'free.' For him, then, the deterministic assumption of psychology is merely provisional and methodological. This is no place to argue the ethical point; and I only mention the conflict to show that all these special sciences, marked off for convenience from the remaining body of truth (cf. p. 1), must hold their assumptions and results subject to revision in the light of each others' needs. The forum where they hold discussion is called metaphysics. Metaphysics means only an unusually obstinate attempt to think clearly and consistently. The special sciences all deal with data that are full of obscurity and contradiction; but from the point of view of their limited purposes these defects may be overlooked. Hence the disparaging use of the name metaphysics which is so common. To a man with a limited purpose any discussion that is over-subtle for that purpose is branded as 'metaphysical.' A geologist's purposes fall short of understanding Time itself. A mechanist need not know how action and reaction are possible at all. A psychologist has enough to do without asking how both he and the mind which he studies are able to take cognizance of the same outer world. But it is obvious that problems irrelevant from one standpoint may be essential from another. And as soon as one's purpose is the attainment of the maximum of possible insight into the world as a whole, the metaphysical puzzles become the most urgent ones of all. Psychology contributes to general philosophy her full share of these; and I propose in this last chapter to indicate briefly which of them seem the more important. And first, of the

Relation of Consciousness to the Brain.—When psychology is treated as a natural science (after the fashion in which it has been treated in this book), 'states of mind' are taken for granted, as data immediately given in experience; and the working hypothesis (see p. 6) is the mere empirical law that to the entire state of the brain at any moment one unique state of mind always 'corresponds.' This does very well till we begin to be metaphysical and ask ourselves just what we mean by such a word as 'corresponds.' This notion appears dark in the extreme, the moment we seek to translate it into something more intimate than mere parallel variation. Some think they make the notion of it clearer by calling the mental state and the brain the inner and outer 'aspects,' respectively, of 'One and the Same Reality.' Others consider the mental state as the 'reaction' of a unitary being, the Soul, upon the multiple activities which the brain presents. Others again comminute the mystery by supposing each brain-cell to be separately conscious, and the empirically given mental state to be the appearance of all the little consciousnesses fused into one, just as the 'brain' itself is the appearance of all the cells together, when looked at from one point of view.

We may call these three metaphysical attempts the *monistic,* the *spiritualistic,* and the *atomistic* theories respectively. Each has its difficulties, of which it seems to me that those of the spiritualistic theory are *logically* much the least grave. But the spiritualistic theory is quite out of touch with the facts of multiple consciousness, alternate personality, etc. (pp. 207–214). These lend themselves more naturally to the atomistic formulation, for it seems easier to think of a lot of minor consciousnesses now gathering together into one large mass, and now into several smaller ones, than of a Soul now reacting totally, now breaking into several disconnected simultaneous reactions. The localization of brain-functions also makes for the atomistic view. If in my experience, say of a bell, it is my occipital lobes which are the condition of its being seen, and my temporal lobes which are the condition of its being heard, what is more natural than to say that the former *see* it and the latter *hear* it, and then 'combine their information'? In view of the extreme naturalness of such a way of representing the well-established fact that the appearance of the several parts of an object to consciousness at any moment does depend on as many several parts of the brain being then active, all such objections as were urged, on pp. 23, 57, and elsewhere, to the notion that 'parts' of consciousness *can* 'combine' will be rejected as far-fetched, unreal, and 'metaphysical' by the atomistic philosopher. His 'purpose' is to gain a formula which shall unify things in a natural and easy manner, and for such a purpose the atomistic theory seems expressly made to his hand.

But the difficulty with the problem of 'correspondence' is not only that of solving it, it is that of even stating it in elementary terms.

"L'ombre en ce lieu s'amasse, et la nuit est la tonte."

Before we can know just what sort of goings-on occur when thought corresponds to a change in the brain, we must know the *subjects* of the goings-on. We must know which sort of mental fact and which sort of cerebral fact are, so to speak, in immediate juxtaposition. We must find the minimal mental fact whose being **reposes directly** on a brain-fact; and we must similarly find the minimal brain-event which can have a mental counterpart at all. Between the mental and the physical minima thus found there will be an immediate relation, the expression of which, if we had it, would be the elementary psycho-physic law.

Our own formula has escaped the metempiric assumption of psychic atoms by *taking the entire thought* (even of a complex object) *as the minimum with which it deals on the mental* side, and the entire brain as the minimum on the physical side. But the 'entire brain' is not a physical fact at all! It is nothing but our name for the way in which a billion of molecules arranged in certain positions may affect our sense. On the principles of the corpuscular or mechanical philosophy, the only realities are the separate molecules, or at most the cells. Their aggregation into a 'brain' is a fiction of popular speech. Such a figment cannot serve as the objectively real counterpart to any psychic state whatever. Only a genuinely physical fact can so serve, and the molecular fact is the only genuine physical fact. Whereupon we seem, if we are to have an elementary psycho-physic law at all, thrust right back upon something like the mental-atom-theory, for the molecular fact, being an element of the 'brain,' would seem naturally to correspond, not to total thoughts, but to elements of thoughts. Thus the real in psychics seems to 'correspond' to the unreal in physics, and *vice versa;* and our perplexity is extreme.

The Relation of States of Mind to their 'Objects.'—The perplexity is not diminished when we reflect upon our assumption that states of consciousness can *know* (pp. 2–13). From the common-sense point of view (which is that of all the natural sciences) knowledge is an ultimate relation between two mutually external entities, the knower and the known. The world first exists, and then the states of mind; and these gain a cognizance of the world which gets gradually more and more complete. But it is hard to carry through this simple dualism, for idealistic reflections will intrude. Take the states of mind called pure sensations (so far as such may exist), that for example of *blue*, which we may get from looking into the zenith on a clear day. Is the blue a determination of the feeling itself, or of its 'object'? Shall we describe the experience as a quality of our feeling or as our feeling of a quality? Ordinary speech vacillates incessantly on this point. The ambiguous word 'content' has been recently invented instead of 'object,' to escape a decision; for 'content' suggests something not exactly out of the feeling, nor yet exactly identical with the feeling, since the latter remains suggested as the container or vessel. Yet of our feelings as vessels apart from their content we really have no clear notion whatever. The fact is that such an experience as *blue*, as it is immediately given, can only be called by some such neutral name as that of *phenomenon*. It does not *come* to us *immediately* as a relation between two realities, one mental and one physical. It is only when, still thinking of it as the *same* blue (cf. p. 239), we trace relations between it and other things, that it doubles itself, so to speak, and develops in two directions; and, taken in connection with some associates, figures as a physical quality, whilst with others it figures as a feeling in the mind.

Our non-sensational, or conceptual, states of mind, on the other hand, seem to obey a different law. They present themselves immediately as referring beyond themselves. Although they also possess an immediately given 'content,' they have a 'fringe' beyond it (p. 168), and claim to 'represent' something else than it. The 'blue' we have just spoken of, for instance, was, substantively considered, a *word;* but it was a word with a *meaning*. The quality blue was the *object* of the thought, the word was its *content*. The mental state, in short, was not self-sufficient as sensations are, but expressly pointed at something more in which it meant to terminate.

But the moment when, as in sensations, object and conscious state seem to be different ways of considering one and the same fact, it becomes hard to justify our denial that mental states consist of parts. The blue sky, considered physically, is a sum of mutually external parts; why is it not such a sum, when considered as a content of sensation?

The only result that is plain from all this is that the relations of the known and the knower are infinitely complicated, and that a genial, whole-hearted, popular-science way of formulating them will not suffice. The only possible path to understanding them lies through metaphysical subtlety; and Idealism and *Erkenntnisstheorie* must say their say before the natural-science assumption that thoughts 'know' things grows clear.

The changing character of consciousness presents another puzzle. We first assumed conscious 'states' as the units with which psychology deals, and we said later that they were in constant change. Yet any state must have a certain duration to be *effective* at all—a pain which lasted but a hundredth of a second would practically be no pain—and the question comes up, how long may a state last and still be treated as *one* state? In time-perception for example, if the 'present' as known (the 'specious present,' as we called it) may be a dozen seconds long (p. 281), how long need the present as knower be? That is, what is the minimum duration of the consciousness in which those twelve seconds can be apprehended as just past, the minimum which can be called a 'state,' for such a cognitive purpose? Consciousness, as a process in time, offers the paradoxes which have been found in all continuous change. There are no 'states' in such a thing, any more than there are facets in a circle, or places where an arrow 'is' when it flies. The vertical raised upon the time-line on which (p. 285) we represented the past to be 'projected' at any given instant of memory, is only an ideal construction. Yet anything broader than that vertical *is* not, for the *actual* present is only the joint between the past and future and has no breadth of its own. Where everything is change and process, how can we talk of 'state'? Yet how can we do without 'states,' in describing what the vehicles of our knowledge seem to be?

States of consciousness themselves are not verifiable facts. But 'worse remains behind.' Neither common-sense, nor psychology so far as it has yet been written, has ever doubted that the states of consciousness which that science studies are immediate data of experience. 'Things' have been doubted, but thoughts and feelings have never been doubted. The outer world, but never the inner world, has been denied. Everyone assumes that we have direct introspective acquaintance with our thinking activity as such, with our consciousness as something inward and contrasted with the outer objects which it knows. Yet I must confess that for my part I cannot feel sure of this conclusion. Whenever I try to become sensible of my thinking activity as such, what I catch is some bodily fact, an impression coming from my brow, or head, or throat, or nose. It seems as if consciousness as an inner activity were rather a *postulate* than a sensibly given fact, the postulate, namely, of a *knower* as correlative to all this known; and as if '*sciou*sness' might be a better word by which to describe it. But 'sciousness postulated as an hypothesis' is practically a very different thing from 'states of consciousness apprehended with infallible certainty by an inner sense.' For one thing, it throws the question of *who the knower really is* wide open again, and makes the answer which we gave to it at the end of Chapter XII a mere provisional statement from a popular and prejudiced point of view.

Conclusion.—When, then, we talk of 'psychology as a natural science,' we must not assume that that means a sort of psychology that stands at last on solid ground. It means just the reverse; it means a psychology particularly fragile, and into which the waters of metaphysical criticism leak at every joint, a psychology all of whose elementary assumptions and data must be reconsidered in wider connections and translated into other terms. It is, in short, a phrase of diffidence, and not of arrogance; and it is indeed strange to hear people talk triumphantly of 'the New Psychology,' and write 'Histories of Psychology,' when into the real elements and forces which the word covers not the first glimpse of clear insight exists. A string of raw facts; a little gossip and wrangle about opinions; a little classification and generalization on the mere descriptive level; a strong prejudice that we *have* states of mind, and that our brain conditions them: but not a single law in the sense in which physics shows us laws, not a single proposition from which any consequence can causally be deduced. We don't even know the terms between which the elementary laws would obtain if we had them (p. 464). This is no science, it is only the hope of a science. The matter of a science is with us. Something definite happens when to a certain brain-state a certain 'sciousness' corresponds. A genuine glimpse into what it is would be *the* scientific achievement, before which all past achievements would pale. But at present psychology is in the condition of physics before Galileo and the laws of motion, of chemistry before Lavoisier and the notion that mass is preserved in all reactions. The Galileo and the Lavoisier of psychology will be famous men indeed when they come, as come they some day surely will, or past successes are no index to the future. When they do come, however, the necessities of the case will make them 'metaphysical.' Meanwhile the best way in which we can facilitate their advent is to understand how great is the darkness in which we grope, and never to forget that the natural-science assumptions with which we started are provisional and revisable things.

THE END.

INDEX.

Abstract ideas, 240, 25; characters, 353; propositions, 354
Abstraction, 251, see *Distraction*
Accommodation, of crystalline lens, 32; of ear, 49
Acquaintance, 14
Acquisitiveness, 407
Action, what holds attention determines, 448
After-images, 43–5
AGASSIZ, 132
Alexia, 113
ALLEN, GRANT, 104
Alternating personality, 205 ff.
AMIDON, 132
Analysis, 56, 248, 251, 362
Anger, 374
Aphasia, 108, 113, loss of images in, 309
Apperception, 326
Aqueduct of Silvius, 80
Arachnoid membrane, 84
Arbor vitæ, 86
ARISTOTLE, 318
Articular sensibility, 74
Association, Chapter XVI; the order of our ideas, 253; determined by cerebral laws, 255, is not of ideas, but of things thought of, 255; the elementary principle of, 256, the ultimate cause of is habit, 256; indeterminateness of its results, 258, total recall, 259, partial recall and the law of interest, 261, frequency, recency, vividness, and emotional congruity tend to determine the object recalled, 264, focalized recall or by similarity, 267, 364, voluntary trains of thought, 271; problems, 273
Atomistic theories of consciousness, 462
Attention, Chapter XIII; its relation to interest, 170, its physiological ground, 217, narrowness of field of consciousness, 217, to how many things possible, 219; to simultaneous sight and sound, 220, its varieties, 220, voluntary, 224, involuntary, 220, change necessary to, 226; its relation to genius, 227, physiological conditions of, 228, the sense-organ must be adapted, 229, the idea of the object must be aroused, 232; pedagogic remarks, 236, attention and free-will, 237, what holds attention determines action, 448; volitional effort is effort of attention, 450
Auditory centre in brain, 113
Auditory type of imagination, 306
AUSTEN, Miss, 261
Automaton theory, 10, 101
AZAM, 210

BAHNSEN, 147
BAIN, 145, 367, 370
BERKLEY, 302, 303, 347
BINET, 318, 332
Black, 45–6
Blind Spot, 31

469

BLIX, 64, 68
Blood-supply, cerebral, 130
Bodily expression, cause of emotions, 375
BRACE, JULIA, 252
Brain, the functions of, Chapter VIII, 91
Brain, its connection with mind, 5-7. its relations to outer forces, 9; relations of consciousness to, 462
Brain, structure of, Chapter VII, 78 ff.; vesicles, 78 ff.; dissection of sheep's, 81; how to preserve, 83; functions of, Chapter VIII, 91 ff.
BRIDGMAN, LAURA, 252, 308
BROCA, 109, 113, 115
Broca's convolution, 109
BRODHUN, 46
BROOKS, Prof. W. K., 412
Brutes, reasoning of, 367

Calamus scriptorius, 84
Canals, semicircular, 50
CARPENTER, 223, 224
CATTELL, 125, 126, 127
Caudate nucleus, 81, 86
Centres, nerve, 92
Cerebellum, its relation to equilibrium, 76, its anatomy, 79, 84
Cerebral laws, of association, 255
Cerebral process, see *Neural Process*
Cerebrum, see *Brain*, *Hemisphere*
Changing character of consciousness, 152, 466
CHARCOT, 113, 309
Choice, see *Interest*
Coalescence of different sensations into the same 'thing,' 339
Cochlea, 51, 52
Cognition, see *Reasoning*
Cold, sensations of, 63 ff.; nerves of, 64
Color, 40-3
Commissures, 84
Commissure, middle, 88 ff.; anterior, 88; posterior, 88

Comparison of magnitudes, 342
Compounding of sensations, 23, 43, 57
Compound objects, analysis of, 248
Concatenated acts, dependent on habit, 140
Conceiving, mode of, what is meant by, 354
Conceptions, Chapter XIV; defined, 239; their permanence, 239; different states of mind can mean the same, 239; abstract, universal, and problematic, 240; the thought of 'the same' is not the same thought over again, 243
Conceptual order different from perceptual, 243
Consciousness, stream of, Chapter XI, 151; four characters in, 152; personal, 152; is in constant change, 152, 466; same state of mind never occurs twice, 154; consciousness is continuous, 157; substantive and transitive states of, 160; interested in one part of its object more than another, 170; double consciousness, 206 ff.; narrowness of field of, 217; relations of to brain, 462
Consciousness and Movement, Chapter XXIII; all consciousness is motor, 370
Concomitants, law of varying, 251
Consent, in willing, 452
Continuity of object of consciousness, 157
Contrast, 25, 44-5
Convergence of eyeballs, 31, 33
Convolutions, motor, 106
Corpora fimbriata, 86
Corpora quadrigemma, 79, 86, 89
Corpus albicans, 84
Corpus callosum, 81, 84
Corpus striatum, 81, 86, 108
Cortex, 11, note
Cortex, localization in, 104; motor region of, 106
Corti's organ, 52

INDEX. 471

Cramming, 295
Crura of brain, 79, 84, 108
Curiosity, 407
Currents, in nerves, 10
CZERMAK, 70

DARWIN, 388, 389
Deafness, mental, 113
DELAOE, 76
Deliberation, 448
Delusions of insane, 207
Dermal senses, 60 ff
Determinism and psychology, 461
Decision, five types, 429
Differences, 24, directly felt, 245, not resolvable into composition, 245, inferred, 248
Diffusion of movements, the law of, 371
Dimension, third, 342, 346
Discharge, nervous, 120
Discord, 58
Discrimination, Chapter XV, 59, touch, 62, defined, 244, conditions which favor, 245, sensation of difference, 246, differences inferred, 248, analysis of compound objects, 249, to be easily singled out a quality should already be separately known, 250; dissociation by varying concomitants, 251 practice improves discrimination, 252, of space, 338 See *Difference*
'Disparate' retinal points, 35
Dissection, of sheep's brain, 81
Distance, as seen, 39, between members of series, 24; in space, see *Third dimension*
Distraction, 218 ff.
Division of space, 338
DONALDSON, 64
Double consciousness, 206 ff.
Double images, 36
Double personality, 205
Duality of brain, 205
DUMONT, 135
Dura mater, 82
Duration, the primitive object in time-perception, 280, our estimation of short, 281

Ear, 47 ff.
Effort, feeling of, 434; feels like an original force, 442, volitional effort is effort of attention, 450, ethical importance of the phenomena of effort, 458
Ego, see *Self*
Embryological sketch, Chapter VII, 78
Emotion, Chapter XXIV, compared with instincts, 373, varieties of, innumerable, 374, causes of varieties, 375, 381, results from bodily expression, 375, this view not materialistic, 380; the subtler emotions, 384, fear, 385, genesis of reactions, 388
Emotional congruity, determines association, 264
Empirical self, see *Self*
Emulation, 406
End-organs, 10, of touch, 60, of temperature, 64, of pressure, 60, of pain, 67
Environment, 3
Essence of reason, always for subjective interest, 358
Essential characters, in reason, 354
Ethical importance of effort, 458
Exaggerated impulsion, causes an explosive will, 439
EXNER, 123, 281
Experience, 218, 244
Explosive will, from defective inhibition, 437, from exaggerated impulsion, 439
Expression, bodily, cause of emotions, 375
Extensity, primitive to all sensation, 335
Exteriority of objects, 15
External world, 15
Extirpation of higher nerve-centres, 95 ff.
Eye, its anatomy, 28-30

Familiarity, sense of, see *Recognition*
Fear, 385, 406, 407
FECHNER, 21, 229

Feeling of effort, 434
FÉRÉ, 311
FERRIER, 132
Fissure of Rolando, seat of motor incitations, 106
Fissure of Sylvius, 108
Foramen of Monro, 88
Force, original, effort feels like, 442
Forgetting, 300
Fornix, 81, 86, 87, 89
Fovea centralis, 31
FRANKLIN, 121
FRANZ, Dr., 308
Freedom of the will, 237
Free-will and attention, 237; relates solely to effort of attention, 455, insoluble on strictly psychologic grounds, 456; ethical importance of the phenomena of effort, 458
Frequency, determines association, 264
"Fringes" of mental objects, 163 ff
Frogs' lower centres, 95
Functions of the Brain, Chapter VIII, 91; nervous functions, general idea of, 91
Fusion of mental states, 197, 245, 339
Fusion, of sensations, 23, 43, 57

GALTON, 126, 265, 303, 306
Genius, 227, 327
GOETHE, 146, 157
GOLDSCHEIDER, 11, 64, 68
GOLTZ, 100
GUITEAU, 185
GURNEY, EDMUND, 331, 334

Habit, Chapter X, 134 ff.; has a physical basis, 134; due to plasticity, 135; due to pathways through nerve-centres, 136; effects of, 128; practical use of, 138; depends on sensations not attended to, 141; ethical and pedagogical importance of 142 ff.; habit the ultimate cause of association, 256
HAGENAUER, 386

HALL, ROBERT, 223
Hallucinations, 330 ff.
HAMILTON, 260, 268
Harmony, 58
HARTLEY, 255
Hearing, 47 ff.; centre of, in cortex, 113
Heat-sensations, 63 ff.; nerves of, 64
HELMHOLTZ, 26, 42, 43, 55, 56, 58, 121, 226, 227, 231, 233, 234, 321
Hemispheres, general notion of, 97; chief seat of memory, 98, effects of deprivation of, on frogs, 92, on pigeons, 96
HERBART, 222, 326
HERBARTIAN SCHOOL, 157
HERING, 24, 26
HERZEN, 123, 124
HIPPOCAMPI, 88
HODGSON, 262, 264, 280, 283
HOLBROOK, 297
HORSLEY, 107, 118
HUME, 161, 244
Hunger, sensations of, 69
HUXLEY, 143
Hypnotic conditions, 301

Ideas, the theory of, 154 ff.; never come twice the same, 154; they do not permanently exist, 157; abstract ideas, 240, 251; universal 240; order of ideas by association, 253
'Identical retinal points,' 35
Identity, personal, 201; mutations of, 205 ff.; alternating personality, 205
Ideo-motor action the type of all volition, 432
Illusions, 317 ff., 330
Images, mental, compared with sensations, 14; double, in vision, 36; 'after-images,' 43–5; visual, 302, auditory, 306; motor, 307; tactile, 308
Imagination, Chapter XIX; defined, 302; differs in individuals, 302; Galton's statistics of, 302; visual, 302; auditory, 306 motor, 307; tactile, 308; path-

logical differences, 308; cerebral process of, 310; not locally distinct from that of sensation, 310
Imitation, 406
Inattention, 218, 236
Increase of stimulus, 20; serial, 24
Infundibulum, 82, 84, 88
Inhibition, defective, causes an Explosive Will, 437
Inhibition of instincts by habits, 399
Insane delusions, 207
Instinct, Chapter XXV; emotions compared with, 373; definition of, 391; every instinct is an impulse, 392, not always blind or invariable, 395; modified by experience, 396, two principles of non-uniformity, 398; man has more than beasts, 398, 406; transitory, 402; of children, 406, fear, 407
Intellect, part played by, in space-perception, 349
Intensity of sensations, 16
Interest, selects certain objects and determines thoughts 170; influence in association, 262
Introspection, 118

JANET 211, 212, 301
JACKSON, HUGHLINGS, 105, 117
Joints, their sensbility, 74

KADINSKY, 330
Knowledge, theory of, 2, 464, 467; two kinds of, 14
KÖNIG, 46
KRISHABER, 208

Labyrinth, 47, 49-52
LANGE, K, 329
Laws, cerebral, of association, 255
Law, Weber's, 17; —, Fechner's 21; —, of relativity, 24
LAZARUS, 300, 323
Lenticular nucleus, 81
LEWES, 11, 232, 326
Likeness, 243, 364
LINDSAY, Dr., 418

Localization of Functions in the hemispheres, 104 ff
Localization, Skin, 61
Locations, in environment, 340; serial order of, 341
LOCKE, 244, 302, 357
LOCKEAN SCHOOL, 157
Locomotion, instinct of, 406
LOMBARD, 131
Longituditional fissure, 84
LOTZE, 175
Love, 407
Lower Centres, of frogs and pigeons, 95 ff
LUDWIG, 130

MACH, 75
Mamillary bodies, 84
Man's intellectual distinction from brutes, 367
MANTEGAZZA, 390
MARTIN, 40, 44, 45, 49, 52, 53, 60, 61, 65, 69
MARTINEAU, 251
Materialism and emotion, 380
MATTEUCI, 120
MAUDSLEY, 138
Measurement, of sensations, 22; of space, 342
'Mediumships,' 212
Medulla oblongata, 84, 108
Memory, Chapter XVIII; hemispheres physical seat of; 98; defined, 287, analysis of the phenomenon of memory, 287 ff.; return of a mental image is not memory, 289; association explains recall and retention, 289; brain-scheme of, 291; conditions of good memory, 292; multiple associations favor, 294; effects of cramming on, 295; how to improve memory, 298, recognition, 299, forgetting, 300; hypnotics, 301
Mental blindness, 112
Mental images, 14
Mental operations, simultaneous, 219
Mental states, cannot fuse, 197; relation of, to their objects, 464
MERKEL, 59, 66

INDEX.

Metaphysics, what the word means, 461
MEYER, G. H., 308, 311
MEYNERT, 105, 117
MILL, JAMES, 196, 276, 289
MILL, J. S., 147, 157
Mimicry, 406
Mind depends on brain conditions, 3-7; states of, their relation to their objects, 464; see *Consciousness*.
Modesty, 407
Monistic theories of consciousness, 462
MORGAN, LLOYD, 368
MOSSO, 130, 131
Motion, sensations of, Chapter VI, 70 ff.; feeling of motion over surfaces, 70
Motor aphasia, 108
Motor region of cortex, 106
Motor type of imagination, 307
Movement, consciousness and, II, Chapter I; images of movement, 307; all consciousness is motor, 370
MUNK, 110
MUNSTERBERG, 23, 311
Muscular sensation, 65 ff.; relations to space, 66, 74; muscular centre in cortex, 106
MUSSEY, DR., 440

NAUNYN, 115
Nerve-currents, 9
Nervous discharge, 120
Nerve-endings in the skin, 60; in muscles and tendons, 66-67; Pain, 67 ff.; nerve-centres, 92
Nerves, general functions of, 91 ff.
Neural activity, general conditions of, Chapter IX, 120; nervous discharge, 120
Neural functions, general idea of, 91
Neural process, in habit, 134 ff.; in association, 255 ff.; in memory, 291; in imagination, 310; in perception, 329
Nucleus lenticularis, 81, 108; caudatus, 81, 108

Object, the, of sensation, 13-15; of thought, 154, 163; one part of, more interesting than another, 170; object must change to hold attention, 226; objects as signs and as realities, 345; relation of states of mind to their object, 464
Occipited lobes, seat of visual centre, 110
Old-fogyism vs. genius, 327
Olfactory lobes, 82, 84
Olivary bodies, 85
Optic nerve, 82, 89
Optic tracts, 84
Original force, effort feels like one, 442
Overtones, 55

Pain, 67 ff.; pain and pleasure as springs of action, 444
PASCAL, 223
Past time, known in a present feeling, 285; the immediate past is a portion of the present duration-block, 280
PAULHAN, 219, 220
Pedagogic remarks on habit, 143; on attention, 236
Peduncles, 84, 85, 86
Perception, Chapter XX; compared with sensation, 312; involves reproductive processes, 312; the perceptive state of mind is not a compound, 313; perception is of definite and probable things, 316; illusory perceptions, 317; physiological process of perception, 329
Perception of Space, Chapter XXI.
PEREZ, M., 408
Personal Identity, 201; mutations of, 205 ff.; alternating personality, 205 ff.
Personality, alterations of, 205 ff.
Philosophy, Psychology and, Epilogue, 461
Phosphorus and thought, 132
Pia mater, 82
Pigeons' lower centres, 96
Pitch, 54

Pituitary body, 82, 89
Place, a series of positions, 341
Plasticity, as basis of habit, defined, 135
PLATO, 240
Play, 407
Pleasure, and pain, as springs of action, 444
Psychology and Philosophy, Epilogue, 461
Pons Varolii, 79, 84, 108
Positions, place a series of, 341
Practice, improves discrimination, 252
Present, the present moment, 280
Pressure sense, 60
PREYER, 406
Probability determines what object shall be perceived, 316, 329
Problematic conceptions, 240
Problems, solution of, 272
Projection of sensations, eccentric, 15
Psychology, defined, 1; a natural science, 2; what data it assumes 2, Psychology and Philosophy, Chapter XXVII.
Psycho-physio law, 17, 24, 46, 59, 66, 67
Pugnacity, 406
PURKINJE, 75
Pyramids, 85

Quality, 13, 23, 25, 56

Raehlmann, 349
Rationality, 173
Reaction time 120 ff
Real magnitude, determined by æsthetic and practical interests, 344
Real space, 337
Reason, 254
Reasoning Chapter XXIII; what it is 351; involves use of abstract characters, 353; what is meant by an essential character, 354, the essence is always for a subjective interest, 358; two great points in reasoning,

360, sagacity, 362; help from association by similarity, 364; reasoning power of brutes, 367
Recall, 289
Recency, determines association, 264
'Recepts,' 368
Recognition, 299
Recollection, 289 ff.
Redintegration, 264
Reflex acts, defined, 92, reaction-time measures one, 123; concatenated habits are constituted by a chain of, 140
REID, 313
Relations, between objects, 162, feelings of, 162
'Relativity of knowledge,' 24
Reproduction in memory, 289 ff.; voluntary, 271
Resemblance, 243
Retention in memory, 289
Retentiveness, organic, 291; it is unchangeable 296
Retina, peripheral parts of, act as sentinels, 73
Revival in memory, 289 ff.
RIBOT 300
RICHET, 410
Rivalry of selves, 186
ROBERTSON Prof CROOM, 318
Rolando, fissure of, 106
ROMANES 128, 322, 367
ROSENTHAL, 11
ROUSSEAU, 148
Rotation, sense of, 75

Sagacity, 362
Sameness, 201, 202
SCHAEFER, 107, 110, 118
SCHIFF, 131
SCHNEIDER, 72 372, 392
Science, natural, 1
SCOTT, Prof., 311
Sea-sickness, accidental origin, 390
Seat of consciousness, 5
Selection, 10; a cardinal function of consciousness, 170
Self, The, Chapter XII; not primary, 176; the empirical self, 176, its constituents, 177; the

material self, 177; the social self, 179; the spiritual self, 181; self-appreciation, 182; self-seeking, bodily, social, and spiritual, 184; rivalry of the mes, 186; their hierarchy, 190; teleology of self-interest, 193; the I, or 'pure ego,' 195; thoughts are not compounded of 'fused' sensations, 196; the soul as a combining medium, 200; the sense of personal identity, 201; explained by identity of function in successive passing thoughts, 203; mutations of the self, 205; insane delusions, 207; alternating personalities, 210; mediumships, 212; who is the thinker? 215
Self-appreciation, 182
Self-interest, theological uses of, 193; teleological character of, 193
Selves, their rivalry, 186
Semicircular canals, 50
Semicircular canals, their relation to sensations of rotation, 75
Sensations, in General, Chapter II, p. 9; distinguished from perceptions, 12; from images, 14; *first* things in consciousness, 12; make us acquainted with qualities, 14; their exteriority, 15; intensity of sensations, 16; their measurement, 21; they are not compounds, 23
Sensations, of touch, 60; of skin, 60 ff.; of smell, 69; of pain, 67; of heat, 63; of cold, 63; of hunger, 69; of thirst, 69; of motion, 70; muscular, 65; of taste, 69; of pressure, 60; of joints, 74; of movement through space, 75; of rotation, 75; of translation, 76
Sense of time, see *Time*
Sensory centres in the cortex, 113 ff.
Septum lucidum, 87
Serial order of locations, 341

Shame, 374
Sheep's brain, dissection of, 81
Sight, 28 ff.; see *Vision*
Signs, 40; sensations are, to us of other sensations, whose space-value is held to be more real, 345 ff.
Similarity, association by, 267, 364; see *Likeness*
Size, 40
Skin—senses, 60 ff.; localizing power of, 61; discrimination of points on, 247
Smell, 69; centre of, in cortex, 116
SMITH, T. C , 311
Sociability, 407
Soul, the, as ego or thinker, 196; as a combining medium, 200, 203
Sound, 53-59; images of, 306
Space, Perception of, Chapter XXI; extensity in three dimensions primitive to all sensation, 335; construction of real space, 337; the processes which it involves: (1) Subdivision, 338; (2) Coalescence of different sensible data into one 'thing,' 339; (3) Location in an environment, 342; objects which are signs, and objects which are realities, 345; the third dimension, 346; Berkeley's theory of distance, 346; part played by intellect in space-perception, 349
Space, relation of muscular sense to, 66, 74
SPALDING, 401 ff.
Span of consciousness, 219, 286
Specific energies, 11
Speech, centres of, in cortex, 109; thought possible without it, 169; see *Aphasia*
SPENCER, 103, 387, 390
Spinal cord, conduction of pain by, 68; centre of defensive movements, 93
Spiritual substance, see *Soul*
Spiritualistic theories of consciousness, 462

Spontaneous trains of thought, 257; examples, 257 ff., 271
STARR, 107, 113, 115
STEINTHAL, 327.
Stream of Consciousness, Chapter XI, 151
STRICKER, 307
Subdivision of space, 338
Substantive states of mind, 160
Succession vs duration, 280, not known by successive feelings, 285
Summation of stimuli, 128
Surfaces, feeling of motion over, 70

Tactile centre in cortex, 116
Tactile images, 308
TAINE, 208
Taste, 69, centre of, in cortex, 116
Teleological character of consciousness, 4; of self-interest, 193
Temperature-sense, 63 ff.
Terminal organs, 10, 30, 52
Thalami, 80, 86, 89, 108
Thermometry, cerebral, 131
Thing,' coalescence of sensations to form the same, 339
Thinking principle, see *Soul*
Third dimension of space, 346
Thirst sensations of, 69
THOMSON, Dr. ALLEN, 129
Thought, the 'Topic' of, 167; stream of, 151, can be carried on in any terms, 167; unity of, 196; spontaneous trains of, 257; the entire thought the minimum, 464
'Timbre,' 55
Time, sense of, Chapter XVII, begins with duration 280; no sense of empty time, 281; compared with perception of space, 282, discrete flow of time, 282; long intervals conceived symbolically, 283, we measure duration by events that succeed in it, 283; variations in our estimations of its length, 283; cerebral processes of, 286

Touch, 60 ff ; centre of, in cortex 116, images of, 308
Transcendental self or ego, 196
Transitive states of mind, 160
Translation, sense of, 76
Trapezium, 85
TURNER, Dr. J. E., 440
Tympanum, 48
Types of decision, 429

Unity of the passing thought, 196
Universal conceptions, 240
URBANTSCHITCH, 25

Valve of Vieussens, 80, 86
Variability of the emotions, 381
Varying concomitants, law of disassociation by, 251
Ventricles, 79 ff.
VIERORDT, 71
Vision, 28 ff ; binocular, 33-9; of solidity, 37
Visual centre of cortex, 110, 115
Visual imagination, 302
Visualizing power, 302
Vividness, determines association, 264
Volition, see *Will*.
VOLKMANN, 285
Voluminousness, primitive, of sensations, 335
Voluntary acts, defined, 92; voluntary attention, 224; voluntary trains of thought, 271

Weber's law, 17, 24, 46, 59
Weber's law—weight, 66; pain, 67
Weight, sensibility to, 66 ff.
WERNICKE 109, 113, 115
WESLEY, 223
WHEATSTONE, 347
WIGAN, 300
Will, Chapter XXVI; voluntary acts, 415, they are secondary performances, 415, no third kind of idea is called for, 418; the motor-cue, 420, ideo-motor action, 432; action after deliberation, 428; five types of decision, 429; feeling of effort.

434; healthiness of will, 435; defects of, 436; the explosive will: (1) from defective inhibition, 437; (2) from exaggerated impulsion, 439; the obstructed will, 441; effort feels like an original force, 442; pleasure and pain as springs of action, 444; what holds attention determines action, 448; will is a relation between the mind and its ideas, 449; volitional effort is effort of attention, 450; free-will, 455; ethical importance of effort, 458

Willing terminates with the prevalence of the idea, 449

WUNDT, 11, 18, 25, 58, 122, 123, 125, 127, 220, 281

i

www.ingramcontent.com/pod-product-compliance
Ingram Content Group UK Ltd.
Pitfield, Milton Keynes, MK11 3LW, UK
UKHW020245240426
12048UKWH00026B/1615